DIARY OF GENERAL PATRICK GORDON OF AUCHLEUCHRIES
1635 – 1699
VOLUME I: 1635 – 1659

Edited by
Dmitry Fedosov

Foreword by Paul Dukes

Editorial Board:
Paul Bushkovitch, Paul Dukes, Dmitry Fedosov,
Irina Garkusha, Graeme Herd, Mikhail Ryzhenkov

Published by
The AHRC Centre for Irish and Scottish Studies
University of Aberdeen

Arts & Humanities Research Council

Published in 2009 by
The AHRC Centre for Irish and Scottish Studies
19 College Bounds
University of Aberdeen
AB24 3UG

Arts & Humanities
Research Council

ISBN 978-1-906108-04-5

Printed and bound in Great Britain by
CPI Antony Rowe, Chippenham and Eastbourne

Portrait
des Generalen Patrick Gordon.

Contents

Foreword *Paul Dukes*	vii
The Chronicle of a Scottish 'Soldier of Fortune' *Dmitry Fedosov*	xv
Editor's note on the text	xli
Description of the Manuscript *Mikhail Ryzhenkov*	xliii
Author's preface	3
1635-1640	4
1644-1646	5
1648-1651	6
1653	10
1654	18
1655	21
1656	73
1657	133
1658	160
1659	169
1656	169
1657	184
1658	243
1659	276
Index of persons and places	283

Foreword

The importance of Patrick Gordon's diary for our understanding of seventeenth-century history has long been recognised. Comparatively recently, in 1967, Professor Konovalov of Oxford University, who located and published some of Gordon's other papers, expressed the hope that "a co-ordinated effort, if necessary on an international scale", would produce "a complete and reliable edition" of the diary. Two years later, I. G. Tishin, then director of the Military Historical Archive in Moscow in which the six volumes of the manuscript are kept, declared that a full translation "would help historians to use it more fully in the interests of learning".[1]

Tishin's aspiration is being fulfilled through the labours of Dr. D. G. Fedosov, who is also playing a leading part in the realisation of the hopes of Konovalov. Since Dr. Fedosov has not only made a painstaking transcription of the Diary but also researched the provenance and the context, it is surely appropriate for him to write the *Introduction*. However, a *Foreword* amplifying some aspects of the background to the present publication of the original may not go amiss. For there have been earlier attempts to publish it, beginning in the early nineteenth century.

Sending an excuse for his delay in the submission of the fourth canto of *Childe Harold* from Venice in the summer of 1818, another *émigré* from North-East Scotland, Lord Byron, wrote to his publisher Mr. John Murray:

Then you've General Gordon
Who "girded his sword on"
To serve with a Muscovite Master,
And help him to polish
A nation so *owlish*
They thought shaving their beards a disaster.[2]

---

[1] S. Konovalov, "Sixteen Further Letters of Patrick Gordon", *Oxford Slavonic Papers*, XIII, 1967, p.72; I. Tishin, "Dnevnik Patrika Gordona", *Sovetskie arkhivy*, 2, 1969, p. 112.

[2] Lord Byron, *The Complete Poetical Works* (ed. Jerome J. McGann), 7 vols., Oxford, 1980–1993, IV, 1986, p.161.

Evidently, an advertisement of Mr. Murray's projected publications had reached Byron in Venice. As Dr. Fedosov makes clear in his *Introduction*, corroboration of the Patrick Gordon project came from a Russian visitor to London who began the intriguing process leading towards the first substantial publication in Moscow and St. Petersburg.

Meanwhile, whatever plans fell through in London, even bare knowledge of Gordon and his diary appears to have been absent from his homeland. This is surprising, as there had been considerable antiquarian activity in Scotland since the late eighteenth century, while Sir Walter Scott described the 1830s as an "age of clubs". The Roxburghe, Bannatyne and Maitland Clubs all included historical publication among their activities. Then, in 1839, the Spalding Club was founded in Aberdeen, aiming to emulate the achievements of the others to the south. Among its founders was John Hill Burton, later Historiographer-Royal for Scotland, and Joseph Robertson, journalist and scholar. Unfortunately, both of these, like several other members, lived in distant Edinburgh, remote from the main antiquarian concerns of the new society.[3]

It was not surprising, therefore, that replying to an enquiry in 1850, Joseph Robertson confessed that "I cannot help you to [*sic*] much about the Czar Peter's general, Patrick Gordon". Robertson observed that Gordon came on the scene too late to be noticed by the northern chroniclers of the seventeenth century before going on to remark that:

> He was so little known or remembered in Scotland in the middle of the next century that he is not even named by the author of the "Concise History of the House of Gordon" printed at Aberdeen in 1754, who, however, speaks of "Sir Thomas Gordon high Admiral of Russia" and of "the generals, John and Alexander Gordons" [*sic*],

---

[3] Donald J. Withrington, "Aberdeen Antiquaries: The Founding of the Spalding Club in 1839", *Aberdeen University Review*, XLIV, 1971–2, pp.42–8. The first President, the Earl of Aberdeen, feared that the Club might be too closely associated with the town of Spalding in Lincolnshire rather than with John Spalding, the Scottish chronicler, author of *Memorialls of the Trubles in Scotland and in England, A. D. 1624–1645.*

not less famous by land than the admiral was by sea in the same service.

Robertson suggested that "John" was probably a mistake for "Patrick", before proceeding to say something about Alexander Gordon of Auchintoul and his publications, and then to narrate the following curious episode:

> Some years ago, Dr. Hamel – a physician in the Czar's service – endeavoured to trace out the history of Patrick Gordon, and of some other Aberdeenshire adventurers in Muscovy, by inquiries on the spot. But he was then on the wrong scent as to Patrick Gordon's birth place. He imagined it to be "Crichie" – but then came to question which Crichie, for there are in Aberdeenshire some half-a-dozen places of the name. I gave him a note of their localities and history, and one day, not long afterwards, he burst in upon me shrieking "I have found it – it is Lord Aberdeen's Kreeky". But he adduced nothing to show that this Crichie had belonged to the Gordons in the early years of the 17th century. I suppose the "Crochdan" of some Russian memorialist had led him to seek for "Crichie" instead of "Cruden". I gave him notes of some half-dozen Patrick Gordons of the period as to which he was inquiring, but I don't remember that he identified any one of them with the Czar's Field Marshal.

Concluding with a few remarks about the history of Gordon's relatives and the estate of Auchintoul, Robertson sent off his response to a letter from Cosmo Innes, the historian, who had been enquiring about the tsar's general on behalf of a Mr. I. Lock, who appears to have been acting for Lord Ellesmere. Sending the response on to Lock, Innes wrote: "I put your note into the best hands we have for Abdn. local things.... Mr. Robertson's guesses at the names of places I could confirm, but the rest of the information is almost new to me".[4]

---

[4] National Archives of Scotland, GD268/87/2–3.

Without any recorded help from Scottish correspondents, or even from Dr. Hamel, the Russian German Dr. M. C. Posselt soon completed a three-volume translation into German.[5] Favourable notices of Dr. Posselt's version appeared in the *Quarterly Review* for March 1852 and the *Edinburgh Review* for July 1856. The first was probably by Lord Ellesmere, writing of "the most stormy vicissitudes of a life of military service, which in many particulars might have been suggested to Schiller the *Dragoon* of the Prologue to Wallenstein, or to Scott that equally felicitous and more finished creation of genius – the inimitable Dalgetty".[6] The second, anonymous review suggests that "Gordon's is the diary of a man of great talent and sound sense, Pepys's the diary of a puppy and a courtier".[7]

Now that the fame of the Diary had spread back to Scotland, the President of the Spalding Club, the Earl of Aberdeen, the "First Lord of the Treasury", was soon persuaded to make an application to the Court of St. Petersburg for a transcript of all the passages that related to Gordon's native country and its southern neighbour. These were duly sent, and published in 1859 under the editorship of Joseph Robertson as *Passages from the Diary of General Patrick Gordon of Auchleuchries, A. D. 1635–A.D. 1699*.[8] Although *Passages* reproduced some of the weaknesses of Posselt's work and added some of its own, it was used extensively for many years afterwards by a wide range of authors.

This was more or less the situation in 1964, at which point I must crave indulgence for some personal recollections following my arrival at the University of Aberdeen. Soon aware of the significance of the Diary for Russian, European and British history, I made a considerable number of

---

[5] See Dr. Fedosov's *Introduction* for a fuller account and an indication of the weaknesses of Dr. Posselt's version.
[6] "Diary of General Patrick Gordon", *The Quarterly Review*, Vol. XC, No. 180, 1852, pp. 314–332, quotation p. 316.
[7] "The Diary of General Patrick Gordon", *The Edinburgh Review*, Vol. CIV, No..212, 1856, pp.24–51, quotation from p. 27.
[8] For a fuller account of the circumstances of this publication, see Paul Dukes, "Patrick Gordon's Diary: The Spalding Version", in Roger Bartlett, Lindsey Hughes, eds., *Russian Society and Culture and the Long Eighteenth Century: Essays in Honour of Anthony G. Cross*, Münster, 2004.

efforts to achieve access to it. After a number of years, I was able to read a copy in the Russian National Library, Leningrad, after a further number to inspect the original in the Military-Historical Archive in Moscow. I made copious transcriptions, distributing them among the students taking courses on the Scots in Russia and Eastern Europe, several of whom went on to do outstanding postgraduate work. One of them, Graeme Herd, completed a PhD Dissertation entitled *General Patrick Gordon of Auchleuchries: A Scot in Russian Service* by 1995, commended by the external examiner the late Lindsey Hughes for its incisive and thorough treatment of its subject. Dr. Herd has made several further contributions, for example pointing out that Charles Whitworth made the first explicit use of the Diary as a primary source in 1704 during his description of the Azov campaigns a few years earlier.[9] Moreover, he has assiduously collected photocopies of the complete Diary, and generously shared them with myself and other colleagues. In addition, he presented to Dr. Fedosov a complete transcription of the *Passages*, a task undertaken by his father's Chinese secretaries in Brunei.

Some years earlier, in 1990, I had the good fortune to meet in Moscow this enthusiast for all things Scottish, Dmitry Fedosov, who has since extended lavish hospitality to myself and many others of us visiting Russia which we have attempted to reciprocate back in Scotland. Making the acquaintance of the Diary, Fedosov soon began the epic labours of transcription and analysis which are now bearing fruit.

A few words on Patrick Gordon's early years from his birth on 31 March 1635 to his departure from Aberdeen on 13 June 1651, when he watched the sun set on the NE Scottish coast from a ship bound for Danzig.. These years are given no more than summary treatment in the Diary itself. A mystery immediately arises. Why should Gordon's parents, in the words of their son 'heritours and proprietours of the same lands of Auchluichries' choose to move on not once but four times in just over ten years? A first point to make is that Gordon does not write that his parents moved, only that his father did. This description could be normal in a

---

[9] Graeme P. Herd, "Peter I and the Conquest of Azov, 1695–1696', in Lindsey Hughes, ed. and intro., *Peter the Great and the West: New Perspectives*, London, 2001.

patriarchal society, but it is nevertheless noteworthy that Gordon makes no mention of his father and mother being together after the first departure from Auchleuchries. Moreover, as he was preparing to take ship, his parents said farewell to him separately. Could it be that the parents were not happy together, indeed lived apart? A firm piece of evidence here is that, according to the records of the presbytery of Ellon for January 1642, John Gordon, Patrick's father, confessed that he had been "delinquent with Margaret Gawains [and was] willing to satisfy the ordinance of the kirk." So, Patrick's father could have moved frequently because of matrimonial difficulties.

A second possibility is that John Gordon needed to leave Auchleuchries and live elsewhere temporarily in order to reduce his considerable debts. For while he appears to have paid off money owed by his father-in-law at his assumption of the ownership of Auchleuchries, indeed was soon lending money to a Robert Innes of Balvennie, within four years he was borrowing 3000 pounds Scots.[10]

Thirdly, we must take into consideration the "great troubles" that Patrick refers to in the first few pages of his diary. In a footnote to his Preface to *Passages* on p. xix, Joseph Robertson points out that "John Gordon of Auchleuchries, his brother Mr. Thomas, and one or two of his tenants, appear among the followers of Sir John Gordon of Haddo in a raid against the Covenanters of Buchan, in April 1644...." Here was an opportunity, conceivably, for the Roman Catholic Gordons to assert their independence and for John in particular to exact revenge for his harrying at the hands of the Ellon presbytery. The difficulty for Roman Catholics was not to cease, however, after Patrick Gordon's departure from NE Scotland in 1651. We know the later fate of his uncle from the records of the parish of Ellon that on 14 January 1655: "The said day the minister did intimat... ye excommunication of James Gordon in Auchlochries for his poprie".[11] Before 1651, Patrick himself was obliged to attend different

---

[10] Delinquency and debt in T. Mair, *Narratives and Extracts from the Records of the Presbytery of Ellon*, Aberdeen, 1897, p. 161.

[11] Ibid., p. 115. I owe the references in footnotes 9 and 10 to Susan Crombie, author of an excellent MA thesis on Patrick Gordon and his family circle.

schools, because of religious difficulties, in 1644, for example, when, in his own words "because of the great troubles both befor and now, all publick schooles were abandoned." In spite of them, however, we should recall Patrick's own remark that his first primary education at the school at the kirk of Cruden from 1640 to 1644 took him as far in Latin as *"Multiplex uno sensu* in the first part of Despauter's Grammer". This progress through a standard text of the time was no small achievement, and was followed by five more years of teaching at other places up to 1649, explicitly mentioned in Patrick's list of reasons for wanting to leave home at the age of sixteen in 1651.

In conclusion, let me just reassert that the importance of Gordon's service in Muscovy from 1661 to 1699 and of his Diary as a historical source for the same period make it a matter of significance to search for a fuller understanding of his early years in NE Scotland from 1635 to 1651. His allegiance to the Roman Catholic Church and to the Stuart dynasty, his interest in the estate of Auchleuchries and other aspects of family affairs back home are persistent themes in his diary and his letters. This much is certain. We can also speculate about how his character traits, his courage, his parsimoniousness and his fidelity, were formed by the experiences of his youth, as well as his life-long interest in learning.

Beyond all doubt, however, the rediscovery of Patrick Gordon in his native land in the middle of the nineteenth century led on to a fuller appreciation of the man and his career in NE Scotland from the late twentieth, when connections between NE Scotland and Russia such as those pioneered by Robertson, Posselt and Hamel were also updated and extended. Both the history of the publication of the Diary and the contents of that outstanding piece of work illustrate clearly the absolute necessity of international collaboration and the paramount significance of international history.

To cut an extremely long story abruptly short, there have been almost as many problems in achieving publication of the Diary as there were earlier in achieving access to it. Without doubt, the usefulness of the work for fellow scholars would have been much reduced if, following some suggestions, we had agreed to bring out excerpts rather than the whole, in six volumes, as the author himself wrote it. A hundred and fifty years after *Passages* were published in Aberdeen, the first volume of the complete Diary is appearing here, and Patrick Gordon himself could be said to have come home.

The editorial board consists of the following scholars, three from Russia, three from the West: Dr. D. G. Fedosov, Senior Researcher at the Institute of General History, Russian Academy of Sciences, Dr. I. O. Garkusha, Director of the Russian State Military-Historical Archive, and Dr. M. R. Ryzhenkov, Director of the Russian State Archive of Ancient Acts; Professor Paul Bushkovitch, Professor of History, Yale University, Emeritus Professor Paul Dukes, University of Aberdeen, and Dr. Graeme P. Herd, formerly of the University of Aberdeen, currently Faculty Member, Geneva Centre for Security Policy. We are extremely grateful to Academician A. O. Chubarian, Director, Institute of General History, Russian Academy of Sciences, and Professor V. P. Kozlov, Chief Archivist of Russia, for facilitating publication of the Diary. The editors wish to express deep gratitude to Professor Cairns Craig, the Director of the AHRC Centre for Irish and Scottish Studies, University of Aberdeen, and Jonathan Cameron, its Administrator, for assuming the onerous task of publishing the Diary. With a benefactor who wishes to remain anonymous kindly agreeing to be its guarantor, we launch the enterprise with a dedication to the memory of a dear friend, the late Lindsey Hughes.

The Chronicle of a Scottish 'Soldier of Fortune'

Dmitry Fedosov

"A treasure unappreciated, predominantly historical material, yielding to no act in trustworthiness, replete with a multitude of most interesting particulars!"[1] – such is the judgement pronounced on Patrick Gordon's Diary by the outstanding Russian historian N.G. Ustrialov. Another great authority, S.M. Soloviev, regarded Gordon as "one of the most remarkable men" ever employed by the tsars, and was grateful to him for "recording his adventures and existence day by day, leaving to us curious tidings of himself, of his brothers in arms, and of Russia before the age of transformation"[2] – and, we must add, of many other things, Muscovite and otherwise.

Hardly anyone well versed in Russian or European history of the early modern period is unaware of the name of Tsar Peter the Great's principal foreign advisor, or has never heard of his journal. It is all the more striking that up to now, over three centuries after its creation, this unique monument of our past has yet to be properly published in the original, for all the efforts to do justice to it.[3] Few researchers have had an opportunity to resort to the Diary in manuscript, and even today most of them are compelled to settle for editions which are far from complete and fall short of scientific standards. Besides, both in terms of quantity and quality, less has been written about the author than he deserves, with some

---

[1] N.G. Ustrialov, *Istoriya tsarstvovaniya Petra Velikago*, vol. I (St. Petersburg, 1858), p. lxxxiv.

[2] S.M. Soloviev, *Sochineniya*, book VII (Moscow, 1991), p. 168.

[3] *Passages from the Diary of General Patrick Gordon of Auchleuchries* (Aberdeen, 1859; reprint New York, 1968), the only previous edition of the English original, is still useful, but contains just a small part of the whole; *Tagebuch des Generals Patrick Gordon*, 3 vols. (Moscow-St. Petersburg, 1849–1853) is the German version by M.C. Possel, very faulty and incomplete. My own unabridged translation into Russian is in progress: P. Gordon, *Dnevnik 1635–1659* (Moscow, 2000; reprint 2005); *Dnevnik 1659–1667* (Moscow, 2002; reprint 2003); *Dnevnik 1677–1678* (Moscow, 2005); Volume IV (1684–1689) is finished and ready to be printed, hopefully in 2009, and the penultimate volume (1690–1695) is under way.

notable exceptions.⁴ Indeed, his career is unusually eventful, including long spells of distinguished service for three major powers, Sweden, Poland-Lithuania and Russia, while the man always deemed himself a subject of the fourth, Great Britain, and her Royal House of Stuart.

Patrick Gordon (1635–1699) was born on his family estate of Auchleuchries, near the town of Ellon in Aberdeenshire. The Gordons were among the noblest and most influential clans in Scotland, but as a "yonger son of a yonger brother of a yonger house"⁵, and a Roman Catholic under Presbyterian dominance, Patrick decided to seek his fortune abroad, like thousands of his compatriots. In June 1651, too green to fight for his rightful king at the age of sixteen, on the brink of Cromwell's triumphant invasion he sailed from his strife-ridden homeland for Gdańsk. It took a while to become a "son of Mars", and first came two years at the Jesuit College of Braunsberg (Braniewo) in Eastern Prussia. Although he never finished the course and dismissed this period of study in a few curt lines, Patrick seems to have been an able and diligent scholar. He gradually mastered oral and written Latin, and later German, Polish (taking lessons even in jail) and Russian. An avid reader all his life, he knew, among others, Livy, Ovid, Dionysius Cato, Walter of Chatillon, Thomas à Kempis, Ariosto, Caesar Baronius, Cervantes, Marlowe, Camden and Sigmund von Herberstein.⁶ But his spirit could not "endure a still and strict way of liveing"⁷ and soon yielded to warlike inclinations, so natural for a

---

⁴ See P. Dukes, "Scottish Soldiers in Muscovy", in *The Caledonian Phalanx: Scots in Russia* (Edinburgh, 1987), pp. 18–23; idem, "Patrick Gordon and His Family Circle: Some Unpublished Letters", *Scottish Slavonic Review*, no. 10 (1988), pp. 19–49; G.P. Herd, *General Patrick Gordon of Auchleuchries: A Scot in Russian Service*. Ph.D. Dissertation (University of Aberdeen, 1995); D. Fedosov, "Cock of the East: A Gordon Blade Abroad" in *Russia: War, Peace and Diplomacy. Essays in Honour of John Erickson* (London, 2004), pp. 1–10; A. Brückner, *Patrick Gordon i yego dnevnik* (St. Petersburg, 1878).

⁵ *Diary*, I, fol. 3 v. He was a scion of the Gordons of Haddo, whose origins date back to the thirteenth century.

⁶ Judging by quotations and hints in his journal. In 1686 Gordon recorded seeing "Hamlet" in London (*Diary*, IV, fol. 125 v.), apparently the earliest known reference to Shakespeare by a resident of Russia.

⁷ *Diary*, I, fol. 5.

penniless young Scot. After some travels Gordon reached Hamburg, and in the spring of 1655 joined the Duke of Sachsen-Lauenburg's regiment of horse employed by King Charles X of Sweden, who was about to descend on Poland and spark off the Northern War of 1655–60.

With no experience, privileges or pay, and no German or Swedish to understand his comrades, the novice had to start from the very bottom, and could only rely on his own mettle. But origin proved a great advantage, for wherever he went – Baltic ports, Polish castles, German taverns, Russian garrisons or British palaces – fellow Scots were always there.[8] Being obliged to them in many ways, Gordon, for his part, never failed to lend a hand to a countryman, saving, for instance, a Corporal Balfour from execution, or securing the advancement of many others. "Good Scots hearts and swords" (*Diary*, I, fol. 161) are the main heroes throughout his journal, and the diarist himself turned out as *bonnie* a *fechter* as they come. According to the patent sealed by the renowned commander of the age, Prince Jerzy Lubomirski, Grand Marshal of Poland, the officer then in charge of his dragoons "has gained praise and honour, and was most equal to the name of the Scottish nation, famed everywhere for military prowess".[9] In fact, all his superiors, whether Swedes, Poles or Russians, were always very reluctant to part with him.

From his maiden campaign in 1655 the young soldier of fortune (as he styled himself) readily volunteered for reconnaissance missions and vanguard battles, which cost him several wounds. Gordon's earnest chronicle testifies to his bravery, composure and resilience both in war and peace. These episodes are not exaggerated or embellished, quite the opposite. Since the Diary was "not intended for publick view" (fol. 2 v.), it made little sense to vaunt or deceive. Reading his accounts of hot and bloody engagements, we often learn of the author's own role at the very last, almost by chance. We can only guess how he fared in a cavalry skirmish between the

---

[8] By my count Gordon mentions 127 named Scots alone in Volume I of his Diary and 118 in Volume II, mostly soldiers on the continent. No wonder in some Swedish and Polish units officers preferred Scottish broadswords and pistols, while the Scots pint was used to measure the beer allowance.

[9] The patent is dated 2 July 1661 in Warsaw (*Diary*, II, fol. 116 v.).

Swedes and Danzigers in January 1657, until an entry elsewhere reveals that he got a sword slash in the head. The battle of Chudnov (Cudnów), one of the greatest in the Russo-Polish war, is emotionally described at length, but only the concluding phrase dryly tells us that Gordon was hit by two musket shots. "Courage carryeth throw!"[10] was his motto. Of course, to judge a man solely by his own words can be misleading, but Gordon's high reputation is well borne out by other sources and testimonies of those who knew him.[11] The latter, as well as historians from different countries and ages, who dealt with the subject, are unanimous: here was a true brave, devoid of vanity or bragging.

The Swedish army, reformed by King Gustav Adolf and reinforced by Charles X, was believed to be the best in Europe, a model of discipline and tactical art. Raw recruits were sternly treated, and even for minor offences Gordon's back quickly felt the successive impact of a colonel's cane, lieutenant's small sword and corporal's broadsword. Constant jeers from his German comrades, "meere bowres come from the flaile" (fol. 21), made his plight even worse. But Patrick never forgot his noble lineage (Gordons of Haddo and Ogilvies of Cullen) and managed to assert himself so that no one could offend him unpunished. A sense of dignity always remained, which in time made him acquire the best military equipment, gallant attire and a suite of attendants including Polish gentlemen. This feeling usually led Gordon to join the van for the offensive, and to cover his comrades in retreat; such were his actions during the Polish pursuit of his small party between Przasnysz and Mława, against the Russians and Cossacks at Chudnov and Slobodishcha, or against the Turks and Tatars at Chigirin.

The first officer's rank, that of an ensign under the Swedes, took two and a half years to attain, but talents of a leader became manifest from early on. Significantly, the Swedish Field Marshal Count Robert Douglas entrusted the recruitment of his "Life Company" to none other than Gordon, who later upheld its interests before King Charles X himself. Besides, Patrick strove to improve his knowledge of the art of war; he

---

[10] Ibid., fol. 37 v.
[11] See, for instance, Johann Georg Korb, *Diarium Itineris in Moscoviam* (Vienna, 1700), or various translations of this work.

says that during the siege of Warsaw, in addition to his duties, "I went often to the leaguer, especially when I heard of any action or assault to be, on purpose to inure my self to dangers and better my understanding in martiall effaires".[12] Very soon, by the end of the Northern War in 1660, he turned into a seasoned veteran, increasingly valued by the high command. Having besieged the town of Graudenz (Grudziądz), Hetman Lubomirski asked his advice on deployment of forces, followed it and captured the stronghold in just a week. Thus came "the full trust of persons of different nations and ranks", and "respect wherewith [Gordon's] name was pronounced by warriors of three nations".[13]

Patrick Gordon was no saint, and not all of his deeds merit praise. His code of honour was that of a mercenary gentleman, which had little against horse- and cattle-stealing or pillage of the populace, especially subjects of a hostile crown. "Sometimes he rather naively confesses to ulterior motives and leanings for intrigue".[14] We can also suspect that the Diary does not give an exhaustive account of its author's sins. Nevertheless, he admits that "many things justly deserve a publick judgement and punishment from God Almighty", calls horse-stealing "a most hainous crime, punishable by all civill and even martiall law", and makes an excuse that "one can scarce be a souldier without being an oppressour and comitting many crimes and enormityes".[15] For a long while he could not obtain a penny from the Swedes, and some of the more scrupulous cavaliers in their employ starved to death or went insane. Although Gordon usually seized a good chance to fill his purse, he was neither heartless nor avaricious. The cases mentioned above belong to the early stage of his career. Having become an officer with regular pay, he did not allow such "shifts" either to himself or his men.

As for changing sides, at that period it was quite customary, and under certain conditions (expiry of terms set for ransom or exchange

---

[12] *Diary*, I, fol. 66.
[13] Words of M.C. Posselt, German editor of the Diary. *Dnevnik Generala Patrika Gordona*, pt. I (Moscow, 1892), p. 7.
[14] A. Brückner, *Patrick Gordon i yego dnevnik*, p. 134.
[15] *Diary*, I, fols. 52, 125–125 v.

of prisoners) perfectly legal. Largely because of his "youthfull bravery", in just over three years Patrick was captured six times by nearly all sides, Poles, Brandenburgers, Danzigers and "Imperialists"! He managed to escape twice, got exchanged once, and thrice gained freedom by agreeing to enemy proposals. Various reasons of his, given in the Diary, though not always consistent, amount to the conclusion that this made more sense than to face execution or rot in jail. Neither Poles nor Swedes blamed the Scot for his conduct when he returned to their banner, and welcomed him back. In all fairness I have to stress that on taking a pledge of allegiance to any crown he served it with loyalty and dedication, often putting his very life at risk. For all his movements to and fro, he is not known to have broken an oath.

Other features can be added to the portrait. Devout in his youth, Gordon grew ever more so; one of his greatest accomplishments was the foundation from 1684 of the first Roman Catholic church in Muscovy.[16] His "nature was always averse to intemperancy", and although he could spend a night "in no Christian exercise"[17], the excesses common to his trade and circle were unlike him. An adroit duellist and courteous cavalier, he enjoyed a dance with a lady, a glass of good wine, a game at cards or a horse race, but never had a reputation of a rake or a *bretteur*. He also appears to have been good and witty company, well endowed with a sense of humour even in extremity or deadly menace. Closely pursued by a far superior force and about to break through a bog, he encouraged fellow Scots "to fight at least for a dry place to dy on, that it might not be said wee dyed in a gutter".[18] But something quite different lay in store.

In 1659, having been captured for the last time, Gordon faced a choice. Jan Sobieski, future King of Poland and liberator of Vienna, promised him a company of dragoons based on rich Sobieski estates. But the prisoner proudly replied that he left home "to seeke honour, and that by lying

---

[16] See D.V. Tsvetayev, *Istoriya sooruzheniya pervago kostiola v Moskve* (Moscow, 1886), although this valuable work is militantly anti-Catholic and unjustly hostile to Gordon.
[17] *Diary*, I, fols. 12 v., 44.
[18] Ibid., fol. 181 v.

upon lands and in quarters nothing of that nature was to be expected".[19] The Scot was then handed over to Prince Jerzy Lubomirski, who virtually held sway over the Polish government and armed forces. This magnate too had his initial offer turned down, because Gordon absolutely refused to serve in the former rank of ensign, finally accepting that of a quartermaster of dragoons.

The Diary, especially the first two volumes, is a wealth of evidence on diverse aspects of Polish and Swedish history (even though its author never set foot in Sweden proper), but it is only recently that historians from these and other countries have begun to pay serious attention to this source and appreciate its richness.[20] Nevertheless, Gordon's future and chief exploits lay in Russia, which he served for nearly forty years until his final hour.

In 1661 the hardy Scot left Poland to offer his sword to Tsar Alexey Mikhailovich, and turned up in Moscow to enroll as major in his countryman Daniel Crawford's regiment of foot.[21] The Russian envoy in Poland, Z.F. Leontiev, who after many persuasions managed to entice him over from the Austrians, could not foresee the importance of the acquisition, for that "stranger of the Scottish land" was to secure the throne for his pupil, the greatest of Russian rulers. As for Gordon, he never imagined he was going to distant Muscovy for good, and his first impressions of that realm and its inhabitants were so unfavourable that he bitterly repented the move.

However, endless wars with Poland-Lithuania and the Ottoman Empire offered many prospects for advancement. In February 1665 Gordon received a colonel's rank, and a year later the Tsar dispatched with him a letter to King Charles II in London, where he displayed his diplomatic

---

[19] Ibid., fol. 239.
[20] See R. Romański, *Cudnów 1660* (Warszawa, 1996); W. Kowalski, "Patrick Gordon z Auchleuchries i jego ogląd staropolskiego świata" in *Staropolski ogląd świata – problem inności* (Toruń, 2007), pp. 81–105.
[21] Patrick was not the first of his clan in Muscovite employ. Captains Alexander and William, *Rittmeister* Robert, Ensign Alexander, Sergeant James and Private Thomas, all Gordons, arrived in Moscow by winter 1631/2 and took part in the War of Smolensk (Russian State Archive of Ancient Acts, F. 210, op. 1, № 78).

skills. Subsequently he quartered with his regiment in the garrisons of Southern Russia and Ukraine, such as Trubchevsk, Briansk, Novy Oskol, Sevsk and Pereyaslav, often threatened by Cossack riots and Tatar raids. In 1669–70 he got leave to go about his private affairs to his homeland, after an absence of almost two decades, and became a freeman of Aberdeen.

Gordon's valour and military expertise were brilliantly demonstrated in the Chigirin campaigns of 1677 and 1678. Heading the defence of the Hetman's capital of Right-Bank Ukraine against the Ottoman host, with his men outnumbered by ten to one, after desperate resistance he personally set fire to the powder magazine, and was among the last to leave the fortress. This earned him the rank of major general and commander of the garrison in Kiev, a crucial post he held until 1686. At this time he also revealed extraordinary skills of a military engineer.

The Crimean campaigns brought Gordon the dignity of full general, the highest in Russian military hierarchy. In August 1689, as the dean of foreign officers, he led them to join Tsar Peter at the Trinity-St. Sergy's Monastery, which sealed the overthrow of Peter's half-sister Sophia. As a result, the first visits ever made by a Russian monarch to a foreigner (inconceivable until then!) were those of Peter to Gordon, and the general shortly became the tsar's nearest councillor, especially in the field of military reform. He got the command of one of the best regular units, the Butyrsky Regiment of Selected Soldiers, supervised Peter's manoeuvres and battles, contributed to the formation of the Guards (a term Gordon himself first applied to the tsar's "stable boys") along with the Navy in Pereslavl and Archangel, where, in the rank of rear admiral, he translated into English the earliest code of Russian naval signals. At the second siege of the key Ottoman citadel of Azov in 1696 Gordon advocated the unusual plan of taking it by means of a "movable" earthen rampart, which soon forced the Turks to capitulate.

The last and perhaps greatest service rendered by the Scot to the Tsar came in June 1698. During Peter's absence on his Grand Embassy to the West, Gordon succeeded in routing the rebel *streltsy*, bound for the capital, near the Resurrection Monastery; before ordering his men to open fire, Gordon intrepidly rode to the enemy camp to negotiate with the rebels, one of whose avowed goals was to "hack the Foreign Quarter" of Moscow, the general's home. The Muscovite government duly lavished "Piotr Ivanovich", as he was now styled, with large salaries in money and kind as well as gifts and privileges, including the unusual right to import Western spirits duty-free. The tsar has also granted to him two large villages in the district of Riazan, so that he also became a Russian landlord. However, his career in Muscovy was not cloudless: persistent solicitations for dismissal so vexed the Russian "Prime Minister", Prince V.V. Golitsyn, that he once threatened to demote Gordon from general to ensign and to banish him to Siberia! All this is well illustrated in the Diary, which is naturally autobiographical.

Although Gordon with good reason regarded himself first and foremost as a soldier, he speaks too modestly of his involvement in affairs of state ("with those of state I have medled very litle, being out of my spheare"[22]). Having made his personal acquaintance, King James II (VII) conferred on him the rank of British Envoy Extraordinary in Moscow, where this appointment was understandably declined by the tsars. But from the late 1680s onwards, due to his high standing, Gordon could and did exert considerable influence on Russian politics. For instance, after the so-called "Glorious Revolution" of 1688–9 and deposition of the Stuarts, he for long succeeded in thwarting the recognition of William of Orange as king by Tsars Ivan and Peter. De facto he became the Jacobite representative in Russia and established the strength of this party at Russian court until the mid-eighteenth century. Its prominent members included Alexander Gordon of Auchintoul, the tsar's major-general and author of the informative "History of Peter the Great"[23], and Admiral Thomas Gordon, Chief Commander of the Port of Kronshtadt; the former was Patrick's son-in-law, the latter, some suppose, his nephew.

The chieftain of the Russian Gordons, a considerable sept in his later years, got married twice; both his wives, Catherine van Bockhoven and Elizabeth Roonaer, sprang from Roman Catholic Netherlandish military

---

[22] *Diary*, I, fol. 2 v.
[23] A. Gordon of A[u]chintoul, *The History of Peter the Great, Emperor of Russia*, 2 Vols (Aberdeen, 1755). Auchintoul commanded the Jacobite centre at Sheriffmuir.

families settled in Moscow. Of their numerous progeny three sons and two daughters have survived childhood. The eldest son, John, having enlisted in his youth as ensign in the tsar's army, soon left for Scotland to live on the family estate of Auchleuchries, although he managed the place negligently; in 1698 he revisited his parental home in Moscow. The second son, James (Yakov), resembled his father by his boldness and passion for warlike pursuits; discarding his studies, in 1689 he joined the Jacobite rising and was gravely wounded at Killiecrankie; on return to Tsar Peter's standard, and after his father's demise, he assumed command of the Butyrsky Regiment, but during the Russian defeat at Narva was captured by the Swedes; in 1702 he fled from Stockholm and led the Russian van at the storming of Nöteborg (Oreshek); covered with wounds, he reached the rank of brigadier, while his father's achievements made him Count of the Holy Roman Empire and Knight of Malta[24]; he died without issue in Moscow in 1722. Patrick's third son, Theodore (Fiodor), also served in the Butyrsky Regiment and in the course of the Great Northern War was promoted to colonel; most of the family papers, including several volumes of the Diary, evidently passed to Theodore's son, a modest St. Petersburg official, whose Christian name is still unknown. Both of Patrick's daughters, Catherine and Mary, twice wedded Scottish and German officers serving the tsar, but were soon widowed and lost all their children. Thus the family, which looked certain to join the highest nobility of the Russian Empire, became extinct in the male line, although later descendants on the distaff side have been traced by Dr. Oleg Nozdrin.

Even those who fully acknowledged the merits of Patrick Gordon sometimes thought that he "served *in* Russia, but not *for* Russia".[25] At best, this is only partly true. Indeed, he tirelessly petitioned for return to his homeland, where he desired to end his days, but the Muscovite government persevered in keeping him so adamantly as if he were absolutely

---

[24] Count James Gordon was the first native of Russia to become a knight of the Order of St. John of Jerusalem (in 1706), styling himself a "Muscovite" (Archives of the Order of Malta, National Library of Malta, 265, fol. 180).

[25] N.V. Charykov. *Posol'stvo v Rim i sluzhba v Moskve Pavla Meneziya* (St. Petersburg, 1906), p. 559.

irreplaceable. He remained a loyal adherent of the House of Stuart and a pious son of the Church of Rome. Still, there cannot be any doubt that he fulfilled his duty with honesty and dedication. One of his biographers rightly observed that he was ready "every minute to sacrifice his own life and those of others for the sake of Russia and her military honour".[26] Moreover, he maintained a very close and sincere friendship with Tsar Peter, who frequently visited his trusty general and could not contain tears by his deathbed. On 29 November 1699 "the eyes of him who had left Scotland a poor unfriended wanderer were closed by the hands of an Emperor".[27] The burial in the Catholic church, which Gordon had founded in Moscow, was one of the grandest ceremonies of Peter's entire reign.[28] It also happened to be the first time a Russian Orthodox monarch attended a Roman Catholic service, the ultimate token of Gordon's success. And how can we refrain from ascribing to him a role in the adoption in the late 1690s of the saltire as a national emblem of Russia, in her naval flag and the first and highest Order of St. Andrew, most remarkable signs of Scottish influence?[29]

Gordon's personal qualities and merit were unanimously lauded by his contemporaries, whether Westerners or Russians. Here is the testimony of the Imperial diplomat Johann Georg Korb. "Gordon was graced with prudence, mature discretion and provident diligence in all things. Not boastful of his renown, and distinguished for civility and amiableness of

---

[26] A. Brückner, *Patrick Gordon i yego dnevnik*, p. 37.

[27] *Passages from the Diary*, p. 193.

[28] On Gordon's final years and burial see J.G. Korb, *Diarium Itineris in Moscoviam* (Russian edn.: *Dnevnik puteshestviya v Moskoviyu* (St. Petersburg, 1906)).

[29] In colour the Russian naval flag, discarded by the Bolsheviks and recently restored, is the exact reverse of the Scots Saltire. The Order of St. Andrew is suspiciously alike that of the Thistle in nearly every respect (choice of Patron and symbols, green mantle, black hat with white plume, and twelve original knights!). In fact, the first statutes of the former plainly acknowledge the debt to the latter (See D. Fedosov, "K triokhsotletiyu pervogo rossiyskogo ordena", *Sredniye Veka*, No. 62 (Moscow, 2001), pp. 247–74). Gordon is nowhere mentioned as a Knight of St. Andrew, but there is a fascinating portrait (State Historical Museum, Moscow) of him in old age with a blue ribbon over his shoulder, which, in this case, can hardly belong to any other decoration. He could well have been made knight in 1699, which went unrecorded, so that further research is needed to confirm this.

manner, Gordon was especially able to attract to his side the Muscovites, who are by nature ill-disposed to foreigners and hostile to their fame. Therefore, when internal strife arose, his house became a safe and reliable refuge for the natives themselves. Often styled by the Monarch with the name of "Father" (*Patris*), esteemed by the boyars, honoured by the councillors, dear to the gentry and loved by the commonalty, he won such respect from all, which could hardly be claimed by an alien".[30] The tsar himself is credited with these words at Gordon's interment: "Myself and the realm have lost an assiduous, faithful and brave general. If it had not been for Gordon, Muscovy would have been in great calamity [apparently meaning the *streltsy* mutiny]. I am giving him just a handful of earth, but he gave me a whole expanse of land with Azov". A.K. Nartov, who recorded the tribute, adds to it: "This foreigner, according to those who personally knew him, was beloved not only by Peter the Great, but also by his subjects. His death was generally regretted".[31]

Unfortunately, Gordon's vast written legacy has not been preserved in its entirety. We have also lost some of its most precious parts, forming the journal which he kept throughout virtually his whole career. Just like its author's life, the fate of the Diary is worthy both of scholarly studies and historical novels[32]. Of the six surviving volumes, numbers IV and V entered the former Moscow Archive of the College of Foreign Affairs among the papers of the disgraced Russian Vice Chancellor, Count A.I. Ostermann, who was exiled to Siberia in 1741. Four other volumes (I, II, III and VI) were acquired in 1759 from Patrick Gordon's heirs[33] by Baron A.S. Stroganov. From him these passed to the noted Russo-German historian and collector, Gerhard Friedrich Müller (1705–1783), after whose death they also ended up in the Archive of the College of Foreign Affairs and, finally, in the Military Scientific Archive of the General Staff. Today

---

[30] J.G. Korb, *Dnevnik puteshestviya v Moskoviyu*, p. 255.

[31] "Rasskazy Nartova o Petre Velikom" in *Sbornik Otdeleniya russkago yazyka i slovesnosti Imperatorskoy Akademii Nauk*, LII, № 8 (St. Petersburg, 1891), pp. 104–5.

[32] See Baroness S. Buxhoeveden, *A Cavalier in Muscovy* (London, 1932).

[33] From the widow of his grandson, accountant of the St. Petersburg Academy of Sciences and translator to the Admiralty College. The lady was unaware of other volumes.

its successor, the Russian State Archive of Military History in Moscow, preserves all six bound manuscripts of the Diary (Fond 846, opis' 15, nos. 1–6). The rest seems to be irretrievably lost, although the search was conducted both in Russia and abroad. Some experts, notably M.R. Ryzhenkov, even doubt that the missing volumes ever existed, but I find it hard to accept that Gordon, given his precision and tenacity in recording his life and times, could entirely neglect so much of importance for so many years – for example, the first *streltsy* mutiny in Moscow or the great siege of Vienna by the Turks. On the other hand, Russian and foreign archives contain a considerable number of documents shedding more light on Gordon, along with his correspondence; some of this material has been published.[34]

Although Gordon kept his notes for his own use, their significance seems to have been already felt by some of his contemporaries. In 1724, possibly at the behest of Emperor Peter I himself, who encouraged historians of his reign and could well have known of his general's annals, Ostermann attempted their first Russian translation from the original. A certain Volkov, whom he hired for the purpose, managed to translate just a small fragment dated 1684–5. Several years later Academician Gottlieb Siegfried Bayer (1694–1738) had recourse to the Diary in order to study the Crimean and Azov campaigns, then the above-mentioned G.F. Müller decided to translate it into German and entrusted the labour to his assistant, Johann Stritter. The latter avidly took to the task, but in the belief that this source was mostly important for the military history of Russia he cut or omitted everything else. Besides, for some reason Stritter altered the style from the author's own to the third person, while his knowledge of English, Scots and seventeenth-century palaeography left much to be desired, which led to numerous mistakes. In the end, it was not so much

---

[34] Russian State Archive of Ancient Acts, FF. 9, 11, 142, 150, 158, 159, 210 etc.; S. Konovalov (ed.), "Patrick Gordon's Dispatches from Russia, 1667", *Oxford Slavonic Papers*, XI (1964), pp. 8–16; idem, "Sixteen Further Letters of General Patrick Gordon", ibid., XIII (1967), pp. 72–95; P. Dukes, "Patrick Gordon and His Family Circle: Some Unpublished Letters", *Scottish Slavonic Review*, no. 10 (1988), pp. 19–49. Besides, I have found deeds of factory, issued by Patrick Gordon in 1670 and 1686, in the National Archives of Scotland.

a translation, but a rather free summary or abstract. Lack of funds and death of the translator prevented the completion and publication of this work, which was more Stritter's than Gordon's.

Müller also wrote the first scholarly essay on the Diary (in French).[35] This was partly published in *Opyt trudov Volnago rossiyskago sobraniya pri Imperatorskom Moskovskom Universitete* (pt. IV, 1778). By the end of the eighteenth century several more works printed in Russia dealt with Gordon's journal. Nonetheless, for all the attention paid to Gordon at that period or later on, he mostly remained in the shadow of other companions of Peter the Great, especially François Lefort. Thus, I.I. Golikov described the Scot as a "colleague of the famous Genevan", and allotted to the former's biography just a half of the space given to the latter.[36] In fact, Lefort, being a generation younger, was accepted into Muscovite employ 17 years later than Gordon and long served as his subordinate, let alone the Genevan's comparatively less impressive talents and merits. It is fitting, however, that today Gordon's Diary is found in the Moscow palace of his Swiss friend and kinsman, in the edifice which the Scot visited and which houses the Archive of Military History.

Gordon's journal attracted some of his compatriots as well. In 1784 it was being copied by one John Ridley, on commission of an unnamed nobleman.[37] From one of Lord Byron's verse epistles[38] it follows that in 1818 his publisher J. Murray was preparing an edition of the Petrine general's Diary; the celebrated poet was, of course, a Gordon on his mother's side and bore this name himself, so that his testimony is especially significant. The projected edition never appeared, but this episode in the story of the Diary did have a sequel. In 1835 the eminent Russian man of letters A.I. Turgenev wrote: "During my sojourn in London the well-known bookseller Murray, friend and publisher of Byron, yielded to me

---

[35] *Mémoires du Général Gordon écrits par lui-même* (1766).
[36] I.I. Golikov, *Istoricheskoye izobrazheniye zhizni i vsekh del slavnago zhenevtsa... Leforta... i sosluzhebnika yego,.. znamenitago shotlandtsa voysk Yego zhe Velichestva generala anshefa Patrika Gordona, izvestnago u nas pod imenem Petra Ivanovicha Gordona* (Moscow, 1800).
[37] *Zapiski russkikh liudey. Sobytiya vremion Petra Velikago.* Izd. I.P. Sakharova (St. Petersburg, 1841). Prilozheniya (appendix), p. 97.
[38] See Paul Dukes, *Foreword*.

a manuscript I have found by him, containing the detailed "Journal of General Gordon", a Scot who served under the double tsardom and then under Peter I. In this journal, seemingly autographic, he is chronologically and daily setting down... every occurrence of his time... Gordon's notes can be of interest not just for the history of that time, and particularly for biographers of Peter the Great, but also for those dealing with the history of Russian state administration in general... Restoring this manuscript to Russia, I desire that it would serve as material for the future historian of the reforms of Peter I, and, furthermore, as proof of my loyalty and love for my fatherland".[39]

What A.I. Turgenev initially took for the original proved to be a copy transcribed from the last three volumes in the late eighteenth century.[40] On return to St. Petersburg he lost no time in sharing this exciting find with many of his acquaintances. On 21 December 1836 Turgenev says in his own daybook: "Koehler's son is translating my Gordon, according to the Most High [Emperor's] command, and has also ordered the original from the Archive. My copy [was made] from the archival [manuscript]... Today about Gordon. My digest was made use of. Promised to Pushkin about Scotland".[41] Not surprisingly, Pushkin's name emerges here as well – just then he was collecting the sources on the age of Peter the Great.

On the same subject we also have a statement from Dmitry Koehler (1807–1839), a chancellery official with the Russian War Ministry: "[17 December 1836]. Was at a ball by [Major General Baron E.F.] Meyendorf. He and his wife spoke to Pushkin about the assignment given me, to translate for the Emperor the manuscript by General Gordon. I was not dancing, and stayed in the anteroom. Suddenly, Aleksandr Sergeyevich [Pushkin] came out with Meyendorf, impatiently asking him: "Mais où est-il donc? Où est-il donc?" Egor Fiodorovich introduced us. Inquiries went on about the size and contents of the manuscript. Pushkin was surprised to learn that I have six volumes in 4o, and said: "The Emperor told

---

[39] A.I. Turgenev, *Khronika russkogo. Dnevniki* (Moscow, 1964), p. 103.
[40] This MS can be seen in the Russian National Library, St. Petersburg, Dept. of Manuscripts, F. 949, № 16.
[41] *A.S. Pushkin v vospominaniyakh sovremennikov*, II (Moscow, 1974), pp.172–3.

me of this manuscript as of a rarity, but I did not know it is so extensive". He asked whether I had other similar studies in mind on completion of the translation, and implored to visit him". At their next meeting Pushkin urged Koehler with regard to Gordon's Diary: "Carry on with it, you will do a great service", and offered his help to the translator, promising to show him an extract from Gordon in German anent the *streltsy*.[42]

It is clear, then, that our source was highly esteemed not just by the leading cultural figures of Russia, but also by Emperor Nicholas I, who commanded Koehler to translate the original and discussed the project with Pushkin. But evil fate still opposed the undertaking. Pushkin, who seemed bent on following N.M. Karamzin on the road from literature to history, fell in a duel a few weeks later, while Koehler outlived him by just two and a half years.

Having studied Turgenev's copy, Koehler learned of the extant original Diary from an article by Professor M.P. Pogodin[43], whose famous collection included Stritter's "summary". On the Emperor's orders all six volumes were transferred from Moscow, and Koehler set to work. He was assisted by the scholarly elite of St. Petersburg as well as the highest dignitaries of the Empire, including the War Minister, Count A.I. Chernyshev, Secretary of State M.M. Briskorn and Admiral A.S. Greig; the latter, a man of Scots descent, suggested that the lost volumes of the Diary could be traced in Gordon's homeland. Apart from his research in Russian archives, the translator sent inquiries to Britain, Austria and Sweden. In 1837–8 the first "five parts" of the translation were presented to the Emperor, for which Koehler received gifts. However, his "incredible labours" and personal tribulations led to "extreme derangement of mental and physical powers", a suicide attempt and, finally, death in a mental asylum.[44] Koehler had time to render into Russian and

---

[42] Diary of D.E. Koehler, Russian State Archive of Military History, F. 846, op. 16, № 1150, fols. 37, 40.

[43] "O russkikh podyachikh XVII v.", *Biblioteka dlia chteniya*, V (1834), p. 11. This article is based on Gordon's Diary.

[44] Russian State Archive of Military History, F. 846, op.16, № 1150; F. 1, op.1, № 12135.

submit to the Emperor the first three volumes, which were favourably received, while the other three were completed by his widow and colleagues at the War Ministry, apparently with less success. Publication of the whole was permitted after censorship, but this had no effect because of the large expenses involved.[45] At present the whereabouts of just one of Koehler's volumes is known (number II, in two books, 1837).[46] In the 1840s this entire translation, along with the original manuscript of the Diary, was kept in the Emperor's private library in the Hermitage[47], but is then lost sight of.

Koehler's cause was continued by another Russian German, M.C. Posselt (1805–1875), with support from Prince M.A. Obolensky, Director of the Moscow Chief Archive of the Ministry of Foreign Affairs. However, Posselt got back to the idea of German translation, which he put into action. In 1849–53 he produced in both Imperial capitals a three-volume edition of the Diary[48], the most complete to date, and still used by historians. But for all its scale and imposing features, one has to agree that this project proved "far from satisfactory"[49], based as it was on Stritter's obsolete and defective "exposition". True, Posselt made use of the original, substantially enlarged the volume of translated text and supplied it with helpful introduction, notes and appendices. In his own translation, from 1691, he allowed Gordon to tell his story in the first person. Nevertheless, the editor also committed a lot of mistakes (in particular, with regard to Scots words and phrases), while his gaps in the original text amount to

---

[45] Ibid., F. 1, op. 1, № 10392. I am grateful to Mrs. L.I. Petrzhak for drawing my attention to this important file.

[46] Russian State Library, Moscow, Dept. of Manuscripts, F. 19/V, № 1 a-b. It is obviously a copy made for Count A.I. Chernyshev.

[47] Russian State Historical Archive, St. Petersburg, F. 472, op. 17, № 299. According to this document, in early 1846 the St. Petersburg Academy of Sciences petitioned the Emperor to lend it "the manuscripts of Patrick Gordon's journal for extraction therefrom of evidence urgently needful for the Academy"; Nicholas I did not allow the Diary to leave the Hermitage, but granted permission to peruse it in the palace.

[48] *Tagebuch des Generals Patrick Gordon*. Bd. I (Moskau, 1849); Bd. II–III (St. Petersburg, 1851–53).

[49] M.P. Alekseyev, *Russko-angliyskiye literaturnyye sviazi* (Moscow, 1982), p. 104.

dozens of pages, substituted by concise retelling in his own words. The author's letters were torn from their places and only partly printed in bulk at the end with no indication of their provenance. Thus, the source was again subjected to merciless and arbitrary abridgement, especially the first two volumes dedicated to Gordon's pre-Muscovite period. For all his assiduity, Posselt did not think it necessary to correct Stritter, and often failed to declare the cuts they both chose to make, interspersing the original with passages of their own.

All subsequently published fragments of the Diary are indebted to Posselt in some way or another, including the Spalding Club edition of 1859.[50] The long-awaited Russian versions of the late nineteenth and early twentieth century[51] are based on reverse translations from German, not on the original, so that their quality suffers accordingly, let alone the fact that they do not go beyond the Chigirin campaigns of the 1670s. As a result, until very recently no complete scholarly edition of Gordon's Diary existed in any language, which should have made Russians agree with reproaches to "the thankless country in which the writer was condemned to breathe his last".[52]

Still, such a prominent historical figure as Patrick Gordon could never suffer oblivion. In 1878 A.G. Brückner, Posselt's colleague at the University of Dorpat and the study of the Petrine period, published a large essay devoted to Gordon's biography and his Diary. This work remains one of the best ever written in Russian on the subject. Its author is very eulogistic of the achievements of "the most skilled of Peter's generals" and "patriarch of the [Moscow's] Foreign Quarter": "Hardly any other foreigner present in Russia in the seventeenth century had such importance as Patrick Gordon. Due to the length of time he spent in Russia, his participation in the most crucial events, and the position he occupied in the realm and society, he deserves more attention than many other, better known, contemporaries... Among the sources for the history of that

---

[50] See Paul Dukes, *Foreword*.
[51] *Kiev v 1684–1685 godakh po opisaniyu sluzhilago inozemtsa Patrikiya Gordona* (Kiev, 1875); P. Gordon, *Dnevnik*, 2 pts. (Moscow, 1892); *Russkaya starina*, 1916–1918.
[52] *Passages from the Diary*, p. ix.

epoch Gordon's Diary has one of the prime places... [and] surpasses all works of a similar kind".[53]

Criticising Posselt's defects, Brückner regretfully observes: "Given the immense size of the original, one can scarcely count on a new edition, more satisfactory for the demands of science... The difficulty of the authentic tongue of the Diary, and its volume, would hardly permit many historians to use this source in a proper manner. If... the German edition has been comparatively little taken into consideration, it can even be said, only by way of exception, by researchers in seventeenth-century history, still less can we count on the scholarly investigation of the English original of the Diary".[54] The dimensions of this source are formidable indeed, but Posselt, Brückner and some other authorities are unfair to accuse Gordon of "extremely bad and arbitrary orthography", or of alleged abundance of distortions and obscure places. Quite the contrary, his handwriting, idiom and style are pretty clear and consistent, especially by seventeenth-century standards, while the overwhelming majority of terms and names do not pose serious problems, although some inaccuracies are naturally to be met with.

The journal of Patrick Gordon, without any exaggeration, is a unique monument. Russian annals (*letopisi*) of the period are, as a rule, anonymous and very limited in their contents. The very genre of daily notes about one's service or private life was practically unknown in Russia prior to the eighteenth century. Perhaps the only exception is the memoirs formerly attributed to I.A. Zheliabuzhsky (embracing 1682–1711)[55], which does not stand comparison to Gordon in any respect. As for contemporary works on Muscovy by other foreigners, addressed to the general reader and, arguably, endowed with greater literary virtues (Olearius, Meyerberg, Collins, Foy de la Neuville etc.), the Russo-Scottish commander still has the advantage in the chronological precision of events, in his competence

---

[53] A. Brückner, *Patrick Gordon i yego dnevnik*, p. 1.
[54] Ibid., p. 5.
[55] *Zapiski I.A. Zheliabuzhskago* in *Zapiski russkikh liudey* (St. Petersburg, 1841). I am extremely grateful to Paul Bushkovitch for pointing out that I. A. Zheliabuzhsky died in 1692.

and "inside" knowledge. Besides, let us not forget the wider context, since apart from Russia Gordon also served Sweden and the Polish-Lithuanian Commonwealth, and clung to British citizenship. He travelled all over the tsar's European dominions from Archangel to Azov, as well as through many Western countries. By the way, in the West likewise, private journals of the seventeenth century, as distinct from polished memoirs intended for print, are rather rare, which makes Gordon's evidence still more precious.

Even being just a trooper, he vigilantly followed the military and political developments in Europe, striving to gather reliable accounts of whatever he missed himself, and to digest the course of events. Thereafter, relying on the whole network of his confidants and correspondents, spread over almost every major city between Russia and Britain, the diarist received prompt and precise communications on European affairs. Another of Gordon's undeniable virtues is impartiality. Despite his lengthy service for different crowns, he did not become a blind partisan of any of them; he often paid tribute to the enemy, did not hush up the follies, vices and cruelties of his comrades, and confessed his own guilt.

The six surviving manuscript tomes of the Diary, which amount in total to 3,183 pages, cover almost the whole life-span of the author, from his birth in 1635 until 1699, when he, already weak with age and illness, seems to have abandoned his notes.[56] The chronological division by volumes is as follows: I. 1635–1659; II. 1659–1667; III. 1677–1678; IV. 1684–1690; V. 1690–1695; VI. 1695–1698. Two, three or more parts dated 1667–1676 and 1678–1683 are lacking. There are also many smaller gaps in each case.

Virtually the entire Diary is written by the author himself, in a neat, intelligible hand, although the density of the text greatly varies even within a few pages. Corrections, errors (repeats or evident omissions of words or letters) and marginal notes are not many. The years of childhood and youth are only briefly dealt with, and detailed entries begin in 1655, when Gordon enlisted into military service. It was obviously then that he decided

---

[56] However, from other sources we know that during the last year of his life Gordon was not confined to bed, but sometimes attended public ceremonies and entertained the tsar and other guests. Perhaps the last chapter of the Diary, begun in 1699, did not come down to us.

to take up the pen as well as the sword. In many places, especially for the early years, there are clear signs of subsequent revision. The restless life of a soldier, entailing campaigns, battles, imprisonments, fires etc., did not favour the preservation of notebooks or personal papers, so that the author must have been repeatedly obliged to restore, rewrite and supplement them. But we can be certain that the Diary was begun earlier than some experts used to believe: Gordon himself says that during the battle of Warsaw in July 1656 he recorded everything he heard at the Polish council of war on the very same day, and the previous year he regrets his failure to set down his impressions of the Pomeranian campaign because of illness. A closer look at Volume 1 reveals that our manuscript is a fair copy compiled by the diarist some years after the events he describes.[57] The reasons for his occasional abrupt alternating between his own story and public affairs (fols. 79v, 125) are a matter of conjecture, but the present edition strictly adheres to the original in this and other respects. Whatever later changes he could have made to his original notes, the frequently detailed and lively narrative, the abundance of dates, names and figures convince us that Gordon strove to stay on a hot scent of things, as far as he could.

Since Gordon came from the North-East of Scotland, lived and studied there and never visited England until his mature years, it might seem strange that he chose to write in English, not Scots. Besides, his attachment to his native country is fully apparent, and he normally makes a pronounced distinction between the Scots and the English. Part of the answer may lie in the fact that his studies at school and college were conducted in Latin, while English was mastered by means of literary works, and considered a hallmark of a refined man of letters. Nevertheless, Gordon was perfectly fluent in his native tongue, which often shows in the orthography and vocabulary of his journal and correspondence. Examples are numerous and common: *as* for *than*; such forms as *cam*, *mad* and *ar*, terms military (*ensignie*, *cartow*) and others (*Januar*, *Saturnday*, *braw*, *travale*, *merk*, *skemler*, *hosenet*, *infare* etc.). All this often defied translators and

---

[57] See M. R. Ryzhenkov's Description of the Manuscript below.

editors, who either made mistakes or simply dropped the incomprehensible terms or phrases, for instance, *burnt bairns fire dreid*. Linguistically this source, with all its impregnations in German, Polish, Russian and other tongues, is no less intriguing than historically, and so far has been even less appreciated in the former sense.

Gordon's style betrays an educated officer, rather than a man of letters; it is restrained, artless, not always smooth, sometimes dryish, but it cannot be called poor. The diarist was well polished for his time and circle, free with several languages, very fond of books, music and theatre and, as Graeme Herd has shown, was a long-standing correspondent of the London Gazette, Britain's first newspaper.[58]

The contents and tone of the Diary undergo gradual changes. With time it gives less vent to personal thoughts and emotions, and in later years becomes more terse and dispassionate. It is much more than a straightforward chronological record. Before us we have not just a narrative source preserving the memory of a multitude of events across more than half of Europe during half a century, but also a valuable collection of documents. Herein we find testimonials of service, petitions, bills, regimental accounts, plans and drawings (in Volume III), international treaties, official and private letters, descriptions of campaigns and battles, various essays and memoranda etc. The greatest detail is allotted to the Northern War of 1655–60, the tragic period of the Flood for Poland-Lithuania, when almost all neighbours rose in arms against it, as well as to the Chigirin and Azov campaigns of the Russians. Each volume has its own culmination points, where Gordon's views and feelings are more fully expressed. Thus, grasping the importance of the occasion and as if rallying the remainder of his strength, he gives a particular and emotional account of the last *streltsy* revolt in 1698.

Throughout such a vast journal it was difficult to maintain a uniform approach and to avoid a certain monotony, especially since Gordon

---

[58] G.P. Herd, *General Patrick Gordon of Auchleuchries (1635–1699): A Scot in Russian Service*. Unpubl. Ph.D. Dissertation (University of Aberdeen, 1995). See also A.B. Pernal, "London Gazette as a primary source for the biography of General Patrick Gordon", *The Canadian Journal of History*, April 2003.

touched upon both momentous and commonplace things, and now and then simply lacked time or chance to capture them. Besides, his innate canniness and prudence made him keep quiet on some matters, if only because the journal could fall into hostile hands. One may regret that meeting the celebrities of his age, monarchs, commanders or noblemen, the diarist is almost silent about their appearance or character, and often prefers not to disclose the themes of their conversations.

Gordon belonged to the same generation as Tsar Alexey Mikhailovich of Russia, Kings Charles II and James II of Great Britain, King Jan Sobieski of Poland, Peter the Great's "Prince-Caesar" Fiodor Romodanovsky and Hetman Yury Khmelnytsky of Ukraine – and was personally acquainted with all of them. He was almost the same age as the French military engineer Sebastien de Vauban, the English writer John Dryden, the Dutch painter Jan Vermeer and the Danish-German composer Dietrich Buxtehude – and, visiting the places where they lived and worked, could have well satisfied his curiosity by getting familiar with their creations. On the other hand, many lines of his chronicle are devoted to rather tedious enumerations of his revenues and expenses, or to distances between the towns and villages lying on his route. Still, I wholly agree with the opinion of the Scottish historian J. Robertson that "we should rather marvel at the journalist's persevering assiduity in writing so much, than blame him for not writing more".[59] For even the most routine information on, say, the prices in Krakow, Moscow or Edinburgh is not devoid of interest.

Gordon's Diary is a veritable kaleidoscope of seventeenth-century history and daily life, to which the author's numerous adventures impart a lot of colour. The range of evidence which can be gleaned from it is extremely wide, from military tactics and armament to monetary circulation, from politics and diplomacy to medicine and the occult. There are also not a few lively and poignant episodes and portraits, such as those of the Polish gentleman Jan Stocki, Trooper James Montgomery, Colonel Alexander Anderson or Prince Jerzy Lubomirski (in Volume II); they show that the diarist could command a more artistic and imaginative style if he chose

---

[59] *Passages from the Diary*, p. xvi.

to. Not least, here is a fascinating record of the Scottish Diaspora; all his life and in all his travels Patrick Gordon could feel at home thanks to his compatriots, and his clansmen alone, whom he encountered between Aberdeenshire and Muscovy, are several dozen.

What follows is the beginning of the first unabridged publication in its original language of one of the greatest surviving seventeenth-century chronicles. For the time being, it is not the editor's task to collate or check Gordon's testimony as against other sources, to correct or make up for his imperfections. Given the enormity of material, this is possible only as a joint effort by scholars representing different countries and trends. This work has already begun, and in most cases, whenever his statements can be corroborated, and despite some inevitable flaws, Gordon proves a very conscientious and reliable witness.[60] My own experience, after working with the Diary as well as in the Russian and British archives for nearly twenty years, is decidedly in favour of this point of view.

To conclude, my pleasant duty is to express sincere gratitude to the staff of the Russian State Archive of Military History and Russian State Archive of Ancient Acts, especially to I.O. Garkusha and M.R. Ryzhenkov, for the opportunity to have constant access to the original manuscript of Gordon's Diary and other treasures of these collections; to my Scottish friends and fellow historians, particularly Paul Dukes, John Erickson, the Dalyell family, the Reid family, Graeme Herd, Murray Frame and Frank McGuire for their manifold help and hearty hospitality during my work in Scotland; to my colleagues at the Institute of General History, Russian Academy of Sciences, and at the Moscow Caledonian Club, and to my own kin for their faithful support and patience. Lastly, I should note that my quest of the life and times of Patrick Gordon was much advanced in 2002 by a Royal Society of Edinburgh/Caledonian Research Foundation fellowship, for which I was nominated by John Erickson and Paul Dukes. I could not wish for better recommendations, and the best token of

---

[60] M.C. Posselt, comparing the Diary's data with authoritative contemporary works, *De Rebus a Carolo Gustavo Sveciae Rege Gestis Commentariorum* by Samuel Pufendorf and *Annalium Poloniae climacter secundus* by Wespazjan Kochowski, often gives preference to Gordon.

gratitude I can offer is the full scholarly edition of Gordon's journal both in Russian and English, which is my ultimate goal.

Editor's Note on the Text

The text of Patrick Gordon's Diary is transcribed, collated, edited and reproduced in its entirety from the original autograph manuscript kept in the Russian State Archive of Military History, Moscow. Every care has been taken to preserve the author's spelling as faithfully as possible, with just a few most evident slips emended and repeated words excluded. The original punctuation has been taken into account and modified, since Gordon hardly uses any question, exclamation or quotation marks. Paragraphs have been introduced where they seemed appropriate. The capitals, rather wayward in the original, have been standardized. Foreign words (not English or Scots) are given in italics, and omissions indicated by ellipses. Except for some obvious or uncertain cases, most abbreviations, contractions and initials have been extended in square brackets, which are also used for editorial additions and conjectures. The author's own notes and significant corrections as well as variant readings of any substance are mentioned in the commentary.

Description of the Manuscript

Mikhail Ryzhenkov

For its first complete edition in the original language it is appropriate to give at least a brief description of the autograph Volume I of Patrick Gordon's Diary preserved in the Russian State Archive of Military History. This is indeed a necessary element of analysis whenever a documentary source is brought to the attention of scholars worldwide. This will possibly allow us to ascertain the date of the manuscript and the circumstances of its compilation.

Volume I is written on paper in quarto, folded into sections and later bound together. The text appears on both sides of folios, and the space it occupies amounts to 16.5–17 by 12–13 cm; the sizes of margins are: top 1.5–2.5 cm, right and left 1.5–2 cm, bottom 0.5–1.5 cm. This arrangement proves that the text was initially written on pages of this very format. Judging by the hand, the entire volume belongs to one person, while comparison with other documents by Patrick Gordon makes it clear that we are dealing with his autograph. The contents of this volume do not make an impression of daily entries, but the sequence of fragments executed with different pens and ink (ranging in tone from light brown to nearly black) shows that the notes were written in several stages, from 10 to about 50 folios at a time. Pagination of the whole volume was marked by the author in one go, apparently before sending it to the binder.

The study of watermarks in Volume I is complicated by the format of the bound manuscript, because in the case of 4to the filigree, usually placed in the middle of a half-sheet, is hidden by the spine, leaving just a part of it visible. However, even these fragments lead us to certain conclusions. Mainly Dutch and, to a lesser extent, French and German paper, widespread in Russia in the second half of the seventeenth century, was used here.

The first folios bear watermarks with the coat of arms of Amsterdam (fols. 1, 20), the jester's head with a collar of 7 (fols. 10, 11) or 5 (fol. 15) bells, and the Paschal Lamb with a cross (fol. 17). Identical Dutch paper was increasingly imported to Russia via Archangel from the 1660s onwards.[1] This serves as indirect proof that Volume I, as we know it, was compiled by the diarist after he moved to Russia. There are even more grounds for such a supposition. From fol. 72 onwards we often meet with the filigree depicting a lady and a cavalier, inscribed "ALLEMODEPAPPIER", which so far has not been traced in documents dated earlier than the 1670s.[2] Even if we take into account Gordon's direct contacts with foreign merchants, and the possibility of paper being old stock, it could still be assumed that the Volume I we have was produced no earlier than the late 1660s. Further indications of this are watermarks with the double eagle (fols. 134, 137, 245)[3], the letters CDG[4], and the anchor within or without a circle (fols. 198, 199). Naturally, filigrees enable us to determine just the lower chronological limit in the history of a given source.

All this, of course, does not rule out that Gordon had at his disposal some earlier notes of his, contemporary with the events described, otherwise it is hard to explain the high level of detail and precision in dates and figures, which are remarkable features of the Diary. However, the text that is available to us was written or copied (possibly with some editing by the author) 10 or 15 years after these events. Readers should bear it in mind.

The binding of Volume I is of particular interest. It is absolutely unique and has no parallels in the catalogues of old Russian books and manuscripts. This is scarcely surprising. S.A. Klepikov, an outstanding expert in the field, observed that "by the end of the seventeenth century individual binding for noble persons became widespread, which greatly differed in style, material and appearance from those of the Moscow Printing House and the Trinity-St.Sergy's Lavra".[5]

---

[1] N.P. Likhachev, *Paleograficheskoye znacheniye bumazhnykh vodianykh znakov*, pt. I (St. Petersburg, 1899), pp. 3–5.
[2] T.V. Dianova & L.M. Kostiukhina, *Filigrani XVII veka po rukopisnym istochnikam GIM. Katalog* (Moscow, 1988), no. 1256.
[3] Ibid., nos. 1037–1041.
[4] W.A. Churchill, *Watermarks in Paper in Holland, England, France etc. in the XVII and XVIII Centuries and their Interconnection* (Amsterdam, 1935), nos. 110, 412.
[5] S.A. Klepikov, "Iz istorii russkogo khudozhestvennogo perepliota" in *Kniga. Issledovaniya i materialy*, sb. I (Moscow, 1959), pp. 137–9.

The dimensions of front and back covers are virtually the same: length 20.6 cm, width 16.5 cm; the inner book with covers is 3.7 cm thick. The binding is of solid leather, smooth and dark, over cardboard. It was restored after 1836, as attested by paper flyleaves with the watermarks "Е.Б.Ф. 1836" (Elizavetinskaya Paper Mill near St. Petersburg). Restoration must have been linked with the translation carried out by D.E. Koehler. The ends of the inner book are covered with red paint, with no other decoration on the edge. There are no laid-on protective or ornamental elements either. Both covers have straps, two on each one. The spine is smooth and undecorated; stamped designs appear only on the covers.

The front cover is framed with a border of plant ornamentation, alternating with crowned heads in round medallions (three on each side). There is a similar double border on the back cover, with the ornament also filling the central square.

The lozenge in the middle of the front cover contains (with traces of gilding) the seated figure of youthful Christ, the image known as the Saviour Emmanuel. The beardless youth with a halo is sitting with legs crossed, his head bent on his left hand, while his right holds the orb crowned with a cross. We can be sure that Jesus is depicted here by the monograms on both sides of the head as well as by images of cherubs. Above, the words "АΣ УСНУХ" are stamped; "Σ" must be the reversed Russian "З", which, in Church Slavonic, gives us the beginning of verse 5, Psalm 3: "*I laid me down* and slept; I awaked; for the Lord sustained me".

It is doubtful that the binder himself chose the image and the quotation unconnected with the contents of the manuscript. On the other hand, some experts point out that in the medieval and early modern period the front-cover centrepiece is comparable to an ex-libris: "the appearance of any centrepiece on a binding was no accident, on the contrary, it already reflected the existing symbolic and literary tradition of the Middle Ages".[6] Gordon himself confesses that, each time he found himself in a hopeless position, he was saved only by devout prayer to the Lord (*Diary*, I, fol. 6; see also fols. 24v–26 and 161–162, where he is in mortal danger while

---

[6] V.V. Kalugin, "Simvolika siuzhetnogo srednika" in *Germenevtika drevnerusskoy literatury*, sb. II (Moscow, 1989), p. 33.

asleep). This is also the apparent meaning of the psalm quoted on the cover, which must have been suggested by the diarist himself. The image of youthful Christ, rather rare in Russian iconography, could be a sign of the Ukrainian school. It has been observed that in the late seventeenth century the ornamentation and details of Russian book-covers were strongly influenced by the fanciful and lavish Ukrainian baroque.[7] The binding in question could well have been made in Ukraine proper, where Gordon spent several years. In any case, the Cyrillic quotation supports the idea that although the events related in Volume I occurred outside Russia, Patrick Gordon completed his manuscript when already in Russian service.

---

[7] S.A. Klepikov, op. cit., p. 141.

VOLUME I

1635 – 1659

Author's preface

{f. 2 verso} I am not ignorant that it is thought as hard a taske for any man to writt the story of his owne lyfe, and narrative of his actions, as for ane artist truly to draw his owne picture; yet, haveing proposed to my self to writt only by way of a journall, without makeing any reflections by blameing or commending any of the passages of my lyfe (following herein the counsell of Cato, *"Nec te laudaveris, nec te culpaveris ipse"*[1]), I think it not uneasy; especially not intending it for publick view, as also leaving to others, if any shall take paines to read it, the free censure of any thing here done. I have mentioned no more of publick effaires as came to my knowledge, relateing rumours for such and truths for verity. Some publick effaires (military I meane, for with those of state I have medled very litle, being out of my spheare) I have touched in a continued series, and others interlaced with the story of my owne lyfe (defective, I confess, and that for want of documents and intelligence) being such things the most whereof I have been present at and seen my self. To conclude, I cannot tell you a better or truer reason for writeing this, as that it is to please my owne fancy, not being curious of pleasing any bodyes else, seing *omnibus placere*[2] hath been reckoned as yet among the *impossibilia*[3].

Words and phrases from the original are in italics.

[1] Do not praise or blame yourself (Lat.). The original saying begins: "Nec te collaudes…" (*Disticha Catonis*, II, 16). The supposed author is Dionysius Cato (3rd–4th c. AD).
[2] To please all (Lat.).
[3] Impossibilities (Lat.).

{3} **A.D. 1635**

In the year of our Redemption one thowsand six hundred thirty and fyve, on the last day of March[4], about 3 aclock afternoone, being Easter Tuesday, in Easter Achluichries[5], within the parish of Crochdan[6] and the shirefdome of Aberdeene, I was borne; my parents, John Gordon[7] and Mary Ogilvie, heritours and proprietours of the same lands of Achluichries.

1640

I was sent to the schoole at the kirk of Crochdan on Lambe masse day[8], and put to lodge and dyet by a widdow called Margaret Allan, my schoolmaster being William Logan.

Here I, together with my eldest brother[9], stayed foure yeares, haveing proceeded to *"Multiplex uno sensu"* in the first part of Despauters grammer[10].

---

[4] Until the middle of the eighteenth century Britain used the Julian, Old Style calendar. However, when in Poland, Patrick Gordon often used the Gregorian (New Style) calendar already adopted by Roman Catholics, ten days in advance of the Julian in the seventeenth century. Thus, he was born on 10 April New Style.

[5] Auchleuchries (Gaelic: Achadh luachrach, "field of rushes") near Ellon, Aberdeenshire. This estate was held by the Gordons of the Lords Hay, Earls of Erroll.

[6] Cruden.

[7] Patrick's father, John Gordon of Auchleuchries, was born ca. 1610 and died shortly before 30 May 1682.

[8] *Lambe masse day* or Lammas, one of the four quarterly term days in Scotland, falls on 1 August. Of Anglo-Saxon derivation, it means 'loaf mass' or 'bread mass', so called because offerings were formerly made on this day of the first fruits of the harvest.

[9] Patrick's eldest brother George, born in 1634, died between 1654 and 1660.

[10] Jean Despauter, or van Pauteren (1460–1520), famous Flemish grammarian, whose works went through many editions. See Ioannis Despauterii Ninivitae, Grammaticae Institutionis Lib. VII docte et concinne in compendium redacti per Sebastianum Duisburgensem, lib. III "De heteroclitis". Edinburgh, 1617, p. 89.

1644

My father, dwelling in Achridy[11], in the parish of Ellon, I was sent to that schoole, my schoolm[aste]r the same, being translated hither, being lodged and dyeted in Alex[ande]r Scrogges his house.

I was at this schoole about a year, when, because of the great troubles both befor and now[12], all publick schooles were abandoned. My father tooke a schoolm[aste]r called Georg Murray into his house, who teached us halfe {3v} a year very well.

1646

My father removeing to Hony-Crooke[13], wee were sent againe to the schoole of Ellon, and lodged in John Mill his house, o[u]r schoolm[aste]r being Mr. Hary Tom.

Here wee learned about a year. My father in the meane tyme removed to Achmade[14], and afterward to his owne lands and dwelled in Westertowne[15].

---

[11] Auchreddie.

[12] Since May 1639 Patrick Gordon's native North-East of Scotland became the scene of bitter conflict between Covenanters and Royalists (the Trot of Turriff took place just a few miles from Auchleuchries). This led to full-scale Civil War, and Aberdeenshire loomed large in the Marquis of Montrose's campaigns. Most Gordons, including the clan chief Marquis of Huntly, supported the King. In 1644 Patrick's father and unkle took part in armed raids, but their leader, Sir John Gordon of Haddo, was seized and executed by the Covenanters. The opposing forces wrought great devastation on the country (see John Spalding, The History of the Troubles and Memorable Transactions in Scotland. Aberdeen, 1829).

[13] *Hony-Crooke*, whose name in the original took quite a while to decipher, no longer exists.

[14] Auchmaud.

[15] Westertoun of Auchleuchries.

1648

Wee were sent againe to the schoole of Crowdan; our schoolm[aste]r Mr. Alex[ande]r Frazer, who teached us about a yeare.

1649

Mr. Andrew Browne succeeding schoolm[aste]r, I, with my brothers, were continued at schoole, and lodged and dyeted in Alex[ande]r Garioch his house, near two yeares[16].

1651

I was taken from schoole; and, staying at home, did wait upon my father.

Haveing thus, by the most loveing care of my deare parents, attained to as much learning as the ordinary countrey schools affoords, and being unwilling, because of my dissenting in religion[17], to go to the university in Scotland, I resolved, partly to dissolve the bonds of a youthfull affection, wherein I was entangled, by banishing my self from the object; partly to obtaine my liberty, which I fondly conceited to be restrained, by the carefull inspection of my loveing parents; but, most of all, my patrimony being but small, as being the yonger son of a yonger brother of a yonger house; I resolved, I say, to go to some forreigne countrey, not careing much on what pretence, or to which countrey I should go, seing I had no knowne ffriend in any forreigne place.

---

[16] On 10 September 1650 the author's name is first mentioned in an official document: in Patrick's presence his debt-ridden father granted to his sister Ann and her husband, James Gordon of Greinmyre, the Mains of Auchleuchries with the mill etc., redeemably by payment of 2,500 merks Scots (Particular Register of Seisins for Aberdeenshire, vol. XIV, ff. 437–9).

[17] The Gordons of Auchleuchries were Roman Catholic.

Being thus resolved, there wanted nothing but to have the leave and furtherance of my parents, which I obtained by the intercession of my unkle, and haveing notice of a ship at Aberdeen bound shortly for {4} Dantzick[18], I made a progresse into the countrey amongst my ffriends and tooke my leave of them.

On the third of June, after a sadd parting with my loveing mother, brothers and sister[19], I tooke my jorney to Aberdeen in company of my father and unkle, who after two dayes stay, wherein I was furnished with cloaths, money and necesseries, returned. My mother came fowre dayes thereafter, of whom I received the benediction and tooke my leave.

On the 12th ditto I went aboord and stayed at anchor all night in the roade. The shipp was a large merchants shipp, with 18 gunnes, belonging to Dantzick, the shipper called Jacob Barthman.

On the 13th the merchants and passengers came aboard and towards night, notwithstanding it was calme and misty, wee weighed anchor and with the tyde made a slow passage. About sunsett it cleared up, whereof haveing notice below deck, wee made hast above, and with many sighes and teares bidd our native countrey farewell, which even then seemed to be in a mourning for our departure; but shortly, by a brisk gale of westerly wind, wee were deprived of all sight thereof. Haveing, to ease our minds, laid our selves downe to rest, wee were called up by the noise which the mariners made, because of some shippes approaching, who, being come near, were knowne to be Hollanders. They enquired what wee were, from whence come and whither bound. To all which, receiving satisfaction, they asked if wee had any Parliament men aboard and if wee had seen an English shipp which had escaped them in the mist[20]. To both which was answered {4v} "No"; so after salutation with great gunnes, according to the manner at sea, wee parted, keeping our course East and by North two dayes with a favorable gale. Then wee were by

---

[18] Gdańsk, Poland.
[19] Patrick had four brothers: George (elder), the younger being John (ca.1637–after 1698), James (d. 1691) and Alexander (d. 1665), and one sister, Elizabeth (1644– after 1698).
[20] At this period Anglo-Dutch tensions grew worse, leading to the war of 1652–54.

contrary winds forced very farr to the North, and after two weekes, had a sight of Norway. The wind then being a litle better, wee sailed along that coast, passing by the Neus to Skagen in Jutland, then by the Illand Lezow[21], the Trindell, and the litle illand Anout[22], then by a rock called the Kole, where the shippers exact a discretion of every one who hath not passed that way befor; the mariners are ordinarily lett downe thrice from the end of the maine re into the sea[23]. Wee came in the evening to the roade befor Elsenure[24], and anchored about halfe a Dutch mile[25] from the strand or shore.

The next day wee went ashore and dined in a Scotsmans house[26] very well for twelve pence a man, and at night returned to the shipp. On the morrow about noone, the shipp being cleared, wee hoised saile, and made good way with a fresh gale of wind by the Illands Ween and Roan on o[u]r left hand, and the citty Copenhagen, the King of Denmarks[27] residence, on o[u]r right, holding our course by Valsterboom[28] [and] the Illand Bornholme over to the coast of Pomerell[29].

On the 18th July, new stile, wee had a sight of the coast. In the evening was a great calme, and in the night great raine and thunder, so that wee made no way. The next day wee passed by the Heel, and a litle after began to throw out our ballast, which was sand and stones. The next day being also calme, and being near the shore, wee were towed near the land by boats, and anchored befor the Munde, a strong fort. Some of us went ashore and walked to Dantzick on foot, being a Dutch {5} mile from the

---

[21] Læsø.
[22] Anholt.
[23] A similar description of "baptism at sea" can be found in A.O. Exquemelin's "The Buccaneers of America". *Re* means yard.
[24] Helsingør, Denmark.
[25] *Dutch* usually means "German" in the Diary. German mile (24,000 German feet) equalled 7,532.5 meters in Northern Germany.
[26] Every major port on the Baltic route had a sizeable colony of Scots. Already in the mid-sixteenth century they constituted nearly 14% of the population of Helsingør (T. Riis, Should Auld Acquaintance Be Forgot... Odense, 1988, vol. I, p. 155).
[27] Frederik III (1609–1670), King of Denmark and Norway from 1648.
[28] Falsterbo.
[29] Eastern Pomerania.

citty, whither wee arrived at noone and lodged in a Scotsmans house in the Holy Ghost street, our landlord being called John Donaldsone[30]. Here I stayed eight dayes.

On Fridday, with a gentleman Thomas Menezes and 3 other Dutch men, wee bespoke the ordinary coach for Konigsberg[31], and Mr. Menezes and I payed each for our share to Brawnsberg[32] a doller and a halfe. On Saturnday at 8 acloak wee tooke our jorney, and came the same night to Elving[33], being 9 miles, and the next day timely to Frawensberg[34], 5 miles; where meeting with o[u]r good friend Mr. Robert Blackhall[35], who was priest and vicar to one of the chanons there, by his perswasion we let our coach go, and stayed all night.

This towne lyeth on the lake called the Frish haffe, being every where open, and all along the foot of an hill, whereon the *Dume*[36] standeth, wherein ar, as I remember, 8 channons, who have most pleasant houses and orchards towards the fields. (Here Copernicus water worke)[37]. The next day, being well entertained by Fa[the]r Blackhall, and hireing an open waggon, Father Blackhall, Mr. Menezes and I rode to Brawnsberg, being a mile, most of the way being through a wood.

---

[30] Here and later on Gordon regularly comes across his compatriots. A part of Gdańsk, mentioned below, was actually called "Schottland". In Poland in the first half of the seventeenth century the number of Scots was estimated to have reached 30,000, most of them pedlars, but many serving in the army, as Gordon was to find out. See A.F. Steuart, Papers Relating to the Scots in Poland. Edinburgh, 1915, and the works of Anna Biegańska.

[31] Modern Kaliningrad, Russia.

[32] Braniewo, Poland.

[33] Elblag.

[34] Frombork.

[35] In the late 1630s one Robert Blackhall was an "outstanding Papist" in the parish of Cruden. Cf. A Breiffe Narration of the Services done to Three Noble Ladyes by Gilbert Blakhal, Preist of the Scots Mission in France, in the Low Countries and in Scotland, 1631–1649. Aberdeen, 1844, p. 68: "I did confesse and communicat all the Catholiks that were ther, and from Aberdein to Buchan, a mater of 19 or 20 miles, wher I had but fyve Catholick houses to go to... and Cruden... The distance betwixt theis houses obliged me to stay a night in each of them to say messe, confesse, communicat and exhort the Catholicks be way of a short preaching".

[36] Cathedral (German: Dom).

[37] Author's note on the margin.

Brawnsberg lyeth in the B[isho]prick of Vermia[38], on the river Passary[39], which a mile from thence falleth in the Frish-haffe. Over the river is the New towne, which is divided in two streets, one towards Koningsberg, the other along the river upwards. The townes ar joined by a bridge, the old towne walled, the new open every where. Here wee tooke up our lodging by Mr. Menezes his brother, who was a priest and called Alexander Michal Menezes, whose charge was a small church in the new towne.

Here being at my studies in the Colledge of the Jesuits[40], albeit I wanted not for any thing, the Jesuits alwayes bestowing extraordinary paines, and takeing great care in educateing youth, yet could not my humor endure such a still and strict way of liveing.

[1653]

Wherefor takeing my leave, I resolved to returne {5v} home againe, and on a Tuesday, about ten acloak, I took my jorney on foot to save expences, for I had no mor money left but 7 reichs dollers and a halfe, and one suit of cloaths which I had one. So takeing my cloake and a litle bagge wherein were my linnens and some bookes, with a staffe in my hand I pilgrim'd it away all alone. I had not learned any Dutch, by reason of our speaking Latine in the Colledge, only had enquired and written downe some words necessary for askeing the way, victualls, and such like. My portmantell I caryed for ease on my back, betwixt villages, or when I did see no body; but comeing to any village or meeting any body, I tooke it under my arme. Thus accoutred, I went privately round the old towne, P. Menezes only convoying me to the high way. I walked the well knowne

---

[38] Warmia (Ermland).
[39] Passarge (German), Pasłęka (Polish).
[40] The Jesuit College of Braniewo (Braunsberg), whose buildings still partly survive, was founded in 1565 by Cardinal Stanislaus Hosius (hence Collegium Hosianum), and had a high reputation in Poland and beyond. Despite his sound schooling there, Gordon seems not to have officially matriculated nor did he complete the course of studies.

way through the wood to Frawensberg, pleasing my self either with trifling fancies or such objects as offered in the way.

Being come to Frawensberg, I resolved not to go to Father Blackhall for fear of being chidden for leaving the Colledge, he haveing alwayes diswaded me from takeing any other course as to be a scholler and turne religious. And so excuseing my self to him hereafter by a letter, pretending my being in company who would by no meanes make any stopp there, I went through the towne without going in any where; and keeping the high roade, about halfe a mile of[f], I did meet a coach with some gentlemen in it, who, stopping, look't very earnestly upon me, and asked me in Dutch something, which I not understanding passed by on my way. A mile and a half further, at the entring of a wood the way divideing, I was doubtfull which to hold, yet the midle being the likelyest I entred that. After I had gone a pretty way into the wood, and doubting whether I was right or not, I began with serious thoughts to consider my present condition, {6} calling to mind from whence I was come, from my most loveing parents and ffriends, and where I was now, among strangers, whose language I understood not, travelling my self knew not well whither, haveing but 7 dollers by me which could not last long, and when that was gone, I knew not where to gett a farthing more [for] the great jorney and voyage which I intended. To serve or work I thought it a disparagement, and to begg a greater. With these and such like thoughts I grew so pensive and sadd, that, sitting downe, I began to lament and bewaile my miserable condition. Then haveing my recourse to God Almighty, I with many teares implored his assistance, craveing also the intercession of the Blessed Virgin and all the Saincts in heaven. Then getting up, I went forward, continuing in prayer with great fervency, when on a suddaine, from the right hand, came an old man rideing, whose gray haires might exact and force reverence from the haughtiest heart. He, seing me crying, in crosseing my way said to me in Dutch, which I understood so: "Cry not, my child, God will comfort you". I was very astonished at his suddaine appearance and words, and also ashamed that any body should see me in such a plight. However, keepeing on my way, I began to recollect my self, and to think that God had sent this old man of purpose to divert me from such passionate fitts;

the conceitt whereof made me rouse up my self and walke on more chearfully. And, truly, as well now as very many times hereafter, as you shall hear, when, in my necessities or any extremity, I betooke my self to God Almighty by prayer, I found His extraordinary assistance.

At night I came to a village and tooke up my lodgeing in the *krue*[41] or alehouse. When I came in, I called for halfe a stowp of beer, the table being covered. The landlord asked {6v} me diverse questions, to which I could returne no anser, because I did not understand him. Only I told him from whence I came and whither I was bound. He desired me to sitt downe and eat with him, to which I readily condiscended, and calleing for another halfe of beer, which and supper being ended, I asked on[e] of the maids where I should ly, and she laughing, went and fetched me a bundle of fresh straw, and told me I might ly in an empty waggon in the place where the waggons and horses were; to the which I went, and makeing my straw bed, I laid my cloake one halfe under and the other above me, with my coat and portmantle under my head; and so, being exceedingly wearyed, I laid me downe. But by and by came the maid, and reaching me a pillow, began to laugh downright, then jumped away in such hast as if she had been afrayed of some infection. I made but one sleep the whole night, and gott up halfe an houre befor the sunne, and bringing in my pillow to the roome, asked what I had to pay. The landlady told me a stowp of beer, which I payed, and then asked what I had to pay for victualls; and she answering "nothing", I thanked and went on my way.

This place being a mile or litle more from Elving, one halfe whereof was downe a hill, about 8 acloak I came into the towne, where I made no stay, only buying some excellent white bread called *semels*[42] and apples, I walked directly through. When I was without the towne, I made a halt, to see if I could light on any company going that way; when by and by came two sturdy fellowes, of whom I enquired if they were going to Dantzick, and they answering "yea", wee jogged on together. These were alwayes troubling me with questions, to the which I could answer nothing, only that I understood not Dutch. {7} Haveing walked a mile, on[e] of these

---

[41] Krug (German) – inn or tavern.
[42] Semmel (German) – wheat bread or bun.

fellowes left us; the other being a dogged-like bare fellow, who was still eying my cloaths and cloak, and our way being towards a black like thick wood, I began to conceit that this fellow had brought me out of the way, and intended to lead me into that wood, and there to murther me for my cloaths, or any thing else he thought to find by me. This conceit of mine strongly encreasing, wee came to a little house, where he asked me if I would drink any beer. I told him I had no money; so he calling for beer, I took out my purse, wherein were 7 or 8 *grosses*, all in small shillings[43], which I of purpose shewed him, telling him it was all I had to bring me to Dantzick. I called for small beer for 2 shillings, which, haveing drunk, my guide and fellow traveller (whom I would have very faine been ridd of if I could) brought me on a way towards the left hand, and by and by to a village.

Wee went into the inne, where my fellow traveller called for beer, and I for small beer; whereat the landlady wondering, was satisfyed at last by the information she received from the fellow that cam with me. At my comeing in, I saw, in the other roome, a fellow standing befor a pack, measuring of lace; and haveing heard in Brawnsberg that there were diverse Scottishmen who used this kind of trade in Prussia, I began to suspect that this was a countreyman. The landlady understanding that I could speak no Dutch, nor Polls either, called out this packman, who haveing asked me something in Dutch, and receiving my usuall answer, that I understood no Dutch, he asked me what countreyman I was. I told him, a Scottishman. Then askeing me, very confidently, from whence I came, whither I was going, what course of lyfe I intended to take, and why I travelled in company of {7v} that fellow, whom he knew, as he said, to be a robber, and wondring that I had travelled so farr with him unrobd, and told me, if I had a mind for Dantzick, I should go along with him to his house, which was but a mile of, and stay three or foure dayes, and he would take me upon a waggon to Dantzick. I answered to every thing as circumspectly as I could, and thanked him for his kind profer, telling him I must be precisely in Dantzick the next day. He urged my going along

---

[43] Grosz and szeląg, small Polish coins.

with him, and the mor he urged, the mor jealous I was that he had some designe upon me; and so, shifting him fairely of, I made ready to be gone. My countreyman diswaded me from going any farther with that fellow, but I told him that I had found nothing in him as yet, and intended at night to hire a waggon for the next day.

So wee went away together, and came to a house called Weyershoffe, and being sett downe in the inne, which is hard by, my fellow traveller told me that he was to stay there; whereat I seemed sorry, but he enquireing, lighted upon other two fellowes, who were bound for Dantzick, to whom he recommended me, and so wee parted. These fellowes tooke a near by way, ferrying over many ditches, and passeing others upon planks; and came towards night to a village about a quarter of a mile from the Wistle[44]. Here I lodged all night, supping on such ordinary fare as they use there.

The next morning I was not able to go any further. My feet, not being used to such hard travell, was full of blisters, and the skinne of[f] in many places; wherefor, going out to the high way, which lay by the end of the village, I waited upon some occasion of hireing a waggon. There droved by, in short tyme, diverse waggons or *kolesses*[45], as they call them, none whereof would take me along. At last came a very civill man, haveing another sitting by him, at whom I asked in the best manner I could, if he would take me along to Dantzik, and what {8} he would take for fraught; who, first askeing halfe a doller, at last told me he would take no less as a reichs ort[46]; which I promiseing, went to the inne, and paying for my supper, fetch my portmantle, and gott me upon the *kolesse*. Here, as every where, I was troubled with questions, which I did not understand. Wee crossed the Wistle in a *prumme*[47], and gott to Dantzick by 11 acloak, being 3 miles from the *prumme*; where, paying my fraught, I went to seek out my old lodging which, after much wandring up and downe, I found, where I was kindly welcom'd by my landlady, who was a notable resolute woman.

---

[44] Vistula, Wisła.
[45] Kolasa (Polish).
[46] *Ort* = ¼ Taler.
[47] Pram, flat-bottomed boat.

Here I found my self in great anxiety and perplexity, not knowing what to begin; for all the ships were gone, and so no hopes left of getting home to my owne countrey; no acquaintance of whom I could borrow any money to subsist with untill the next shipping; my cloaths and linnens beginning to looke bare; and, the worst of all, no person to whom I could reveale my necessities, being bashfull and ashamed that any should know that I was redacted to such straights. But my landlady guessing, by my retirednes and melancholious behaviour, my condition, began to presse me to declare my intentions. I told her my resolution was to returne to my parents as soone as I could; which my intention she communicateing to diverse of my countreymen who frequented her house, and withall, that she thought me to be scarce of money; so, the next day at dinner, these merchants began to perswade me to turne merchant, to the which I, fynding my nature averse, answered in fair termes, however, not being willing to disoblidge any. They began to tell me, that it would be 9 or 10 moneths ere I should fynd ane occasion by sea to Scotland; to travell by land would be very expensive, and to stay there no lesse. But findeing me averse to engage my self, and resolute to returne home, they left of, and told me I had best travell up to Polland, where I might, one way or another, passe the ensuing winter, and then take what course I thought fittest in the spring; and that there was a countrey man and namesake of mine {8v} liveing in a towne called Culm[48], about 20 miles of[f], who was a very civill man, and would be very glad of my company; which counsell I embraced, and desired their assistance in findeing an occasion thither.

The next day, I was informed of a flatt-bottomed vessell, ordinarily called *skute*[49], which was to returne to Swets[50], a mile from Culm; which way of travelling, albeit longsome and irkesome, yet because cheape, I willingly choosed. So upon a Tuesday […][51] *Augusti*, haveing contented my landlady for my dyet and lodging, being very favourably used, I walked to the vessell, wherein I was to travell; and about two houres befor sunsett,

---

[48] Chełmno.
[49] Szkuta (Polish).
[50] Świecie (Polish), Schwetz (German).
[51] Gaps in original MS are indicated thus.

haveing all ready, wee sett forward. This, as I said before, was a flatt-bottomed vessell, which is so made because of the many shallow places in the river Vistula. It was about 50 or 60 ordinary paces in length, and breadth conforme. There were 15 or 20 Polles, or rather Russes, in the boat, who could not speak a word Dutch; only he who had the command of them could speak a litle. I took up my lodgeing in the most convenient place I could find, being in the open part of the boat, being guarded from the raine by the long hanging cover of the cabine. Here was no hopes of any exercise but lying and sitting, there being no convenience for walkeing, only where the steurmans place was, which was very cumbersome. My best pastime was my booke; only sometimes I went on land and walked a good pace befor, going in now and then to some boures house or another, wher I bought milk. I had very litle pleasure for the most part of the way; the Vistula being hemmed and kept in with great dammes on either side, which hinder the prospect of the countrey, only the toppes of the houses and trees were to be seen.

About 4 miles, being so much by water, and three by land, wee passed by a towne, on our right hand, called Dirshaw[52], lying on a high ground, and fortified with walles. A mile and a halfe below this towne the Vistula divideth, on[e] arme going for Dantzick, another falleth into the Frish Haffe. The point at the division, called Dantziker Hooft[53], {9} hath been diverse tymes fortifyed and garrisoned, to the great detriment of the adjacent countrey. About 2 miles further wee passed by that arme called Nogat, which falleth also in the Frish Haffe, after it hath passed by Marienburg[54] and divided the Great from the Elbings *werder*[55]. The point here is called Monto Spitts[56], and hath been also fortifyed and garrisoned in the warres. About two miles further wee passed by the Meve[57], on our right hand, lying on a high ground, and fortifyed with stone walles. About a mile off,

---

[52] Tczew.
[53] Danziger Haupt (German), Głowa Gdańska (Polish).
[54] Malbork.
[55] Island, especially on a river (German).
[56] Montauer Spitz.
[57] Gniew.

on the left hand, Marienwerder[58], a towne fortifyed with a stone wall, and belonging to the Duke and Elector of Brandeburg[59], did show itself. Some 4 miles further, wee passed by another towne, called Nyenborg[60], situate also on a high ground, and fortifyed with a stone or brick wall; and, 3 miles further, by Graudents[61], a well fortified towne, with a castle, which being situate on a high ground, hath a very faire prospect over a most fertile and well inhabited countrey. 3 miles further wee came to Swetsh, which lyeth in a low ground, and hath, it seemes, in former times, been well fortifyed with a brick wall, [but] had only now a castle, half ruined. It lyeth off from the river to the right hand, by a litle rivelet called [Schwarzwasser]. Here I was conducted, by one of these who came along with me, to the house of John Smith, a merchant, and very civill man, where I lodged all night, and was very well entertained. The next day I gott a waggon, and after noon, I crossed the Wistula by a *prumme*, which is a flatt bottom'd vessell, wherein waggons, horses, and every thing else ar transported over rivers in this countrey.

Towards night I came to Culm, being a mile from Swets, and was conducted to my namesake his house. This Culm is very ancient and hath been of great account in former tymes, which may appear by its giveing name to all that district; and the common law, which is observed throughout all Prussia, is ordinarily called Culmish law. It was fortifyed by the [...] wi [...] with a very strong brick wall of a large circumference. It is but meanly inhabited, and slenderly builded; only about the market place are some very faire houses, with wealthy indwellers. Albeit it hath many gates, yet hath it but three which they make use {9v} of, one which leadeth to the river, the other to Culmsee[62] and Grawdents, the third to Torun[63]. It is under the jurisdiction of a bishop, who hath his title from it, and resideth in a towne about 15 miles from thence, called

---

[58] Kwidzyń.
[59] Friedrich Wilhelm Hohenzollern (1620–1688), Elector of Brandenburg and Duke of Prussia from 1640, known as the Great Elector.
[60] Nowe.
[61] Grudziądz.
[62] Chełmża.
[63] Toruń (Polish), Thorn (German). Gordon uses both versions.

Libava⁶⁴. It hath its owne magistrates and peculiar lawes and very great and ancient priviledges. It is very pleasantly situated on a large corner of the high continent. Below, towards the river, and all along the side of the hill, towards Graudents, ar many fair orchards and gardens, as also by the river a large suburb, called the Fishery. It hath within the towne 3 monasteryes, a Dominican, Franciscan, and of Votaresses, and a large cathedrall. There ar fair lands belonging to the towne, which is divided among the burgers, who of beer brewing and buying of cornes for the most part have their livelyhood.

Here I passed the tyme the winter, when falling in acquaintance with one John Dick, who was prentice to a merchant called Robert Sleich, I was perswaded by him to travell further up into Polland; and because I was much inclined to be a souldier, he told me that Duke Jan Radzewill had a lyfe company, all or most Scotsmen⁶⁵, where we would without doubt be accommodated.

[1654]

So, takeing my leave of ffriends here, I began againe a jorney on foot in company of the afors[ai]d John Dick, who had left his service. My stock was much the same as I had when I came from Brawnsberg, haveing gott 4 dollers from a ffriend upon my way; but my habit was farr changed, for towards the winter I had translated my cloak into a Polls upper coat, and lyned it with sheepskines. The first night wee went to a village and lodged by a Skotsman, who lived there. The next day wee passed by a gentlemans house, called Gzin, and so the direct way to Thorun. When wee were within a mile of the town, two waggoners with wood did overtake us, to whom wee, being wearied, gave each 2 pence to let us {10} sitt up to the towne. Wee entred the towne towards night, and

---

⁶⁴ Lubawa.
⁶⁵ Prince Janusz Radziwiłł (1612–1655), Field and Great Hetman of Lithuania, was a Calvinist. His estate of Kiejdany, which Gordon visited later, had a large colony of Scots.

tooke up our lodging in a great house, on the west side of the market place, in the old towne.

Here wee stayed 4 dayes, and then haveing with two Dutchmen, who were bakers, hired a waggon for Warso, giveing each eight florens, wee sett forward on Saturnday, betimes in the morning. The next day wee passed by Cuiafsky Brest[66], so called to distinguish it from another Brest in Littaw[67], through Cowale and Gambin, two litle townes, to Varsaw, which is 30 miles from Thorun.

Wee tooke up our lodgeing in the suburb Lesczinsky, so called from a pallace-like house hard by, built by noblemen of the family of the Lesczinskyes. The *Seym* or Parlament was sitting at this tyme in Varsaw, where wee hoped to have found Duke Radzivill. After wee had stayed 8 dayes, expecting his comeing, wee were informed that he was not to come at all, which put us upon new projects. My comerad had been two or three yeares in the countrey, could speak Polls and Dutch, had some skill in merchandising, and so, for getting a livelyhood, had many wayes the advantage of me. But my purpose of turning souldier here failing me, I resolved to persue my former resolution of returneing to my parents. Here were many merchants of our countreymen, into whose acquaintance I was ashamed to intrude my self, and they shewed but very litle countenance to me, haveing heard of my intention to turne souldier, and fearing lest I should be burthensome or troublesome to them. I had but 8 or 9 florens left, wherewith I was not able to subsist long here, or to travell farr either. I began, however, to enquire for the neerest way for Scotland, and was informed that Posna[68], the cheife citty of Great Polland would be the most convenient place I could go for first; whither an occasion shortly after offered, with a gentleman called [...], who had been at the *Seim* and had bought some horses, so that by the recommendation of a ffriend he promised to take me along and keep me {10v} free of expences, which was a very good occasion considering my condition.

---

[66] Brześć Kujawski.
[67] Brest, Belarus.
[68] Poznań.

So, upon a Tuesday early wee tooke horse, being 3 persons and six horses. The gentleman, his servant and I drove the horses along; but when wee cam to any towne he would have me lead one, and the servant the other two spare horses. The first night wee rode 5 miles and lodged in a village; the next morning through the litle towne […], and dined in Lovits[69], which is a large not well fortifyed towne; the arch-bishops castle-like faire house is fortifyed with a wall and moatt. This night wee lodged in a village; the next night in a litle towne, Piatek; and crosseing the river Warta twice, at the second crossing wee passed by a very fair gentlemans house haveing large orchards and parkes. 4 miles from Posna wee passed through the litle towne Szroda[70], where the *seimiks* or county comittees for choosing of commissioners ar kept, and, being Palme Sunday, according to the new stile observed in Polland, about midday wee passed through a pretty wood of firres about halfe a mile in breadth, the way being straight, about 30 or 40 fathome broad, ascending gently, which made a very pleasant prospect. At the comeing out of this wood wee had a sight of the fair citty of Posna, which wee entred about one acloak afternoone.

Posna or Posen of all the citties in Polland is the most pleasant, being very well scituated, haveing a wholesome aire, and a most fertile countrey round about it. The buildings are all brick, most after the ancient forme, yet very convenient, especially those lately builded. The market place is spacious, haveing a pleasant fountaine in each corner, the shopps all in rowes, each trade apart, and a stately *radthouse*[71]. The streets ar large and kept cleaner as any where else in Polland. It hath on the west side within the towne on a hill a castle built after the ancient manner and someq[uha]t decayed. The river Warta watereth the east side thereof, makeing an iland, w[hi]ch is inhabited by Germans, most whereof being tawners, giveth the name of the Tawners Suburb to it. There is a fair street which leadeth to the *Thume*[72] eastward, being halfe a mile in lentgh [*sic*]; the *Thume* is a stately structure. There are diverse monasteries of both sexes and severall orders

---

[69] Łowicz.
[70] Środa.
[71] Rathaus (German) – city hall.
[72] Cathedral.

and a vast cathedrall, {11} which make a stately show. The suburbs ar large and decored with churches and monasteries. The citty is fortifyed with a brick wall, yet not very tenable by reason of its wastnes. But that which surpasseth all is the civility of the inhabitants, which is occasioned by its vicinity to Germany and the frequent resorting of strangers to the two annuall faires, and every day almost; the Polls also, in emulation of the strangers dwelling amongst them, strive to transcend one another in civility.

The gentleman who brought me along had his house or lodging in the Jewes street, where I dined with him; and after dinner he took me along to a Skotsman called James Lindesay, to whom I had a recommendatory letter. At first he was imperiously inquisitive of my parents, education, travells and intentions. I answered to all his demands with an observant ingenuity. One passage I can not forgett, which was this. When upon his enquiry I had told him what my parents names were, he said in a disdainfull manner: "Gordon and Ogilvie! These ar two great clannes, sure you must be a gentleman!"; to which, albeit I knew it to [be] spoken in derision, I answered nothing, but that I hoped I was not the worse for that. However, afterwards he was kind enough to me. Here I was perswaded by my countreymen to stay and wait some good occasion or other of prosecuteing my jorney.

During my abode in this place I was kindly entertained by my countreymen, to witt, Robert Ferquhar, James Ferguson, James Lindesay, James White, James Watson and others. I was afterwards by their recommendation entertained in the suit of a yong nobleman called Oppalinsky, who was according to the custome of the Polonian nobility going to visitt forreigne countreyes. At my departure my kind countreymen furnished me with money and other necessaries very liberally, so that I was better stocked now as I had been since I cam from my parents.

[1655]

In this noblemans company, as one of his attendants, I came to Hamborgh, being very civilly used the whole way. It was the middle of

Februar when wee arrived here; and the nobleman after eight dayes stay takeing post for Antwerp, I tooke my leave of him.

Here at this tyme were the Sweds officers very busy levying and listing of souldiers. All the innes were full of cavaliers, ranting and carousing. When my lord departed, Wilczitsky, his paedagogue (who spoke good French, Dutch and Latine) agreed with the landlord of the inne {11v} where wee lodged, for my dyet, chamber and bed for 4 merks Lubsch[73] a weeke; only, when there were no other strangers, I was to be content with such ordinary fare as the house affoorded.

Here I stayed 8 weeks, when it chanced a cornet and a quarter master to lodge in the same innes, who haveing enquired at the landlord what I was, and understandeing my condition, began to be very kynd to me, and to shew me all respect in the tyme of dinner and supper, which was the only tyme I was forced to converse with them, I either passeing the other tymes with walkeing or keeping my chamber. In all their discourses they extolled a souldiers lyfe, telling that riches, honour, and all sorts of worldly blessings lay prostrate at a souldiers feet, wanting only his will to stoop and take them up; then, falleing out in commendation of our countreymen, then whom no better sojors were of any nation to be found, and that albeit nature had endued them with a genius fitt for any thing, yet did they despise the ease, advantage or contentment any other trade might bring and embraced that of a souldier, which without all dispute is the most honourable. Albeit I understood most of their discourse, and was well enough pleased therewith, yet was not I able to render any satisfactory answer, negative and affirmative being all I could affoord them; and, being jealous that they had a designe to engadge me, I shunned as much as I could any familiarity or conversation with them.

One day at dinner the quarter master told me that a countreyman of mine was come, called Gardin, which, according as he pronounced it, seemed to me Gordon. He told me he was a *ruitmaster*[74], a very pretty discreet man. In the tyme of my being in this citty I had not sought to be acquainted with any man for severall reasons, but especially for saveing

---

[73] Lübeck marks.
[74] Rittmeister (German) – captain of cavalry.

of expences; but now I could not be at rest untill I had gott notice where this *ruitm[aste]r* lodged, and thereupon resolved to give him a visitt, not without thoughts of engadgeing my self. Being come to his lodging, I enquired for him, and by accident, light upon a servant of his called Andrew, who was a Dutch man, but spoke good English as haveing lived in Scotland some yeares. He brought me immediately above to the *ruitmaster*, who was in company with two or three other officers. I told him that, hearing of a person of such quality as he was being come to this citty, I could not be satisfyed with my self, untill I had payed my respects {12} to him with a visitt, hopeing that he would pardon my abrupt intrudeing my self into his company at such a time, when perhaps he was bussied with weighty effaires. He answered me that I was very welcome, and that he had no such weighty effaires as could hinder him for giveing that entertainment which was due to a ffriend, especially a countreyman and stranger. And haveing desired me to sitt downe, he began to enquire of my parents, wherein haveing received satisfaction, he asked me if I knew one Major Gardin. I told him I had heard of him, but had not the honour of his acquaintance. He told me that he was his brother, and that I must be their kinsman; then, calling for a glasse of wine, began to be very merry, remembring all friends in Scotland, and then, falling to particular healths, in a short tyme wee were all pretty well warmed. All along both he and the other officers were a battering downe my resolution for Scotland, telling me that I would be laught at when I should come home, and that they would tell me I had been over sea to see what aclock it was, and returned as wise as I went out; and what comfort or content could any man of spirit, who had nothing to care for, have to stay at home, when the countrey was enthralled by an imperious insulting enemy[75], and no way of redresse left. The only way for those who bore honourable minds was to passe the tyme abroad and better their judgments by purchaseing experience at least. But what needed many perswasions, it being a course to the which I was naturally enclined? So that, without any further circumstances, I gave my promise

---

[75] Oliver Cromwell's rule in Britain was, of course, regarded as usurpation by the Royalists.

to go along, and that without makeing any capitulation (so ignorant I was of such matters at that tyme).

The next morning, when I had slept out and began to reflect upon my last nights engagement, I found my self in such a labirinth of perplexed thoughts, that I knew not how to wind my self out of them. However, of necessity, according to my promise and duty, I must go wait on my *ruitmaster*; whither being come, he brought me below to the stable and showed me his horses, there being three prime horses for his owne sadle, any of which, he told me, should be {12v} at my service and for my use, and that his servants should be as ready to take and bring my horse as his, and that he would use me as a loveing kinsman, with many fair promises more, which setled my wavering thoughts; so that, now come what will, I resolved to try my fortune this way. The *ruitm[aste]r*, his occasions carying him from this citty to Stade, I stayed in my old lodging, not at my owne but his charges now. He told me that in a few dayes he would call for me.

Here I continued a fortnight, when by intemperancy (to the which my nature was alwayes averse) or by some other accident, I fell into a feaver, which the phisitians commonly call the remitting feaver, which continued me bedfast eight dayes, and then turned to a tertian ague. After I had stayed 3 weeks longer, which made up in all 13 weeks, I rode with the *ruitm[aste]r* to Ratzeburg, the residence of the Dukes of Saxen-Lawenburg, on[e] whereof called Frantz Artman[76] was our collonell, and from thence the next day to Lubeck, where the *ruitm[aste]r* left me, I not being able to travell. After 4 or 5 dayes stay, the *ruitm[aste]r*, being on his march, sent for me. I was in this march in a very pittyfull condition, being hardly able to ride that day which I was free of the ague; and that day I had it, I was forced to ly on an open waggon above the *ruitm[aste]rs* baggage, and was very glad of such a convenience.

Wee continued our march through Pomeren to Stetin[77]. I am sorry that I can give no exact account of my jorney and march now through this

---

[76] Franz Erdmann (1629–1666) succeeded to the Duchy of Sachsen-Lauenburg in 1665.
[77] Szczecin.

pleasant and fruitfull countrey, being hindred in my jorney to Hamborg by rideing in a closse waggon and want of the Dutch language, and now by my tedious sicknes, which tooke away all appetite to any curiosity. Wee had very good accomodation on this march; and by that tyme that I was come near Stetin I was pretty well {13} recovered. I was sent befor to Stetin to buy some necessaries as swords and boots for some troupers who wanted.

1655, July 14. I rode out of Stetin and the next morning came to the army, when they were drawing up in a large meadow. It consisted of 34 brigades of foot and 7,000 *ruiters*[78], being in all about 17,000 men, with a gallant traine of artillery. It was a most delightfull and braw show, the *ruiters* being very well mounted, and the foot well cloathed and armed, and above all the officers in extraordinary good equippage.

Befor I proceed any further I must digresse a litle and sett downe the reasons which the K[ing] of Sweden alleadged for his invadeing of Polland[79]. Which, albeit sett downe at large in his declarations and letters to other princes, yet lest you should not have the opportunity of seing these papers, I shall give you a briefe relation thereof, as also of such passages in the army, or in other parts relateing to this expedition, as came to my knowledge; which, however defective, may give you some light to the knowledge of the principall and chieffe actions of this expedition.

In the first place he alleadged the permission, connivance or rather private encouragement of Collonell Herman Boote to invade Liefland[80] An[no] D[omi]ni 1639, he haveing marched through diverse provinces of Polland wherein they could have hindred him.

2. The incursion of Colonell Crakaw in Pomeren, they permitting him to march through their territories and furnishing him with men and amunition out of Putsky[81].

3. K[ing] Wladislaw[82] his letters by Shonbergen, a gentleman of his

---

[78] Reuter (German) – cavalryman.
[79] Karl X Gustav (1622–1660), King of Sweden from 1654, was about to invade Poland and begin the Northern War of 1655–60.
[80] Livland, Livonia.
[81] Puck.
[82] Władysław IV (1595–1648), King of Poland and Grand Duke of Lithuania from 1632.

chamber, to the people of Oesel[83] perswadeing them to revolt. {13v}

4. The like to the people of Liefland, all this being in King Wladislaus his tyme.

5. That this present King Johannes Casimirus[84], notwithstanding he was recommended by the Queen of Sweden[85] to the estates of Polland and courted for a perpetuall peace, he did first in his letters desist to writt to the Queen in Latin, because in that language, according to the Stumsdorffes treaty, the title was taken from the Poll and given to the Swed[86], and this of purpose to overthrow the fundamentall ground of that treaty.

6. That he had perswaded the Lieflanders to revolt and had consulted how to gaine Riga.

That the Kosaks had been courted to invade and make incursions into Liefland.

That the Polls had dallyed with the Sweds at the two Lubeck treatyes, only to gaine tyme and raise up more enemyes against them; their unsincerity appearing herein: at their first meeting in their plenipotentiary letters was much untruth, and the King of Polland had appropriated to himself the Swedish title, and after the comissioners had acknowledged the fault, and promised to the French ambassadours to bring other and better plenipotentiaryes; yet after so long stay did they bring none and confessed the fault to be their owne, not dareing motion to their King ane alteration so prejudiciall.

At the other treaty their plenipotentiaryes were sealed with a seale whereon the Polls and Swedish armes were, {14} which was repugnant to the treaty of Stumsdorffe, as was very well knowne to Zadzecky, at

---

[83] Saaremaa, modern Estonia.

[84] Jan II Kazimierz (1609–1672), King of Poland and Grand Duke of Lithuania from 1648, abdicated in 1668.

[85] Christina Augusta (1626–1689), Queen of Sweden from 1632 to 1654, when she abdicated and converted to Catholicism.

[86] From the late sixteenth century Sweden and Poland were ruled by the same dynasty, the House of Vasa, which led to reciprocal claims to both crowns. During the Thirty Years' War (1618–1648) the Truce of Stuhmsdorf was signed between the two countries in 1635, due to last for 26 and a half years .

that tyme Great Chancelour of Polland and then principall of the Polls embassy[87], and to the ambassadours of Great Brittaine and Holland. And albeit the Sweds ambassadours did openly declare that they would have if possible and wait for an amended plenipotentiary, which notwithstanding the paines of the mediatours could not be obtained.

As lykewise however by the dispatching of Canasilius[88] into Sweden the King of Polland had caused declare, that he would send his and the Repub[lican] ambassadours, who should finish the treaty of an everlasting peace in His Ma[jes]ties presence, which the Sw[edish] King granted, provideing they should come immediately or in all hast (to the which he was not bound, being frustrated twice before). But in stead of these came none but an envoy called John Morstein[89], who had no full power to treat and conclude ane everlasting peace, only a creditive which had this prejudice in it: under *"in An[no] Regni"* (which was the K[ing] of Polland) was insinuated that he was King of Sweden, and that the title on the back of the creditive, which was due according to the Stumsd[orf] treaty was disanulled, besides severall other things omitted in the title, which according to the treaty was requisite to be observed, and was prejudiciall to the equality of both the Kings.

That the King of Pol[and] had brought into the Baltick Sea forreigne warr ships, and sought to enter in league with diverse princes and people dwelling thereon, Sweden only excluded. Which appeared to be of purpose against the Sweden, seing in the Stumfdorffs treaty it was concluded, that neither the King of Pol[and] nor Rep[ublic], nor the King of Swed[en] nor Rep[ublic] {14v} should dureing the truce make use of any martiall fleet in the Baltick, which by the treaty of G[ustavus] Mag[nus][90] with the citty of Dantzick and the security of the Dukes of Prussia and Curland is knowne, and was at that tyme no wayes necessary, the Balticque being then peacable.

These were the pretences of the King of Sweden for his invadeing of

---

[87] Jakub Zadzik (1582–1642), Great Crown Chancellor, Bishop of Krakow.
[88] Henri de Canasilles, secretary and diplomatic agent of King Jan II Kazimierz.
[89] Jan Andrzej Morsztyn.
[90] Gustav II Adolf (1594–1632), King of Sweden from 1611.

Polland. It would be too tedious to mention the Polnish objections and reasons, and the Swedish replications, but, to tell you briefly, the maine reason was this. The Swedish King, haveing been bred a souldier, and haveing now obtained the crowne by the resignation of his cousin Queen Christina, would needs begin his reigne with some notable action. He knew that the remembrance of the honour and riches obtained by many cavaliers in the German warrs under the Swedish conduct would bring great confluence of souldiers to him, when it should be knowne that he was to arme, which by reason of the late universall peace in Germany and the many forces lately disbanded would be mor easily effectuated. Haveing in his conceit already formed an army, there was no prince or people, except Polland, to which he could have the least pretence (albeit princes, indeed, never want pretensions to satisfy their ambition, and will have their pretences lookt upon as solid and just reasons). Besides, he could never gett such an occasion, perhaps, as now, Polland haveing been for some years tossed by their prevailing rebellious Cosakes, who had not only gott the Tartars to joyne with them, but had the last year procured the Moscovite to espouse their interest, who with very great armyes had made a great impression in Littaw and at this tyme had brought most of it under his subjection[91]. He wanted not also good intelligence {15} and encouragement from some of the discontented Polnish nobility, and Radzievsky, the banished under chancellour of Polland[92], added fuell to his ambition; so that such a tyme accompanyed with such advantages was not to be omitted.

The Swedish *Ricksrades*[93] were very forward and levyed 3 regiments on their owne expences. Cromuell[94] also (who was never backward to make work abroad, that strangers should not have leisure to pry into his designes and actions at home) advanced money for the which foure regiments were levyed in *stiff*[95] Bremen and Verden.

---

[91] In 1654, after the Cossack Hetman Bohdan Khmelnitsky and Left-Bank Ukraine swore fealty to Russia, Tsar Alexey Mikhailovich started a successful war against Poland-Lithuania.
[92] Hieronim Radziejowski (1612–1667), Crown Vice-Chancellor in 1651–52.
[93] Riksråd, upper parliamentary house in Sweden.
[94] Oliver Cromwell (1599–1658), Lord Protector of England from 1653.
[95] District or fief (German). The Duchies of Bremen and Verden belonged to the

But see here a list of most of the regiments who advanced first into Polland:

Of Horse	companies
Curd Christoph, *Graffe* von Konigsmark	9
Graffe Pontus de la Guardie[96], coll[onel]	9
Maior Generall Betker[97]	10
Christian von Bretlach, coll[onel]	9
Hertzog Frantz Hartman von Saxen Lawenburg	4
Maior Schlachte 1 comp[any]; Maior Broberge	1
Of Foot	
Felt Marshall Wittemberg[98]	10
Gen-ll Maior Wurtz	8
Gen-ll Maior Horn	8
Graffe von Hanaw	8
Collonell Fabian de Versen	8
Graffe Oxenstern 6 esquadrons	
Lt. Coll[onel] Ludwig	5

These were all levyed in the *stifts* Bremen and Verden, Hamborg, Lubeck and thereabouts, except Wittembergs. {15v}

There landed at Wolgast the Uplandish, East Gottish, Sinklers and Baniers regiments as also Coll[onel] Larkins, all of horse; this Coll[onel] Larkin commanded the Westgottish [regiment]. Coll[onel] Fabian Barnes[99] and Coll[onel] Taube, Maior Gen-ll Muller, Coll[onel]s Engell, Rosa, Bowrman and many more afterwards arrived, of whom I cannot give an exact acco[un]t. The King also gave out patents for compleeting an army of 40,000 men.

But herein I have exceeded the method of a journall, which I only at first intended. Then, to returne.

Swedish Crown from 1648 to 1712.
[96] Count Pontus Fredrik De la Gardie (1630–1692), in whose regiment Gordon was to serve.
[97] Hans von Böddeker (Bötticher).
[98] Count Arvid Wittenberg (1606-1657), Swedish Field Marshal and Privy Councillor.
[99] Properly, Berends (M. Nagielski, Warszawa 1656. Warszawa, 1990, s. 240).

1655, July 16. The army under the command of Felt Marshall Wittemberg marched to Uchtenhage and Suider mills from whence a trompeter was sent to the Polls army lying at Ustzie[100] and the Snide mills, on the River Notez, with letters to desire them to render themselves under the King of Sweden his protection.

17. Wee marched through Freyerwald and over the Rusische Moule.

18. Wee lay still this day. The Felt Marshall haveing conveened the chieffe officers of the army, told them, that seing this expedition was intended against Polland, it was necessary to instruct their souldiery (many whereof were undisciplined) how to behave themselves upon all occasions, but especially when they should come to joyne battell or fight with the Polls; that they should not regard their shouting and noise, but keep closse together, because the Polls, being excellent horsemen, ar very nimble upon all occasions, but ar afrayed to deale with closse troups and partyes. And albeit he no wayes doubted the sufficiency of the commanders, yet did he think good to admonish them, seing they wer to deale with a new enemy, who was unlike to the Germans, and they should deale {16} gently with the inhabitants, whereby they that render themselves would be better content, the leaguer be furnished with necessaries, and others moved to submitt. Who should do otherwise should runn the hazard of loosing himself.

The commanders promised to do their best and be very carefull of all.

19. The army marched very early over Wangerin[101] and leaguered by Bernsdorffe.

20. Wee marched over the Trago[102] a quarter of a mile above Tramborg[103] and leaguered by Falckenborgh[104].

21. Wee marched by Falck[enburg] and Henrichsdorff, a great mile from the other. On the halfe way wee marched through a litle forrest, which is held to be the border. Wee leaguered by Tempelsborgh[105]. Takeing

---

[100] Ujście.
[101] Węgorzyno.
[102] River Drage (German), Drawa (Polish).
[103] Dramburg (German), Drawsko Pomorskie (Polish).
[104] Falkenburg (German), Złocieniec (Polish).
[105] Tempelburg (German), Czaplinek (Polish).

possession of the castle of Dracheim, which the Polls had slighted, Maior Saxen was left here with 50 men and some ammunition to keep the countrey in contribution. This same day returned our trompeter with two letters, containing that, seing there was an honourable ambassy from the King and the Republick of Polland sent to Sweden, with power enough to take away all differences, the happy successe whereof to an everlasting peace they dayly expected; wherefor they did not beleeve that any hostility in the meane time should be used towards them, concludeing with amicable gratulation from the Pollonian gentry to the Field Marshall. The trompeter said he was well entertained and receaved ten ducats in gift.

Wee could have gone a nearer way to Polland, but went this, because the bridge at Niewwedel was not ready, and the other way wee must have taryed longer in the Elector of Brandeburgh his lands. Moreover, o[u]r army being provided of bread, beer and salt for six dayes, wee receaved in the Dukes after Pomer[ania] and New Mark-land freely 50,000 pund of bread and 100 tunnes of beer.

23. Wee marched from Dracheim the way to Krone and pitched o[u]r leaguer in the field by Hoffstet. From hence there was a troop sent out to perswade the countrey people to stay at home and to furnish the {16v} army with provisions and necessaries. These comeing to Weyershoffe, scituate in a peni-insul and belonging to Ludowick Weyer, *Woywod*[106] of Pomer, which finding empty they put a garrison in it, but the night thereafter they were almost surprised by a party of 500 Polls, these in the towne being taken, some few escapeing to the castle.

24. The army marched towards Veze, and being advanced a litle, the Field Marshal drew up the army in battaile array in a large field, placeing betwixt every troup of commanded horsemen 50 foot, which made a gallant show (the baggage being after). In this manner the army advanced, and by the damme the avantguard engaged with the Polls, takeing and killing some; two collours also, the one red the other white, were taken. And marching over the damme in sight of the Polls leaguer on the other side of the river, they tooke an advantagious place hard by

---

[106] Wojewoda (Polish), or Palatine, – governor of a province, member of the Polish Senate.

and planted two pieces of cannon, wherewith shooting continually into the Pollonians leaguer, some collours[107] of foot were forced to quite their stations.

25. In the morning early there came a trumpeter from the Polls *woywods* to the field marshall, desireing an accord. Then were ten of each syde deputed to conferr betwixt the leaguers, but could come to no agreement befor noone, but afterwards, nine other being sent, agreed, by the mediation of the Under Chancellour Radzievsky, on the following conditiones, the ratification being reserved to His Majesty:

1. The Countyes of Posna and Calish[108] shall from this day forwards be under the protection of the King of Sweden, they promising such loyalty and subjection to him, as to the King of Polland formerly.
2. The King of Sweden shall have all the Regalities, viz. the free disposall of all the Crowne and spirituall lands in the whole land, with the tolls and rents thereof, according as they had been in the tyme of the King of Polland.
3. The citties of Posna, Calish, Mezeritz, Kostzian[109] and all forts in the Kings lands and elsewhere, which His Ma[jes]tie finds convenient, shall be rendred and put in His Ma[jes]ties possession.
4. They consent that His Ma[jes]tie shall have the free disposall of the foot belonging to the two counties.

In the name of His Ma[jes]tie these things were promised:

1. That all and every one of whatsoever quality or condition shall have the free excercise of their Religion and to use it unmolested in their churches. {17}
2. That every person shall enjoy the priviledges, freedome and places given them formerly by their Kings.

---

[107] *Collours* here, as elsewhere in the Diary, means Polish chorągwie (banners) – military units or companies.
[108] Kalisz.
[109] Międzyrzecz and Kościan.

3. That no winter quarters, farr lesse any violence, harme, robbery, or spoiling of corne shall be imposed or suffered, and if any such be done through the insolency of the souldiery, to be severly punished.

4. Lastly, the chambers of justice and all old right or law matters shall runne in the name of the King of Sweden, and the places and offices, which the Kings of Polland used to bestow, shall be disposed by the King of Sweden as they fall, to the native Polls only, but in case any of the natives of these counties do not approve of this treaty and agreement, and take part or side with the King of Polland, the hereditary lands of such to be at the Kings disposall.

Actum at Uscia the 25 July 1655
signed by:

Christoffel von Brun Opalinsky, *Woywod* of Posna,[110] in his owne and in the name of all the inhabitants of that county
Pawl Gembetsky
Andreas Carlen Grudzinsky, *Woywod* of Calish,[111] in his owne and that counties name
Maximilian Miaskowsky, *Castellan*[112] of Carolen
Woicoch Priaskowsky, *Castellan* of Samptra[113]

On the Sweds part in the chieffe place signed the field marshall etc.

26. Radzievsky and Collonell Mardevelt with 2,000 horse marched towards Posna and quartered all night at Murovanie Goslin[114], three miles from Posna, whither the deputyes from Posna come with assurance of submission and deprecating violence. In the meane tyme Wittembergh with the army advanceth over the r[ive]r Notez, holding his march to Posna.

---

[110] Krzysztof Opaliński (1609–1655), Wojewoda of Poznań, writer of satires.
[111] Andrzej Karol Grudziński (1611–1678), Wojewoda of Kalisz.
[112] Kasztelan (Polish).
[113] Probably Szamotuły (German: Samter).
[114] Murowana Goślina.

29. Radzievsky entereth Posna in a military pompe, the *Woywod* of Winowratsaw[115] being gone from thence 3 dayes befor, and haveing protested against the treaty and rendition at Snide millne or Ustczie. There entred with Radzievsky, besides his domestiques, a hundred commanded *ruiters* who were quartered in the towne, the party {17v} being leaguered a mile short of the *Dume* or *Thume*. Here I spent the time in visiting and makeing merry with my former ffriends and acquaintances, but there was litle mirth in their mindes, as I could well perceive.

Aug[ust] 2. The field marshal with the army leaguered by Posna, and the former party under the command of Coll[onel] (afterwards Major Generall) Betker marched to Szroda 4 miles, drawing out a formall leaguer for the army in a field by a small brook, a quarter of a mile from the towne. But the next morneing after the party removed from Posna I returned with *Ruitm-r* Gardin and *Ruitm-r* Duncan, as also a lieutennant, ane Egiptian[116], and two Germans, a quarterm[aste]r and a corporall, who all went without licences. And albeit all returned the next day to the party, yet were they missed, and at their comeing the two *ruitm-rs* put in arrest, and with great entreaty of Coll[onel] Hessen and other ffriends escaped a tryall. But the other three, being put under the guard, were tryed after at a councell of warr and condemned to dy, yet got that favour at last to throw the dice, and the lot befell the lieutennant, who was hanged on a growing oake on the other side of the brooke; there being the same morning hanged on the same oak a boy of 14 or 15 years of age, for throwing only a stone at a Poll, who with a guard was makeing search among the regiments for some horses which had been taken from him.

The *ruitm[aste]r* had left me in Posna for provideing some necessaries for him, which haveing provided, I returned in company of four troupers belonging to o[u]r regiment, by whose perswasion I went along with them out of our way to see what wee could catch, and falling on a gentlemans house, albeit wee found no body at home, yet in a thicket hard by wee gott six pretty good nagges and some slight baggage in the house,

---

[115] Inowrocław.
[116] Gypsy.

for it seemes they had conveyed all their best things and goods out of the way. One of these horses I gott for my share.

The field marshall haveing stayed 4 dayes at Posna refreshing the souldiers with provisions from the citty, and haveing receaved a good summe of money also, he left Collonell Duderstatt commendant therein with 1,200 foot and 300 horse, and advancing to Szroda, he encamped there,

[August] 7. makeing a circumvallation. Upon his arrivall many {18} gentlemen came in, complaining of robbery and all sort of violence done to them, which (the persons being knowne and laid hold one) were most severely punished, and even the smallest crime with ignominious deaths. Two dayes after the arrivall of the army I had like to have come in a great misfortune, for the gentleman whose horses wee had taken in o[u]r returne from Posna, haveing exhibited a complaint, receaved a safeguard to search through the army for his horses and those who had taken them. It chanced that I with others of o[u]r regiment were rideing out of the leaguer for forrage, when this gentleman with his safeguard seased on one of o[u]r troupers with one of the horses, which wee had taken. I seing my comorad caryed away against his will and not minding for what cause, made hast after him to rescue him, which the rest seing, poasted after me and with much ado perswaded me to desist by informeing me of the mutuall and common danger, which I litle imagined, and scarsely could understand them by reason I understood not their language. And so the poor fellow, which was taken, was hanged the same day, and wee for fear hideing o[u]r selves for some dayes thereafter.

Two dayes thereafter the field marshall caused hang his owne chirurgeon, a pretty yong man, for killing the suffragan of Gnesna[117], a person of above 60 yeares of age. This surgeon with these who were with him, being in number 20, gott a great deale of money and rich booty. He was hanged on a new gallowes on a hill opposite to the field marshall his quarters. Some of these who were with him were catched and executed, but most escaped.

---

[117] Gniezno.

Such was the severity, I will not say tiranny, of this field marshall, that for the least crime he that was catched must dy; and I did see a foot souldier who, haveing gone into a poor cottage, and fetching out a pott with milk, the field marshall chanceing to come by in his coach, the fellow for fear let the pott fall out of his hands, the woman of the house following him out crying, rather {18v} for fear as for any harme she gott, which appeared by her great lamentation and falling downe on her knees begging, when she see the poor fellow by the command of the generall laid hold on and presently hanged on the gate. And I have had it from sure hands that betwixt Stetin and Conin[118], where the King came to us, there were about 470 persons executed, most whereof for very small crimes, which was too much severity in a army not under pay, and was so judged by the King himself, who was heard to blame Wittembergh oftentimes afterwards for his extreme rigour.

In this leaguer wee were untill, haveing notice of the Kings arrivall at Posna, wee dislodged and quartered by

19. a litle towne called Pisdra[119], 4 miles;

20. the next day wee marched early and encamped by another towne called Sluptca[120], 4 miles.

21. The next day wee marched and encamped on a high ground along the River Warta over against Conin. From hence a party of 250 horse under the command of Collonel Engel was sent out and, engageing with a party of 300 Polls by Colla[121], at the first onset routed them, killing many and takeing some. The prisoners informed that the King of Polland was come to Lovits. Here I was wounded in the left syde w[i]t[h] a shott, but not dangerously.

24. The army by day light advanced out of the leaguer and was drawne in one lyne of battaile and equall front, and the King haveing lodged 2 miles from thence, came rideing along the front of the army from the left to the right hand, accompanyed with many great officers, his guard of

---

[118] Konin.
[119] Pyzdry.
[120] Słupca.
[121] Koło.

Trabants[122] and of horse, with severall troups of commanded men. Being come to the right hand at his pavilion, two salvees were given with 44 piece of cannon and small shott of the whole army, horse, foot and dragouns.

25. The next day wee lay still, getting orders to be

26. in readines to march. The army marched over the River Varta through Conin and encamped a mile of the towne.

27. Wee marched to a litle towne Colla where, againe crossing the River Varta by a bridge, wee encamped all along the river side. From hence was a strong party of 2,500 horse commanded out under the command of the Prince of Anhalt[123], with whom were Radzievsky, {19} Maior Generall Muller, yong Konigsmark and divers other collonels. Wee marched all night and by day light came in sight of a

28. litle towne called Uniewa[124], which towne haveing capitulated, was spared and dragouns placed at the entryes of the streets, that the troups passing through should do no harme. Wee encamped on a field without the towne and had provisions, as beer and bread, enough brought us out of the towne, whereof wee stood in great necessity. Haveing refreshed our selves, about midday wee began to march to the left hand towards Lenshits[125]. At night, being a mile or thereabouts from the towne, wee were drawne up on a large field, and a small party sent out for intelligence. This whole night wee stayed in our rankes in great silence without any fires, the one halfe of the night one halfe of the party were mounted, the other standing or lying by their horses with the bridles in their hands, and so

29. releeving each other. The next day early the small party returning brought intelligence, that all the gentry of the countrey were drawing together and that the King of Polland was expected from Varso thither. Whereupon our party returned, sending out skouts to skoure the countrey on all quarters. The same day the army, which had come with the King

---

[122] Trabanten (German) – bodyguards.
[123] Johann Georg, Prince of Anhalt-Dessau (1627–1693), later Field Marshal of Brandenburg-Prussia.
[124] Uniejów.
[125] Łęczyca.

through Pomeren, came to the leaguer, consisting of 6,000 men, with whom came Wrangel[126] and Steinbock[127] Field Marshals, and Douglas, Generall of the Cavaliery[128].

And the day befor an ambassadour from the King and Republick of Polland had audience by His Ma[jes]tie; his name was Christophorus Przeimsky. He had a harangue to this purpose: that the King of Polland was not a litle astonished at this suddain invasion of the Sweden befor the truce was expired, seing he had many tymes sued and used all meanes to obtaine a good understanding with that Crowne, and to that purpose had at present a plenipotentiary in Sweden. Neither could he in his owne opinion see any reasonable motive of their present invasion. As for their pretences published in their proclamations, any impartiall person might easily see that they were grounded upon strained consequences and aggravated to justify their premeditate invasion. But {19v} if it be either out of hate or envy towards the King or Republick of Poll[and], or out of a desire and hope to obtaine great riches and treasure, or by subduing of Polland to enlarge their dominions and encrease their fame and honour, they were first to consider the injustice and then the vanity of such ambitious desires, seing His Ma[jes]tie of Polland did not know wherein he had wronged or offended, but had allwayes studied to keep good neighbourship with all and especially with the Crowne of Sweden. Morover he did not beleeve that so great a King would begin a warr for the hopes of riches and treasure, of which meaning if he were, he would find himself hugely deceaved, seing Polland was exhausted by an intestine and forraigne warr, and it is well knowne that the Polls wealth consists most in their military equippage and houshold plenishing and husbandry. Lastly, if it were to obtaine honour and fame and encrease of his dominions, it were more honourable to seek that of some other nation, and not of Polland,

---

[126] Count Karl Gustav Wrangel (1613–1676), Swedish Field Marshal and Admiral.
[127] Count Gustav Otto Stenbock (1614–1685), Swedish Field Marshal and Admiral.
[128] Robert Douglas (1611–1662), like his protégé Patrick Gordon, was a "younger son of a younger brother of a younger house" in Scotland (Douglas of Whittinghame). He served the Swedish Crown since 1631, rising to become Count of Skenninge and, in 1657, Field Marshal.

already weakened by a long and contin[u]ing warr against their rebellious Cosakes and the Tartars, and now lately driven to the utmost extremities by the invasion of the numerous armyes of the Moskoviter. Neither were it probable that he could obtaine a peacable possession of that by conquest, which befor by a hereditary possession and voluntary election had proved unsuccesfull by reason of the diversity of religion, speech, habits, manners, fashions and statutes. All which he desired His Majesty of Sweden to consider, and to preferr an honourable and advantagious peace befor an unjust and doubtfull warr. And for the present he desired a suspension of the warr, promiseing in his masters name all satisfaction, if they would advance no further.

The King of Sweden answered by the P[resident] Beerenklaw[129], that he much admired that the King of Polland and his counsell desired now to know the reasons and motives of this warr, {20} he haveing already in his proclamations[130] given notice thereof to the whole world, and was never defficient on his part to further a just peace, of which opinion he was still, and desired the ambassadour to informe his master thereof. After severall discourses the King said that Stetin was too farr of, and that his cousin should choose another place, to which the ambassadour answered that, as the case stood, some place betwixt the leaguers were fittest, seing they were but twelve miles from another. Whereat the King smileing said, "Seing wee ar so near another, I will take that trouble for my cousin, and go and meet him rather, hopeing shortly to have the honour to visitt him". Therewith the ambassadour with a Pollonian confidence and courage arose and takeing his leave went out of the pavilion, whom the P[resident] Beerenklaw following, desired to give in his desires in writting, that they might give the fitter and mor formall answer, which promising, he was convoyed back in His Ma[jes]ties coach from the leaguer to the towne Colla.

30. The party under the Pr[ince] of Anhalt returned into the leaguer, and here I must relate how unfortunate I was on this party, and thereby my course of lyfe at that tyme. Understand then, that my *ruitmaster* haveing

---
[129] Matthias Björenklau or Bärenklau (1607–1671), Swedish diplomat.
[130] *Manifestoes* crossed out in MS.

by his faire and sugred words gott me perswaded to embrace a souldiers lyfe, I remained by him as a domestick. In the tyme of my sicknes and on o[u]r march to Stetin and to the Polls borders he was very kind to me, and my lyfe was somewhat compatible. But how soone wee came into Polland and that wee had neither free quarter nor pay, nor any thing to be had for money in most places, wee were forced to make what shift wee could, and that with the imminent hazard of our lives many tymes, and being out on our purchase with the troupers of o[u]r regiment, and sometimes differences falling out, as in such cases often happen. I imagined that the troupers ought to cary me a greater, or at least an equall respect, knowing me to be a friend of the *ruitmasters* and remaining by him {20v} as a free person, and not in the quality of a servant. But it seemes they understood it otherwise, for in our branglings sometimes they would object to me, that I ought not to compete with them, who were souldiers and His Ma[jes]ties servants, whereas I was only a servant to a private officer, or at the best but a *morode broeder*[131], as they termed it.

Haveing had some quarrels about this, I began to consider with my self and bethink of a remedy, for even then I began to see my self in a worse case as a trouper. For in necessity, because the company was weak, I was put sometimes to do the duty of a trouper, my paines in provideing victualls and forrage more as any. And what purchase or booty I gott, I could not possesse it because the *ruitm[aste]r* took all, at least the best part of it. And then it was the mor honourable way to preferment, to be inrolled and serve for a souldier. Haveing therefor one day made a shift to make one of o[u]r troupers understand my condition and intention, he advised me to informe the lieutennant of the company, who was a Dutch man and a good old souldier. I comeing to him and showing him that I was desirous rather to serve for a trouper and have my name enrolled, as to be in the condition I was, he, it seemes, being at some enimity with the *ruitm[aste]r*, assured me that at Stetin my name was put in the muster-roll, and that I should henceforth take my quarters and place by the company; and that the *ruitmaster* could not, neither would hinder me.

---

[131] Marodebruder (German) – marauder, straggler.

So the next day, haveing been out for purchase upon my owne horse which I had gott in my returne from Posna to Szroda, and haveing also mad shift for sadle and pistolls of my owne, I tooke up my quarters by the company, desireing the lieutennant to make all well with the *ruitm[aste]r*, which was done with some reluctancy and grudging.

Being now established a sone of Mars, I found the proverb true: out of the frying pan into the fire. For as to duty, it was so hard that in a week I had the guard 4 nights, and in some weeks scarce one night free, to the which not being used, it seemed at {21} first intollerable. And then was it great paines and labour to provide necessary provisions for my self and forrage for my horse, for haveing some tymes with difficulty either on the march with the regiment, or on the guard provided some victuals and comeing to the leaguer somewhat late, befor I could gett any thing dressed, and my horse looked to, heavy sleepe and wearinesse would so possesse my senses that all appetite was gone. Or haveing rather devoured as eaten something, I went to rest under heavens canopy, where befor I had halfe satisfyed nature with sleep, the *Pozell*[132], ravaillye and the corporalls clamouring rouzed me up to make ready my self and horse. But on the guard one or two releefes at most gave us litle respite from the sentry to provide necessaries or rest our bodyes. And that which helped to augment my miseries more, was my being amongst strangers and wanting the language of those with whom I was necessitated to converse. For being in comoradship with the other troupers, who were but meere bowres come from the flaile, every one was oblidged to provide necessaries by turnes dayly and do such worke as building of hutts, dressing victualls, bringing wood and water, and that with alacrity without grudgeing; in all which, albeit I strived to exceed my comorads, yet seemed they dissatisfyed, and the odde turne or taske was alwayes mine. And, which was worse, because I was bashfull and loath to resent every injury, or to be heard, or called troublesome, all which invited my comorades to a sort of imperiousnesse and contempt of me, and by scoffing or jeering at my actions or language vexed me exceedingly.

---

[132] For all the effort, this term defies explanation. It could be a distortion or some German dialect word.

In this case not knowing what to do, I chanced on[e] day to be in company with a Scotsman called William Lawder, a reformado[133] lieutennant who had served in the German warres, and was pretty well acquainted with {21v} their humours and natures, and revealing my condition to this person, I asked his counsell concerning my comorads their behaviour towards me. Who gave me this advice, that I should not by any meanes let the least injury go unresented, and that whensoever I did perceive them jeering, scoffing or laughing, and had the least occasion or presumption to think that it was at me, I should question them peremptorily whither they meant me or not. If they denyed, then to make no more of it, but if they avouched it or spoke ambiguously, then presently to pick a quarrell with them either by affronting words or a boxe on the eare, either of which without doubt would draw on a duell. Wherein whether I gott the better or the worse, all would be one, for therein they would see my courage, and that I would not put up an afront, and then would rather choose to be quiet as to runne such a hazard knowing me to be troublesome.

This his counsell I presently followed, which after great trouble and many quarrells brought me to such contentment, that openly they durst not say any thing which might move laughter. But presently they used meanes to make me understand their meaning and carryed pretty faire with me always thereafter. For in lesse as three weekes I fought six duells with sundry persons, wherein I had twice the better and 4 times the worse, yet could they and the seconds perceive, that it was not want of courage, but dexterity and strentgh [*sic*], that made me have the worse. And this all befor I arrived at Colla.

Now come I to the misfortunes on the party from Colla. The night befor I had been on the guard and slept but very litle, and was no sooner come into the leaguer but I was commanded upon this party. Yong *Grave* Konigsmark commanded 10 troupes of the commanded horsemen. I was in the 2d troupe, and marching in the night, being very sleepy, my horse, whither of himself or being driven out by some of these I rode {22} by, caryed me out of the troupe I rode in by the other troupe, and rested

---

[133] Officer deprived of command by reorganisation or disbandment of his unit, but retaining rank and receiving full or half pay.

not untill he came on the right hand of the coll[onel], who it seemes was sleeping also. But he awakening and seing one rideing on his right hand, asked who it was, and I, being sound asleep and not knowing but I was in the trowpe among my comorades, and thinking that they were vexing me, answered not at first. But he calling more roughly againe and againe, I said in Dutch, "Hold your peace", litle thinking it was the collonell. Which he hearing and knowing me to be some trowper strayed out of my ranke, with a small cane he had he struck me twice or thrice, befor I could gett my self recovered or awakened, my horse carying me a great way from him. When I recollected my self and drew nearer, I perceived it was the collonell, to whom I durst not say any thing, but returned to my trowpe and then began to question those I had been rideing by for leading or driving my horse out of the trowpe; who all denyed, alleadging themselves to have been asleep also. But I suspecting one, with whom I had been at oddes in former tymes, challenged him, who not denying absolutely what he had done, when it was day light, wee went aside into a small bush and fought it out with broad swords, where my foot slipping, I gott a small scratch in the forehead, and so were parted, it being ordinary to fight only for the first blood.

Marching through Unieva about sunne riseing, and being exceeding hungry, wee were not permitted to enter into any house, and being past the market place in a street which leadeth to the port, there was a sellar doore broken up by some of o[u]r sojors. Which perceiving, I gave my horse to one of my comorads and gott downe to the cellar, where were ten or 12 barrells of new beere all workeing. I staying someq[uha]t long in seeking some vessell to draw beer {22v} in, and not finding any, I drew into my hatt, but befor I could recover the foot of the staires, the strong smell of the working beare tooke the breath from me, and if those who were by me had not helped me to the fresh aire, I think verily I had dyed.

Being come out into the street and following the trowpe on foot, I espyed a gate open at which I entred, and passing thorow a closse or yard, I leapt over a wall into a street and by chance came into a bakers house, where was a table full of bread of wheat newly taken out of the oven. I presently snatching up one fell a eating, which the landlord seeing presented me with another, but I was resolved to have all. So, going to the bed, I tooke the cover from a bolster, which the fellow seing, offered to hinder me, but I offering to my sword, he and wyfe and all run out of doores. I haveing filled the sack, returned the way I came and, getting out of the towne, came to my comorades who made me very welcome, being as hungry as I.

About halfe ane houre after, beer and bread was brought out of the towne to us. It was my turne to stand sentry a foot by the collonell, who being told that I was the person he had beat in the night on the march, called for me and drunk to me, makeing me drink out a great bowle of beer. He made some sort of apology for what he had done, but I not understanding well what he said, was dismissed.

In o[u]r returne the next morning I was commanded with a lieutennant, there being 40 in all, on a skout watch to the right hand of the party. Haveing ridden a mile and a halfe, wee came to a village, the priest whereof brought out to us beer in a great pale, to which every one thronging and one acquaintance drinking to another, it was {23} a long time befor it came to me. In the meane tyme wee had a larum, a company of 150 Polls haveing, whilst we were here, passed through the other end of the village, the lieutennant in great rage driving us from the house in the nick when I had the pale at my head. And he beating every one promiscuously with a drawne small sword, and comeing towards me, I for hast lett the pale fall out of my hand, which enraging him more, he followed me and beat me thrice crosse the back with his sword, so that being but thinne clothed, I thought he had cutted me in to the puddings. All which I must take in good part and not mutter a word.

Wee marched all this day on the right hand of the great party. Only about midday wee took a small repast at a gentlmans house in a great village, where wee found no body at home. Towards evening I with ten more were commanded with a corporall further to the right hand. About ane houre after sunne sett wee came to a village and there tooke up our station by a hedge at the back of the village. My lott was to go first to sentry, whereof I was glad, for in the meane tyme my comerads were to provide provender for my horse and victuals, if any to be had. Being returned from sentry, I laid me downe to sleep, which oppressed me so (haveing slept but litle in 3 nights befor), that about midnight o[u]r sentry fireing, and the corporall with the rest getting to horse and haveing scoured the fields, returned, I not haveing heard any thing. Whereat the corporall being enraged, and finding me sleeping still, without any expostulation belaboured me so with his broad sword (according to the Swedish manner) that I was in ane amazement, not knowing whether it was enemy or ffriend, and at the first drawing {23v} my sword and standing to my defence, which occasioned his greater rage and me more blowes. Whereby recollecting my self, I put up my sword and gave good words, which was well for me, for the Swedish discipline of all other in such cases of command is the strictest. Befor evening wee came to the leaguer and dispersed our selves to our respective regiments.

[August] 31. The next day early wee marched upon the first motion of the artillery and foot. The great kettle drummes, which being so great that 9 or 10 hogsheads of liquor could be contained in each of them, and were caryed on a large waggon drawne with six horses, the drummer sitting and, when beating, standing behind; these beat halfe an English mile to give notice to the army and the guards, which way the army marched, and were easily to be heard two Dutch miles. This day the right wing marched first, then the artillery and foot, the left wing afterwards, the wings changing the vanne day about. At night wee encamped by a litle towne called Oparow.

Sept. 1. Wee marched early. About noone our avantguard advancing out of a litle wood, discovered on the other side of a large marish by a village smoake and by and by some horsmen. The collonell, who had the avauntguard, commanded a major with a 100 horsemen to go as quietly to the passe as he could and, if possible, to engage them, notice being also given to the King. As the regiments marched out of the wood, they were drawne up in battell array.

In the meane tyme the major, advancing to the passe, and the foretrowpes or avantgard following {24} and being come neere, there came downe the hill on the other side of the passe about 20 horsemen very confidently. But perceiving what wee were by o[u]r order and the advancing of the other trowpes, they betook them to their heeles. The passe was about 300 fathome broad, not deep and good ground, which wee passeing in great hast, some of the best horsed were sent to persue them, but could not overtake any of the gentlemen. Only some servants were killed and some taken by the village, and some luggage and provision. These were the gentry of the Varsawish *poviat*[134], or province. The prisoners informed that the King of Polland passed by on the Saturnday befor towards Piatok, where he now lay with some forces. Upon which intelligence a strong party was commanded thither under the command of

2. Coll[onel] [...] who, comeing thither, found nothing but an empty leaguer, the King haveing, upon the alarum given by the fors[ai]d gentry, marched away in great hast toward Przedbors[135] in the night.

The army haveing marched over the pass, encamped on a high ground, the litle towne Sobota being on the other side of the pass. Here I must relate another great misfortune.

5. On Sunday the 5th, being scarse of provender and provision and not knowing how long wee were to stay here (for the Sweds {24v} cary all their business very closs), I with another comorad rode out to provide, it being our turne. Wee passed this marish and brooke at a milne halfe a mile below the towne, and haveing ridden about 3 miles, wee came to a village, where wee found no body at home, but all sort of provision in abundance. So, haveing gott a large waggon, wee filled it with oats, sheep, geese, hens and other provision as much as o[u]r horses could draw. Being halfe way on o[u]r returne, the waggon began to shatter and shortly after was so spoiled and broken that wee could not gett it brought forward, so that wee knew not what to do. At last wee resolved to cast lotts, who should ride to the leaguer and fetch a waggon, the other being to stay by the provision, which wee were loth to part with.

It was my lott to stay, it being now growne darke. Haveing tyed my horse to the broken waggon, I walked up and downe an houre or two, in which tyme many straglers who had been out for forrage passed by. At last, being very weary, I tooke my horse in my hand and satt downe by

---

[134] Powiat (Polish) – district.
[135] Przedbórz.

the waggon, expecting the returne of my comorade and, being weary and sleepy, at last about an howre after midnight I did fall into such a sound sleep, as the travale[136] or dying in the leaguer (which was not a mile of) did not awaken me, neither the great noise of trumpets and drummes at the {25} marching of the army. Which, however, gave advertisement to the bowres in the woods lurking of the armyes removall, who came flocking to the leaguer, where by their tymely comeing and takeing possession of what was left many could well recruit their losses. 10 or 12 of these comeing the way where I lay or rather satt asleep, seing no body neer me, nor any lyke to come that way, the army in their view marching a contrary way, consulted, it seemes, to lay hold on me and, takeing what I had, to murther me. In order to this some tooke possession of my horse, whilst others, haveing gott my sword from me, laid hands on me.

I was even then troubled with a most fearfull dreame, and being now awakened by their hard gripeing of me, and not by any noise they made, and seing my self besett in this manner, it was not a fear, terror or perplexity that seased me, but ane amazement and astonishment. Of resistance and entreating them I was made alike incapable, of the one by the strentgh of 3 or 4 fellowes holding me fast, and of the other by the amazement wherein I was. But they tearing rather as takeing of all my cloaths in great hast, pressed from me abundance of teares, which I would have willingly retained but could not.

There was ane old man amongst them who, it seemes, pittying my condition and yong yeares, began to diswade them from murthering me, whom two of them vehemently opposed; which contest continuing some while, I began to recollect {25v} my self. But, not being able to speake, I only recommended my self to God Almighty, whose assistance as at many other tymes I now found.

In the tyme of their contest the two who were most violent offered diverse tymes to knock out my braines with their clubes, which the rest opposed but very faintly, and these two urging reasons: as that I, being let go to the army, would informe of my usage, and then a party might

---

[136] "T" seems to be added here, so that it is either *reveille* or *travallie* – Scots for clatter or noise.

be sent back to burne and kill and destroy all they found, and that they should consider what hard measure they, their wives, children and countrey receaved from the Sweds. All which methinks I perfectly understood, and perceiveing by the demeanour of the most part of them that they began to yeeld to their perswasions, I began to think how I could escape from them. One of them held me strongly by the left arme, and whilst some of the rest alwayes were offering to beat me either with their fists or clubbes, I shunned them by winding about him who held me, who, albeit a strong ill looking fellow, it seemes, was none of the worst natures. In one of these windings, shunning the stroake of a club, whether by chance or fearing the stroak of the club himself, he let go his hold of me. Which I no sooner perceived but I betook me to my heeles and runne directly forward, though not the way to the leaguer, which in such ane amazement I could not consider. However, in the lentgh of a furlong I outrun them all a 3d part thereof, fear adding admirable {26} swiftnes. At first some of the nimblest breaking loose after me, they lett their clubbes drive after me, one whereof after it had hitt the ground did strike me so on the thighes that it had almost overturned me.

When I was gott a good way of and hearing no body following me, I looked about and see 3 or 4 of them standing at the place where they gott me, and the rest returning to them, but could not see my horse whom, it seemes, they had convoyed away at first. Which was well for me, for any one of them might have overtaken me thereon and killed me with my owne pistoll, sword or a club, I haveing nothing wherewith to defend my self. But considering that the horse could not be farr of and that they might as yet follow me, I made what hast I could the neerest way to the marish, which haveing passed, I made up to the army, haveing nothing on but my shirt and drawers.

To such a hazard of my lyfe and losse, which I afterwards with great travell, difficulty and many hazards hardly recovered, was I by my owne folly and carelesnes brought to. Being come to the baggage of the army all besuttled and bemired and naked almost, I was not mor desirous to know where the waggons wer that belonged to the regiment wherein I served, as they were to enquire what had befalne me. Wherein haveing satisfyed them with a short relation, {26v} they told me that the Duke of Saxen-Lawenburg his regiment

6. was marched with the other army to the right hand under the command of the Field Marshall Wittemberg, whither I mad great hast, and haveing run about a Dutch mile, I came first to the baggage of Coll. Bretlaw his regiment and by and by to o[u]r owne. And meeting with a *markettenters*[137] waggon, the good woman gave me the lend of an old Polls coat; from another I gott a pair of Polls boots, and from a third a cappe. I stayed by the baggage untill wee came to o[u]r leaguer, which was on a field on the further side of a litle towne called Jezow, where I had but a cold welcome from my *ruitm-r* and lieutennant, and in stead of being pittyed was well laught at by my comorads. All which I was forced to endure with patience at this tyme, not knowing how to helpe my self.

Here I understood that the King was marched towards Lovits and Varso, and Field-Marshall Steinbock with him, haveing about 6,000 men, and that our army was ordered to follow the King towards Krakow.

7. The army marched early, and my comorads not offering me any assistance wherewith to come forward, and I disdaining to begg any of them, I stayed untill all the baggage and army was marched (only the rereguard). And then going through the army, I made choice of a horse (whereof there were no small store left), which I thought had spirit {27} enough, but was pittifully galled. And seeking among the huts, I found the stock of a Polls sadle which from diverse places I fitted with girths and stirrops, and being so mounted I followed the army. And haveing ridden and driven about a mile, I turned of to the right hand to seek some booty. Being come all alone about a mile and a halfe to the right hand of the army, I espied a village and therein a gentlmans house wherein was not any thing, all being taken away. I only by chance found in a bed under some pease straw an old *shable*[138] and a paire of yellow Polls boots, both which were very necessary, I haveing no armes, and my boots I had on not good. I durst not hazard to ride any further for fear of my horse failing, and falling among the bowres, so returned to the leaguer about sunne sett, at Rava.

---

[137] Marketender (German) – sutler.
[138] Szabla (Polish) – sabre.

8. The next day the army lay still. I walked in to the Jesuits closter which was plundered out and nothing left, only an excellent library, of which the field marshalls secretary haveing the custody, I was admitted by him to help to choose some speciall books for the f. marshalls use, whereby I had the occasion to put up some for my self. Afterwards I went to the castle and visited two Jesuits old men who were there, the rest being fled towards Silesia. I gave to these some reliques which I had found upon the ground in the monastery. As I returned {27v} out of the castle, I see a fellow lying by the gate and a smoake comeing out of his mouth as out of a [...][139], which was terrible to behold. The people comeing flocking about him, one perswaded to powre milk into his throat, which in hast being brought and powred downe his throat, he began to womit and shortly after to recover, though never I beleeve to be so well as formerly. All which, as I heard, proceeded of drinking too much brandewine.

In the afternoone I went to see a duell betwixt a lieutennant and cornet of *Graffe* Pontus de la Gardie his regiment, the lieutennant (who was a Catholick) being chalenged for admonishing the other not to weare a sharbracke or saddle cloth made of a surplus. The lieut. behaved himself very couragiously, killing the others horse and wounding himself (the duell being on horseback). This same cornet, being a great church robber, was afterwards killed by the boures at Krakow.

9. Wee marched at the usuall tyme and leaguered by a litle towne called St. Bresini[140].

10. Wee marched and leaguered on a high ground hard by a litle towne called Inovlodzs[141]. Here was a pretty castle wherein was left a garrison of a 100 men under a Finnes captaine called St[...]felt; our ordinary march being about four miles Polnish a day.

11. Being Saturnday, wee crossed the river [...], which runneth on the one side of the towne and falleth in the r[iver] Pilcza[142], which cometh by

---

[139] Gordon, a devout Roman Catholic, avoided infernal allusions.
[140] Brzeziny.
[141] Inowłódz.
[142] Pilica.

the other side, just underneath the towne, the first by foord and the other by bridge.

{28} Being on our march, a small party of the Polls did fall in on the rear of o[u]r baggage and presently retiring without doing any considerable harme. The regiment of *Graffe* Pontus de la Gardie, commanded by Lt. Collonell Forgell, made presently after them for it had the rereguard, and perceiving them to be gone a great way, he sent back the standards and unadvisedly persued them.

It was my lott also to be on the arrereguard among the commanded troops, and being with a corporall and 12 others on the side scowting, the lt. collonell in his persute perceiving us, tooke us along with him. After wee had ridden a mile and a halfe to the right hand of the army, and being among some thick bushes, o[u]r foretroop gave us notice of the enemyes approach. Wee drew up amongst these bushes, being about 250 horse in all, when immediately a party of the enemy about 300 horse advanced towards us with a resolution to charge, as wee thought, but being come neere us, they let fly some shott at us, as wee at them, and wheeling of to the right hand of us, they gott in betwixt us and the army. Which the lt. coll. perceiving, made a halt and sending out *Ruitm-r* James Duncan to discover if there wer any more forces, and to returne speedily, for he was resolved to make his way back to the army, suspecting no good.

The *ruitm-r* with 30 horsmen (whereof I was one) had not ridden farr but he discovered 18 or 20 collours advanceing towards us, whereupon he sent to the lt. collonell, and in a trice was engaged with his troope by these. {28v} The Polls chargeing furiously upon our small troope, albeit wee did what wee could to keep closse, yet were charged through and put into disorder with the losse of some men. The *ruitm-r* with a few recovered the regiment with the Polls at his heeles. The lt. coll. and all the rest, as I heard afterwards, behaved themselves very couragiously, but being overpowred with numbers, and the 300, which wee did see at first, falling in on the rere, they were presently put into disorder and confusion and fled, but none escaped (the Polls being exceeding well mounted).[143]

---

[143] This whole episode is a good example of the favourite Polish tactics of ensnaring regular units with light cavalry.

The Polls gave good quarters at first, but a cornet being taken by a gentleman, a *Towarsis*[144] as they call them, it seemes the cornet, perceiving some likelyhood of escapeing and haveing a pistoll charged (which the gentleman had too negligently let him keep), killed him, but was himself overtaken and with many more upon this acco[un]t killed. There were taken prisoners the lt. collonell, Major Konigsmark (who was shott in the arme), 2 *ruitm-rs* Stein and Duncan, 5 lieutennants, 3 cornets and 120 inferiour officers and troopers, none escapeing, only a corporall and 8 troopers, who being in the foretroope when it was disordered, escaped by chance through the bushes undiscovered. I my self was on[e] of these eight, haveing received a most dangerous shott in my left syde under my ribbs.

After wee were a litle way of, wee could hear {29} very well when the regiment was engaged and routed, but made no stay, hasting to the army as fast as our horses could carry us. The army haveing had the alarum, wee found drawne up in a great field, and wee were immediately brought to the Field Marshall Wittemberg, who being troubled with the gout or podagra, was standing in the boot of his coach ready to sitt up on his horse. The corporall drawing neer, the f.m. asked him what was become of the regiment. The corporall answered, "I and these (pointing to us) are only escaped", whereat the f.m. chafingly replyed, "The divell could have taken you with the rest". Then, enquireing of the enemyes strentgh and where wee were engaged, the corporall informing what he knew, was with us dismissed to o[u]r quarters, which was on a field by a litle towne called Opoczno.

A strong party was sent out, and the army in the evening came into the leaguer. The f. marshall this night sent notice to the King, who was now in Varso, that the Polls army was neer, and what else had passed. I being come to my comorades, the *ruitm-r* presently sent for the Dukes chirurgeon, who searching my wound for the bullet could not find it. He only applyed a plaster with a tent of a finger long. The next morning the surgeon after some search found the bullet and said, he hoped, there was no danger. All the tyme he was dressing of me I knew not of any {29v} thing, being in a swoune, and for a weeke there after swouned

---

[144] Towarzysz (Polish) – literally, comrade. In the Polish army, a member of a national cavalry unit (choragiew), usually a gentleman.

12. alwayes when I was dressed. And indeed the surgeon at my *ruitm-rs* request administred very good medicines and waited on dilligently. He said also it was happy that I had not eaten any thing that day, otherwise I had been in great danger. Among other things he did not permitt me to eat any thing the next day, only gave me warme beer with mans grease in it, at other tymes with dogs grease and constantly with oyle d'olive, dyeting me very sparingly. Neither did my *ruitm-r* let me want for any thing which was to be had, so that beyond expectation I recovered shortly.

13. A party was sent out to wiew the place where wee were routed and to bury the dead, which they did, bringing two cornets and some others to the leaguer, who the next day were buryed with vollies of shott after the souldiers fashion.

14. The King came to the army and Duglas with him, haveing a convoy of 500 horse and 300 dragounes.

16. The army marched. This day I rode in the *ruitm-rs* hanging waggon, which I had purchased and given to him that day wee came to Inovlodzs. When the army had marched about a mile, our foretroopes engaged with a party of the enemy, who being in ambush by their suddaine eruption forced ours to a disorderly retreat, without any great losse. The King, haveing intelligence of the Polls {30} army being neare, drew up the army in two battailes or lynes, besides commanded men in foretroopes and a strong rereguard. In the first battaile or lyne the squadrons of horse were flanked with pikemen and musquetiers, the other was of pikemen and musquetiers, and the wings horse and dragouns.

In the meane tyme I, not finding my self well at ease in the waggon, as also willing to see what passed, gott upon my horse, which being a very easy goer, I found my self at better ease as in the waggon. The army advanced on a high ground through ploughed lands, and being neer the descent, wee discovered the Polls army drawne up on a plaine low ground, haveing the easy ascent of a hill on their right hand with a litle towne called Zarnaw[145], and on their left hand a litle wood. Behind them was a wooddy countrey, and from the foot of the high ground whereon wee

---

[145] Żarnów.

wer to their army were low bushes. The Polls had no foot at all, only 4 or fyve companies of dragounes. Their [h]usars, being 3 or 4 companies, were divided in the wings and body, the King himself with his lyfeguard of strangers on a litle hill behind the army.

The Swedish army, marching downe the hill in very good order, with their regiment pieces befor the regiments as usuall, and the great artillery betwixt the battailles, but comeing to the {30v} skirt of the hill, most of the artillery were planted there befor the baggage, and fireing over the army advancing on the low ground, did the Polls some, though no considerable harme by reason of the distance and inequality of the ground. The army being advanced within a musquet shott of the Polls, the King, Generall Duglas and the *Graffe* von Sultzbach rideing continually about ordering and exhorting the army, the Polls not being in unity nor comeing to any resolution among themselves, and being loth to engage with such a well ordered army, haveing neither foot nor artillery, suddainly retreated or rather runn away. The Sweds followed but slowly for fear of an ambush, and were once alarumed as if the enemy was gott behind us, so that some regiments were commanded back to secure the rere.

The Polls made great hast away throug[h] a wood and marish, where many left their horses sticking and fled on foot. On the other side of the wood was a passe where, the passage being narrow, some weake resistance was made by the Kings lyfeguard of strangers, 2 or 3 whereof were taken. The Polls tooke the right hand towards Przedbors. A party of 3,000 horse were sent after them who, overtakeing some of their baggage, got good booty. The King with the army stayed all night at this passe.

{31} 17. The army marched and leaguered by a village on a high ground.

18. Wee marched over a passe by an iron milne and leaguered in a field by a towne called Radoshits[146].

19. Being Sunday, wee removed not, only a party of dragounes were sent out to clear the way.

20. Wee leaguered by Malogost[147], a litle, well scituated towne.

[146] Radoszyce.
[147] Małogoszcz.

21. Wee leaguered in a valley beyond a litle towne called Jendrzejowa[148]. Here wee had intelligence that the King of Polland with all the forces he could make were rendevowing at Krakow.

22. Wee marched along the r[iver] Nida, then turning to the right hand by the litle towne Xiaz[149], wee leaguered by Miechow.

23. Wee leaguered by Slomnikow[150]. By this tyme I was pretty well

24. recovered, rideing alwayes at my owne ease in what place of the army I fancyed best.

25. Haveing marched two miles, our foretroopes were engaged, but the Polls mad no stay, neither did ours persue for fear of being intrapped. When wee came to a high ground, wee perceived the north suburb of Krakow all on fire. For the King, makeing hast away, left the command of the castle and citty to Czarnetsky[151] with a good garrison, who immediately set fire on this suburb, that it might not help us nor be hinderance to them. Wee leaguered at the foot of a hill along a rivolet, a good halfe mile from the citty.

26. Generall Duglas, being sent by the King with a strong party to wiew the west side of the citty, {31v} which he did, and crossed the Wistula above Krakow. The army stayed untill 10 acloack, in which tyme I escaped a great misfortune. For haveing come late into the leaguer, and not knowing of being so near Krakow, I tooke up my quarters with a reformado major called N. Bow in ane orchard neer Generall Duglas his quarter. And haveing sleeped somewhat longer in the morning as ordinary, befor wee were ready Generall Duglas was gone, and as wee were informed (though untruly), in persuite of the Polls, whereupon wee resolved to follow in hopes of getting some booty.

Being come out of the leaguer to the rivelet which, it seemes, by the great depth of a ditch wherein it runneth, hath been drawne this way from its ordinary course, here wee discovered a great body of horse, and

---

[148] Jędrzejów.
[149] Książ.
[150] Słomniki.
[151] Stefan Czarniecki (1599–1665), one of the greatest Polish commanders of his time, from 1657 Wojewoda of Ruthenia (Lwów province).

thinking to ryde to them, wee could find no foord, neither rideing a pretty way up the brooke could perceive any. At last, comeing to a great planke which was laid a crosse for people to passe over a foot, I being impatient, hazarded and rode over it, though not without danger. Which startled and vexed my comorad, that he did fall a railing at me from the other syde, which made me (to pacify him) ride along the brooke untill, comeing to a mil[n]e, he passed there. But comeing nearer the body of horse, wee perceived it to be the maine guard, which wee resolved not to come near. And meeting a trowper returned from the party, he informed us which way they were gone, and that they were not farr of.

So, haveing passed by a double sentry with some difficulty, being in a large field and perceiving through the smock of the burning Clepars[152] many steeples and towers, wee begane to censure the {32} Polls of folly for burneing and destroying their owne countrey, especially such a brave towne as this appeared to be. And comeing nearer, wee resolved to ride through and take a wiew of the ruines thereof and then to make hast, not doubting to overtake the generall, he being not farr of, and this appearing not much out of the way, so (not knowing any thing but wee wer about 3 miles from Krakow as yet) wee rode on through the leaguer, which the Polls had deserted the day befor, and was fortyfyed towards the fields with ane entrenchment.

When wee were entred into the suburbe, and seing the many steeples and towers appear more clear, wee began to doubt if wee were not mistaken, but askeing a woman who was searching among the ruines, how the towne was called, and she answering "Clepars", this confirmed us in o[u]r first opinion. Wee had not ridden farr downe the street when, I espying two sojors in blew livery crosseing the street, told the maior, who said, "If ther be two, there may be 20, let us returne", but I replying, "What, shall wee be afrayed of two? Let us go forwards". When wee were about that place where I saw the two sojors, wee were kept up by a guard of 10 or 12 persons, who began to question us what wee were. I perceiving them to be Polls, answered that wee belonged to the Polls army

---

[152] Kleparz, a suburb of Krakow.

and were stayed behind, desireing them if they had any drink to give us some. They desired us to alight, which wee denyed, then questioning us to what regiment wee belonged, I not answering to them {32v} directly, because I knew not whom to name. One steps forth, some small officer or another, and asserts with an oath that we ar Sweds, and going to the maior takes his pistolls out of his hulsters. And albeit I called to him not to give them, yet he did not offer to resist, as haveing all the tyme not understood what wee said and thinking (as he excused himself afterwards) a great offence to resist a guard, especially our owne, as he tooke this to be, I speaking so friendly to them, which I behoved to do, being within their danger, and not knowing how to be ridd of them, 4 or 5 standing ready with cok't matches.

This corporall haveing taken the majors pistolls from him, presently drawes his cimitar, but he seing this wheels of and in the turning hindred me, I being cop't up betwixt him and a stone wall. So that he, missing him, struck at me, and I bowing forward to avoid the stroak, and the horse being in motion, he cutted me through coat and breeches and gave me a light wound in the breech, and glad I was to have escaped so.

Wee would have gladly returned the way wee came, but at the very first they had stopped that way, so that wee were forced to keep downe the way towards the towne, these sending the hue and cry after us, yet not shooting at us, which was to be admired. Wee ridd as hard as we could, the maior being befor me when, beholding a large gate with a draw bridge drawne up and a stone wall as thick besett with armed men as it could hold, the maior being short sighted, and {33} I seing a street leading from the gate another way, called to the maior to wheele to the left hand, yet were wee forced to come within lesse as 20 fathoms of the gate. They gave a confused noise from the walls, which I answered only with: "Wee are friends, do not shoot!" But when wee turned our backes to them and made hast up the other street, then was I afrayed and expected to have a volley of shott sent after us, but heard none, only one from these who followed us downe the other street. Being gott a good way of, this street was stopped with the rubbage of a great house which was fallen and was yet burning, so that there was no possibility of getting thorow, so that wee were forced to turne of to the left hand through a churchyard. At the first entry our horses wee led easily over a woodden trally or grate, but the other being iron, wee knew not what to do. But haveing no tyme to dally, I perswaded the maior to spread his clocke over the trally, so the horses passed easyly without any great harme done to the clock.

In the meane tyme wee heard a great noise from the towne-wards, but wee plyed our way untill wee gott without their danger. Haveing past their trenches, wee halted to resolve which way wee should take, I being for following the generall, and the maior to returne to the leaguer {33v} without all delay. But I tarrying a litle to looke to my old wound, he chaffingly told me I might go and choose another comorad, for he would none of such who would ride over foot-bridges and storme townes alone, and laying all the blame on me of the danger wee had been in and the lossing of his pistolls. Whilst wee were quarrelling, I espyed 20 or 30 Polls at full speed makeing towards us, which tooke of our quarrelling and sett us a running. Comeing to the sentryes, wee gave them the alarum, and they by fyreing and retreating to the guards put all in a hurly burly. In the meane tyme, knowing that wee should be questioned for this, wee made hast to the baggage in the leaguer, which was then beginning to remove. Here wee sheltered our selves the best way wee could, and albeit search was made, yet they could not find us.

A short mile below the leaguer wee crossed the r[iver] Vistula by foord and quartered not farr from Casimirs[153], another suburb of Krakow, but environed with a wall, and within a Jewish town apart. This afternoone the King rideing about to wiew the citty and castle, a page belonging to […] was killed with a cannon bullet within five fathome of him, and the first sentry of horse, who was put upon a high *Mogill*[154] (where, {34} they report, […] lyeth buryed), was killed with a cannon bullet from the red tower on the south west side of the castell. However another was put presently in his place, at whom and others his successors above a 100 shott were spent to no purpose.

---

[153] Kazimierz.
[154] Mogiła (Polish) – tomb or burial mound.

27. Being Moonday, the suburb or rather towne of Casimirs rendred, paying a round summe of money, and the Jewes payed a great summe apart. This day wee did meet with our comorad John Holstein, whom wee had left by Jendrzejowa, and associating to our selves Lt. W[illia]m Lawder, wee tooke up our quarters in a house which was farr distant from any other among some bushes, wherein wee see no body but 5 or 6 women and children, wee being glad of the convenience and they of our protection.

28. The army marched over the r[iver] Vistula againe and leaguered in the Dembe[155], so called from the oakes growing there. I furnishing my self with plasters and salves, returned to my quarters, where in a fortnights tyme my wound was perfectly healed.

The King in this tyme marched to Voynits[156], where he had gott notice that the *quartianers*[157] were in a body still, and routed them. Returning by Visnits[158], he tooke it and a good store of artillery, 35 pieces, the King of Polland being fled by the way of Sandets[159] to Scepusia[160] and thence into Silesia. In the tyme that the King of Sweden was from the army, haveing 4,000 horse and dragouns with him, which

{34v} Oct[ober]. was nine dayes, the guards about the citty of Krakow were not releeved.

After the King returned he caused approaches to be made on the east and south side of the citty, which Czarnetsky, who was governour both of citty and castle, endeavoured to impede as much as possible by sallies and excursions, in one whereof he caused burne the suburb Stradomia. In another he tooke a monastery which the Sweds had manned, which three dayes after the Sweds retake, and the Polls againe by a sally take it and burne and demolish it.

---

[155] Probably Dębniki.

[156] Wojnicz.

[157] Wojsko kwarciane (quarter army) – regular units raised in Poland since 1562, so called because they were paid a quarter of the income of the royal estates.

[158] Wiśnicz.

[159] Sącz (Polish), Sandez (German).

[160] Spisz (Polish), Spiš (Slovak), Zips (German), Szepes (Hungarian), once a region of Poland and Hungary, now part of Slovakia.

10. Generall Duglas was sent with a party of 2,000 horse and dragouns to clear the hills of the gentlmen and bowres, who did great harme to our forragers, and were said to be 10 or 12,000 men in the woods. Haveing marched an easy march, wee made an halt in the evening to feed o[u]r horses. About two houres befor midnight wee marched.

11. About sunriseing wee entred a wood where was very strait ground, and descending downe into a valley by a litle brooke, wee made a halt, where wee gott good store of rey and oat sheaves from a small village hard by, to feed our horses, but nothing for our selves. Wee had not rest much above an houre, when our guards gave us the alarum, and were beat into the body, where being rallyed and reinforced with fresh troopes, the enemy was beat into the wood againe. But wee were in a very disadvantagious place, for the Polls had not only the wood to shelter them, but also a very steep hill one on [*sic*] syde of us, from whence they rolled great stones downe upon us. Most of them were on foot and kept themselves in their strait ground, so that our {35} horsemen were not able to do any service; and they were a great deale nimbler as our dragouns.

Being at unequall skirmishing about ane houre, the generall resolved to returne the way he came, and haveing ordered the nimblest horsemen with some dragounes on foot in the arrearguard, wee retreated back the way wee came. Which the Polls perceiving, they did fall on upon all hands, so that wee had enough to do to keep them from breaking in thorow our troopes, so that about a quarter of a mile wee were in great danger and perplexity. Being gott without the wood, wee faced about with some troopes and skirmished with them untill our dragounes mounted.

At one of these encounters it was my badd luck againe to be shott through the right legg a litle below the garter, and my horse killed under me with the same shott. How soone I perceived my horse hurt, I made hast to gett befor, fearing the worst. When I gott up to the front, which was a good halfe mile from the wood, the generall began to rally the troops and draw them up under the shelter of a small hill overgrowne with thick bushes. Wee had lost some men in the woods, and the generall being incensed, was resolved to be revenged. Wherefor sending order to the troops in the reare to retreat speedily with some show of confusion, to draw them from the wood within danger, which had its wished successe. For not only the Polls horsemen but the foot in great multitudes, but disorderly and makeing a terrible noise, persued our people a good way. The generall perceiving them at a stand, with great celerity wheeled about the hill and did fall in among them befor they were {35v} awarre, who being astonished made but small resistance. The horsmen being beset presently fled another way, leaving the foot to shift for themselves, a great multitude whereof were killed in their flight back to the wood. The horse escaped without much damage, being primely mounted and farr lighter as ours. About 1,600 were killed.

I was not present at the execution, my horse fainting under me befor the charge. The generall caused give to me, and to twelve or 15 more whose horses were killed, horses which were taken from the enemy. The generall sent Coll[onel] Konigsmark with a party to persue further these Polls untill they were quite dispersed, who getting intelligence that many of them were gott into the castle of Landskron[161], he marched thither and, summoning the castle, they rendred upon discretion. But haveing gott them, he caused hang them all, being about 400, for the which he was afterwards in great trouble. The generall returned to the leaguer.

12. In the meane tyme my legge was so swelled that my boot was ripp'd up when I came into the leaguer.

13. I gott a quarter in Casimirs.

The Polls *quartianers* send their deputies to treat and gett good conditions. The principall men among the *quartianers* were Konietspolsky[162], the Crowne Ensigne Jan Siobesky *Starosta* Yavorofsky[163], Jan Sapi[e]ha. After the rendition of Krakow these Polls joined with the Sweds and marched down to Prussia.

17. The deputies belonging to the garrison and city of Krakow conclude their treaty on these conditions:

---

[161] Lanckorona.
[162] Aleksander Koniecpolski (1620–1659), Wojewoda of Sandomierz.
[163] Jan Sobieski (1629–1696), famous commander, King of Poland and Grand Duke of Lithuania from 1674 as Jan III. Starosta was a royal official in charge of a territorial unit.

{36} 1. The free publick excercise of the Catholick religion. The channery, churches, colledges, monasteries, hospitalls and all religious houses and persons to be free from all violence, plundering, inquartering unlesse great necessity urge it, and all sorts of persons whatsoever to be free from all force or harme, provideing they do not practice any thing against the Crowne of Sweden, but remaine true and obedient, and such contribution to be payed from the church lands as from other.

2. The officers and gentlmen belonging to the castle and county shall have freedome and security in their persons, goods and lands, and if they remaine within the Kingdome, to swear to continue true, peacable and obedient to the Swedish King. And if any will depart out of the Kingdome and quite his dignity and office, it shall be free for him to go with all he hath.

3. The citty of Krakow with all the citizens and indwellers shall retaine their priviledges and freedomes inviolated, which the former Kings have given them, as also

4. The Academy[164] shall keep the rights and freedomes, which have been confirmed in the Kingdoms constitutions, as also their rents.

5. The Governour Czarnetsky, *Castellan* of Kyow, with the Commendant Collonell Wulffe and all officers of warr and souldiers with bagge and baggage, flying collours, beating drumms, 12 peeces of cannon, shall march out of the towne on the 19 instant *st. novo* at 8 acloak in the morning free and securely. In the meane tyme, so soone as this accord shal be subscrived, sealed and exchanged, the citty gate towards Stradomia, {36v} as also the gates of St. Nicholas and Tzworetsky with the turrets betwixt these gates, be cleared for the King to besett.

6. The garrison to have quarters for 4 weekes in the Kings lands on the Silesia borders, in Zator, Osweczin[165], Kosichewa[166], Bendzin[167] etc., provideing they practice not hostility against the Swedish King and army, and to preserve from all harme and plunder the inhabitants and travelling

---

[164] The University of Krakow.
[165] Oświęcim.
[166] Possibly Koziegłowy.
[167] Będzin.

persons, and for this to leave sufficient pledges. After 4 weekes be expired they shall be free to depart whither they please. Yet if the Polnish King do not entertaine them into service, they shall make offer thereof to the Swedish King befor any other.

7. The foot, which had been drawn out of the countrey to this garrison, shall with their officers and armes freely depart to their homes, yet that they live peacably and practice no hostility privately or publickly against the Swedish King.

8. The Kings domesticks and servants shall be safely convoyed to His Ma[jes]tie by a trompeter and have passes.

9. The prisoners taken on both sides in the tyme of the siege shall be released, and the Moskovite prisoners to be delivered to the Swedish King.

10. All the publick writtings and registers of chancery and revenue etc. and the regalia and the court documents, whither hidd in citty or castell, shal be delivered into the Swedish Kings commissaries hand unspoiled and unfalsified, and all artillery (except those mentioned in the 5th article), ammunition, proveant with all warlick instruments and necessaries, whether in castell or citty, be left, and nothing taken along but what properly doth belong {37} to the governour, officers and sojors; and to this effect, and that in the castle or citty no fire, mines or any other dangerous businesse be not placed or left, the governour shall give sufficient pledges.

[October] 19. The garrison marched out, about 6,000 strong, according to the accord, with flying collours, 12 peeces of cannon, 20 tunne of powder and a great deale of baggage. In the castle and citty were found 96 mettall pieces. The citty gave 300,000 reichs dollers *brandshats*[168], as they call it.

About the tyme that the army lay at Krakow these things passed in other places. Three thowsand horse and foot under the command of the Maior Generalls Muller and Wresovitz were sent to lay siege to the famous monastery of Czenstochow[169], which in the end proved fruitlesse.

---

[168] Brandschatzung (German) – contribution.
[169] Częstochowa. Its Pauline Monastery of Jasna Góra, led by Prior Augustyn Kordecki, bravely withstood the Swedish siege from 18 November to 27 December 1655.

Landgraffe Friderich of Hessen, commonly called Madd Frits, who had marryed the Swedish Kings sister, comeing towards Kostzian in Great Polland, sent his secretary and trumpeter befor, who not returning, he rode forward himself, and being with all signes of respect permitted to enter, in the very entry was killed by a shott, the Polls haveing a few dayes befor surprised the towne and killed governour and garrison.

The King of Sweden sent ambassadours to Ragotsky, the Prince of Transilvania[170], and to Chmielnitsky, the Generall of the Kosakes[171], who was by Reus-Lamberg[172] with his army. Both promised friendship, and Chmielnitsky desired to know whither he should go with his army to be serviceable to His Ma[jes]tie.

The King also writt from Casimirs 12° Oct. to the Roman Emperour[173], who thereupon sent *Graffe* Pottingen with rich presents, being 2 Turkish horses whose decks were valued at 20,000 r[eichs] dollers. The Emperour offered himself mediatour at the King of Pollands desire, the French ambasadour offering the like. {37v} The King of Polland was at this tyme in Opolia[174] in Silesia.

Felt Marshall Steinbock beats the Massours[175] and takes some townes in Massovia and Cujavia.

As to my owne particular, my *ruitmaster* upon some discontent desired his passe from the Duke, who in some passion promised it to him, and I used meanes to obtaine myne from the *ruitm-r*. However, dureing the siege the *ruitm-r* was againe reconciled to the Duke, but I kept my self free, untill the army was to depart from Krakow towards their winter quarters, and then I engadged for a volontier by *Ruitm-r* James Duncan under *Graffe*

---

[170] György II Rákóczi (1621–1660), Prince of Transylvania from 1648.
[171] Bohdan Khmelnytsky (ca.1595–1657), Hetman of Ukraine. In 1648 he led the Cossack rising against Poland-Lithuania and in 1654 swore fealty to the Tsar of Russia.
[172] Lemberg (German), Lwów (Polish), Lviv (Ukrainian), once centre of the Polish province (Województwo) of Ruthenia.
[173] Ferdinand III Habsburg (1608–1657), Emperor of the Holy Roman (German) Empire from 1637.
[174] Opole.
[175] Mazovians.

Pontus de la Gardie his regiment, which was said to gett good winter quarters because it had been ruined under Opoczno.

The King with the army marched towards Varso, Generall Major Vurtz being left governour in Krakow with about 4,000 horse and foot. Lt. Coll. Stewart was commendant in the castle.

The regiment of *Gr.* Pontus de la Gardie marched to the winter quarters in New Sandets. I not being able then to travell, followed 5 or 6 dayes afterwards, and lodged the first night among our new made ffriends the *quartianers*, not without danger of our lives, but wee could not avoid it, being come out of our way, and within their danger. The next day wee dined in a small towne called Rimanova[176], which is ten miles from Krakow, and towards night came to Sandets, 2 miles further. {38} The regiment was commanded by *Ruitm-r* Lighton, the lt. collonell and major not being returned out of prison.

This towne being a regality belonged to Constantin Lubomirsky, the yongest sone of the deceassed *Woywoda* Krakowsky. The river Dunajets, which cometh out of the Karpathian mountains, runneth on the west syde thereof. It is by nature fortifyed on two sides more, and the whole environed with a wall sufficient against any suddaine assault, though not tenable against a siege of a formed army. On the west side also is the noblemans house environed with a pallisade. In the towne were some iron cannon, which wee caused mount and planted in convenient places. Wee were not welcome guests to this towne and countrey, which wee could very well perceive by their behaviour.

How soone the lt. collonel came, he sent out partyes and gott good summes of money from the townes thereabout and sett the countrey in contribution, which for four or five weeks was pretty well payed, but afterwards came in but very slowly. A party of 20 horsmen being sent out to force the defficients, the bowres out of the woods did fall upon them and killed nine of them, the rest escapeing, and two or 3 dayes after 3 of our men were killed within halfe a mile of the towne. This, and not one of the countrey people comeing into the market as they were wont, as also the

---

[176] Obviously Limanowa, not Rymanów, which is too far away.

flight of some of the townes people, made us suspect no good. Hereupon the lt. collonel tooke all armes from the burgers and made them swear loyalty, caused repair the wall, keep good watch, as

{38v} Dec[embe]r. also a guard of 24 trowpers with a lieutennant upon the market place in readines, who every morning befor the gates were free to be entred marched out at the north west gate round the towne, searching the suburb and recognoscing about halfe a mile round the towne, returned at the other gate. And every company had so much of the towne wall to defend, and every thing ordered as well as possible, but our men, haveing been many of them prisoners, were naked and not furnished with such weapons as was needful.

The lt. collonel, haveing gott notice from ane Arrian gentleman called Slichting[177], that the countrey people called *Goraly* (that is, Highlanders), and the *Rusnatsy*, i.e. Russes, were gathering to a head with some gentlemen and intended no good to us, he suddainly in the night tyme sent away his lady and the best of his goods to Krakow. Two nights thereafter wee had an alarum, some fyres haveing been seen in the wood. A party sent out the next day found the fyres, but no body by them.

12. But on the 12th of December, being Sunday, in the 2d houre of the night, our guards discovering many fyres on the north e[ast] syde of the towne in the woods, gave the alarum, so that every man went to his post. A party of a hundred horse being sent out for intelligence, attacted their guards and brought away some prisoners among whom was a gentleman could speak Dutch. These informed us, being some of them put to the rack and others threatned, that there {39} were about 2 or 3,000 bowres together, 200 dragouns belonging to the Bishop of Krakow and other noblmen, some gentlmen, among whom two brothers Vonsovitses were the chieffe; that they intended to fall upon the Arrian gentlmans house which was a mile below the towne and take it, and then to assault

---

[177] Members of the Minor Reformed Church in Poland were known as *arianie* (Arians, also Polish Brethren, Antitrinitarians or Socinians). Prominent among them was Jonasz Schlichting (1592–1661), author of many theological works. Banished by the Sejm in 1647, he came back to Krakow with the Swedes. All Arians were finally expelled from Poland in 1658.

the towne; that the bowres best armes were sythes stretched out upon long poles, some ryfled gunnes and small axes.

The lieutennant collonell (who was a very valiant gentleman, but very unfortunate in this warr) called a counsell of warr of the chieffe officers, where it was concluded by day light to march out with all the forces wee could make and attact them, and not suffer them to take in the gentlemans house.

13. In order to this the lt. collonell himself and major with all the officers (except those who had been upon the party and the guards) and about 240 trowpers marched out towards the same place where they leaguered the night befor. The ports of the towne were shutt, but the draw bridges not drawne up, and wee very secure in the towne, expecting the successe of our party. Neither had our maine guard recognosced and visited the suburb as usuall. It seemes the enemy, receaving invitation and intelligence from their ffriends in the towne, after the camisado[178] done on them by our people in the fore part of the night, had convoyed themselves very silently and covertly into the suburb. And because wee used ordinarily to search the houses only, they hidd themselves in the barnes and out houses, and how soone they perceived our party out of sight, they {39v} sent halfe a dozen of good shooters who, traversing as near the port as they could in a negligent manner as if they had been bowres belonging to the suburb, were not taken notice of by our sentries on the walles, when on a suddaine turning themselves and fixeing, killed two of our sentries without any great noise. (Their ryfled gunnes, being heavy and takeing a very litle bullet not much bigger as a good pease, and not much powder, shoot very just without makeing a loud report, the peculiar name of lock [?] is *czeshinka*[179]).

These sentryes being killed, they advance in great hast to the gate, and whilst some with their axes are cutting up a hole in the gate, others provide ladders and scale the wall and, finding no resistance, enter. My quarters being near this gate, I heard a noise and, going out to know

---

[178] Attack under cover of darkness.
[179] Such wheel-lock guns were called *cieszynka* after the Silesian town of Cieszyn (Teschen).

what it was, a woman cam running up the street crying that the Polls were beating up the port. But going a litle further to know the certainty, a trowper came running confirmeing it and telling that they were scaleing the wall also. I running back to my quarters, gave notice to those who were in the quarters. It was my bad fortune this morning to cause take of the shooes from my best horse to sharpe them, haveing a litle nagge sadled with a Dutch sadle newly stuffed, the girths being slackened. Upon which mounting, I came to the gate with 10 or 12 more, *Ruitm-r* Donklaw comeing to us also.

A cannon stood {40} opposite to the gate, which the *ruitm-r* offered to fyre, but being poisoned by some of the burgers, would not go of. In the meane tyme the enemy, haveing made a large hole in the gate throw which they had put 10 or 12 ryfeld pieces, gave a salve among us wounding two men and a horse, which dispersed us. I returned to my quarters for my other horse and rideing into the forehouse, desired my landlord to bring him forth, which he stubbornly refused, but at lentgh my boy brought him to me (I being afrayed to light my self). I no sooner rode out of the doore but I see the enemy come flocking up the street with their white coats and black cappes, all on foot. I made as fast as I could towards the market place, but was in great danger befor I gott thither, for the nagge on which I rode, being a pacer, had no speed, and they persuing me hotly had very neer overtaken me. And also by their shooting and flinging of small axes (wherein they have a singular art) they so irritated the horse which I had in my hand, that haveing nothing in his head but a halter, he had almost pulled me of the horse.

Being come to the market place, I took tyme to looke about, when seeing the guard mounting, and others running to the other gate and noblemans house, I made thither also. In passing by my *ruitm-rs* lodging, Maior Bow abovementioned was comeing out on horseback, to whom I called, "Forgett not your booke, maior, for wee are like to be all undone today". For he {40v} used to tell me and others his confidents, that he had a book, which could teach halfe a dozen of good fellowes a rich livelyhood in some great citty if each had but a stock of a hundred ducats. This occasioned much good sport afterwards.

When I came to the other gate, I see the *ruitm-rs* Donklaw and Duncan forcing our people to a stand, perceiving then that wee should have some bickering for it yet, and remembring in what danger I had been on the litle nagge, every nimble rogue being able to overtake me, I choosed rather to hazard on my best horse, though he wanted shooes, it being indeed very slippery. I had no sooner sadled and given my other horse to one on foot who asked him of me, but the *ruitm-rs*, haveing gott together a troup of 20 or 24 horse, were advancing towards the market place.

When wee came to the market place, which was full of the rogues, wee presently charged in amongst them and drove them to the other side beyond the *radthouse*. But a cry ariseing that they were running downe the other street to gett betwixt us and the gate, wee retired the way wee came. In this retreat my horse did fall with me, and the sadle, being newly stuffed and not well girthed, turned, yet by that *Ruitm-r* Duncan had cleared the other street and placed a guard at the foot thereof to secure our retreat, I was ready, and advanced up to the market place {41} againe with the troop, which was now thinner. When wee were near the market place wee see a free *ruiter* called Hans Yurgen (whom the *ruitm-r* had sent in for the standart at o[u]r first charge) comeing out with it by the enemy presently killed, and o[u]r collours taken, whom wee were not able to help.

When wee were gott to the market place, it was even full of the rogues, no lesse as two or three thousand to my thinking. At this charge wee effected but litle, the enemy encloseing us on all hands, so that some were killed and *Ruitm-r* Duncan with great danger charging back againe through a thick company who were gathered to oppose us, helped to make good our retreat downe the street, the enemy persuing us very hard. At the end of the street were some of our men on foot with muskets, who fired up the street promiscuously among us and the enemy. Near the end of the street, as wee were wheeling to repulse the enemy, my horse did againe fall with me, the sadle also overturning, and albeit the *ruitm-r*, being forced to retire and seing me fall, made a halt untill I should recover my horse, yet could not gett stayed untill I was ready. I seing the *ruitm-r* gone, and not being able in such a distraction and hast to get my sadle fitted and girthed, was forced to cut the girths and leave it. It was Gods providence that the enemy, being afrayed of o[u]r men shooting up the street, left the middle of the street and advanced under the shelter and covers of the houses.

At my sitting up I gott a stroake (with an axe, I think), which had almost overturned me againe, but recovering my self I made what hast I could to the gate, which from the other street was already possessed by the {41v} enemy, who were busy killing all who came in their way, and many, not knowing that they had possessed the gate, came running into their hands and receaved their last.

Being come to the gate and perceiving it full of the enemies at such work as I said, I first not makeing any stay bequeathed my self to the protection of the Almighty God. I put my horse to it, haveing my sword over my head to guard it, my horse being of good courage, rushed in through the gate in the wall and overthrowing some in the way. In the pallisado without the wall there was a port with two leaves, and another lesser on the right hand. Two or three (whom I knew afterwards to be the Bishop of Krakows dragouns) were shutting the bigg port, which perceiving I made towards the lesser, but befor I could reach it, some let drive at me with such weapons as they had. And one haveing a sythe on a pole stretched out, struck me with all his might overthwart my head (I not being able to shun it), so that, had not a good Bredaes hatt[180] abated the violence of the stroak, he had surely cleft me to the shoulders. However, I receaved a great wound and was so stounded and astonished with it that I was a pretty way without the gate befor I cam to my self, my mercifull God makeing my horse the instrument to bring me of, who was in a manner in a trance. As I recovered my self I perceived our ffriends below the hill, and comeing thither all bebloodied, the *ruitm-r* in few words expressed how glad he was that I, whom he thought really to have been lost, was escaped.

The {42} *ruitm-rs* resolved to get over the pallisado on foot to the castle or noblemans house, and hold out that untill our party should returne. Being dismounted and ready with all to ascend, the lt. collonells servants came running out at the back doore (posterne) and informed of the enemies takeing possession of the house also. One of these servants when

---

[180] Probably, a hat made in Breda in the Netherlands.

he came out shutt the door after him to hinder the pursuit, which was the losse of many who might have escaped that way.

Here againe wee were taken with another fear. Our party returning another way, wee imagined them to be the enemies horse. Wee made through the river, the better horsed being forced by the officers to transport those who were escaped out of the towne on foot, most whereof were Egiptian women (there being more of such stuffe under this regiment as under any other in the army). The first I caryed over behind me was a Scotsman called Alehous, o[u]r regiment waggonm[aste]r. At the second tyme they put up a *zigan* or Egiptian wyfe behind me and, being neer the river all makeing great hast, they put up another bigg girle befor me. The river was deep, and these women out of fear not sitting sure, had almost drawne me of into the river, so that I was forced to let my feet hang in the river for surer sitting, and haveing but shooes on I wett my feet whereby I did freeze them in the night.

By this [time] wee perceived these horsemen which wee saw to be our owne people. The enemy within the towne fired two cannon, on[e] from {42v} the castle, another from the gate, which being high styled did no harme. On the south syde of the towne an unskilfull fellow fired some bagges of powder lying in the carriage of a cannon, which made a great noise. One thing which I understood afterwards contributed to the safety of us all who were who [*sic*] escaped out of the towne, which I here cannot omitt. There were among those our enemies 2 or 300 dragouns and foot well armed, who at the first assault were ordained to go round the towne to the other port or gate and there attacque and hinder our flight, which if they had performed, not on of us had escaped. But they being halfe way round the towne and hearing the towne taken and the bowres entred, they thought it better to returne and enter at the gate which was taken as go to the other, where the[y] were sure to gett some blowes and perhaps litle or no booty, which they did, and this gave us a free passage.

Our people being come to us, made no stay but presently marched of, takeing our way towards Krakow. About halfe a mile from the towne wee plundred a gentlmans house, where I gott some linnen which was very steddable to me afterwards. In the eve[n]ing wee came to a small towne

Rimanowa, where makeing no stay, wee marched over a mountaine and came to a village called Grabia, which is 6 miles from Krakow and halfe way from our garrison. This night was very cold, and it would have grieved any heart to see the poor infants throwne away and lying by the way, none helping them.

My feet {43} as is said being wett, and I not able to walke by reason of the great paine in my head, were frozen, which I perceived not untill I came to the fire. Our quarter was a great *kruke* or alehouse or innes, such as is in these parts. Wee made great fires by our horses, and I had the liberty because of my wound to stay in the roome with the officers, there being above 20 persons more, which was all it could hold. I had my wound dressed by one of our surgeons, who not haveing materialls to sew it up (for a great piece of flesh was hanging over behind), occasioned the festering of it thereafter, when I was in prison.

14. Wee marched early and quartered in a village a mile and a halfe from Krakow, where wee had slender accommodation in such cold weather in pittifull black stoves. Here wee stayed two dayes and then marched[181] and lodged on the other side of Krakow near the place of o[u]r leaguer when wee first came to Krakow. Here wee stayed two nights and then, haveing gott our quarters allotted us in the castle, wee marched [thither].

The regiment drawing up in the suburb, some difference did fall out betwixt our lieutennant called Barnes (who was an English man) and the lieutennant of *Ruitm-r* Halberstatt his trowpe, about precedency, if I remember rightly (our *ruitm-r* being upon a party). O[u]r lieut. rideing up to the other fell, it seemes, a quarrelling {43v} with him. The other, being a sharp man, upon some word or other drew his sword, struck him and keeping closse to him that he could not draw his, drove him back to the company. I seing this, called out, "What, a Gods name, shall wee see and suffer this?!", and no body stirring, I rode out of the trowpe and with my drawne sword put the lieut-t to his guard. *Ruitm-r* Halberstadt upon this came rideing up with a cock'd pistoll and presented it to my brest, my countrey-men who were in our troope calling all this tyme to me to retire,

---

[181] Crossed out in MS: into Casimirs, where we stayed about a week. Wee marched out afterwards…

and if I were made to medle in such things. Whereupon, I seing my lieut. with his sword now drawne upon his guard, and some other officers come to parting, retired the fairest way I could into the troope.

This night wee quartered in Casimirs. The next day my lieut. fought a duell with the other and cam of but with small creditt. Wee stayed here about a week and then marched into the castell to our quarters. I stayed in the towne with my lieut. in one quarter. Two dayes afterwards wee went with a strong party to Prossowits[182] and had intelligence that the King of Polland was come out of Silesia to the Scepts and takeing his way toward Crosna[183], and that the Tartars would assist him.

Upon our returne to Krakow partyes were sent out to bring in provision out of these places, which being farr of denyed contribution. Returning from on of these partyes upon a Fridday at night, I understood the regiment to be marched that morning.

{44}   **1656**

Ja[nua]ry.

The next morning, haveing sold some booty which I had gott on the party, in the afternoone, intending to follow the party, I came in company and spent the most part of the night in no Christian excercise.

The next morning I made hast to begone after the regiment in company of Lieut. Barnes, two other reformado officers and two servants. Being come near a litle towne on a hill called Dupshits[184], about 5 miles from Krakow, I was sent to the towne to desire a guide. The gentleman who was governour of the towne (it being a regality), called Jordan, with some reluctancy granted us a guide, being a gentlman on horse, who knew no further of o[u]r partyes march but that they had quartered at Grabia the night befor. Neither could wee in Krakow nor by the way by diligent enquiry gett any intelligence, what their intent was and whither they

---

[182] Proszowice.
[183] Krosno.
[184] Dobczyce.

intended. Being come to Grabia, wee found the march divided to the right and left hand, the greater number being gone to the left hand or rather directly forward. Here wee consulted which way to take, and because it was thought and reported in Krakow, that this expedition was to be revenged on Sandets and that cannon was to be brought from Wisnits thither, wee concluded it to be so and fancied the foot with the greater number to be gone towards Wisnits for the cannon, and that o[u]r regiment, as being best acquainted with the countrey, was gone the directest way to environ the towne.

Upon this probable {44v} conjecture wee tooke the right hand way. Being come to the tope of a hill, wee espied a horseman afarr of makeing great hast away towards a gentlmans house and village; this wee guessed to be a sentry. About sunsett wee did meet 3 countrey fellows, of whom enquiring for our people, they informed us that they were marched through Rimanowa and, as it was thought, intended to returne and quarter there, and that they were not above a hundred horse. Whereby wee perceived that it was but a party of commanded men, and wished then wee had taken the other way, such parties being commonly well horsed and useing quick dispatch, but our horses haveing ridden 10 Dutch miles without baiting, not being able to hold out if wee should returne.

Wee resolved to go forwards and bait our horses in the towne untill the party returned, or lodge all night if the party stayed there, I being sent befor with our guide to take up a quarter. When I came into the towne, I see ten or twelve of the burgers standing together on the market place, whom I asked concerning our party. They told me that about an houre ago they went through the towne and that they thought they would returne and lodge there. Whereupon, takeing up quarters in the *voyts*[185] house where I had dined once befor, I left our guide to provide necessaries for us, and I returned to meet the lieut[enant].

Being come without the towne, I expected their comeing. After a litle stay I rode back almost {45} to the place where I left them, but seing no body, I imagined that they had taken another way into the towne, it being

---

[185] Wójt (Polish) – village elder.

every where open. So, returning to our lodging and finding them not, I began to fear the worst. And hearing from the landlord, who was a very honest man, that our party, haveing taken some gentlmen a mile from the towne, were returned by the other side of the towne in great hast, I called to our guide that he would come along and follow the party, but he excused himself not knowing the way, and that his horse was not able to travell without being fed, and perswaded me to stay and feed our horses untill the moone rise.

It being now darke, I not being willing to stay, enquired for a guide to conduct me to Wisnits, offering any money, but none would undertake it. Whereupon I rode out of the towne againe intending to hazard alone. Befor the towne a woman, who had taken notice of my going and returning, told me that befor my first comeing out of the towne she saw 4 Sweds comeing towards the towne, and that meeting with some straglers from the party they turned back in great hast. I held on my way wishing to meet with one person alone, whom I might force to conduct me.

Haveing rode halfe an English mile, I came to some houses lying scattered along the side of a steep hill and well hedged in towards the way. Here I espyed a fellow in a lane, of whom I enquired if he had seen any Sweds passe that way. He answered me calmly, but I did not understand well what he said. At first I thought to lay hold of him and force him to shew me the way, but drawing neare to him I perceived he had an axe in his hand and a great club trailing after him, which he was makeing ready {45v} to manage. I seing this pulled out a pistoll and threatned to shoot him if he would not go along with me, but he skipping over the hedge began to whistle and raise a great noise, so that in an instant he was answered from all corners, and in a trice the hue and cry set after me.

I made hast to be gone, but it being exceeding dark and rugged way, could not make great speed, so that befor I reached the end of the village, they had the gate of the enclosure from the fields shut and manned, and hearing me comeing on they shott twice at me. I seing no possibility of forceing my passage, being alone and loth to fall in the hands of the boures, with whom there is as litle civility as mercy, resolved to returne, and being now without their danger, began to consider that it was my best way to ride round the towne if possible and come in as quietly as I could to my lodging, which I did, so that no body perceived me.

In the roome were 7 or 8 countrey fellowes drinking at a by table. I caused get water and provender for my horse and then some victualls for my self, intending when the moone should rise to be gone with my guide. Haveing eaten, I became so sleepy and weary, that I was not able to hold up my head. My landlord was very civill and assured me that I needed fear no danger from any of the towns people. So I lay downe on the bench to take a litle rest.

About midnight I was awakened by a most fearfull dreame, for methought my horse was growne so leane and weary, that he was not able to creep out the way, and being in a very pittyfull dirty place {46} I was sett upon by a great many wolves who had the visages of men, and that after a long pursuit they pulled me downe among them and were ready to devour me.

Being awakened and com to my self, I called to the gentleman who was with me, telling him that I wished wee were gone and that I would give my horse to be in Visnits. He answered that he had slept but litle and was possessed with a great fear. Whilst he was yet speaking wee heard on knocking at the utter doore softly, asking for beer. I, suspecting no good, caused bring a candle, and forbidd to let any body in, and calling for the landlord asked what way I could escape. For he told me that without doubt gentlmen were come to the towne and had gotten notice of my being there, and told me if they had not besett the back gate, that were the only way.

I presently mounted, takeing my guide along (whose horse I was faine to bridle, he being not afrayed but astonished). My landlord going befor to make up the gate, found it besett with ten or twelve men on horseback besides others on foot. I seing no meanes to escape, returned and resolved to mantaine the roome untill I should at least get good quarters. So, quitting our horses, wee betook ourselves to the roome and barracadoing the doore, into which there was a small glassen window just opposite to the utter doore, I put the gentlman to maintaine the windowes which were in on end of the house.

The enemy, finding no entrance by faire meanes, were beginning to force open the doore. The landlord {46v} and they were in the meane tyme capitulating, he desireing that they would do me no harme, I being a very yong man, and they calling to him to diswade me from makeing any resistance, I calling to the landlord to make open the doore or let them break it open, for I would see who durst enter, which they hearing, became calmer and desired the landlord to assure me, that if I would not make resistance, they would do me no harme. And one of them calling out aloud to me in broken Dutch to take quarters, I answered, "If good quarter, I would yeeld". Which they confirming with oathes and putting their fingers acrosse, I bidd the gentlman draw the table from the doore. I laying my pistoll downe on the table, satt downe on the bench opposite to the doore and expected their comeing.

How soone my guide had opened the doore, they came rushing in, and 4 or 5 of them presented karabins to my brest, so that I thought verily they would kill me, yet could not my heart yeeld to begg submissively of them, that they would spare my lyfe. There was among them one gentlman called Jan Stotsky, who it seemes had more authority as the rest. He interposeing himself, tooke me into his custody and makeing no stay here, mounted me on a naughty litle nagge and brought me to his house, about a mile from the towne. Being about {47} two aclock after midnight, he brought me into an inner roome where his wyfe lay on a bed, and he caused spread downe a carpet upon straw for himself and me and locked the doore with a paddlock. The gentleman himself sleeped very soundly, and his wyfe would needs entertaine discourse with me, whereof I understood but litle. She told me that she had a brother or near kinsman who had been a generall in Germany, and many things more.

About break of day the gentlman caused make ready his horses and bring some victualls for me, telling me he knew the fashion of strangers to eat early in the morning, but I had no stomack. Then began he to tell me that he was to deliver me of in New Sandets, where I would be kept under a strict watch of the *Hayduckes*[186], and that I would be narrowly

---

[186] Hajdúk (Hungarian and Polish) – foot soldiers, originally Hungarian.

searched even to my shirt, and if I had any thing of worth by me, money or jewels, it would be taken from me, and that I would gett but a pittifull allowance of victualls. Wherefor I should do well to give any thing I had to him, and he would releeve my necessities in prison and would do his best to procure liberty for me to come and live by him on his lands untill the King, generall or Lubomirsky should give order concerning me. I knowing that he could command what he desired so ffriendly, this being only that I should not divulge to his comorads any thing he should gett from me, gave him my purse wherein were 9 ducats, 4 dollers and about 8 florens of small money. He told the money as if he had been borrowing of it, and renewing his former promises of suplying my necessities, insinuating how civilly he had used me, and that if I had fallen in anothers {47v} hands, my cloaths being so good, had not escaped, telling me all in broken Latin, that I could understand him the better. I then with too much credulity trusting to his generosity and fearing the search he spoke of, produced my hidden treasure, which I had privily by me. It was two gold bracelets with enameled locks, a small chaine of an ell and a halfe long, 3 rings with stones, one a large saphire, the other two diamonds, 4 dozen of small silver overgilt buttons, a toad-stone and some other trifles, in all to the value of 150 ducats or more.

When he saw this he could not containe his joy, nor his wyfe conceale her gladnes. Then had I many religious protestations how much they would do for me, but being now bright day, he made hast to be gone, telling me slightly that I needed not tell any body what he had gott from me. By the way those who had been at my takeing came to him.

And so, being a very cold morning, and colder comfort to me to have such badd luck on the first Moonday of the new-year, wee came to the towne; the gentlman, where I had lodged, being mounted on my horse (which was a yong tall sprightly beast well worth 25 or 30 pieces), rode vaporing befor, then 5 gentlemen in a rank, I then alone on a naughty litle beast, after 10 or 12 servants. As it seemes, they brought me through the street where I had my quarters last befor our su[r]prisall, where the people knowing me seemed rather to commiserate as insult over my condition, especially the women who by nature are tender hearted.

One Captaine Kollete, a Dutch man, had the command of the towne at that tyme and, being at dinner by the *podstarost*[187], {48} I was brought to him, who examining me first of the occasion of my comeing from Krakow, the manner of my being taken, but especially whither our party was bound, I answered to all in plaine truth so much as I knew. As for the party, I knew of no other designe unlesse it were to come to this towne, wherewith he and the rest seemed not satisfyed, and sent me with a guard to his owne quarters where I had a very good dinner.

About two aclock afternoone a serjeant with 12 musquetiers brought me from thence towards the *radt*-house, whither being come, the serjeant with 6 musquetiers descended with me into a vault, leaving the other six above. In the vault were 3 or 4 sturdy fellowes standing, and a small fire. The serjeant then told me that notwithstanding I had been urged to declare the truth, what designe the party had, that I would not, wherefor it was ordained that I should be put on the rack to make me confesse the verity.

I hearing this was astonished and stood mute a while, then recollecting my self I desired the serjeant (who seemed to be a good natured creature, albeit his phisiognomy presaged no such thing) to informe the commendant and those with him, that I had told the plaine truth already so farr as I knew, that I was not in Krakow when the party went out, neither had seen it to know how strong. Nor could I and those with me, either in Krakow or upon the way, learne any thing else of their designe, as I had told already, and that the commendant, being a souldier, knew very well how closse the Sweds are; and that none upon a party of what quality soever is acquainted with the maine designe except he who commandeth in chieffe, nor he either, oftentimes haveing a sealed order which he is to break open in presence of the chieffe officers when he comes to such a place. Wherfor {48v} they might well beleeve that I, who was no officer, could not know any thing.

With these reasons the serjeant seeming convinced, said he would go and informe the commendant and councell thereof. After a short stay he returned and told that they were not satisfyed herewith, affirming that they

---

[187] Podstarosta (Polish) – deputy of starosta.

had just now gott other intelligence as I had brought, and that I did but ly to them, wherefor to the rack I must. I answered that I had told nothing positively concerning the party, only what I heard, and therein might be deceived, as it seemes I was. But he insisted and told that upon the rack I would sing another song, and therewith gave order to the fellowes to strippe me of my cloaths, and withall showing me how they would use me, and that they would not only skrew out my limbes, but burne my sides with pitchy torches or *fackles*[188] which they had ready.

Hereat I was exceedingly afrighted and could not containe my self, but with aboundance of teares cryed out, "Rather to cut of my head, or shoot me dead, as spoile my body so!", assuring them, although they should teare me in pieces, I could tell them nothing else. So after many threats on their part and protestations on myne the serjeant said he would go once more to the commendant.

After a quarter of ane houres stay he returned and began to threaten me afresh, but seing me constant, he left of. Neither had any of the fellowes laid an hand upon me. As he brought me out of the vault it was past sunsett, and a number of people were standing without, some wherof, especially the women, even pittyed my condition with teares. Being brought to the commendants lodging and put under a guard in a litle roome, I was {49} so terrifyed, and the fear brought such a change upon me, that neither meat nor drink could go downe with me.

Under this guard I continued untill Saturnday, in which tyme I had gott notice that there were some Swedish prisoners in the *radt*-house, among whom my old comorad John Holsteine. This moved me, being very solitary, to desire to be among the rest, for *"solamen miseris socios habuisse doloris"*[189], which I obtained. So on Saturnday, being the market day, I was brought through a great confluence of people to the *radt*-house, whither being come and welcomed by my comorade and others, many people who had not seen me in passing thronged in to see me. Some of the gentry men and women were admitted, who according to

---

[188] Fackel (German) – torch.
[189] "It is a comfort to the unfortunate to have had companions in woe". Quotation from Christopher Marlowe's *The Tragical History of Doctor Faustus* (I, 5).

their good natures bestowed something on me, so that this day I receaved about 4 florens.

In this prison were 15 persons of all sorts, one whereof was a corporall called Friderich Hoode, a native of the *stift* Bremen and had wyfe and children there, another my old acquaintance and comorad John Holstein, a 3d a Dutch man borne in Prussia, who spoke Dutch and Polls perfectly, which availed me much in learning these languages whilst I was here, a 4th a simple fellow borne in Polland, his father a Scotsman. This fellow afterwards maryed one of the townes officers (or rather servants, as they call them there) daughters and so acquired his liberty. The rest were Polls who had served the Sweds, fellowes base and of no acco[un]t.

Towards evening the corporall had a quarrell with one of these fellowes and gave him a boxe on the eare, which the jaylor relating to the burger master (under whose jurisdiction wee now were), order came to put the corporall into the dungeon and me with him to bear him company. Whereat I expostulateing with the jaylour, received no other satisfaction but that I should repent my petitioning to be under their guard. {49v} So that I perceived they tooke my comeing thither as great a burthen to them as I it a bondage to my self.

The corporall and I being brought out, were lett downe by ropes into a dungeon 4 or 5 fathome deep and were told to go to the right hand, where was a vault without a doore. Being entred here, wee found it so exceedingly cold that wee did not know what to do. The darknes and unevennes of the floore would not permitt us to walke. After a long silent weeping wee began to gather some thing like straw or chaffe and lay downe, he holding my feet in his armes and I his in myne for fear of freezing. Then began wee to relate the many misfortunes and disasters and a progresse of o[u]r lives hitherto, in which discourse and the like wee passed the night without sleeping any.

About ten aclock the jaylor, letting downe a rope, called on me to come up. I tyed the rope about my midle, was hoised up, leaving the corporall very pensive, who never the lesse two houres afterwards was brought up. Then were the corporall, the Englisman, the Prussian and my self locked together with a heavy iron bolt and chaine by one foot, and two and two together by the hand, which was a great trouble and paine to us. For when any one of us had a mind to go aside, all must go along and patiently wait untill he had done his businesse.

This day came the gentlman, who tooke me and gott my money and jewells, and gave me a visitt. He sent for aquavitae and entertained me and told me he had given money and provisions to my first landlady, who being a very good woman would not let me want. My landlady came afterwards and told me that he had sent only a goose and given her 20 pence.

After this I never saw nor heard from my good gentlman, only {50} three or fowre yeares thereafter, when being in the Polls service I came this way, I heard this story of him, which for the inhumanity thereof I must relate. His father being an aged gentlman of good acco[un]t, who in his lyfetime, seing his children come to be men, provided honourable matches for them, especially for this and another sonne, and gave to them such parcells of his lands and goods as might affoord them a competent livelyhood, reserving to himselfe his dwelling house and a small village only and, as it seemes, some money, plate and jewels, which he had layd up or hidden in some place. These two inhumane sonnes, whether grieving to see their father live so long or fearing that he would dispose of this small treasure to his other children, who were more dutifull, resolved on a cruell exploit. They disguise themselves with halfe a dozen of their trustiest servants lyke highlanders, come, besett and enter their fathers house, lay hold on the old man and by cruell torments force him to tell where his goods were hidd. Whilst they were tormenting him the aged man, by their maskes as also by the voice of Jan who animated the servants loth and, it seemes, abhorring such cruelty, suspecting who they were, said to this Jan, "Sonne, sonne, dost thou envy me the few dayes I have to live? God will not let the[e] go unpunished!"

After they had gott what they cam for they departed to their homes, and the next day, when it was divulged that robbers had been at their fathers house, they posted thither, dissemblingly lamenting exceedingly. Their father at first tooke no notice, but grieved the mor to see such egregious dissimulation, at last declared openly that none but his two sonnes had done this act, {50v} that he knew the voice of his unnaturall sonne

Jan or John, and that by many circumstances, as their behaviour, the stature and proportion of their bodies, and servants, it could be none other. This gave the hearers such strong presumptions and suspition that their deep dissimulation could not evince, so that, departing from thence to their houses, they resolved to make their escape, which they did with wiwes and families. The old man dyed a week thereafter, and of them nothing to be heard, only that they went to Moravia and lived there obscurely.

But to returne to the relation of my owne condition dureing the tyme of my imprisonment, which was so miserable as I am hardly able to expresse. And first concerning our dyet, our middayes portion was a dish of dry turnips boyled without salt or any other seasoning amongst nine of us, every ones share being 5 or 6 spoonfulls and a loafe of bread worth two *grosses*, which served rather to whetten our appetites as allay our hunger. At evening wee had a dish of buckwheat groats boyled thick without either salt, soure, bread or other kitchin meat. And this our allowance was sometimes mor untimely, sparing and uncleanly (but seldom larger unlesse upon some festivalls), given according to the humour of our entertainer, who was the burger master regnant, they being here changed monthly. My landlady now and then furnished me privately without the knowledge of her husband (who was a drunken surly curr and caryed no goodwill to me) with a small well dressed dish, which might have satisfyed me alone at such times very well, but there being a community among us fowre who were chained together, it availed litle.

Our beds were on the cold pavement, haveing a litle straw under us, which was become like chaffe and was small ease to us, {51} and in a short time was so mixed with vermine that wee made it our sorrowfull pastime sometimes to see them cary the straw up and downe the roome, the want of clean linnen, fresh aire and drinking of water engendring them abundantly. The extreame cold also was not the least of o[u]r miseries, and to add more sorrow to our aflictions, the ruder sort of Polls comeing now and then in out of curiosity to see us, did revile and abuse us. And the drunken burgers in the night tyme visiteing the guards, and among others us, entertained us very inhumanly and many tymes with sadd stroakes.

And that which perplexed us most of all was the fear of death wherewith wee were daily threatned, if any evidence should be brought in against us of robbing of churches, ravishing of women, killing in cold blood, or of such hainous crimes, whereof albeit for my owne part I knew my self free, yet knew I not what misinterpretations, allegeances and false proofs might be brought in against us by our enemies in whose power wee were. Once two burgers came and declared to us, that seing our Sweds in Wisnits had starved to death some of their people with cold and hunger, they would proceed so with us. But haveing gott liberty to speak, wee shewed the case to be different, seing the prisoners in Wisnits were no sojors, wanted lawfull comissions, were only bowres, *snaphanes*[190], and so no where reputed worthy of quarter, farr lesse good usage in prison. With this scarsely seeming satisfyed, they departed.

And that there was a generall rumour of some such thing intended against us, may appear by the profers of marriage that some of the lowest condition of women made to some of us, whereby wee might be freed from such danger. {51v} For it is a custome in Polland for a virgin to releeve a condemned person, haveing first obtained licence of the magistrates, which is seldome denyed unlesse the malefactor be too notorious. And this is done ordinarily when he hath kneeled downe to receive the stroake of justice, then cometh the maide with a long white towell which she throweth over him, and then if he consent to marry her they are immediately brought to the church and wedded. Yet have I heard of one who, riseing up and lookeing earnestly on his bride and guessing by her phisiognomy her badd conditions, kneeled downe againe and willed the headsman to do his duty.

But to returne. One of these suiters, being serving maid to one of the burgermasters, after the sending of two or three choice dishes of victuals for two dayes together at midday and evening, the third day she caused the jaylour require a catagorick answer, which some diswaded, and to give some hopes whereby wee might get some more of her victualls, w[hi]ch upon an absolute refusall wee were like to want, but I would by no meanes,

---

[190] Snaphaan (Dutch) – highwayman.

accounting it not good to jest in such matters. The same method others keeped, who were all alike served.

In this prison I was detained 13 weeks, when by looking out of a window and speaking to some Sweds who were newly taken, the next day wee were all taken out, o[u]r irons being first strucke of, and carryed to a straiter place where wee had scarce so much roome as to ly one, yet must of necessity reserve a corner for easing of nature. In this place was no light but what wee had from a longish narrow window 2 fathome from the ground, whereby wee could not read or see on another scarse. To this roome wer two doores, one whereof was a strong iron grate, the other of iron also closse.

{52} When I was brought in here, I must confesse, I began to misdoubt the worst, the sense whereof pressed forth abundance of teares from me as well as the rest, but much more when two or three dayes thereafter wee were advertised at night to make ourselves ready for confession against the ensuing morning, insinuating not obscurely as regratting our condition, that there was some mischieffe at hand. The night wee passed very distractedly, sometimes with many teares and exclamations lamenting our sadd misfortunes, then privately examining our former lives and tacitely reconcileing o[u]rselves to God Almighty.

For my owne part, after I had called my self to a strict acco[un]t of all the passages and progresse of my by past lyfe, wherein albeit I found many things justly deserving a publick judgement and punishment from God Almighty, yet did I find his gratious spirit giveing such motions of confidence and assureance of mercy, that I became very resolute and couragious.

The next morning, our jaylors attending us, my comorad John Holstein and I desired that for the more devotions sake wee might be permitted to confesse and communicate in the monastery or in the cathedrall church, which was not permitted, and wee brought above to the *radt*-house where wee who were Catholickes confessed and receaved the B[lessed] Sacrament from a Franciscan fryer, to whom I remonstrated our sadd condition and the great guilt that would ly on these who against all divine and humane law would murther us in cold blood, being prisoners of warr and souldiers of fortune. He seemed to be very sensible of o[u]r misery, bidd us be of good courage and comfort, and promised to recommend our {52v} case as farr as in him lay.

Being remanded to our prison, wee passed the tyme for some few dayes in such contemplations as best befitted our miserable condition. 5 or 6 dayes thereafter Father Innes, Provinciall of the Franciscan Order in Polland, being in his annuall progresse and comeing by chance hither, came to the prison to us, and calling for me with Holstein he began to chide me soundly upon two acco[un]ts. First, that being a Catholick, I did with hereticks fight against the Catholick religion; next, that being a Scotsman, I would fight against Polland, where our countreymen had such large priviledges, protection, and where many getting large estates enjoyed great freedome. I made my apology as submissive as I could, that I understood the King of Swedens quarrell to be a businesse of state, not of religion, and that I haveing engaged my self in the Sweds service befor I knew whither they would direct their armes, could not thereafter free my self. That to expiate this offence, if I could obtaine service here, I should strive to shew such fidelity and courage as might merit both trust and good entertainment.

After some other discourses he promised to interceed for me with the *starost* who was lately come to towne, whereof wee did not know. For this same day I found meanes by one who had served the Sweds and was now stallmaster to the commendant, to gett a petition convoyed privately to the commendant, Collonell Gerlechofsky, in all o[u]r names, for service, my good {53} landlady haveing furnished me with paper and my owne pocket inkhorne, which she had preserfed when the towne was gained from us.

The commendant being the next day invited to dinner by the *starost*, as also Father Innes, our businesse was brought so farr as the *starost* gave order to send for us. Wee being brought to the court, after a litle attendance, the *starost* with some gentlemen comeing to the windowes, he ordered us to send up one to him. Wee desired a lieutennant called commonly Bowle Hans, an old man, who had been al along in prison with us, after he had recovered of his sicknes. Him wee desired to speak very submissively and to promise in our names all fidelity if wee could be accepted into service.

He comeing befor the *starost* and being asked if wee were willing to serve the Crowne of Polland, answered that wee were in their power now, they might do with us as they would. This answer so displeased the nobleman that he presently ordered us to prison againe, whereat wee were all hugely dejected. Haveing marched of some few paces, by the intercession of Father Innes I was called back againe. Being come under the window, the *starost* himself asked me in Latine if I would serve the Crowne of Polland. I answered, "Most willingly". He asked me farther if I would rather serve under the Kings guards or under him. I replyed, rather under him. Then againe he asked me if I would stay here in garrison or go to the fields with him. I said, I being a {53v} yong man, had rather, if it were his will, serve in the fields, where honour and preferment is soonest acquired. Then asked he me if there were any more among us of my opinion. I told him with some confidence that there were two more who might be trusted, wherewith I was dismissed.

    The corporal, Holstein and my self were carryed to the prison from whence wee came, and the rest unto the dungeon wherein I had been on night with the corporall. O[u]r conductors assured us three, that the *starost* being to march the next day, wee should be sent for and released. But the next day being come and nothing to be heard of o[u]r releasment, wee began to doubt whether it were not a bare promise as wee had had severall tymes befor, and this day seemed longer to us as any week befor.

    However the next day very early wee were sent for and had horses and sadles given us, and about 10 aclock marched out of the towne after the *starost* among his company of dragouns, which were about 80 men, all Polls with blew cloaks after the Dutch manner and fashion, the captaine being a Dutch man called Zacharias Mitlach. The ensigne could speak Dutch, but was a Poll. The day of my releasment was Fridday, haveing been about 17 weeks in prison, untill by the gracious goodnes of God and the assistance of good people I was released.

    Haveing marched a mile, the *starost* made a halt at the *podstarosts* house, and wee had a tunne of beer sent out to us. At night wee quartered in a litle towne called Gribowa[191], where by the change of aire and fresh

---

[191] Grybów.

victualls I grew somq[uha]t sickely, and truly, when I came out I was hardly able to stand upon {54} my feet for weaknes. However by temperancy and good dyet I shortly recovered my former strentgh. Yet for all this were wee not trusted, for haveing each of us a quarter, wee were all three ordered to remaine all night by a corporall under a guard.

This nobleman, under whose command wee now were, was the yongest of the three Lubomirskyes then in Polland, the eldest being Crowne stallmaster or master of horses, and afterwards *Woywod* of Krakow as his father had been. The 2d, being the famousest of all, was Crowne marshall and field generall[192]. This yongest, called Constantine, was Crowne cupbearer. They all three entitled themselves earles in Visnits and Yaroslaw. The yongest had farr different qualities from the other two, being extreamely covetous and niggard and loveing ease.

Wee marched by the townes Bicz, Reshowa, Landshut,[193] Przeworsk to Yaroslaw, where wee stayed 8 dayes. I haveing been employed and sent befor here for makeing of quarters, found the meanes to provide my self of pistolls and a Dutch sword. Wee marched afterwards to Samostze[194], crossing the r[iver] Saan under Yaroslaw, and then to Lublin, where the King of Polland, being come from Lvowa, rendevouzed his army. Here wee stayed about 8 dayes and marched to Varso, which the Littawish army held beleaguered already 3 weeks. But now I shall relate the progresse of the warr briefly untill this siedge.

The King of Sweden, marching with his army by Varso towards Prussia, the Romane Emperour and French King[195] their ambassadours being with him, the countrey every[where] submitted. The Woywodship or Palatinate of Sendomires obtained safeguards, not only the townes but {54v} the private gentlemen also. The military persons every where submitting, tooke the oath of fidelity, the Crowne Generall Potocky[196] and the Crown

---

[192] Prince Jerzy Sebastian Lubomirski (1616–1667), eminent Polish commander and politician, Grand Crown Marshal and Field Crown Hetman. He was soon to become Gordon's patron.
[193] Biecz, Rzeszów and Łańcut.
[194] Zamość.
[195] Louis XIV (1638–1715), King of France from 1643.
[196] Stanisław Rewera Potocki (1579–1667), Great Crown Hetman from 1654.

Field Generall Landskoronsky[197] not excepted. Generall Duglas remained in Sandomirs to settle that quarter, the King being advanced near unto Prussia, where the Felt Marshall Steinbock after the rendition of Varso and the beating of the Massovish forces had secured some places on the Polls syde of the Vistula, and now with Radziefsky taketh Strasburgh[198]. From whence the King advanced to Thorne, Radziefsky being sent befor with some forces, most Polls; hath diverse conferences with the magistrates, which end in a surrender, and the King maketh his entrance into the towne the 5th of December, M[ajor] Gen[era]ll Mardefelt being made commendant with 3 regiments: Coll[onels] Gerfelts, Nairnes and Fittinghoffes.

Here the King gave audience to the ambassadours of the Roman Emperour, the Mosko and Transilvania. Graudents is also rendred to M. Gen-ll Leuwenhooft. Here also the King had notice p[e]r post of the birth of the yong Prince, who was borne November 24 *stilo veteri* betwixt 12 and 1 in the night and was named Carolus[199]. His godfathers were the Pr[ince]s Electours of Saxony, Brandeburg and Heidelberg, the Dukes of Shleswick-Holstein and Wirtemberg, with the Pfalts-Graffe Adolph Johann[200]; the Godmothers: the Electresse of Saxony, the Dutchesses of Altenburg, Holstein, Mechelburg of Gustrow, and *Graffe* Magnus [De la Gardie] his lady.

{55} The Prince Elector of Brandeburgh had at this tyme a compleat army in Prussia in a leaguer, consisting of 23,272 men and 80 piece of cannon. From Thorne the King, haveing sent to demand the rendition of Marienburgh and Elbing as also to Dantzick, demanding 2 millions of money and that they will swear fidelity and give the Wistul-munde[201] for security, he sent also to the Duke, offering ane accomodation. Whereupon commissioners meet at Reden[202], but effect nothing, whereupon the King advanceth from Reden and hath Elbing rendred to him. But the Palatine

---

[197] Stanisław Lanckoroński (ca.1597–1657), Field Crown Hetman from 1654.
[198] Brodnica.
[199] Prince Karl (1655–1697),King of Sweden as Karl XI from 1660.
[200] Prince Adolf Johann (1629–1689), Count Palatine, Swedish Generalissimus, brother of King Karl X Gustav of Sweden.
[201] Weichselmünde (German), Wisłoujście (Polish).
[202] Rehden (German), Radzyń Chełmiński (Polish).

of Pomer and Coll. Sparr resolving to hold out Marienburgh, Prince Adolph with Felt Marshall Steinbock are sent to beleaguer it, who not long thereafter had the towne rendred by the burgers, and in the 4th week the castle by composition, notwithstanding the Dantzickers were on their way with a strong party to their succours.

Upon the fruitles treaty of Reden the King sent to *Graffe* Magnus de la Gardie to advance towards Prussia, and now resolves to march for a conjunction. The Brandeburghs army, about 16,000 strong, lying at Brawnsberg, haveing notice of the Kings march, retire towards Konigsberg, where the Duke himself lay with a strong reserve. {55v} Maior Generall Laurens von der Linde[203] was left commendant in Elbing with a considerable garrison. The King being on his march, after some intercourses and overtures by the Duke for another treaty, sends the Chancelour Oxenstern[204] to Konigsberg, against whose rhetorick and forcible perswasions the Duke not being able to hold out. Upon Gen-ll Kannenbergs comeing into the Kings leaguer a treaty is entred into and concluded, many particulars whereof, as is thought, were not divulged, but those which came to publick wiew were the following:

1. The Elector shall not be oblidged to take the oath of allegeance to the King befor he be chosen and crowned King of Polland in a publick parliament.

2. The Electors oath shall not be changed without the consent of the estates of Polland.

3. In the absence of the King the Elector shall erect a new judicatory of 6 councellours and a president, from whom appeales may be made to the King of Polland.

4. The Electors army shall be disbanded and let over to the King of Sweden, who promiseth not to use it otherwise as against the King of Polland.

5. For the losse that the Sweds have done the Elector shall have the Bishopdome of Wermeland.

---

[203] Baron Lorens von der Linde (1610–1670), who soon became Swedish field marshal.
[204] Count Erik Oxenstierna (1624–1656), Chancellor of Sweden from 1654.

6. The Elector hath granted to the Swedish King the halfe of the Pillawish toll.

7. The said Pillaw[205] to be garrisoned with halfe Sweds and halfe Brandeburgish.

8. The free excercise of the reformed religion and a church to be built for them in Konigsberg is granted. {56}

9. The towne of Dantzick is not included in this treaty.

10. Within 4 weeks after the ratification of this treaty the Elector shall free Marienburgh of the garrison and deliver the same into the Kings possession.

11. The toll of the Pillaw shall not be hightened on condition that all goods going out and into Polland shall be brought by the way of Elbing.

12. The warr ships of His Ma[jes]tie in necessity ar permitted to come into the Pillaw free and unmolested.

13. When this treaty betwixt the King and the Elector shall be ratifyed, then shall the league with Holland against the Crowne Sweden and allyes be broken and dissolved.

The Swedish chancelour as also the M. Gen-ll Kannenbergh receaved royall presents. However the Hollanders (whose ambassadours were arrived to mediate a peace between the Crowns of Sweden and Polland) were not well satisfyed with the Duke for this agreement, as also the Prussian *Riddershaft*, or gentry, as done without their consent and fearing some of the private articles prejudiciall to their priviledges.

At this tyme also Collonell Dubald who had been commendant in Dantzick came over to the Sweden, promiseing to effect great matters. The Dantzickers prepare for defence, burne the suburbes, as Nobis-kruge, Newkirk and the *closter*[206] of the *Fratres Misericordiae*, and afterwards the Motla[u] street and Scotland side to Petershagen and New Garten, refuseing absolutely the Swedish yoake. {56v} In the meane tyme the King of Swed[en] and the Elector meeting at Holland[207] and

---

[205] Pillau, modern Baltiysk, Russia.
[206] Kloster (German) – monastery.
[207] Preussisch Holland (German), Pasłęk (Polish).

Bartenstein[208] make merry, drinking brothership with many protestations and promises of a stricter allyance and league. But after such a gale of prosperity the Swedish King did meet with a very adverse storme occasioned by the returne of the King of Polland out of Silesia and the revolt of the Polls army. And here I must digresse and brieffly relate the reasons why the Polls were so easily wonne to syde with the Sweden, and why now they so soone returned to the obedience of their former prince, as I have heard it often from great and very judicious persons.

The Polls had for some yeares befor this been struging with many difficulties occasioned by the revolt of their naturall subjects the Cosakes who, haveing associated to themselves the Crim Tartars, had put many afronts upon the Polls and ruined their armies at Zwanec, Glinam, Pilavets and at Zbaras and Zborow[209] forceth the King to a peace on the following conditions:

1. There shall be an everlasting peace, friendship and brothership betwixt the King of Polland and the Chan[210] and his family.

2. The usuall yearly pension for the Chan to be brought to Camieniets Podolsky[211] and duly delivered there.

3. The King upon the Chans entreaty shall forgive the Zaporovish Cosakes[212], confirme their old rights with a new priviledge, make the ordinary number of priviledged Cosakes to be 40,000. The *Starosty* of Czegrin[213] shall be given to Chmielnitsky, when they shall {57} acknowledge their misdemeanours, ask the K[ings] pardon, which Chmielnitsky very submissively did.

4. On the other side the Chan shall be obliged to assist the King of Polland with his army against all enemies.

---

[208] Bartoszyce.
[209] Ukrainian towns of Zhvanets, Hliniany, Piliavtsy, Zbarazh and Zboriv. The treaty of Zboriv between King Jan II Kazimierz of Poland and Bohdan Khmelnytsky, Hetman of Ukraine, was signed in August 1649.
[210] Islam III Geray, Khan of Crimea from 1644 to 1654.
[211] Kamianets-Podilskyi, Ukraine.
[212] Cossacks of Zaporizhska Sich.
[213] Chyhyryn, Ukraine.

5. To free the Kingdome of Polland from all infalls, invasions, losses and robberies of his Tartars.

6. To march of and disband their armies, permitting the beleaguered army at Zbaras to come without all molestation to His Majesty.

7. The Greekish religion, goods and churches shall remaine in the same state as formerly, and all this to be ratifyed in the next parliament.

But this agreement lasted not long when, new jealousies arising, the Cosakes advance with a mighty army into Polland and at Beresteczko in Volhinia ar routed by the Polls[214]. And then, perceiving themselves unable to hold out long against the Polls, they submitt and renders themselves to the Moskovite, conjureing them by vertue of the same religion to protect and assist them. The Moskovite, glad of such ane occasion to diminish the power of, if not altogether to conquest the Polls, receave them into their protection and presently quarrell with the Poll. And in the year of our salvation 1654 commence the warr, marching with mighty armyes into Polland and Littaw, so that the Polls, being now attacqued on the one side by so powerfull an enemy as the Moskoviter, on the other side by the Cosakes and Tartars, and one a third by the Swede, confusion and a panick fear so possessed them, that they were at the utmost extremity. For this year the Moskovite beat Duke {57v} Radzivill, tooke in the Vilna[215] and the remnant of Littaw, plundered Lublin, beleaguered Reusse Lemberg and made incursions as farr as Varso and Jaroslav. So that there was not a corner in Polland which was not overrun by their enemies, the King after his retreat from Krakow haveing no where to shelter himself in his owne Kingdome, and so was forced to flee to Silesia; the army in the meane tyme being deserted by their prince and their generalls, not knowing of any winter quarters or other subsistance. Neither wanted the souldiery their owne discontents, as their want of pay, which they imputed to the evill management of the republicks effaires and the treasure, as also their badd fortune against their owne slaves and other enemies. All which they atributed to the badd luck of their prince, besides a jealousy that

---
[214] The battle of Berestechko was fought on 28–30 June 1651.
[215] Vilnius (Lithuanian), Wilno (Polish).

these troubles had been under hand fomented by the court, especially the Cosakes, out of designe to humble them and create a power upon occasion to curbe their exorbitant libertyes.

All these moved the army and many particular persons, wanting their prince, strive who should anticipate and first gaine the favour of the fortunate King by a timely submission; three quartals or quarters of a years pay and good winter quarters haveing been promised to the army, in place whereof some gratuities and giftes were distributed among the grandees and the leading persons, and a long tedious march into Prussia for their winter quarters. The King also had let fall words to this purpose in Sandomires, that it could not be well in Polland untill the power and priviledges of the great churchmen and small gentry were dimi[ni]shed, which words being divulged, the Polls interpreted to a setled resolution {58} in the King of Sweden, if he came to be King of Polland, that he would conquerour-like overturne both church and state, and settle religion and lawes according to his owne fancy.

All these things breeding discontent among the Polls, and haveing now gott notice that the King of Polland was returned out of Silesia and marched for Reusse Lemberg, the grandees of the army and magistrates of all the townes of Prussia haveing also from the King receaved invitation to returne to their former alledgeance, Koniecpolsky, Sobiesky with the army, some few companies excepted, on a suddaine revolted and marched up to Polland, which so vexed the King of Sweden that, notwithstanding the season of the year, postponeing all other businesses, he marched up after them with ane army of 10,000 men and artillery conforme towards Varso, passeing the r[iver] Vistula at Casimirs, where his brother Pr[ince] Adolph by a fall from his horse broke his legge and was convoyed back to Varso by Coll. Sinkler with his regiment.

18 Feb[ruary]. At Columby[216] the Polls, haveing joyned with Czarnetsky, being in all 80 collours, face the Sweds, and retire with some losse, many being drowned in the r[iver] [...] as they passed. The two hetmans three weeks before had fled from Lublin to the King. Gen. Duglas was forced

---

[216] Gołąb, where the Swedes won the battle on 8(18) February 1656.

also to leave Sandomirs, for upon the King of Pollands returne from Silesia, the gentry not being able to endure the insolency of the Sweds, especially their sacriledge, revolted, and especially these of the Palatinate of Sandomires, killing all their safeguards, which were thought to be about a 1,000 men, were up in armes, which made Duglas make hast to his King, leaving the castle only garrisoned.

After the Polls were routed at Columby the King of Sweden marcheth {58v} to Lublin and so onwards to Samoystsky[217], the lord whereof standing to his defence, batteryes were made and cannon planted and the towne plyed with shott for two dayes. The King sending to demand the rendition of the towne, was answered by the lord that the towne being his owne proper inheritance, he could by no justice be pressed to deliver it to any. As to His Ma-tie of Sweden, he had hitherto been a spectatour and used no act of hostility, only stood in his owne defence, and that when His Ma-tie should be King of Polland, he and all in his power should be at his devotion. With which answer the King seeming satisfyed, prepared to depart.

Here at a councell it was debated which way to take, and whether they should march for Russe Lemberg, where the King was said to be with a potent army. The couragious and high minded Swedish King is said to have been very earnest for marching thitherwards, but most of the councell being of another opinion, a resolution was taken for marching to Jaroslaw, because of the vicinity to Transilvania, with whose prince an alliance was neer concluded, and for the convenience of transporting the artillery and ammunition downe the r[iver]s Saan and Vistula in the approaching spring.

Mart. 2. The King with the army arriving at Yaroslaw, sends a party to surprise Premisl[218], [...] miles from thence, but ar repulsed. Here and on the march many Polls dropped away as they could find opportunity, some whereof being catched, were hanged and harquebussired. There remained only by the K[ing] of Sweden of men of note Koritsky and Nemerowitz, the first whereof continued untill the peace was concluded and then by vertue of the amnestia returned and receaved imployment.

---

[217] Zamość.
[218] Przemyśl.

The Swedish {59} King getting intelligence that all the countrey were riseing in armes, and that the Crowne army under Lubomirsky and Czarnetsky and the Littawish army also were advancing to cope him up,

12. marcheth from Yaroslaw, the artillery and ammunition downe the river Saan, intending to crosse the r[iver] Vistula at Sandomirs, but comeing to the river he found himself hemmed in on all sides. For on the other syde of the Saan were the Littawish army, and on the other side of the Vistula the Crowne Marshall Lubomirsky and Czarnetsky with the *quartianers*, and behind him were the whole countrey up in armes, so that here he was in a manner besiedged.

The Sweds intending to make a bridge over the river Vistula at Sandomirs, ar hindred by the Polls, who wanted nothing but a good body of foot to have made an end of the warr at this tyme. And truly the King of Sweden in all this warr was never in such hazard as here. He sendeth to his brother at Varso to send as many forces as possible to his assistance. In the meane tyme the army, lying in a low ground, by partyes furnish themselves with forrage and provisions as well as they can. The Polls haveing taken the towne of Sandomires, and the Sweds retired into the castle, the Polls runne as blind folded to storme the castle, but were at first repulsed with the losse of one Capt. Collet (who, when I was brought prisoner to Sandets, was commendant there, and was now shott on the bridge).

However, the King of Sweden haveing no hopes of crosseing the Vistula here, and knowing the castle not to be tenable and at this tyme uselesse, gave orders to desert the castle and give the Polls a Swedish drink, as they call it. Whereupon the powder being laid in the vaults with a traine, the Sweds retire to some vessels they had lying ready under the castle, and notwithstanding they were

{59v} *Mart.* attacqued by the Polls guards at the river side, yet escaped they to the army. The Polls in the towne perceiving the Sweds flying out of the castle, make hast to gett in, but in halfe an houres tyme it was a sadd song, for the powder being fired, all was blowne up. Here dyed about 500 Polls, yet of the meaner sort, as being voluntiers.

The Swedish King haveing made show or attempt to make a bridge over the Vistula, at last commandeth a thowsand foot to passe the Saan in the night and to intrench on the other side, haveing made a battery the day befor on the side where the army lay; whereon some cannon being planted and playing to the other side, made the Littawish remove their stations further of from the river. So that the other day, the foot being entrenched on the other syde with some field pieces, and vessels and materialls being made ready befor to a bridge, it was instantly perfected and the army marched over, the Littawers makeing litle or no resistance.

The Polls had indeed at this tyme the Sweds in a hosenet, and never did meet with such ane occasion againe. And here they were sensible how necessary foot and dragouns are, without whom no great action can be well effected. And reports were blazed abroad even into forreigne countreyes not only of the Swedish army being ruined, but of the death of the King himself. However, albeit with great difficulty, he came of with honour, makeing his passage by maine force through his enemies, and by slow marches with wearyed army arrived in safety to the Prague by Varso.

But the Polls on the other syde of the Vistula, seing the King escaped and haveing notice of an army comeing to his assistance, march with {60} great hast to intercept them. For Prince Adolph haveing received notice of the Kings distresse and orders for assistance, mustered about 2,500 men and sent them under the command of the *Margraffe* von Baden and *Graffe* Slippenbach, who comeing to Varky[219] sent imediately to Radomy[220] orders to the commendant there to desert that garrison and march without all delay to a conjunction. But this commendant being a tirrannous, avaricious man, haveing received orders in the evening, tarryed all night and a good deale of the morning disposeing of his ill gotten goods, which was the ruine of that small army. For the *Margraffe* haveing gott intelligence of the approach of the Polls army by a party of a 150 horse sent out under the command of a maior, very few whereof returned, but was forced to stay six houres longer as he should, waiting for this commendant and garrison, who being come, and the Polls showing themselves already on the other side of the river, the *Margraffe* ordereth to throw of the bridge, the baggage to march of towards Varso, and he retired softly himself. But the

---

[219] Warka.
[220] Radom.

Polls being come to the river and finding the bridge broken downe, and not brooking delayes, they swimme the river on their horses, the burgers in the meane time bringing materialls and repairing the bridge.

The Polls putting themselves in some order and advancing out to the fields, which are here very large, and the Sweds being retired neere to the woods, the speed of the Polls horses brought them quickly to ane engadgement. The Sweds retiring and seconding other in good discipline, put the Polls many tymes to

{60v} Apr[il]. a stand, whereof being impatient and loth that they should recover the wood in such order, desperately charged a squadron of horse commanded by Maior John Watson, who being new levyed men of Coll. Sr Samwell Bosa his regiment, and albeit well mounted, were notwithstanding brought in confusion. But being seconded by a gallant troope of horsemen, most whereof were Scottish men commanded by *Ruitm-r* John Meldrum, Watson had tyme to retire, but not to rally againe. Meldrum haveing put that body of the Polls to a stand, wheeled about in order to a retreat, but finding none to second him, for by this tyme all were fled, and the Polls falling into his rear, he was necessitated to wheele and charge againe, but now was forced to a retreat in some confusion. The Polls beating up his reare very hard, here he lossed his standard, his lieutennant taken and the most halfe of his troope killed.

The Polls now advancing to the chase on all hands, receave a check from the musketiers in the wood, whom the *Margraffe* had here ordered to make a stand to repell, at least to retard, the pursuite of the Polls. They were about 400 in number under the command of their Lt. Collonell Riter, who had been commendant in Radomy, and were all Finnes. These by their continuall fireings makeing resistance at the entry of the wood, many of the Polls sought other wayes to follow the chase, in the end the Finnes being forced to take quarter by the Crowne marshalls dragounes and others, who alighting fired the grasse, very combustible at this season of the year; which so terrified them, that notwithstanding the threats of their officers they threw downe their armes and gott quarters, some only in the first heat being killed, the lt. collonell being {61} thereafter in cold blood killed for haveing caused hang some gentlmen whilst he was commendant in Radomy. The souldiers were sent to Lubomly[221] and afterwards served under the Crowne marshalls regiment of foot.

The Polls had the following of the Sweds till within a mile of Varso. At a passe most of the slaughter was made and booty gott, for the Swedish baggage being stopped here, all became a prey to the Polls, there being many women also, whose lamentable cryes none of the flying Sweds could or durst take notice of, farr lesse able to assist. The *Margraffe* himselfe retired into the castle of Czirsk[222] with 5 or 600 men, and scarse so many more gott to Varso, the rest being all killed and taken. Varky is 8 miles from Varso, and the passe where the baggage was taken and most slaughter made 5.

The Prince Adolph from Varso sendeth notice and orders to all garrisons to be upon their guards, as to Lovits, which is 12 miles from Varso, and to M. Gen-ll Israell[223] who with his regiment of horse lay in quarters not farr from thence. The Polls haveing made a bravado befor Varso, march with great celerity towards Lovits and by the break of day catch some Sweds a napping in the towne, and M. Gen-ll Israel comeing marching with his regiment with great difficulty, the losse of three standards and his baggage, getteth into the castle. His lady being also taken, who seing no way to escape, leapt out of her coach and gott up into a sutlers waggon, telling when she was taken that she was a sutlers wyfe and that her husband had escaped into the castle and would give any reasonable ransome for her; the Poll who had her beleeving all, she being a corpulent woman and {61v} attired not unlike such sort of people, craved leave to have her ransomed, which obtained, he agreed with her for 100 ducats, to the which she with some seeming difficulty condiscended, writing a note or supplication to the collonell, to cause seek up her husband and move him to ransome her. The trumpeter brought another with him haveing the promised ransome, upon the delivery whereof he receaved the lady, who had not passed so lightly had they knowne who she was.

---

[221] Luboml, Ukraine.
[222] Czersk.
[223] Israel Ridderhjelm, Swedish general.

The Polls from hence march to Great Polland to move that part to returne to its alledgeance. In the meane tyme the King of Sweden in the Prague giveth audience to the Romane Emperours ambassadour *Graffe* Pottingen, and leaving Felt Marshall Wittemberg being sickly in Varso with a sufficient garrison and all the sick people and women, he departeth with his brother, Wrangell and

May 1. Duglas to Thorne, where he arrived the 1 of May.

The Queen of Sweden[224] being with 6 warr ships landed at the Pillaw some dayes befor and receaved most magnificently by the Elector of Brandeburgh, and with the Reichs chancelour convoyed to Elbing by water, whither the King getting notice hasted.

The Sweds also a litle befor this had gott a fearfull rubb in Samogitia, for about 3,000 being quartered up and downe the countrey were all slaine, their Generall Liewenhaupt escapeing to Riga. At this tyme also the Romane Emperours ambassadour Allagrett ab Allagretis, a spirituall person, obtained {62} of the Emperour of Russia[225] a yeares truce with the Polls and a resolution to fall upon the Sweds, which gave the Polls some breath.

300 Sweds in Polls Lissna[226] in Great Polland, wanting ammunition as was said, desert the towne takeing most of the inhabitants with them, which Czarnetsky investeth, haveing in his march from Varso passed by Thorne. The Sweds in Lublin capitulated to be convoyed to Varso, which was but slenderly kept, and the corps of *Graffe* Voldemar, the King of Denmarkes bastard sonne (who had been once in great esteeme in Russia)[227] left there, but afterwards convoyed thence.

But somewhat to mitigate the misfortunes of the King of Sweden, two French secretaries arrive from the King of France with 8 tunne of gold, and the Swedish ambassadour Coyet returneth from England with

---

[224] Hedwig Eleonora, consort of King Karl X Gustav.
[225] Alexey Mikhailovich (1629–1676), Tsar of Russia from 1645.
[226] Leszno.
[227] Valdemar, natural son of King Christian IV of Denmark, formerly stayed in Moscow while engaged to Irina, daughter of Tsar Mikhail, but the wedding did not take place. He was wounded at Lublin and died there.

good satisfaction; 2,500 Scottish men under the command of my Lord Cranstoune[228] arrive at Stade and Pillaw. A Hollands ambassadour, who had travelled up through Polland seeking the King, had now audience in Marienburgh. Felt Marshall Steinbock retakes Brambergh[229]. Prince Adolph, Wrangell and Duglas with about 5,000 Sweds face the Polls at Snina[230], where the *Starost* Dziallinsky is taken and the Polls retire with some losse, and againe at Gniesna with the same fortune. After which Lubomirsky and Czarnetsky, haveing moved the gentry of the three palatinates of Great Polland to march to the siedge of Varso, they thereafter march thither also, and the Sweds to Prussia.

Steinbock haveing taken the Oliva, Putsky, Sluchow[231] and Konits[232], cometh to the Hoft. The King in the meane time {62v} with 5,000 men cometh to Prust, taketh in Grebin, a house belonging to Dantzick, and in it 50 men. From thence he cometh to the Gutland or Stiblawes fort, wherein were 350 men, which not rendring upon summons, is stormed and at the 3d assault taken, 120 of the Dantzickers w[i]t[h] their capt[ain] being killed. The King haveing thus straitned Dantzick, upon hopes of bringing them to a composition sendeth to them, but they absolutely refuse, whereupon the Sweds make a bridge over the Vistula at Keisermark and fortify the Hoft *shantz*[233], striveing to divert the river [ ], wherewith their milnes ar driven, as also the Vistula. But all this could not shake the loyalty of the Dantzickers, who haveing levyed 5 or 6 trowps of horse and haveing a strong garrison of foot, besides the burgers, give the Sweds worke enough and keep their citty free from being blocquired, especially on the Pomerells syde.

I have heard it often reckoned for a great errour, which the King of Sweden committed in the management of this warr, in that immediately after his agreement with the Electour of Brandeburg he did not bend all

---

[228] William, 3rd Lord Cranston.
[229] Bromberg (German), Bydgoszcz (Polish).
[230] Żnin.
[231] Schlochau (German), Człuchów (Polish).
[232] Konitz (German), Chojnice (Polish).
[233] Schanze (German) – earthwork, fortification.

his forces against Dantzick. Then was it thought that at least he might have forced them to a neutrality. But now, when the King of Polland was with a potent army beleaguering Varso, the whole Kingdome againe up in armes for their liberties, a truce with the Moskovites, and jealousies ariseing betwixt them and the Sweden, they would not hear of any capitulateing.

The King of Sweden returneth to Marienburgh to give audience to a Tartars ambassadour, and to treat with the Hollands, haveing sent Pr[ince] Adolph, Wrangell and Duglas with 6,000 men towards Varso, who fortify their leaguer at Novodwor[234], 5 miles from Varso, where the rivers Narew and Bog[235], being joyned, fall into {63} the Vistula. Whilst they lay here they provide materialls and make a bridge over the Vistula. Generall Duglas marched and releeved Tikotzin[236], beleaguered by the Massours, which Gonsiewsky[237] from Varso in vaine attempted to hinder with a strong party marching towards Poltovsko[238].

In Krakow Maior Gen-ll Wurts caused secure some of the p[rinci]p[a]ll citizens and pine them, whereof one dyed, and another was beheaded for corresponding with the Polls. Hereupon he driveth all the spirituall persons out of the citty. In Thorne at this tyme also the Jesuits were driven out, and the krakovian Sweds gott great booty belonging to the Queen of Polland[239].

The King of Sweden despairing of makeing a full conquest of Polland alone, entreth into a stricter league with the Elector of Brandeburgh and sendeth new propositions to the Prince of Transilvania. The articles of the league with the Elector of Brandeburgh were:

1. The Elector shall maintaine 4,000 men in the Swedish leaguer, and the King 6,000 in the Electors, in necessity.

---

[234] Nowy Dwór.
[235] Bug.
[236] Tykocin.
[237] Wincenty Korwin Gosiewski (ca.1620–1662), Field Hetman of Lithuania.
[238] Pułtusk.
[239] Maria Ludovica, consort of King Jan II Kazimierz.

2. The King shall deliver to the Elector for him and his heires the three palatinates of Great Polland with all the townes and lands thereto belonging.

3. This league shall be defensive in Great and Litle Polland against all enemies whatsoever.

4. The King to have the chieffe command of the army, excepting when the army marcheth into the territories of the Duke[240], then shall the Duke or his officers command over the Dukes forces.

5. The Duke shall hold in vassallage for him and his heires male the Dutchie of Prussia and Bishoprick of Vermia, giveing to the King a yearly acknowledgment of 40,000 reichs thalers.

6. His Ma-tie shall no wayes appropriate to himself the fors[ai]d lands, but shall deliver all places that are or shall be taken with all that are therein, provisions, {63v} ammunition and military instruments fo[u]nd therein to be payed for.

7. What the Duke shall recover from the Moskovite shall not now, but in the future be determined.

After the concludeing of these articles the Dukes ambassadours returned to Konigsbergh, by whom the King desired an interview with the Duke in Holland, which was readily accepted. And the King haveing dispatched a Moskovitish envoy unsatisfyed[241], and a Turkish with some content, departed for Prusse-Holland, whither the Duke being come and the allyance ratifyed, much friendly entertainment and mirth passed one both sydes, the solemnity of brothership being also here celebrated. Amidst these jollities the Duke condiscendeth to joine his army with the King of Sweden and march personally towards Varso to fight the Polls and releeve Varso, which accordingly shortly after he performed. But now it is tyme to leave the King and the Duke to gather, joyne and march their forces towards Varso, and returne to the siedge, whither from all quarters I have brought the exasperated partyes.

---

[240] Duke of Prussia, i.e. Elector of Brandenburg.
[241] The mission of Russian envoy Nazary Alfimov could not prevent the Russo-Swedish war of 1656–58.

Befor the arrivall of the King of Polland at Varso the Littawish army (as is s[ai]d) had beleaguered or rather blocquired it 3 weeks. How soone the King came, posts ar taken, approaches made and batteries raised, at 3 places especially, one in the Krakovish suburb, the other to the north west of the Bishop of Krakowes house and the third towards the New towne by the Dominicanes cloister, all being joyned by ane irregular lyne of communication. {64} Varso being neither by nature nor art well fortifyed, as lying in a plaine on three sydes, the walls weak and ditch dry, the Sweds made use of some monasteries and houses in place of outworkes, as in the Krakowish suburb the nunnes and Bernardines monasteries, Radzievskies house, towards the west, the Bishop of Krakowes house, and at the New towne the Dominicanes monastery, all which they guarded.

Junii 4. On Whitsunday about noone the Sweds sallyed out with two trowpes of horse commanded by Collonell Forgel and 200 foot. The horse passed as farr as the old earthen wall towards the *zeich* house[242], whilst the foot beat the guards from the battery, nailed 2 cannon, drew two along near to the towne ditch and retired with the losse but of 5 or 6 persons. This made the Polls more wary thereafter. Some choice cannon were brought from Samoistczie, among which one called "Smock" shott exceeding sharp.

The Bishop of Krakowes palace being taken by storme, out of which the Sweds retired with small losse, batteries were raised against Radzievskyes palace, the west part of the towne wall and the New towne port. The Polls being not well stored with foot and dragownes, in their assaults made use of their free servants and all others who either in hope of booty, out of hatred, desire of revenge, esteeme or other reason would engadge; there being many gentlemen *towarises*, willing undertakers, who in the disguised habite of servants both ledd them on and animated them; most of the blinds, ladders and {64v} other necessaries and instruments for assaults being prepared by the few dragowns and foot, whose task for the most part only was to guards [*sic*] their posts and cannon, and to be a reserve in case upon a violent repulse any dangerous [action] should be made.

---

[242] Zeughaus (German) – arsenal.

In one generall assault which continued about 4 houres the Polls were beat of with great losse, leaving their blinds and other materialls behind them. Yet some hundreds had gott downe by the Gnoyova Gora to the *spichliers*[243], or corne houses, and taken a post slenderly guarded there. But upon the approach of the commendant with a company of choice foot they were beat of againe, and about 200 who had retired into the corne houses forfeited their lives. But shortly after this, the wall on the west syde of the towne being made assaulteable, and a breach made also in Radzievsky his palace, a generall assault was proclaimed in the evening at the giveing of the word by sound of trumpet according to the custome.

July 1. The next morning by day light great numbers of all sort of people were ready for the assault, which continued some houres with greater violence as good order. However, at the breach they entred Radzievskyes palace and drove the Sweds not only from thence, but by a nimble and resolute persuite out of the Bernardines and nunnes monasteryes, which was immediately with a strong guard invested. On the other sydes they were beat of with losse.

The Sweds seing the Polls masters of these places, wherein consisted their strentgh on that side of the towne and from which the Kings palace and the towne were lyable even to small shott, beat a parley, which being accepted, {65} Canterstein and Coll. Forgell came into the Polls leaguer to treat, and with some qualification condiscended to the former articles treated on some dayes befor. They returning into the towne, had only two houres allotted for ratification by the felt marshall: the rabble of the Polls could hardly be perswaded to desist from assaulting againe. But when the two houres were exspired and nothing to be heard from the felt marshall, the signe was given by shooting of two pieces of cannon for the assault.

It is admirable with what celerity and resolution the multitude from all parts conveened, being animated by their former successe, and in hopes of rich booty which had been promised to encourage them. And even when the Sweds commissioners were permitted to come into the leaguer,

---

[243] Speicher (German) – barn, granary.

it was promised to the rabble that they should have a considerable summe of money.

The Sweds, it seemes, knowing the towne now not tenable and hearing the signe for the assault given, presently againe beat a parley and sent the fors[ai]d commissioners with the ratification. The rabble, however, could not be withholden nor hindred from assaulting, notwithstanding the Field Generall Landskoronsky and Czarnetsky used all their endeavours even to the hazard of being afronted. That which at last brought them of was a promise, that the King would presently disburse the promised summe to them. Whereupon they flocked immediately to the Kings court, which was then in the pallace of the Lessinskies, where, when they were put of with faire promises and delayes in hopes that they would at last disperse and be gone, they grew to that insolence that they threatned by scalado[244] to get into the court, seing the gates were shutt, and pull out those who had cheated them with faire promises. Which some of the courtiers hearing, told them that they should have the goods of the Armenians who were in the towne, which words being carryed from one to another, {65v} was understood and taken at last that they had liberty to take all the goods of the Armenians, who had their shops in a market place behind the court. Whereupon they immediately runne all thither and robbed these innocent merchants of all they had, and albeit the Kings guard and others hasted to their rescue, yet came they too late.

The articles of the rendition were these:

1. All officers and souldiers who are borne Sweds or strangers shall march freely of; the Polls or subjects of the Crowne of Polland shall remaine.

2. All who are able to march shall be safely convoyed to Thorne.

3. After the subscription and ratification of the articles of the accord 3 gates of the towne and the castle shal be opened and delivered to the Polls, yet shall the Sweds have liberty to stay three dayes in their quarters and thereafter march out after the souldiers manner.

---

[244] Assault by use of ladders.

4. All the cannon to remaine in the towne.

5. The sick shall be convoyed to the Swedish leaguer at Novodwor by water.

6. The dead also; yet that under this pretext no other thing be taken away.

7. The Sweds shall have liberty to carry all what they have along, except church ornaments and goods.

8. The Swedish women shal be convoyed safely also by water to their army on this condition, that *Graffe* Wittemberg shall endeavour to release all the Polnish women prisoners by the Sweden.

9. All bookes belonging to the Kings bibliotheck shall be restored.

10. The Sweds shall pay all debts contracted by them.

11. All prisoners in the towne to be released. {66}

12. The towne and pallace to be delivered without all practice of being mined.

13. All who march out not to bear armes or enterprize any thing in foure weeks tyme against Polland.

Three dayes thereafter according to this accord there marched out 900 foot or thereabout and 300 horsemen. The foot were lodged in Ujasdow and the horsemen in Ossolinskyes palace, and were afterwards convoyed to Thorne. The women, amongst whom were Gen-ll Duglas his lady and her sister as also the sick and dead persons, were convoyed by water to the army at Novodwor. These persons were, howe[ve]r, detained either for performance of the articles or upon the acco[un]t of the breach of some of the articles, or for some other cause, to witt: *Graffe* Wittemberg Felt Marshall, *Graffe* Benedictus Oxenstern, Canterstein, Slangfelt, Puchar the upper commissary, Forgell and another collonell who was commendant.

Dureing this siedge I was commanded to a safeguard two miles below Varso in a village called Maly (or litle) Lumny, belonging to the Crown stallmaster, my lord his eldest brother. Here I was very well entertained, the old woman the *podstarosts* wyfe being very kind to me; her husband, whose sirname was Archisefsky, being somq[uha]t crabbed.

When the *quartianers* returned from Great Polland, two *towarises* were sent hither also for safeguard with whom, being civill gentlemen, I lived in good amity. Dureing my abode here I went often to the leaguer, especially when I heard of any action or assault to be, on purpose to inure my self to dangers and better my understanding in martiall effaires. Here also I profited much in learning the ground of the Polls language, whereunto the yong gentlwomen in the house helped much, they with some curiosity correcting my speech and giveing me {66v} taskes of love sonnets, ridles and other trifles, which I not unwillingly performed.

In the tyme of my being here I gott notice of a illand in the river Vistula, wherein some boures from the other side sheltered themselves with their goods and cattell under my protection, as belonging to Maly Lumny, and that without my knowledge. Thither I went with 2 or 3 servants in a small boat, and with threats of deserting them and informing of their liveing under no protection, I made them give me 16 florens for bypast and 4 florens a week for the future; as also getting notice of a horse which they had stolne from the Sweds, I took him, paying only 7 florens for him, the rest of the boures putting me on and assisting me to gett him from him who had him in possession.

There were also some gentlmen of Great Lumny and others who had their cattell in one herde with those I had in protection, who not acknowledging me for my pains, and that by the *podstarosts* crabbednes, I found out a way to pay them home. For, being often in the leaguer, I bespoke my acquaintances to come and drive away some cattell, when they were in the field. I haveing my horse alwayes ready sadled, followed and, formally shooting at other, recovered the cattell. Haveing done so once or twice, I told plainly I could not hazard my lyfe against desperate robbers and spoile my horses in protecting or recovering the goods of others, whom I had no order to protect without ane acknowledgement for my paines. So they willingly condiscended to give me a reichs doller for each flight, and two when I recovered all. So that finding this trade currant, I had twice or thrice a week such occasions, shareing alwayes with {67} my acquaintances what I gott by this meanes, as also what they tooke away, which my crabbed *podstarost* did not in the least perceive. For, my correspondents being alwayes at least 6 or 7, and I but with two servants at most, I pretended my inability, and that probable enough, of not catching any of them, and, if *pia fraus*[245] be allowable, this, as *necessaria*, may be so likewise.

But the Sweds haveing made their bridge over the Vistula, wee were all forced to remove into the towne, and I was discharged of my safeguardship with some reluctancy. For my landlord or *podstarosts* daughter haveing been dureing the siedge in Varso by a Scotseman called John Rosse, the *podstarost* hearing of the townes rendition, desired me to conduct his daughter and onely child out of the towne. I, out of a youthfull humor, then and the short tyme I stayed in the village after that, haveing ingratiated my self in her eyes, as in her mothers long ago, it raised, it seemes, a conceit in them of a stricter engadgement, which I with some contentment entertained. The old woman haveing told me once in serious confidence, that when I should leave the warres, she would make me one of her dearest ffriends, to the which I gave an ambiguous answer. And the tyme I lived in Varso untill the battell was lost, my visits, which were frequent, were very acceptable.[246]

The King of Sweden being now arrived with the Elector of Brandeburgh and their forces at their leaguer at Novydwor, began to consult whether they should march over the Vistula and assault the Polls on that syde, or to march on the same side they were, which last prevailed. {67v} The Polls after the rendition of Varso had certaine intelligence of the conjunction of the Swedish King and Elector of Brandeburgh with their armies and of their march towards Varso; wherefor they so disposed their forces on both sides of the river, whereon they had a large bridge of boats with forts on each syde, that upon occasion they might draw all or so much as was requisite to one syde.

The Crowne army stood on the towne syde along the river below the New towne on high ground, the Littawish army on the other syde and the Tartars also. The Littawish army had cast up an intrenchment betwixt the river and the sandy hillocks towards Nieporent with ordinance on its bulwarkes and flankes, this being the front of their army. For the other sydes

---
[245] White lie (Lat.).
[246] Next five lines, blotted out in MS, are unreadable.

of the leaguer small care was taken, the sandy hills and a wood of firres being on their right, the river on their left hand, and the towne of Prague on their rear, which was thought sufficient. Neither had they, indeed, foot to manne a line round their leaguer, and scarse enough to guard their front well. On the towne side their leaguer was fortifyed also, yet with lesse industry, because they had the large old wall about the suburbes in case of necessity. Besides, the wayes of approaching to this syde with an army was mor difficult.

The gentry of the three palatinates of Great Polland had gott liberty to returne home, and most of the rest of the gentry were also gone: the good King and generalls being unwilling in such a ticklish tyme too rigorously to presse their services, a rumour of the Sweds falling into Great Polland giveing some collour for the departure of these.

{68} July 28. Upon Fridday about 10 aclock befor noone, the Polnish King haveing notice of the Swedish and Brandeburgish armies advancing, with the hetmans and army marched along the bridge. The army was drawne up within the trenches. About a mile and a halfe from the leaguer the Polnish guards and voluntiers engaged with the Swedish foretroupes or skoutes, the Polls retireing and the Sweds advancing and pikiering, with the losse and wounds of diverse of the most couragious.

The Swedish avantguarde was commanded by L. Gen. Sparr, who persuing the Polls in good order even to their trenches, which he could not perceive, it being growne darke, so that the Polls being entred at a large gappe not finished as yet, the artillery discharged at once amongst them did great harme, for Coll. [...] Sinkler, a valorous souldier, was killed[247], and diverse others. The Sweds finding themselves nearer as was safe, wheeled of in good order and took up their stations at a convenient distance. About ane houre thereafter, the Swedish cannon being come, they played into our leaguer at adventure for the space of two houres, and then all was quiet till day.

The Swedish army was drawne up in equall front from the river to the wood and within it, the Brandeburgish being on the left wing. The whole

---

[247] Colonel David Sinclair died of wounds the next day.

army consisted of 60 esquadrons of *ruiters* and 4 regiments of dragouns, divided equally in the wings, and 12 brigades of foot, being in all about 24,000, whereof the Sweds made scarce up one halfe.

The Polls army consisted of 8,000 *quartianers*, 16,000 of the countrey gentry, 5,000 Littawers, 6,000 Tartars and 4,000 foot and dragouns, being in all about 40,000. The Polls, tis true, had the advantage in numbers, being of all sorts of people twice as many. But the Sweds and {68v} Brandeburgish had farr the oddes of them in order, discipline and warlike ammunition.

Day light appearing, the Sweds (whose dilligence and vigilancy at all tymes can never be sufficiently commended), haveing in the night tyme discovered and possessed a litle hill among the bushes and planted thereon two pieces, they began to play into our leaguer, whereof they had a full wiew, to avoyd which the Polls drew of from the most eminent places. And two or three trowpes of Polls, whether by command or not, I know not, sett forward towards this hillock with great resolution. But being come within danger, the Sweds welcomed them so with great and small shott that they were glad to wheele of to the left hand, leaving some of their fellowes behind them.

About 9 aclock the King of Polland with the hetmans and principall persons of the army, amongst whom was Sir John Henderson Major Generall[248], held a counsell of warr under heavens canopie, sitting on the trunkes of trees (there haveing been a wood there in former tymes). It were tedious to recount the opinions and reasones of severall persons, all which I heard and noted downe the same day. The result, however, was that, seing the Sweds were come out of their leaguer without provisions more as for 3 or 4 dayes, and so not able to continue long in that posture, the Polls should continue in their leaguer and let the Sweds be at the disadvantage of assaulting their trenches, which were indifferent well guarded with foot and artillery. The Tartars in the meane tyme should hinder them from fetching provision or provender.

About ten aclock the Tartars who were in the woods in the reare of the Swedish army, espying some advantage, assaulted the Swedish guards,

---

[248] Major General Henderson, sent to King Jan Kazimierz by Emperor Ferdinand III, was the main author of the plan of campaign against the Swedes.

beating them into their bodyes. But being circumvented by some troops of horse sent to that purpose and welcomed with {69} great and small shott from the rereguard, they were forced to retire with losse. Many of them being driven in to a marish, were forced to leave their horses, yet some of them, about 40 or 50, breake resolutely through a wing of the Brandeburgish and brought two horsemen prisoners with them to the King of Polland.

Ane houre after this the Queen of Polland came in her coach to the other syde of the bridge, and seeing the Sweds to have the use of the river, she caused two cannon be brought with her owne coach horses downe the banke of the river, walking downe her self on foot, Amazonian-lyke, and caused plant and secure them for annoying the Sweds on the other syde of the river and hindring them from watering, which tooke the wished effect.

About 2 aclock afternoone the Sweds countermarched their army, changeing wings and marching through the woods to take up fresh ground. At their first marching the Polls imagined them to have fled, wherefor the most part of the cavalerie drew out of the leaguer as to a persuite, but being advanced neer to a trench which the Sweds had cast up in the night along the front of their army, the Sweds faced about and thundred among the Polls with great and small shott, so that they retired as fast as they had advanced, marcheing into the leaguer there to exspect the event of this stratageme, as they now tooke it.

About 3 aclock afternoone the Sweds appeared out of the woods in full *battallia*, marching towards Nieporent and haveing taken up sufficient ground in a large plaine *champaigne*, they faced to the right and so ordered their armyes in a battell and a reserve, makeing two large {69v} fronts, haveing the wood now on their right hand. The Polls thought at first that the Sweds, knowing their designe of intending to weary them out, and being scarce of provender, resolved to possesse this Nieporent, being a countrey house of the Kings and mannor well stored with provender. Wherefor they immediately sent Colonell Bockhune[249] with 500 dragouns

---

[249] Johann Heinrich von Alten-Bockum, commander of the Polish King's dragoon guards.

to set fyre on the mannour, and the Littawish army, who had their stations on that syde of the sandy hills towards the mannour, were commanded to draw nearer the body of the army, both which were performed in good order and manner.

The King of Polland with the generalls and other p[rinci]p[a]ll persons of the army, seing from the sandy hills (where they stood) the order of the Swedish and Brandeb[urgish] armyes, and that they stood exspecting battell, and being urged by some hott spirits, resolved to hazard the attacting the left wing of the army, where they had intelligence that the Brandeburgers were, whom they looked upon as worse sojors as the Sweds and against whom, as their owne vassails, they carried a greater spleene, and this succeeding well, to follow the successe as occasione should offer. To this the Littawish husars, in number 500, commanded by [...] Sapiha[250], presented themselves, to {70} second whom 4,000 *quartianers*, halfe *pantzerny*, or armed, and halfe *kosatsky*, or light horsemen, were ordered, under the command of the famous Czarnetsky, the rest of the army being in readines.

The King of Sweden, seing this tempest comeing towards his left wing, immediately advanced thither himself betwixt the battells with his guards of *trabants* and *riters*, and gave orders to all commanders of brigades and regiments that when the husars or lanciers should charge them, they should open and give way to their fury, which he knew was not to be withstood with any force or other policy at that tyme.

The husars advanced with great resolution, but the mentioned reserve at too great a distance in their rear towards the left hand, Czarnetsky either not intending to second them, or seing the improbability of doing any good. A great number of voluntiers also from all parts advanced in a confused manner with a hideous noise and shouting after the husars. The season being dry, the horses raised such a dust that the heavens were obscured and nothing to be seen, but the engageing partyes involved as in a cloud. The Swedish field pieces played upon the Polls all the way as they

---

[250] Paweł Jan Sapieha (1609–1665), Great Hetman of Lithuania, was injured in a fall from his horse and left the field. The hussars' attack was led by Aleksander Połubiński (M. Nagielski, op. cit., s. 129, 162–3).

came {70v} on, and being to the first battell, they found a free passage without any opposition, but such as the small shott in their flankes.

The distance betwixt the battells was large, whither the husars being come, they roamed up and downe as a horse without a rider, and every where assaulted, especially from the reserve with great vollies of small shott. And in this condition the King himself with his guards charged them, even to the endangering of his owne person. These few but gallant and resolute men, being as in a hose nett, attacted on all hands, were as dry fuell with a violent fyre in a short tyme consumed, few fynding the way back againe, the great body of the reserve, as the voluntiers also, not giveing them any help or offering any reall engadgment or charge, but upon the plaine appearance of the losse of these gallant husars, retired confusedly.

After this the Swedish army advanced in full *battalia* forwards the sandy hills, playing continually with their field pieces on these hills, which made the Polls to abandon their stations and their cannon also. So that if the Sweds had continued in their march forward, that night had decided the {71} businesse.

About 6 aclock the Swedish and Brandeburgish armyes marched eastward towards Nieporent, which gave the Polls tyme to reinforce their guards on the sandy hills againe. And seing the Sweds aiming at the wood on the east syde of Prague, they sent Colonell Bockhune with his regiment of dragouns and other forces to take possession of the wood and fortify themselves after the best manner they could; who from the hills thorow the wood in the utmost side thereof did cast a trench and build a brestworke with ordinary flankes and defences.

The King of Polland in the evening crossed the river to Varsaw, and the Sweds and Brandeb[urgers] rested the short night by Nieporent. Befor the breake of day the Polls generalls and other p[rinci]p[a]ll persons of the army sent over their waggons and baggage to Varsaw, foreseeing the event. Which I seing and haveing no charge, only a voluntier, thought it no tyme to stay and so went over also.

About an houre before sunnrising the Swedish and Brandeb[urgish] armyes began to march in full *battalia* towards the wood, and sent out strong [...]²⁵¹ forlorne hopes to attact these in the wood. The Brandeb[urgers] had the avantguard by the Dukes desire. Being come neer the trench, the Polls welcomed them with diverse vollyes of shott, and so after halfe ane houres skirmishing and a short dispute at the trench, the Polls were beat of from their parapet and put to flight.

{71v} The King of Polland (who by day light was come over to the army) with the generalls, upon the first appearance of their enemyes comeing on, drew the front of the army to that quarter and sent such relieffe of foot as they could spare, with their readiest trowpes, to the relieffe of these in the wood. But the Sweds advancing now without opposition and persuing their good fortune in good order, carryed all befor them like a violent inundation.

The Polls seing their trowpes and foot fleiing [*sic*] out of the wood, gave all over for lost. The cavallierie fledd most towards the Prague, beyond which at a passe they were mett by Generall Douglasse with the Sweds cavalliery and stopped, but after some losse the Polls breake throw and escaped. Others tooke the river. The King with many p[rinci]p[a]ll persons of the army and the infantery passed the river by the bridge, the Sweds advancing out of the wood in great bodyes through the Polls leaguer towards the bridge, which was defended by a fort at the end thereof, wherein were about 500 men. These, after some vollies of shott discharged upon the advancing Sweds, retired over the bridge and set fyre thereto in two or three places, which quickly consumed some vessels and so rendred the bridge useless.

{72} The Polls in this battell lost about 2,000 men and above 40 cannon of different syzes. The Sweds and Brandeb[urgers] lost not above 700. The Sweds were buryed where knowne, but the Polls not, in revenge of the Sweds left unburyed by Varky. The Swedish King commanded only Sapiha, the commander of the husars, out of a singular respect to his valour, to be buryed.²⁵² The booty here gotten was not great nor rich, the

---

²⁵¹ No gap in MS, but an evident omission here.
²⁵² The Swedish King has indeed caused bury one of the enemy hussars, who perished near him. His name is variously given in the sources, but it was not Sapicha (Nagielski, op. cit., s. 174–6).

most and all the best being convoyed over the river befor. No person of quality killed on the Swedish syde but Coll. Sinklar; of the Brandeburgish, Maior Generall Kannenberg was wounded with a cannon bullet.

The Pollonian countrey gentry, many whereof had swimme and by one meanes or other passed the river, immediately packt all up and went away. The King also with all the nobility and military persons prepared all to be gone and in the evening after sunsett marched of towards Piositsna[253] and Varky. They left behind them in Varshaw *Graffe* Benedict Oxenstern and the G[enera]ll Commissary Puchar, who were sick. About midnight the burgers of Varshaw came to *Graffe* Oxenstern and desired him to send some of his servants to guard the gates of the towne and to send two along with them to present their keyes to the King of Sweden, which {72v} was immediately granted.

The next day the Sweds haveing repaired the bridge, marched over and tooke possession of the towne, and all the generall and p[rinci]p[a]ll persons of the army had quarters allotted them in the towne, notwithstanding the body of the army removed not, but encamped in the Polls leaguer. Generall Duglasse with 5,000 horse persued the Polls and the fourth day returned without doing any great execution, and at his returne was preferred to be felt marshall lieutennant[254], and that worthily, his services in this warr haveing been all along very signall.

Here I must relate something of my owne fortune at this tyme. One Fridday, upon the first alarum of the aproaching of the Swedish army, I rode to the army on the other syde and then towards the enemy, about a myle from the leaguer, where comeing near to the engadged parties, I did meet diverse returneing wounded, which made me mor eager to see how things passed and upon occasion to try my fortune, but was not permitted to come near by the Polls who told me, that in such a bickering and medly I might be mistaken for an enemy, being in Dutch habite, and counselled me to returne to the {73} leaguer, which I did.

The night I lodged by a markettenter, or suttler, as they call them, and the next day I rode up and downe the whole day with Maior Gen-ll

---

[253] Piaseczno.
[254] Further on Gordon continues to refer to Douglas as general.

Henderson, whereby I had good convenience to hear and see all what I have befor related. In the evening I, perceiving how the businesse would go, strove to gett over the river at the bridge, pretending to be wounded, but the guards did not let me passe.

Then I rode towards the Prague, intending to gett or hire a small boat and swimme my horses, but on the way thither was in an instant besett by a company of rascalls lurking after a hedge, who ere I was aware laid hands on my bridle and pulled my patron-case from me, and had undoubtedly robbed me of all, if I had not freed my self of them with my pistoll, and with great ado recovered my boy, haveing lost his sword. But two others who were with me payed the score, all what they had being taken from them, these rascalls pretending an order for doing so to hinder any from running away.

I returned and laid me downe by the high way not farr from the bridge and watched tyme about with my boy. About the breake of day, I seing the generalls waggons and baggage driveing by with a convoy, amongst {73v} whom were some strangers dispersed betwixt the waggons, which opportunity I embraced and put my self in among the rest, and so gott over without being questioned. Being come to the topp of the hill, I see halfe a dozen of horsemen comeing directly towards me, whom I wished to shun, fearing to be questioned and forced back againe, which I did by another way, very fitly comeing in there. However, one was sent of to know of me what passed. I told what I knew and, being past, I perceived it was the King going to the leaguer, the *isnatshek*[255], or signe, being sunke.

Being come to my quarters and sett up my horses, I went to the river syde by the Dominicans monastery, where I see all that passed as the Polls fledd. In the evening, when all fledd, in such hast I lost my boy in the throng, and being without the towne towards Ujesdowa, I made a halt to find my boy and some strangers to ride along with, fearing in the darke and in such a confusion to be knockt in the head, the Polls then openly curseing all strangers for the Sweds sakes. I had not stayed long when I did meet with two Scotsmen, and after a litle mor stay wee gott together a

---

[255] Znaczek (Polish).

dozen of horse, all strangers, each {74} being glad of anothers company for the same reason. And so rideing along, diverse parties of the Polls overtooke us, who in their rideing by reviled and scolded at us, saying it were well done to cut all our throats, wee being all one with the Sweds. And albeit these things were spoken by the scumme and rascality of the people, yet did it put us in no small fear least, being overpowred at last by such lyke, wee might runne the hazard of our lyves. So wee resolved to stepp asyde and make a halt untill all were past.

While wee stayed here, it was debated amongst us what course wee should take, after many propositions how to proceed in our jorney, and how to be in some part revenged of these and such lyke who abused us. Most concluded to go upon the Lovitz way and ease some of the countrey gentry, who were flying home, of such things as were worth the takeing. And so with one consent wee bended our course that way. In the night tyme wee discovered diverse partyes, who being too strong for us to medle with, wee carryed all fair. About day light wee did meet with 20 or 30 Polls, such adventurers as our selves, {74v} by whose counsell wee went asyde to a village to feed our horses.

In this village, about a mile from Blunia[256], the people were most fled. Wee dispersed our selves through the village as fearing no danger. Only wee strangers had stabled our horses in two houses, somewhat distant from another. Neither had wee set out any guard or sentry as wee should have done, but very securely went walking through the village seeking what wee could gett.

Wee had been litle more as ane houre here, when wee heard ane alarum and some shotts at the further end of the village, which made me and 4 others who were with me make hast to our horses, but had scarsely recovered our quarter, when the village was full of the enemyes, and wee besett on all hands. I bringing my horse out of a low stable, was shott with a pistoll bullet in the left thigh, but being farr shott was not dangerous. Two of my comorads were gott to their horses and out at a back gate through a long lane, but were quickly driven back to us

---

[256] Błonie.

againe by ten or twelve horsmen. And now, wee being besett on all sydes, were forced to accept of quarters, {75} which they courteously offered us. They killed most of the Polls who were with us, two of the Dutch men were also killed and 3 wounded beside my self. There were above a 120 horsemen in this party, most whereof were Brandeburgers and had crossed the river the day before by the bridge at Novodwor and upon notice of the Polls retreat and flight were come so farr for booty and intelligence.

Wee were all brought out into the fields befor some officers who examined us apart. I, to gett better usage, told I had served under Generall Duglas befor, haveing been taken prisoner by Krakow and forced to serve. Wherefor a *ruitmaster* of the Brandeburgers, who as it seemes commanded the party, tooke me to him and told me he would bring me to Duglas. These haveing intelligence from us that the King and all had left Warso, after they had fedd their horses a litle in another village, marched directly thither, whither wee came towards night.

The next day the *ruitm-r* tooke me along with him over the river, where I stayed in his quarters that day and the following night.

[August 2.] The next day, being Wednesday, he tooke me along with him to Generall Duglas, where haveing gotten audience of the {75v} generall (who was just then returned from the pursuite of the Polls), he told his Exc[ellency] that he had taken prisoner a yong man, who said that he had served under his Exc[ellency] befor. Whereupon I was immediately called in, the generall asking me in English, where and when I had served under him. I answered, craveing pardon for makeing use of his Exc[ellency's] name, which I only did to gett better quarter and usage, haveing indeed never had the honour to serve under his Exc[ellency], but had served under others in the Swedish service, and being taken prisoner was forced, after a long and hard imprisonment, to serve the Polls.

The generall hereupon turned himself to the *ruitm-r* and told him he knew me, and desired him to give me my lyberty. The *ruitm-r* told the generall that for his sake he would restore to me my horse and mounting, which was very well taken of the generall, and for which he thanked the *ruitm-r* heartyly.

I went back with the *ruitm-r* and lodged in his quarters, and the next morning, haveing received my horse and armour, I went along to the generall who commanded my horse {76} to be stabled among his owne, and to tarry there. Afternoone the generall called for me and told me that he was to have a lyfe company of Scotsmen; that there were many voluntiers, who had been officers, come over with the Lord Cranstons foot regiments, whom he was to take into the said company, and such other pretty men as he could find; that they should have large priviledges, as not to watch or ward but for their owne private security; to have good and large quarters; that they should be a seminary of officers; and if any ones urgent occasions should call him home to his native countrey, he should upon his desire have his free liberty. All which were good conditions, and faithfully thereafter keep'd to us except the last. He desired me to go about in the army and in the citty of Varshaw and enquire for free persons, who would engage upon such conditions.

The next day I went in to Varshaw and by chance did meet with two Scotsmen, whom I had knowne under the Polls in the tyme of the siege, and passed for reformadoes, but now being metamorphosed into Polonian habite, were scarse and not willing to be {76v} knowne. I accosted them, and after some short suspitious salutations they, to avoide being taken notice of in the streets, invited me into a taverne where by a cup of the best wee began to discourse of our adventures and present condition. What concerned my self, I (according to my naturall custome) told them all plainly, not concealing Gen-ll Duglas his offers.

After wee had stayed a while, three other Scotsmen came in, whether sent for or it being their ordinary place of meeting, I know not. These altogether, after many discourses to and fro, began to reveale to me their conditions and ask my counsell. Yet, it seemes, not trusting me too much either, I knowing and perceiving by their discourse them all to be free persons and to have had a subsistance formerly under the Polls, and now in a fear to be taken notice of and questioned, began to deale more sincerely and confidently with them, perswadeing them to engage and enter themselves under such a company, where they could have such honourable conditions and their liberty when they pleased.

This seeming all to them but Sirens songs, they began to entreat me not to take notice of them or reveale any {77} thing of their being their [*sic*]. But I useing forcible perswasions with some fair threats, brought them so farr that they would take the businesse to consideration and give me an answer the next day, adding after a hearty parting cup that if they must engage, they would find a great deale more. I laying hold of this, told them that the greater the number, it would be more acceptable and cary the greater authority, even to the degree of capitulation. However, I obtained no more as a promise of an answer the next day, and so returned to the leaguer.

The generall haveing been this evening late by his Ma-tie, and convoyed home by some persons of quality, I thought best not to trouble his Exc[ellency], but the next morning very early made my appearance and had admittance whilst he was dressing himself. I told his Exc[ellency] my adventures the day befor, which he desired me to prosecute with great fervency and caused give me some spending money.

Being come into the towne, and after some stay at the appointed place, haveing mett with my ffriends, I found them somewhat sc[r]upulous {77v} at first. But after I had dispelled these clouds with some cups of radiant liquor, I brought them so farr as to send a deputy along with me to the generall to hear these conditions, which I told them, confirmed. I only desired a list of their names. This tooke up some tyme, they sending out to seek up others to engage in the same capitulation, so that to compleete my businesse I was forced to resolve of lodging there all night.

Wee gott on the list 18 persons, besides their deputy Andrew Stretton, who the next morning early went along with me. Being come to the generall and relateing to him how I had prospered, he caused admitt the deputy and confirmed what I had promised with many gracious promises besides, and sent me along with him againe, where after curious search wee found and engaged halfe a dozen more.

Towards evening, haveing parted with my ffriends, I went and gave my landlords daughter and the two yong ladyes with her a visitt. They had their quarters in an apothecaryes house in a back chamber, a yong

Swedish *graffe* haveing his quarters in his house. The yong {78} gentlewomen were astonished to see me. After short and cordiall salutations they would needs engadge me, and that upon the point of honour, to ride to their countrey habitations and bring notice how all passed there, which I performed the next day with some hazard. My landlord not trusting me nor I him much either, did not compear, but my landlady, being sent for to a thick wood in a marish, did come. She entertained me very kindly and gifted me 5 duckats. She told me plainly that the greatest part of their substance was by their daughter, and wished me to bring their daughter and it and those that were with her to a safe place, and then I might command what I pleased, and desired me to take a note of credence along to their daughter to this purpose, which haveing received, I tooke my leave and returned to my yong gentlewomen, who could not expresse their joy.

I shew my note of credence and desired them to resolve against the next day to be gone with me to Prussia. My landlords daughter, knowing herself to be the chieffest price aimed at, shewed herself most scrupulous. The other were exceeding well content, especially the yong widdow, {78v} who fancied to her self things above reason. Haveing left them in this humour, I went to my lodging and the next day, according to my promise, I returned, where I found all upon the hoyty toyty to be gone.

My landlords daughter haveing been counselled and schooled so, that she even offered her consent, but I haveing advised with my pillow, changed the scene and told them in sincere termes that, haveing received so many courtesies of their family and now this extraordinary favour and trust, I would not undertake any thing which might not be agreeable to the confidence which they reposed in me or the gratitude I owed to them. So that haveing ripely considered the nature of the tymes, the state of the present effaires and their conditions as well as my owne, I found that there was no feare of violence or lossing what they had, which were the chieffe causes that mad them put themselves into my protection, whereof my yong yeares and small authority were scarse capable, and wherein by many accidents I might faile them, and so perswaded them {79} to settle themselves in to a resolution of staying, seing I perfectly had learned that the Sweds would be quickly gone from thence without doing violence to any in the towne. And so they might be at liberty, in which condition it were best makeing equall and reall bargaines.

To these and with larger discourse amplifyed reasons they, seing my resolution, acquiesced without appearance of any discontent. Only the yong widdow could not containe her self from bewraying her grieffe, which appeared in this, that at my leave takeing, when the rest gifted me with love-toyes and tokens, she told me I tooke one thing along with me, which made her uncapable of bestowing any thing else upon me.

Some dayes thereafter Feld Marshall Duglas marched and passed the Vistula by a bridge a litle above Sakrotczin[257], where a strict view was taken of all that passed, and so marching to Sacroczin, [...] and to Plotsko[258], from whence wee, divideing our selves in small trowpes or partyes, went out to seeke adventures, and I with 10 or 12 more in stead of better booty drove downe {79v} about 700 oxen and kowes and 1,500 sheepe, which wee sold at Thorne very good cheape, of which money I hadd a 100 r[eichs] dallers for my share. Here wee stayed 8 dayes and then marched to Culmsee and to Grawdents, from whence wee, being 27 in all who came along with the felt marshall, were sent along with *Ruitm-r* John Meldrum to our quarters at Reden 3 miles from thence. This *ruitm-r* had but 18 men with him, the relicques of a former trowpe, most whereof were Skotsmen. (This continued pag. 243)[259].

The King of Sweden upon due consideration with the Electour of Brandeburgh and their counsell resolved to draw their forces (the Sweds, I meane) out of most of the townes, which they had garrisoned in Great and Litle Polland, and so accordingly kept only garrisons in Crakow, Lovits, Posna and Calis in Great Polland, and left in Buck-*shants* above Zacrotczin Maior Andersone with 500 men.

---

[257] Zakroczym.
[258] Płock.
[259] Here Gordon abandons his own story until folio 125 for a detailed description of military affairs.

This maior gott with him 8 piece of cannon, good store of ammunition and a good quantity of provision of cornes out of the storehouses of Varso, but very litle money, with liberty to transport {80} as much salt out of a *sklad* or storehouse hard by as he pleased. All which he very dilligently and industriously caused bring either over to the illand or under the defence of the cannon to the river syde, which thereafter proved his greatest lyvelyhood and the safety of the place. For notwithstanding whilst the army was in the fields about Varso, he had provided himself of such provisions of cattell and cornes as he was able, and thereafter by such small force as he could spare in sending our partyes, brought in now and then necessaryes for lyvelyhood, especially cattell. Yet the Polls at lentgh by their trowpes quartered in Sakrotczin and other places thereabouts cut him so short, that he durst not hazard to send out any more, being destitute of horsemen. So that he was forced at last to spend upon the store which he had providently gathered, which being towards the spring [1657] near an end, he advertised his Ma[jes]tie, desireing relieffe, in stead whereof he received orders to demolish the fort and {80v} by water retire to Thorne, which was a matter of no small difficulty, the illands below in the river being full of gentry and countrey people, who were not unfurnished of shott and weapons, and the passage of the river so uncertaine and full of sands and shelves not to be passed without skilfull pilots, which was wanting.

But whilst the commendant is deviseing how to overcome these difficulties, an occasion offered whereby he gott sufficient relieffe with abundance of all things and preserved the fort, which stood the King in good stead the next summer for transporting of his army. The Polls, to be freed from the losse done by parties out of this garrison, lodged some companies in the adjacent townes as Sakrotzin and Pultowsko (Pultusk), by whose vigilancy the countrey was well secured and the garrison forced to spend upon their provided store, which now near spent, he began to sue for a truce with the neerest garrisons by meanes of some gentlmen whom he had prisoners in the illand, agreeing also with these for a certaine {81} quantity of cornes for their ransome. This being so dexterously caryed, that the Polls upon the first motion embraced it and desired an intercourse of traffick, the great necessity which the countrey had of salt moveing them hereto, whereof the governour was not ignorant. So that the countrey people comeing with provisions and money to fetch salt, he gave and receaved at his owne price, and haveing furnished his storehouses, hearing of the league and juncture of armes with the Prince of Transilvania and the trepidation of the Polls, he was not ignorant. So that the countrey furnished his coffers with good money for the salt.

Whilst the Polls were triumphing for their conquest of Varso, and the Sweds thereafter for the battell gained their, Crakow was blocquired by the countrey gentry and people of that province, haveing their leaguer at Tenits[260], about 3 miles from the citty. The Sweds haveing intelligence of their security and the weaknesse of their guards, resolved to hazard the beating up of their quarters and freeing themselves {81v} of the fame of being besiedged. So, makeing out all the forces they could spare, haveing befor taken good orders and care for quieting and keeping the burgers from enterpriseing any thing, they marched out in the evening towards Tenits and by day light falling upon the Polls scouts, they routed them and followed them into their leaguer with such celerity that the Polls had no tyme of thinking to make any head or resistance, but every man makeing shift for himself, all was in confusion, so that ane absolute victory was gained, with great booty and many prisoners.

About this tyme Colonell Forgell, whom the Polls had sent prisoner from Varso to Zamostcze, haveing agreed for his ransome, was dismissed towards Krakow, and upon the way taken by the Tartars. By intercession of some Polls noblemen, seing his passe, freed and, comeing to Crakow, after a short stay, with some officers and a convoy with much booty, baggage and servants belonging {82} to the officers of that garrison, in all about 500 men, intending for Pomeren, was way-layed by the Polls and after a sharpe fight routed and taken. The Polls gott here great booty, the collonell dyed shortly thereafter of stroakes gott here and at his former takeing by the Tartars.

Calis being straitly besieged by the Polls under the command of Weyer, the *Woywod* or Palatine of Pomeren, the Sweds from Posna sent out such

---

[260] Tyniec.

forces as they could possibly, being upwards of 2,000 under the command of Maior Generall Wresowits. These advancing thither, were mett by a strong party of the Polls who were sent out to recognosce, whom they routed. But the Sweds, fearing an ambush, persued them not farr, their horses also being wearyed by a long and sharp march, so that it was resolved to lodge in a village to refresh them selves and horses, and to march betimes in the morning. The most of this party were {82v} new levyed souldiers, and by negligence or some fatality did not ly in such order nor keep such strong guards as was requisite, as contemning the enemy whom they had routed and chased.

The Polls seing none to persue them, made a stand in a wood not farr from the village where the Sweds lodged. The palatine being come himself, sent some bowres to discover the behaviour and manner of the Sweds encamping and guards, whereof being sufficiently informed, he resolved to beat up their quarters, though he was farr inferiour to them in numbers, as not being above 500 men. So, divideing them in 4 partyes, he sent 3 to fall on in 3 sundry places and stayed with the 4th on the rendevous place, which he had providently and conveniently ordered, that in case of any great resistance he could make a safe and orderly retreat, giveing command that, beating their guards, they should fall in closse with them into the village and fyre it in as many places as they could. All {83} which succeeded so well that, finding litle or no resistance by the guards, who brought in their flight the reserves in confusion, they fyred the village in divers places.

Such a fear and confusion was among the Sweds, that none thought of makeing any head or opposition, but every one shifted for themselves, many swimming a litle river hard by, the only way left to escape. The maior generall halfe naked comeing thither and wanting skill to swime, was either drowned or killed unknowne, for his body was not found, albeit the Polls caused make dilligent search for it. Here the Polls gott great booty and some field pieces. Most of the Sweds were killed or taken either here or in their returne by the countrey people. The beleaguered Sweds were forced thereafter to render.

Neither did fortune stoppe as yet to frowne upon the Sweds, for some jealousyes ariseing betwixt the Moskovite and them about diverse businesses, as that the Moskovite had {83v} put garrisons and exacted contributions of diverse places of Samogitia, to which province the Sweds claimed right, as being first by them conquered and possessed; some small partyes and persons on both sides ruined without reparation, and many mor too tedious here to recite. All which might have been easily composed if a stronger reason of state had not procured a rupture betwixt these princes, which was this: the Roman Emperour had sent his ambassadour to the Tzar of Russia to offer his mediation betwixt the Tzar and the King of Polland. This minister was a spirituall person called Alagrett ab Alagrettis who, following the Tzars court even in the expedition to Littaw, used all meanes to promote the peace betwixt Polland and Russia, and the interest of the Roman Empire and Catholick religion, which had a great dependance upon the fortune of Polland, and behaved himself in this his negotiation so dexterously that, representing most strong reasons to the Tzar and his counsell, he perswaded and obtained a truce with Polland for a year, and the invasion of Sweden.

For the Russes being naturally suspicious and diffident, were growne exceeding jealous of the victoryes and greatnes {84} of the King of Sweden, seing plainly that if he conquered Polland, whereof there was great likelyhood, in short tyme they should be forced to fight against both conjunctly. And so were easily perswaded for their owne security to make a diversion of the Swedish armes by invadeing them at their owne doores, and that so suddainly that they were marched towards Liefland a good way befor it was divulged whither they were bound. And the King of Sweden knew nothing untill Cockenhausen and some other small forts were taken and Riga beleaguered. The Tzar was here in person himself with an army of 100,000 men and store of artillerie and warlick provision.[261]

Aug[ust] 19. At the first approaching the Sweds sallying out with their horse, were beat back with the losse of the *Conte* d' Torren, whose body was sent to his lady two dayes thereafter by a *ruitm-r* who received a 100 ducats in gift.

---

[261] The Russo-Swedish war began in May 1656. The Tsar's forces took Nyenskans, Dünaburg, Kokenhausen and Dorpat, but after their failure at Riga there was little action.

The siege continued near 6 weekes with losse on both sides. The most memorable passage was a sally made by the Sweds on the quarter of *Kniaz* Jacob Kudinikowitz Czirkasky[262] about midday, when the Russes usually after dinner {84v} fall to sleep, which was done with such resolution that they beat the Russes quite out of their trenches, killing many, takeing some prisoners and 18 collours, which they displayed thereafter upon their walls in great bravery.

After this the Tzar commanded Generall Lesly[263] and the stranger colonells to hold a counsell of warr and consider if it was possible to gaine the towne by any meanes, and to give in the result of all with their reasons in writteing; which they did two dayes thereafter, concludeing the impossibility of takeing the towne at this tyme for the following reasons. 1st, the latenesse and unseasonablenes of the year; 2, the scarsity of provisions and impossibility of supplying sufficiently such a multitude in a countrey every where wasted with their numerous armyes; 3, the sicknessesse increasing dayly in the army; 4, the strentgh of the towne, being strongly fortyfyed with walls and rampiers, a deep and broad water ditch, which they could fill and empty at pleasure; 5, the number, resolution and obstinacy of the garrison and inhabitants, the impossibility of hindering {85} relieffe to the towne by sea without great paines, danger and greater tyme as the season of the year could permitt.

These reasons, though relevant enough, were received with some indignation from the Tzar and his counsell, who imagined the strangers able to produce and shew supernaturall meanes for gaining of the towne, and verily beleeved that the strangers would not use their utmost endeavours against the Sweds as their countreymen, they reckoning all strangers to be of one countrey.

This being knowne, one colonell offered to draine the ditch by a milne,

---

[262] Prince Yakov Kudenetovich Cherkassky (d. 1666), scion of a noble Kabardian family, Boyar, Voyevoda, one of the Tsar's chief commanders.

[263] Sir Alexander Leslie of Auchintoul (ca.1595?–1663), Scot who served Poland, Sweden and, from 1630, Muscovy. He headed the reform of the Tsar's army along Western lines, raising the so-called "regiments of foreign order", embraced Orthodoxy with the name of Avraam Ilyich, became Russia's first-ever general, and started a long pedigree of Russian Leslies.

which device was highly applauded, and he encouraged to practice it. But after he had toyled himself and many people 5 or 6 dayes, it was found by geometricall dimensions that the water in the river was higher as that in the ditch, and so was faine to desist.

After this the Tzar caused make preparation for his departure, sending his greatest artillery be water to Cockenhausen, which with great labour and difficulty they brought thither. The army {85v} marched along the river Dwina and was aflicted with many difficultyes and necessityes in passeing through the countreyes, which they had before burned and wasted. Being come into Russia, the Tzar went to Mosko with part of the army, the rest were sent to the garrisons in the conquests.

The King of Sweden in his returne from Varso towards Prussia hearing of the Moskoes Tzar his advancing into Liefland and beleaguering of Riga, commanded Felt Mar[s]hall Lieutennant Duglas with 3 or 4,000 men to go by sea to the relieffe of Riga, who being at the point of departure, newes was brought that the Tzar had deserted the siege. In the meane tyme the Swedish King gave audience to the Hollandish ambassadours in Frawensbergh, who offering their mediation *inter* Sweden and Polland, were dispatched thereafter with complements.

The King of Sweden being informed that the Tartars, who had been at the battell of Varso, were hovering in Littaw and intended {86} ane incursion into Prussia, advised the Elector of Brandeburg to send an army for defence of the borders, who sent thither *Graffe* Waldeck his generall with Duke Boguslaw Radzivill and 9 regiments. The King sent thither Maior Generall Israell with 4 Swedish regiments, who encamped at the brooke lock betwixt Raygrod and Augustowa[264],

October 8. where being attacted by Wincent Korwin Ganshewsky, Field Mar[s]hall of Littaw, with the Littawish army and these Tartars, after some weake resistance they were routed, many killed and taken, among whom were the Duke Radziwill and Maior Generall Israell with some colonells and many other officers. They gott all the ammunition and 7 piece of cannon, *Graffe* Waldeck himself hardly escapeing.

---

[264] Rajgród and Augustów.

Upon the notice of the Littawish army advancing towards Prussia the Sweds and Brandeburgs had drawne their forces together and were advancing towards the borders when, being advertised of this losse, they marched more circumspectly, exspecting more forces who {86v} were on their march from all quarters. And being gott together about 9,000 men under the command of Fieldmarshall Steinbock, *Graffe* Waldeck, Generall Maior Dorflinger and many great comanders, they suddainly set upon the Polls and Tartars at Philippova[265] in the instant when the Polls and Tartars were almost quarrelling about 8,000 reichs dollers, the ransome of the Duke Radziwill, who being in the custody of the Polls, the Tartars would needs have him or the money.

But by the suddaine and resolute attact of the confederats and their owne dissention they were routed, and Duke Radzivill escaped by the connivance or rather furtherance of Ganshewsky and the Polls, who were not such enemyes to their owne natives nor such friends to the Tartars, as to wish such a prince to fall into their hands. The Polls and Tartars retired without any {87} notable losse, as being all horsemen.

Oct[ober] 19. Some few dayes after this *Graffe* Konigsmarke comeing by sea with some forces out of the *stift* Bremen and Pomeren, and in a great misty calme being forced to cast anchor in the road befor Dantzick, was by the treachery of some of his people, who fled and gave notice to Dantzick, surprised and brought in prisoner to Dantzick. Upon his ship were two companies of Scotsmen who, being boorded almost ere they could see any body or know an enemy, offered to resist, but being most under hatches, were overpowred by the Dantzickers who had first covertly advanced in the ship, which the traitors had manned and taken into Dantzick, and so taken for ffriends untill they had grapled with them; who quickly dispersing those above deck, and being seconded by the sloups comeing in, quickly forced these below also. Some officers being in the cabinet with the generall, would have been at sallying out to make resistance, but were inhibited by him, who seing {87v} no good to be done, yeelded.

---

[265] Filipów.

No[vembe]r 2. This with the death of the Swedish Reichs Chancelour *Graffe* Erich Oxenstern, one of the greatest polititians of his tyme, much troubled the King of Sweden. The rest of the ships which were with Konigsmark, hearing of a noise and after by their sloups understanding what had passed, weighed anchor and came to the Pillaw.

The King with the Queene kept court in the channery of Frawensberg as well to be near to the Elector at the Littawish borders, from whence they had this tyme bypast exspected the fors[ai]d invasion. Generall Duglasse lay with an army in the Dantzicker Hooft as well to straiten the Dantzickers as to attend the diverting of the river Vistula from Dantzick into the Fresh Haffe or Lake, by sinking vessels full of stones and driveing in of great stakes and bindeing all with strong plankes, and to worke all the mischieffe possible. Because the indwellers of the Dantzicker *werder* refused to live in their houses and contribute {88} so largely as they required, they cutt the dikes or dammes wherewith the Vistula is kept in and drowned all that fertile and pleasant countrey so farr as in them lay. Yet God did not suffer this practice to have the desired effect, for in the spring thereafter, albeit the river did overflow a great part of the *werder*, yet did it force its passage in the right course notwithstanding all obstacles and opposition, and thereafter the[i]r dikes or dammes were repaired and all brought into the right channell.

But whilst the Sweds are busy here forrageing and plundering by their frequent partyes all the places about Dantzick, and useing all meanes to constraine the Dantzikers to syde with them or at least to be neutrall, the King of Polland, to prevent any thing of that nature and to confirme this his loyall citty, resolved in person to come thither, leaving such forces as he had gott togither to follow at leasure.

No[vembe]r 5. And so, on the 5th instant was received into Dantzick with great magnificence,

{88v} No[vembe]r 17. and on the 17th thereafter entertained royally by the *burgraffe* and presented from the citty with two tunne of gold. The Polls army came and encamped at Langenaw, about 2 miles from Dantzick, and by their forces regaine Konitz and overrun all Pomerell as farr as Stetin.

Hereupon the King of Sweden went to Grawdents and ordered a bridge to be made there over the Vistula, which was by the great shills of ice and stormy weather twice broken when it was near perfected, which misfortunes or apparent impossibility of makeing of it there produced a resolution of makeing it below, at the Meve, where, when all the timber was ready and most of it framed, the frosts became so violent that the river began to freeze over, which they helped by drawing webbs of linnen over the river and constantly watering of it, and in other places strowing straw thinne and watering of it, which in two or three dayes made the ice very thick and strong. So that the Sweds {89} army advancing out of their quarters with a competent artillery marched over the river safely, and by the Meve quartered two nights in the low countrey betwixt Meve and Dirshaw along the river.

The King of Sweden haveing somewhat refreshed his army, in the morning early drew them together and rendevouzed on the high *champaine* ground, and marching in good battaill order about a mile further, made a halt and caused fyre two piece of the biggest cannon wee had, being the Swedish signall, w[hi]ch was immediately answered with three shott from Dantzick, which troubled the King of Sweden a litle, disdaining that the Dantzickers and not the army should answer him, not considering that the King of Polland was in Dantzick.

After an houres stay in this place, from whence Dantzick, Dirshaw, both the *werders* and the Polls guards were to be seen, and the Polls army being but a mile from us not appearing, the King gave orders to march into the Dantzick *werder* and to make the head quarters at Stiblaw, the right wing at Leczko and the left at Gottland, the regiments of horse comeing

{89v} *Dec[emb]ris.* tymely into their quarters, the foot about two howres in the night, and the arrearguards about midnight. The Polls, considering the impossibility of fighting with the Sweds without foot or artillery, marched of in the night tyme, whereof the Sweds had notice in the fifth houre of the night by some fugitives.

Two howres befor day a strong party of the Sweds marched, takeing their way by Grebin towards Prust, from whence about halfe a mile, haveing gott certaine intelligence that the Polls were marched into Pomerell, they returned. And marching by Grebin, a stone house with a ditch belonging to the Dantzickers and manned with 60 men and a lieutennant, some voluntiers rode up in a bravado towards the castle and were shott at without harme. Three Scotsmen rode through all their shott to a house on the hithermost syde of the ditch, one whereof creeping in at a window, brought out good booty of cloaths, and for all their shooting returned in safety to the party, to the no small wonder and grudging of others.

Being returned to our quarters, my lord Cranston was ordered with a 1,000 foot to take in Grebin, whither {90} being come, he caused summon the commendant to render, who seeing all things prepareing and doubting releefe, rendred on condition to march of with their armes.

A prisoner brought this night informed that the Polls had sent in their artillery to Dantzick two dayes befor they marched of. Colonell Ashemberg[266] marched towards Pomerell with a party of 1,500 horsemen, and in the night tyme not farr from Konits falleth into the Polls quarters, fyreth some villages, ruineth D[uke] Dimitre Visniovitsky[267] his and other regiments, and retires with some losse and in great confusion to Sluchow, the trowpes haveing lost [each] other and their guides in the woodes, and persued hotly by the Polls.

1657

The French ambassadour l'Ombres mediating a peace, cometh from the King of Sweden to Dantzick with these overtures as preliminaries to a treaty to be holden at Studt Hoffe:

1. That no mediatours be admitted but the French ambassadours.
2. The King of Sweden will not treat apart, but with all his confederates, for whose ambassadours or commissaries he desireth passeports.

---

[266] Rüdiger von Ascheberg, commander of a cavalry regiment in the Swedish army.
[267] Prince Dymitr Jerzy Wiśniowiecki (1631–1682).

{90v} Januar.

3dly. The King of Sweden will treat jointly with the King of Polland and the states thereof.

4thly. That the treaty and accord be guarandired or surety given that all what is accorded shalbe kept and observed.

5thly. That Field Marshall Wittemberg and the officers detained at the rendition of Warshaw be released befor the treaty.

6thly. That the pretence the K[ing] of Polland hath to *Graffe* Bendt Oxensterne for his appearance be voyd and null, seing he was retaken in Varshaw by force and not dismissed.

The Great Chauncellour of Polland with others had been long ago commissionated to treat, and now the King of Sweden nominated *Graffe* Bengdt Oxenstern, the President Beerenklaw, Field Marshall Wrangell and *Graffe* Slippenbach his commissioners. The Polls, guessing by the high straine of the preliminaries the demands of Sweden, refused to accept of this treaty.

The King of Sweden marcheth to Marienburgh, leaving Field Marshall Lieutennant Duglasse with 5,000 men in the Dantzick-*werder* at Niew Kerch neer the Houft, where he vexeth the Dantzickers and ruineth their {91} *werders* with continuall incursions, one whereof was very notable, on the 4th of Januar, thus.

The Sweds did draw downe about 2,000 horse within a mile of Dantzick, whereof the Dantzickers haveing timely notice, drew out all their cavalliery and some foot, marched in strait ground among the ditches. The *werder* being most overflowed and frozen was so sliddery as glasse, which was a great advantage to the Dantzickers, their horses being sharpe shooed, whereas among the Sweds the tenth man was not able to go upon the ice, let be to charge and wheele, by reason of their badd and unshooed horses. So that when the Dantzickers advanced, the Sweds regiments stayed on a high ground, which was not overflowed, and sent out such as were best mounted: the Kings guard, the generalls lyfe company of Scots with two other trowpes of about 60 horse apeece were only the men could be made use of.

1657 135

The Dantzickers were neer 600 horse divided in 10 or 12 troopes, who in charging some tymes joyned 2 or 3 together. They continued chargeing and recharging with {91v} alternative fortune and without any signall advantage on either syde, only the Sweds gained alwayes ground. But one troope, persuing the Dantzickers too farr, was drawne into a place where 40 or 50 *snaphanes*[268] lay who, fireing lustily upon them, killed 6 men and some horses befor they could gett themselves cleared of them. At this rencounter a Scots corporall was killed and many of that company wounded, 14 more of the Sweds were killed and more as 50 wounded. Wee heard afterwards that of the Dantzickers 26 were killed and more as 60 wounded. It drawing towards evening, both parties marched of.[269]

Maior Generall Dankwort useth all meanes as befor to divert the course of the river Vistula from Dantzick, whereof the Dantzicker haveing informed the Hollands states, who order their ambassadour Maesdam to diswade the King of Sweden from it, seing it would be prejudiciall to the free commerce. To which the King answered, "If I do not molest Dantzicke, will the Dantzickers abstaine {92} from all hostility against me?" The Hollands ambassadour Isbrandt gave in a memoriall to the Elector of Brandeburgh concerning this also, but it was not the Electors interest to diswade it, because if that haven were spoiled, his Pillaw would fare the better.

In the tyme that the King of Sweden was with his army by Dantzick, the Massours haveing collected what forces they could make, fall into Prussia and do great harme, whither Field Marshall Steinbock is sent with a considerable force, who retaliates them, Duglasse being also commanded to Marienburgh and then further to wait on the Polls motions, who being at Gen-ll Steinbocks comeing vanished, the armyes returned; Duglasse being againe ordered with 400 men to ly at Whitekirch to wait upon the Dantzickers,

26. who in the absence of the armyes had taken in Grebin, killing and takeing 50 or 60 men therein, plundered Niewteich[270], Great Lichtenaw

---

[268] Here – marksmen.
[269] In this action Gordon was wounded in the head. See below, fol. 141 r.–v.
[270] Nytych.

and other places, takeing many prisone[r]s and killing {92v} many, especially sickmen in Lichtenaw who were not able to go along, where also they tooke away Gen-ll Duglasse his coach horses.

The King of Sweden had a meeting with the Prince Elector in Holland, where another treaty is projected to be in Brawnsberg. This same tyme the estates of Prussia represent and remonstrate to the Prince Elector many things wherewith he was not well pleased, not knowing how to amend them.

In the meane tyme the Roman Emperours minister d'Isola[271] cometh to Dantzick, desireing ratification of a treaty with Polland. At this tyme dyed in Dantzick Jacob Weyer, *Woywod* or Palatine of Pomeren, and Gen-ll Quarterm-r Percevall, commander in chieffe of the Hollands forces in Dantzick[272].

A party from Dantzick cometh and plundereth out Tolkamet[273]. Gen-ll Duglasse sendeth a maior to treat with the Dantzickers about prisoners at Grebin and to adjust about the prisoners, being 91, whom they had {93} dismissed 3 weekes ago.[274] After 10 dayes stay at Whitekerch Gen-ll Duglasse is remanded to Marienburgh, marcheth to Niewteich, where he stayeth 4 dayes, and then cometh to Marienburg. At this tyme Gen-ll Midleton came to Dantzick; the Scots lying in Dirshaw, most of them ran into Dantzick.

The Crowne Marshall Lubomirsky had the most part of this winter with ane army straitned Krakow, and haveing notice of the great preparations which the Transilvanian Prince Georg Ragotsky was makeing, dispatched two gentlemen, Stanislafsky, a kinsman of his owne, and Sobigorsky, a gentlman of his chamber,

Ja[nua]r 27. to Ragotsky with letters of credence and a very pathetick letter, diswadeing the prince from enterpriseing any thing against Polland; remonst[r]ateing the good opinion and affection which the nobility of

---

[271] Baron Franz Paul von Lisola (1613–1674), distinguished Imperial diplomat.
[272] In July 1656 Holland sent to Gdańsk an auxiliary corps of 1,300 men under General Peter Perceval.
[273] Tolkemit (German), Tolkmicko (Polish).
[274] Gordon was among these prisoners. See fol. 146.

Polland caryed to him, and assuring him that in case of the present King his death he should be the first in consideration; showing him also that the Polls were of such a mind rather all to dy as to be forced to any thing. Wherefor he wished and counselled him not to losse the good opinion the Polls had of him by makeing {93v} a hostile invasion, desireing the prince not to rely on the Swedish promises, allyance or power, but to consider the nature of the tymes, telling him that this summer would change the scene of the warr.

These gentlemen comeing to the prince, found all his forces drawing together towards Polland, but at the receat of these letters being uncertaine what to do, he mustered his forces and called a counsell, where the votes and advices varyed. However, he advanced with his army towards Monchats[275], where he passed the Carpathian mountains which divide Polland from Hungary. It was said that these gentlemen sent from Lubomirsky, when they did see the great preparation, forces and warlike furniture that the prince had, perswaded him to make hast, assureing him that he would find small or no resistance, and that notwithstanding the diswasive letter from Lubomirsky they were privately instructed to assure the prince of no hostility from him, wherewith being encouraged, he embarqued himself in this businesse now actually with more confidence.

In the beginning of February Czarnetsky, comeing with a strong party of light horsemen out of Polland, in his way betwixt Marienwerder and Grawdents happened on a party of 80 Sweds convoying ammunition to Thorne, all whom he takes and kills, and ruined such of the ammunition as he {94} could not get caryed along. Passeing the r[iver] Vistula,

Feb[ruary] 7. he came to Dantzick. Two dayes thereafter the French and Hollands ambassadours had audience by the King of Polland, who declared unto them that out of the desire he had to make an end of this warr, and so to stoppe the further effusion of Christian blood, he would renounce his hereditary right to the Crowne of Sweden and his hereditary lands there, and not use the title of King of Sweden in any thing concerning that Crowne, only to other princes, as also the armes, as being a

---

[275] Mukacheve, Ukraine (Hungarian: Munkács).

descendant of the royall family of Sweden. Yet if any difficulty should be made herein, the peace should not be hindred for that. Further, that he and the Republick of Polland were ready to renounce their right to all the lands, townes and places in Liefland possessed by the Sweden befor this warr by vertue of the Stumsdorfish treaty A.D. 1635, so as they both may use the title of Duke of Liefland. That, on the contrar, the King of Sweden may ingenuously declare what he will do on his syde to the furtherance of the peace. That His Majesty and the Republick of Polland maketh it evidently knowne and declareth that if the King of Sweden will not resolve to restore all he hath conquered in Polland and Prussia without any reservation of losses, expences, interest or other {94v} pretences whatsoever, they will no wayes condiscend to any treaty of peace. And what belongeth to the interest of the Elector of Brandeborgh, he was willing to condiscend to an amnestie of all things past in this warr.

The next day the King departed from Dantzick, marching through Pomerell and Great Polland to Czestochowa, whither most of the nobility came and in counsell concluded to call and hold a parliament there. From hence the King of Polland dispatched a messenger to the Port to complaine of the Prince of Transilvania for his invadeing of Polland.[276] And seing now small hopes of agreement, they concluded to hasten and conclude the treaty with the Roman Emperour for succour, as also invite Denmarke to breake with Sweden.

The King of Sweden haveing intelligence that the Prince of Transilvania had signed the treaty of alliance with him, and haveing rendevouzed his army was on his march to Polland, resolved to march and joine with him. Wherefor haveing taken the oath of allegeance from the citties of Prussia, he sends *Graffe* Slippenbach to the Elector of Brandeburgh for the promised forces to march into Polland with.

In the meane tyme Czarnetsky, being come to Dantzick for the King, made ane incursion into the great *werder* and burnt some villages, returning {95} the same day to Dantzick. This made the Sweden draw some forces together, not knowing what this suddaine returne of the Polls army

---

[276] Until the end of the seventeenth century Transylvania was under the suzerainty of the Ottoman Empire.

did meane and fearing some designe or other on some of the townes of Prussia, who were weary of the Swedish yoake, there haveing been some discontents perceived befor this, which were discovered by their complaints and remonstrances, and sensibly apprehended by the King at the secureing of the Polls Under Chauncellour Hieronimus Radziefsky, who to redeeme his former offences had practised with the Polls to deliver up Elbing and Marienburgh to them, as was said. Whereof the King getting information, caused secure him in the castle of Marienburgh, and now at the resolution of going for Polland ordered to send him to Sweden. Colonell Rosa wase [*sic*] secured also for speaking some words tending to mutiny and diminishing the reputation of the Kings armes.

But these thoughts of the Polls designes soone vanished with their departure from Dantzick with the King. {95v} The Sweds send a strong party over the Vistula to recognosce whither the Polls went, who retakeing Konits returne.

The King of Sweden at this tyme was in great perplexity. For albeit he had finished the accord with the Prince of Transilvania and entred into a more strict league with the Elector of Brandeburgh, who was also included in the allyance with the Transilvanian Prince, and so haveing divided Polland amongst them, as did some tyme the *Triumviri* the Romane Empire, the King being to have the Regall Prussia, Cashube[277] and Pomerell, the Elector of Brandeburgh – Great Polland and the Bishoprick of Warmia, and the prince to make himself King of Polland if he could; all which the King of Sweden, notwithstanding the year befor he had in hopes and almost in effect devoured the Kingdome of Polland, yet now seeing his owne inability and weaknes, was glad to gett the other two embarked in the quarrell, by dimitting that to them, which he knew he himself {96} was not able to keep, and doubted if the other two could. And albeit by these meanes his party was pretty well strengthened, yet there was appearance of great stormes from all quarters.

For he knew that the Polls were entring in a treaty with the Roman Emperour; that Denmarke was entred upon resolutions of makeing

---

[277] Kashubia.

warr and to that purpose had summoned a convention of the estates at Odenzee in Funen[278], whither he and the Elector of Brandeburgh had dispatched their respective messengers to desire a cathegorick answer in 24 houres whither the King of Denmarke would be friend or foe; who were dismissed without any answer, whereby no good could be expected. For the estates of Denmarke haveing really resolved on a warr, granted to the King 40,000 reichs thalers a month to continue for a year, makeing account to have 70,000 men in armes. And such alacrity they shewed that 15 Danish gentlemen promised and engaged each of them {96v} to levy a regiment upon their owne charges.

The Moskovite was in open warr with him in Liefland, and in possession of the best part of Littaw, the truce with Polland being not as yet expired. He knew also that the Turke would not permitt such ane accession of power and strength to fall to the Transilvanian. All these things considered, he ordered the transporting of his Queen for Sweden, and left the chieffe command in Prussia to his brother the Prince Adolph Johan, and with him the *Graffe* von Sultsbach and Felt Marshall Steinbock, who had a litle well formed army by Dantzick. He sent also some forces to Liefland, and the citties and strengths in Prussia well garrisoned. And so, haveing received 4 regiments of horse and dragouns under the command of the *Graffe* von Waldeck from the Elector of Brandeburgh, he ordered his owne regiments to march towards Thorne, Felt Marshall Lieutennant Duglasse haveing the avantgarde, {97} the King remaining behind in Marienborgh to dispatch the ambassadours of forreigne princes and other effaires of state.

The Sweds army with the 4 regiments belonging to the elector were in all about 6 or 7,000 men, all horse and dragounes with some light peeces of ordinance. The season of the year not permitting their encamping in the fields, the regiments for their better livelyhood and convenience marched diverse wayes, lodging in the villages which were not altogether ruined as yet. And truly, this was not one of the least perplexities which the King of Sweden had, that he had not wherewith to pay his army,

---

[278] Odense, Fyn island.

many whereof had neither good horse nor armes. For albeit of late he had receaved a subsidy of some tunnes of gold from France and out of Sweden, all that was litle enough to levy new regiments and recruits for his armyes, to furnish ammunition, maintaine the face of a court, and now and then give a 3d part *lenung*[279], as

{97v} March. they call it, to the foot regiments in garrisons lest they should be burthensome to the inhabitants, the horsmen both in garrison and fields living always by their shifts.

The army, haveing passed through Thorne and Soloyeva[280], encamped first together in the fields 2 miles from thence, and marching thereafter quartered in villages not farr from Cuiavish Brest, and so onwards to Kowalia, where some dayes were given to refresh the army and to exspect some regiments not come up as yet. From hence the army marched towards Sobota and quartered in the towne and adjacent villages.

17. Here the King receaved letters from the Prince of Transilvania, who at his entry into Polland by a short manifest proclaimed the reasons of his invasion being:

1. The just pretension which he had to the succession of the Crowne of Polland.

2. That notwithstanding the many good offices which he had done to the Kingdome {98} of Polland, the Polls estates had been offering their crowne to diverse, and had neglected him.

3. That he had been caressed and desired by diverse of the nobility and gentry to claime it, wherefor he was now come to desire the estates of Polland to declare themselves, which if they would not, he would persecute them with fyre and sword and all the calamities of warr. But if they would declare in his favour, he promised to maintaine all persons of whatsoever quality or condition by their priviledges, libertyes and immunities.

This was armed rhetorick, which could not but sound very harsh in the Polls eares. He had at his comeing in spared every where the lands of the

---

[279] Löhnung (German) – payment.
[280] Służewo.

Lubomirskyes, which gave and bred great suspicion among the Polls, and the more because it was reported that the Crowne and field marshall had sent from his leaguer at Crakow two gentlmen to the prince with letters to invite him to make this invasion. But some straglers {98v} of his army, being cut of by a party sent by the Crowne marshall and excluded out of Landshute, a castle well fortifyed and belonging to him, he caused fyre the towne of Landshut, and his lands thereafter suffer the same extremityes with others, and from thenceforth he had not the two gentlmen, Stanislawsky and Sobigorsky, in such esteeme and trust as befor.

At Sobota also the King of Sweden received intelligence that the Polls army was at Sandomirs, and that the Littawish army under their Generall Sapiha were marched from the borders of Prussia, where they had been attending the motions of the Sweds and Brandeburgians, towards Polland to joyne with the Crowne army. Here lykewise Generall Duglasse falling sick, was convoyed to Lovits, which being 12 miles from hence had a Swedish garrison still.

{99} After 3 dayes stay at Sobota the King marched towards Rava and then towards Peterkow[281], whither a great party of 2,000 horse was sent befor, who summoned the towne and was ansred by the commendant, Maior Lonsky, that he would not render it so lightly. So notice being given in all hast to the King, the army advanced, and being come befor the towne, after the artillerie was planted, the commendant came to a parley, and rendring the towne on tollerable conditions, marched out two dayes thereafter. The King left here rather a safeguard as a garrison, not willing to misse or rather losse men.

The army marched and quartered more closse as usuall, yet in villages. This night wee had a alarum and stood to armes the whole night, and gott intelligence the next day that the Polls army was marched by within halfe a mile of our quarters, takeing the way towards Sandomirs. Wee marched not early the next day and quartered about a myle and a halfe from thence.

{99v} Wee marched towards Predbors and from thence to Radoshits, where a message from the Prince of Transilvania came to the King. Here

---

[281] Piotrków.

wee had notice that the prince was encamped about 12 miles from thence, and had in his army about 20,000 Transilvanians, 5,000 Valachians, 5,000 Moldavians and 6,000 Cosakes; that he had 30 piece of cannon with him and 1,000 waggons with all sort of warlick ammunition.[282]

Here also did Maior Generall Wurts come to the King and received orders to deliver up the towne and castle of Krakow to the Prince of Transilvania when he should require it, and with the garrison march into Prussia or Pomeren, to whither he could come most convenient. Here wee had also notice that the Emperour of Germany Ferdinand the 3d was departed this lyfe; that his sonne Leopoldus, King of Hungaria and Bohemia,[283] was levying to compleet a field army to 32,000 men; that the Polls were now in great hopes of makeing {100} an alliance with this King and the House of Austria, to which they could never perswade the late Emperour to condescend. As I heard that after the battell of Varso he answered the Polls ambassadours thus: that in regard of the peace but lately made with Sweden and the welfare and quiet of the Roman Empire he could not breake with the Crowne of Sweden. Yet in regard of the interest and affection he caryed to the Crowne of Polland, he would use all meanes both himself and by his allyes to perswade or force Sweden to a peace in case of too unreasonable demands. In the meane tyme he would assist them with his best counsell and tell them that by no meanes they should hazard a sett battell with the Sweden, they wanting foot and good discipline, and the Sweds excelling both in the one and the other. Only he advised them with light and small partyes to cut them short of their {100v} forrageing, whereby in short tyme they should be redacted to small numbers and great necessityes, this being very easy for the Polls to do, who are a nimble and light kind of horsmen.

The army, marching from Radoshits, passed by Pienshow[284] where Ragotsy had a safeguard, and comeing into the Palatinate of Sandomirs, the King caused sett all the countrey in fyre in revenge of above a thowsand Sweds killed here upon safeguard in the countrey; and so in

---

[282] Cf. below, fol. 162 v.–163.
[283] Leopold I (1640–1705), Holy Roman (German) Emperor from 1658.
[284] Pińczów.

order to a conjunction with the Prince of Transilvania marcheth towards Swienty Krziz[285], the princes army marching some few miles of on our right hand, so that our forragers did often meet together and make acquaintance.

{101} Upon the last of March the Prince of Transilvania came and did meet with the King of Sweden by a village called Miedzibeze. The prince came along with the King and tooke a view of the army, which was drawne up in one front on a very advantagious peece of ground. The King and prince being clear of the front, two salvees were given, at the first whereof *Graffe* W[illia]m Adolph of Nassaw was killed befor his regiment by a great mischance, yet none knew by whom.

The army marched from hence to Zavichost, where a councell of warr being held, it was resolved to make a bridge over the river Vistula, and go and seeke out the Polls army who were said to be about Lublin. Eight dayes being spent in these consultations and makeing the bridge, the army marched alongst the bridge, and afterwards to Urzendowa[286]. Here intelligence was brought that the Polls were with their army by Varshaw, whereupon orders were given to burne all the superfluous baggage.

So the next day the army marched and passing by Lublin with strong and long marches towards Varshaw, {101v} being within a dayes march of it, wee had intelligence that the Polls were gone to Wengrowa[287] and towards Brest. Upon this the army removed to Wengrowa. Here the prince complained to the King of Sweden of the great theft and robberies commited by the Sweds upon his people. Redresse and justice was promised, and accordingly two who had stollen horses were hanged.

From hence the army marched to Krzemien. The Polls at our encamping appearing on the other syde of the river Bug, the K[ing h]imself mounted and with such as were at hand marched over, but the Polls quickly vanished. However most part of the army with the King stayed in the fields all night.

---

[285] Święty Krzyż.
[286] Urzędów.
[287] Węgrów.

From hence the army marched to Littawish Brest, which at summons refused to render, but after some shott of cannon at it they parlyed, and upon promises to be dismissed with their collours, armes and baggage they rendred.

May 6. So two dayes thereafter the *Castellan* Jawicky with Woyna and about 300 men, most *haydukes*, marched out and were convoyed to Parczew. Here wee {102} had intelligence that the Polls army was encamped by Sokal[288], whither the Prince Ragotzi was very earnest to follow them, but the next day brought other newes which vexed them all.

The King of Sweden being advertised of the great preparations the King of Denmarke had made both by sea and land, and that he was ready to fall in action, as also that the treaty betwixt the Crowne of Polland and the King of Hungary and Bohemia was as good as concluded, resolved to returne, wherewith the Prince Ragotzy was greatly surprized and grieved. However the armyes divide and march back to Krzemien, where some 8 dayes were spent in consultations and exspecting newes from the forces comeing out of Prussia. At last Felt Marshall *Graffe* Steinbock came, haveing left his forces at Sakroczin with 6 halfe cartowes[289] and a good deale of ammunition, one halfe thereof and more haveing been by accident blowne up in a wood, and about 80 men and many {102v} horses therewith killed. Maior Generall Gortsky[290] commanded the Brandeburghs forces who were with him.

The Prince Ragotzy haveing left a strong garrison in Crakow, and now another in Littawish Brest under the command of Maior Generall Gawdy, which townes were by vertue of the accord with the King of Sweden delivered to him, and it being now concluded to march to Varshaw, the regall seat of Polland, where it was said that Czarnetsky was hovering with a flying army, as well to attend the motions of these armyes, as to guard the convention of the estates or parliament now sitting in Czestochowa. The prince, I say, was, however, greatly perplexed to think that the King of Sweden should desert him, and he alone left to

---

[288] Probably Sokoły on the right bank of the Bug. Cf. fol. 173 v.
[289] *Cartow* (Scots) – cannon shooting a ball of a quarter of a hundredweight (12.7 kilos).
[290] Apparently, Joachim Rüdiger Goltz.

undergo the hazard of engageing with the Polls, Germans and Tartars, which last were said also to be come out of the Crime, and hearing also that the Felt Marshall {103} Lubomirsky was fallen in with ane army into Transilvania, where he aflicted that countrey with all the calamities of warr, and that the King of Polland had sent to the Port to complaine of his invasion of Polland, and that the Sultan[291] was not well pleased therewith.

All these indeed considered, it was no wonder if he were troubled, and that with some heate he expostulated with the King of Sweden for embarqueing him in that quarrell and now deserting him. But what could be done? He saw the King of Sweden in as great perplexity and environed with as great difficulties as himself, and nature teacheth that every one take best head to himself.

In the meane tyme, upon their approach to the Vissell, Czarnetsky made show of resisting their comeing over, but the Novodwor skonce in ane illand {103v} stood them in good stead. This skonce had been built the year befor whilst the Swedish army lay at Novydwor not farr from Zakroczin, and after the battell of Warso was given in keeping to Maior Alex[ande]r Anderson with about 200 commanded men out of diverse regiments. (This told pag. 152).[292]

He at his first entry had gathered in as much provisions as he could so long as the army lay about Warshaw. But especially he provided salt, whereof there was abundance in one of the Kings *sklades* or magazines near by, bringing it first to the river syde under the defence of the cannon and then at leasure into the illand. Of bread he had great scarsity in short tyme, whereof haveing advertised the King, he receaved orders to desert it and march downe the river to Thorne. But haveing sent to try if he could passe, it was deemed impossible, the Polls haveing so many illands below in the river wherein they lyved, and by others he was blocqued up. So that intelligence being gott of his departure, it had been impossible for him to have come thorow.

So being forced to manage his provisions so well as he could, at last

---

[291] Mehmed IV (1642–1693), Sultan of the Ottoman Empire from 1648 to 1687.
[292] In fact, Gordon repeats what he already told on fols. 79 v.–81.

the countrey {104} people being in great necessity for want of salt, and haveing learned from some prisoners who had ransomed themselves that there was abundance of salt in the skonce or fort, they made meanes for a treues. And so for salt he received cornes and what other provisions he had need of.

And now this being in the Sweds power, was a great help for the speedy makeing of a bridge over the river. Czarnetsky with his Polls seeing it earnest, marched of in tyme towards Czenstochowa, where a project was for levying of a good army of foot and horse under the command of stranger officers, which afterwards by the pious concessions of the spiritualty tooke effect.

The King of Sweden with the prince and their armyes remained 8 dayes in Warshaw consulting about their effaires, but being both alike necessitated to separate, they parted, seeming good ffriends. The King of Sweden, after the houses in Warshaw which were distributed among the officers were made bare, passed the r[iver] Vistula at Zakroczin and went through the Massowr

Junii v. 3/n. 13. to Strasburgh,

{104v} June v. 8/n. 18. and from thence to Thorne, where he exspecteth the *Grave* von Sultsbach from the Elector of Brandeburgh and the forces, which he had ordered and resolved to take along with him.

The Roman Emperour being deceassed in March, his [son] Leopoldus, King of Hungaria and Bohemia, entred in a strict allyance with the Polls on the following articles:

1. A perpetuall peace shall be betwixt both partyes.

2. The King of Hung[ary] and Bohem[ia] granteth to the King of Polland a succurse and assistance of 16,000 men with sufficient artillery.

3. This army, so long as it shall be needfull in Polland, shal be at the devotion and under the command of the King of Polland, and the joyning with the Polls army be at His M[ajesty's] discretion, yet so that it be dependant on the Kings Ma-tie and on none of the Polls generalls.

4. The King of Polland shall dureing their stay in Polland furnish this

army with provisions and ammunition, and to this purpose a Polnish commissary shall be by them. {105}

5. As to their *stipendium* or pay, the King of Polland shall give the salt mines *assecurationis loco*[293], that the King of Hung. and Boh. shall have in consideration of the expences in the raising of this army in these salt mines a summe of 500,000 ducates, yet that this summe be not payable at once, but in ten yeares.

6. Both Kings to have their administrators in these mynes, and the army to be payed out of the profits of these mines, and the superplus to be dealt together betwixt the two Kings.

7. In case the rents of these mines do not amount to the paying of the fors[ai]d summe of 500,000 ducates and the maintenance of the army, then shall the King of Hung. and Boh. be secured in the pretensions and interest, w[hi]ch the King of Polland hath in the Dukedomes of Opolia and Ratibor[294] so farr as the other security and profits or rents shal be found defective.

8. Such places as shall be taken in by this Austrian army shal be garrisoned by the same to the end of the warr *salvo tamen numero praememorati succursus*[295].

9. Neither party shall make peace or warr without consent of the other. {105v}

10. To this alliance shal be admitted the Princes of the House of Austria, Denmarke, Holland, Musko, Tartars, the Electors and Princes of the Empire if they will, especially the Elector of Brandeburgh with this condition: to restore *ablata*[296], separate from the Sweden and joyne with Polland as a vassall of that Kingdome.

So done May 27, 1657, in Vienna.

This treaty and allyance being concluded, the offer of the French ambassadour l'Ombres for a treaty in the behalfe of the Sweds on condi-

---

[293] In stead of security (Lat.).
[294] Racibórz.
[295] Saving, however, the number of the aforementioned auxiliary force (Lat.).
[296] Things seized or stolen (Lat.).

tion that all the Swedish confederates should be included was rejected, the King of Polland denying to come to any treaty without the consent of the King of Hungaria and Bohemia and his other confederates, and that befor any treaty the Sweds should avoyd his territories.

Czarnetsky, haveing a litle befor retaken Peterkaw from the Sweds, was made by the King *Woywod* of Russia.

The Prince Ragotsy after parting with the King of Sweden at Warshaw made no stay, but marched away and crossed the river Vistula at Casimirs. And haveing notice that {106} the Austrian army was already advanced into Polland, and that Lubomirsky, who had done great harme in Transilvania, in his returne had besett and strongly garrisoned all the Carpathian streights; that the whole countrey of the Podgures[297] were up in armes to hinder or retard his march untill the Austrian army should come; being afrayed to be coped up and environed with these forces, and perswaded by the Cosakes, who were with him and commanded by one Anthon Collof, he declined to the left hand.

The Cosakes promised to conduct him and sent for more forces wherewith they said they would force a passage into Transilvania near to their owne countrey. But, as the poet said, *incidit in Scillam cupidus vitare Charibdim*,[298] so it fell out with the Transilvanians. For being advanced to the borders of Podolia, the Cosakes haveing notice from their countreymen that the Crimish Chan[299] with his Tartars were come into the Ukraina, they deserted the prince and run all home. Yet by such as haveing been out seeking victualls the prince had intelligence of the Tartars being come into the Ukraina, which put him in a greater perplexity as befor. But there being {106v} no tyme to advise long, he marched with great hast towards the right hand againe.

Much about one tyme intelligence was brought that the Tartars and Polls were very neere, wherefor in these difficulties seing litle possibility

---

[297] Podgórze – southern Poland, adjacent to Carpathian mountains.
[298] He falls to Scylla who wants to avoid Charybdis (Lat.) – a quotation from the late 12th-century epic poem *Alexandreis* (V, 301) by Walter of Châtillon. In the original it runs, "Incidit in Scyllam qui vult vitare Charybdim".
[299] Mehmed IV Geray, Khan of Crimea (ruled 1641–1644, 1654–1666).

of getting safe away, in a counsell of warr it was concluded to send and capitulate with the Polls. There was no tyme to treat long, the Transilvanians readily condiscending to any thing the Polls desired. Neither were they unreasonable, so agreeing that all prisoners on both sides should be let free, the townes w[hi]ch the prince held garrisoned in Polland restored, the garrison souldiers to be convoyed to the borders of Transilvania with their collours, armes and their baggage, which they had brought into the countrey with them. For the harme done in Polland the prince is to pay [...] millions of ducates, for fulfilling of which two chieffe noblemen to remaine hostages.

Lubomirsky promised to cause convoy the prince and such as he would take along with him, but for the whole army he would not engage, because the Chan with all his forces were so near, whom he

{107} Aug[ust] 11.[300] durst neither irritate nor disoblidge. Only he promised not to assist the Tartars and in case of a mischance to mediate for favourable usage. These concluded, subscrived, ratifyed and the hostages delivered, the same night the prince with about 1,500 horse marched away and was convoyed in safety by the Polls to his countrey.

The army the next day marched in good order, but full of bad humors because the prince had left them, and in great perplexity, being apprehensive of the danger and difficulties they were fallen into. The chieffe command rested in the Generall Comineanus[301], a nobleman of good courage and experience, who, as it was said, albeit the prince desired and gave him liberty to go along, would not desert the army.

Befor evening the forragierers were beat into the army by the forrunners of the Tartars. By day light the army marched againe, keeping very closse to their *waggonburg*[302], and attacqued now and then by some companies of the Tartars. About midday the Chan with all his forces, being

---

[300] This date refers to events described below, when many Transylvanians became prisoners of the Tatars.
[301] János Kemény (1607–1662) after two years in Tatar prison and death of György II Rákóczi in 1660 was elected Prince of Transylvania. He fell in battle with the Turks.
[302] Wagenburg (German) – a temporary, movable fortification made of army waggons.

about 60,000 men, came {107v} and presented himself befor them, and immediately gave a fearfull charge on them upon all quarters, thinking to breake them. Yet the Hungarians resisted most valiantly and repulsed them diverse tymes that day, forceing them with their great and small shott to keep farther of. The night they passed in great anxiety, being so pent up as they had scarce grasse for their horses and bestiall. Neither did the Tartars allow them any rest, but alarumed them by horrible cryes and shoutings.

By day light they marched and all this day were furiously assaulted by the Tartars who strove to break them, wherefor they were forced to make diverse stands. Many were killed and wounded on both sydes, yet the greatest loss was on the Hungarian syde for the Tartars in their passing by let such showres of arrowes fly, as the day was obscured thereby. They made no great progresse this day, and the night affoorded them but litle rest, being harder pent up as befor. Here they left many waggons, the horses and oxen which drew them being killed, and buryed some of their heavyest cannon that they might be the {108} more expedite to march.

The next day they marched through the same difficulties and a litle after midday came to a litle towne and castle called Mezeboze[303], scituate in a pleasant valley and marish. Here they stayed the night and the next day, being not much infested by the Tartars. Here they consulted what course to take. Some advised to stay there and weary out the Tartars, but the want of provisions for man and horse soone dashed that designe. Besides they were not to expect relieffe from any, for albeit the prince at his departure promised to raise the whole countrey and come to their assistance, yet the better and wiser sort had litle faith or hope in that. Many there were that advised to capitulate for a great summe of money and give hostages, but this was strongly opposed by the more resolute. At last it was resolved to march in maugre of all opposition, hopeing in few dayes to come to such straight ground as might be disadvantagious to the Tartars, they being all horsemen. Neither had the Tartars for all their vigorous charges ever broken them, and now being indifferent well acquainted with their way of fighting, they were in good hopes by resolution to withstand

---

[303] Unidentified place. The Ukrainian town of Medzhibozh is too distant to be meant here.

all their assaults and march {108v} whither they pleased.

So haveing ordered and disposed all in the best manner they could, in the 3d houre of the day they marched away, being about halfe a mile from the towne and furiously assaulted by the Tartars, whom however they valiantly repulsed. Yet the foot who did the best service and were at greatest paines, being most Moldavians, whither seeing among the Tartars many in the habite of Turkes (which stratagem to terrify them the more the Turkes[304] used), or despairing of effecting what was intended, in an instant revolted and went over to the Tartars. This so unexpected accident so astonished the Hungarians as they were a long tyme irresolved what to do. Yet the imminent danger not admitting formalities and orderly consultations, without order and almost in confusion they returned back to the towne, where they entred into serious consultations what course they should take.

The Tartars, being now assured of the victory, resolved, seing the Hungarians could not long hold out for want of provisions, to attact them no mor but only to block them up and keep from fetching in provision or forrage. This day and the next there were some light skirmishes betwixt {109} them, but on the third the Hungarians, despairing of help or freeing themselves, unanimously resolved to capitulate. And so accordingly, it being the 11th of August, they came to a parley, w[hi]ch was soone ended, for the generall and some of the p[rinci]p[a]ll men of the army going out themselves, they were detained by the Tartars, and immediately orders sent to the army to render themselves prisoners of warr. There being no remedy, the Hungarians marched out and delivered their colours and armes, and being lightened of all that they had, were all carryed into the Crim, and afterwards ransomed themselves with great summes of money.

The German army being come into Polland, near the promised number, under the command of N. Hattesfeld as generall[305]. The generall persons wer Feld Marshall Sparre, *Graffe* Montecucculi[306] Lt. Generall over

---

[304] Clearly, Tatars are meant.
[305] Count Melchior Hatzfeld von Gleichen (1593–1658), Imperial field marshal.
[306] Count Raimondo Montecuccoli (1609–1680), Italian commander and military theorist in Austrian service, promoted to field marshal in 1658.

the cavalierie, Susa Lt. G-ll of the infanterie, M[ajor] G-lls Hester and [...]. They advanced towards Crakow, whither being come, the generall sent two trumpets, one to the Sweds, the other to the Hungarians {109v} or Transilvanians. To the Sweds it was told that they had no orders from the King of Hungaria and Bohemia to use any hostility against, wherefor if the governour, according to the orders which he knew he had, would march away out of the castle and towne, he promised to cause conduct them safely to any of the neerest places of the Swedish territories. Which, if refused, then desired he that the Sweds would not assist the Hungarians, whom he had orders to force out of that place, and if they assisted them, he would be compelled, though unwillingly, to proceed with all hostility against both. The Swedish governour Maior Gen-ll Wurtz, a wise man and expert souldier, excused himself from marching out of the castle (which he only had in possession, haveing according to order delivered the towne to the Hungarians), so long as the Hungarians were in the towne, and promised not to give them any assistance.

The Hungarians were required to avoide the towne, which if they would do befor the artillerie should be planted, it was promised that they {110} should be safely convoyed with all what was their owne to the neerest place of their countrey, which they refused. So the Germans artillerie not being come as yet, some dayes were spent in skirmishing and sallyes, wherein some of the Sweds being taken, they were returned to the governour into the castle with admonition not to permitt his people to joyne with the Hungarians and use hostility, which he, excuseing, promised.

The King of Polland being come to the German army befor Crakow, and haveing received the order and warrant which the Prince of Transilvania had given for the rendition of Crakow, he sent it to the governour, who calling a councell of warr, wherein obedience was resolved, they sent to desire a meeting for capitulateing. W[hi]ch being granted, and the ordinary military conditions accorded,

Aug. 22. the Hungarians marched out and were safely convoyed to their countrey. The Sweds also accorded and marched out of the castle with cannon, ammunition, collours flying, drums beating and trumpets sounding, being under 26 foot collours about 1,500 men, 2 companies of dragownes {110v} 80 men, 12 companies of horsemen 672 men, commanded horsemen and musquetieres by the baggage 500, baggage waggons 317, 27 coaches, 46 *colesses*, 132 led horses, 221 women on horseback and on foot. The[y] were convoyed by 9 trowpes of German horse. Czarnetsky haveing notice of their march, followed them with 6,000 horsemen, but could not overtake them. So misseing them, he made an incursion into Pomeren and did great harme there.

Crakow being rendred, the King of Polland with the Imperiall army marched towards Prussia. Maior Gen-ll Gawdy at this tyme, haveing receaved orders from the prince, rendred Littawish Brest to the Polls, and was with his garrison after the usuall military manner convoyed safely to Transilvania.

But to returne to the Sweds. Whilst the King was up in Polland, the fort called Dantzicker Hooft was attempted by Grudzinsky with 5,000 Polls and Dantzickers in vaine. However they blocked it up, untill now by the approach of the King and army into Prussia they marched of. {111}

The *Graffe* von Sultsbach being returned from the Elector of Brandeburgh with small assurance of constancy from that prince, and the regiments which the King resolved to take along with him being conveened, and all things ordered after the best and liklyest way he could for the preservation of Prussia, the King marched from Thorun (walking on foot alongst the bridge accompanied with the magistrates) on the 4th of July. Takeing his march to Bramburgh and to Stetin, he had befor sent Duglasse, who was made felt marshal, and Henrich Horne, being made lt. generall, and Gustaw Gabriel Oxensterne, maior generall, to Sweden to gather forces and secure the borders of Sweden from Danmarke and Norway.

In Prussia were left Prince Adolph Johan, the *Palsgrave*, being Generallissimus, *Graffe* Bent Oxensterne, Feld Marshall Lorentz von der Linde, the yong *Margraffe* von Baden, the Major Generalls Bilaw[307], Dankwort and Wirtzburg. The forces left in Prussia were in Thorun 3,600, in Strasburgh 1,200 with those from Newmarke, {111v} in Grawdentz 800,

---

[307] Bertold Hartwig von Bülow.

in Stume 100, in Marienburgh 2,500, in Dantziker Hooft 1,800, in Elbing 3,000; in all about 13,000. In Thorun *Graffe* Bent Oxensterne commanded as governour, M. G-ll Bilaw commendant, in Strasburgh Colonell Pleitner, in Grawdentz Colonell Puchar, in Stume Coll. Anderson, in Marienburgh Coll. Duderstat commendant; the Generallissimus himself resided here for the most part; here was also M. Gen-ll Wirtzburg. In Dantziker Hooft M. Gen-ll Dankwort commanded, in Elbing Felt Marshall von der Linde governour and the *Margraffe* von Badden commendant. They had also at this tyme diverse other small townes and castles garrisoned, as Touchel[308], Konits, Swetz, Meve, Lipinky, Dirschaw, Newmark, Goluby, Kovaleva and Monto Spits, all which they shortly deserted except the last.

Yet the number of these men in the garrisons decreased dayly by sicknesses and running away. I heard it said that the King gave expresse orders to desert Towchel and Konits to the end that the Polls takeing possession of these places, all hopes should be taken away from these who intended to run out of Prussia into Pomeren. {112}

It is worth the consideration to know how these garrisons were maintained, it being well knowne that the revenues or supplies from Sweden were too litle to maintaine the face of a court, the expences of publick ministers, furnishing of ammunition, gratifying the chieffe and generall persons, and in such an exigence as this warr with Denmarke to furnish money for new levyes and recruits and give a largesse to the souldiers, who were altogether disarmed and dismounted, for furnishing themselves with armes, horses and cloaths. The supplyes from France and England came to the King where he was, nothing from any place was brought to Prussia. It must mantaine itself, which was a very hard matter, the souldiery being hungred and the people harryed, for the countrey with the great armyes roaming up and downe was much wasted and depauperated. All trade and intercourse with other countreyes or places failed, the great herds of cattell driven downe out of Polland brought a murraine on these in Prussia.

The magazines in the townes were indeed furnished with good store of cornes, which affoorded the souldiers two pund of bread a day and

---

[308] Tuchola.

a kan of beere. Very pityfull stuffe, their service, as they call it, which is fyre and candle, salt and sower, in such {112v} places where any thing was to be had, the landlords well conditioned, and few quartered, gave some help. They gathered in contribution from the countrey, especially out of the *werders*, as long as they were able to give any thing. The foot sojors in many places had sometymes a reichs thaler or 3 florens a month, and the horsmen now and then a largesse, and the officers accordingly. Notwithstanding all this, there was great necessity among persons of all quality at the last.

After the King of Swedens departure from Prussia the Swedish effaires began to ebbe, they being cutted short on all hands. The first who shewed themselves were the Massowres who, adventuring over the river Dreventz[309] at a foord, tooke away the governours horses and refused to give any contribution. The Sweds in Thorun haveing notice that they were gathering to a head, sent out Colonell Drake with 500 horse and 200 dragouns to discover their number and designes, and if occasion offered to fight them. The Massowrs haveing by their espialls notice of the Sweds being marched over the r[iver] Dreventz, drew together about 300 horse and 200 pawres on foot, and haveing intelligence how they had lodged themselves by the edge of a wood in a field without any advantage, came very closely and about day {113} light with a great noise did fall in on all sydes, and without much ado routed them, haveing them in chase over the Dreventz untill within a mile of Thorun. The Swedish horsmen made diverse halts, otherwise not a man of the dragouns had escaped. Yet a weeke or two thereafter the Sweds beat a party of the Massours and gott some prisoners wherewith they relieved those who were taken in the former surprise.

The Lord Cranstowne haveing obtained liberty from the King to returne to Scotland, and diverse Swedish officers, who had stayed behind the King and were ordained to follow him, went with a convoy from Thorun and were safely brought to Pomerell.

The Sweds haveing a garrison in Dirshaw and a bridge over the r. Vistula neer the towne, kept all the Dantzik-*werder* almost under contribution,

---

[309] Drwęca.

which was a great losse, hinderance and eye-sore to the Dantzikers. Wherefor they resolved to ruine the bridge and surprise the garrison at Dirshaw. So marching out with 2,000 men and upwards horse and foot very privately, they came near Dirshaw undescryed by any, as they thought. Yet the generallissimus, who lay on the other syde of the bridge in the great *werder*, haveing notice of {113v} their march some houres befor, marched over and stood in good order attending them, haveing not about [*sic*] 1,500 men.

The Dantzickers, whither because of the mist or to refresh their souldiers, being drawne up in order on the high ground, made a halt, in which tyme by great chance and good luck for the Sweds, *Graffe* Waldeck with about 1,000 horsemen being on his march for Pomeren came thither, whom the Sweds perswaded, though with some reluctancy, to syde and engage with them.

The mist clearing up, the armyes were gott so near one another they could not gett of without fighting, neither booted it to think of a retreat. So to it they went, and for ane houre and more it was disputed very hotly, untill the Dantzickers, overpowred at last, retreated into the *werder* at first in some order; yet at last were brought into confusion, especially the horsmen, being not a third part so many as the Sweds and Brandeburgers. Being come into the *werder*, the strait ground, it being all ditched, helped the foot to gett of. The horsmen also made diverse stands at the bridges, whereby the foot gott leasure to shift away. About 300 of the Dantzickers were killed and taken, some collours, 4 cannon shooting bullets of 12 pund, 3 field pieces and all their ammunition with many armes.

{114} Sept[embe]r. This passed, *Graffe* Waldek kept on his march to Pomeren, and as it was said, had notice of the Elector of Brandeburgh his haveing taken a truce for 6 weekes with Polland and confederats. Neither was the Elector well content with him for giveing so ready assistance to the Sweds.

About the same tyme one of the *Graffes* of Waldek was killed in the Massour, and Coll. Rosa and Maior Klinger were executed in Marienburgh, the first for treasonable speeches, and the other for playing fast and loose in the levying of souldiers.

The Polls armyes advancing into Great Polland, had Calis and Posen rendred to them. Gonsiewsky also with the Littawish army advanced towards Prussia, which oblidged the Electour to looke to himself. He had no hopes of any vigorous assistance from the Sweds and knew the Polls with the Germans would be too hard for him, and that his countrey must needs be ruined. Wherefor by meanes of the Baron d'Isola a conference was had betwixt the Elector of Brandeburg and Gonsievsky at the Wellaw[310] and a truce accepted for 6 weeks, in which tyme they were to treat.

19. Neither did that treating last long, a peace being concluded the 19th *Septembris* {114v} upon the following conditions:

1. A firme and perpetuall peace to be betwixt the King and Republick of Polland and the Elector of Brandeburg.

2. Whereas the King of Polland hath had the halfe of the Pillavish toll, it shall be now altogether the Electors.

3. The Elector shal be released of the yearly acknowledgment he was oblidged to give to the King of Polland upon the acco[un]t of the Dukedome of Prussia.

4. No appeales from any of the Dukes vassalls or subjects in Prussia to be to the Polls court, as formerly.

5. The King of Polland accepteth of the Dukes mediation betwixt him and the King of Sweden.

6. The Duke shall not only breake his league with Sweden, but shall if need require give assistance to Polland for regaining of Prussia.

So done at Welaw in Prussia *A. Dni* 1657 *Sept[emb]ris* 19.

Commissioners for Polland were:
Venceslaus de Lesno *Episcopus Warmien[sis]*[311]
Vincentius Corvinus Gosiewsky *Thesaurarius et Campiductor M.D.*

---

[310] Welau – modern Znamensk, Russia.
[311] Bishop of Warmia (Lat.).

Lith[uaniae][312]
>Franciscus d'Isola *Ser[enissimi] Regis Hung[ariae] et Bohemiae, ablegatus pro mediatione*[313]
>{115} Commissioners for the Elector were:
>Otto *liber Baro a Schwerin*[314]
>Laurentius Christophorus Somnits

This treaty was ratifyed in Bramburgh on the 6th of November thereafter, and grounds laid for a nearer and mor strict allyance.

The Polls with the German army marching at leasure downe towards Prussia, the first act of hostility that did fall out betwixt the Sweds and them was at Strasburgh, Field Marshall *Graffe* Duglasse his lyfe company being ruined, the *ruitm-r* and 11 being killed and 14 taken, most whereof were wounded.[315] Upon w[hi]ch the army advanced and leaguered on the Cuiavish or Polnish side of Thorun, and haveing played some dayes on a fort at the end of the bridge, after they had levelled it almost with the ground, they tooke it by storme and in it a Scots lieutenant with about 20 men. Here they did ly about three weekes, some regiments of horse lying in the Massowre and infesting all the places on the Prussia syde of the river Dreventz. At last about the midle of November they dislodged and marched into Great Polland to their quarters.

None did more harme or vexe the Sweds more in Prussia at this tyme as one Michalko, who being a peasants or pawres son in {115v} Prussia had served the Sweds in the quality of a trowper and corporall. Being taken by the Polls in the monastery Pe[l]plin, or as the Sweds said, run away from them, he first gott together some loose people, and being well acquainted with all the wayes and by-roads, he gott good booty of the Sweds, makeing his retreat allwayes to Towchel, Konits or Sluchow. And the Imperialists or Germans being now come into Prussia and keeping Thorun blocked

---

[312] Treasurer and Field Hetman of the Grand Duchy of Lithuania (Lat.).
[313] Envoy for mediation of the Most Serene King of Hungary and Bohemia (Lat.).
[314] Free Baron from Schwerin.
[315] The wounded included Gordon himself. For a detailed description of events on 1 October 1657 see fols. 187–191 below.

up, he gott a number of people together, and garrisoning the castles of Stargard[316] and Lipinky, with a trowpe of light horsemen he skowred up and downe the countrey, doing every where great harme and surprising the Sweds even at the gates of their garrisons like a thunder, and getting away againe no man knew whither, when the first newes that was to be heard of him was that he had done harme in another place and was gone.

But the German army being retired from Thorun, and he come to his garrison of Stargard to consult what course to hold, the Sweds of Thorun haveing notice, marched out in the night tyme and by day light environed the castle, w[hi]ch being unprovided, and not in posture of makeing any long defence or resistance,

{116} No[vembe]r 20. yeelded on condition to have their lyves spared and to be let go free, w[hi]ch was kept. Only Michalko, who went under the title of *ruitmaster*, was detained as a fugitive from the Sweden and sent to Marienburg, where a councell of warr was held upon him. And like enough, albeit there were no very clear evidences, it would have gone hard enough with him, if tymely intercession had not come from the King of Polland for him, which being refused at first, the next tyme was persued with threats of retaliation. So he was dismissed and returned to his old trade, doing more harme as befor. The King of Polland nobilitated him and gave him a commission (w[hi]ch he had not befor), confirming him *ruitmaster*.

1658

The Sweds haveing taken in Lipinky, put Lt. Coll. Bomesdorffe with about a 100 men in garrison therein, and so were not much molested unlesse by the fores[ai]d Michaelko untill the beginning of February, when Maior Generall Hester, comeing with 4,000 horse and dragouns and intending to crosse the Vistula above Monto Spits, whilst the army was drawne up, he rideing over himself with 6 horsemen to view the ground,

---

[316] Starogard.

was surprised and taken by a {116v} Swedish cornet, who was lurking in a thicket near by. Litle resistance was made, the Sweds being choice men sent out of purpose for intelligence. It was not much above a musket shot from the army where he was taken, yet for all the hast they made, they could not get the Sweds overtaken, who haveing gotten such a prey, made all the hast they could to Marienburgh.

After the maior generall was taken, one Spanko, a colonell of dragowners, had the chieffe command, who marching by Stum and Aldmark encamped in a large village by the Elbings *werder*, where he stayed two weekes and, forraging the *werder*, lost many men. He marched afterwards into the Bishopdome of Warmeland, where he stayed the rest of the winter, sending partyes and makeing inroades into the *werder* and countrey about Marienburgh and Elbing.

The Polnish generall commissary, or *pisar polny*, as they call him, Jan Sapiha, came with 3,000 horsemen and wintered in Colum[317], where with small parties he kept the Sweds in Thorun and Grawdents in continuall excercise, the Sweds not daring to come near his garrison, because they were not well mounted and not able to bring {117} out so many men as to make good a retreat in case of a misfortune, so that there passed not any action of note in that quarter all this spring.

The Polls holding a *seym* or parliament in Varshaw, great debates were amongst them about the carrying on of the warr. The Sweds were no mor masters of the fields, but were couped up in garrisons, all very strong and well fortifyed townes, which could not be taken with their horsmen. A good body of German foot of the Imperialists they had, but that was insufficient, and against the nature of true allyance to set them to work alone. To cary on the warr jointly they must levy foot, w[hi]ch was found not only convenient but necessary by all. The number, but especially the meanes to levy them tooke up more tyme. At last they condiscended on the numbers being 14,000 foot, 3,000 horsemen and as many dragowners, all under stranger officers and discipline, besides the recruiting of some old regiments which they had.

---

[317] Kulm (Chełmno).

This number might well be said to be (as it was) no wayes proportionable to their abilities, yet very agreeable with the exigencies and necessity of their effaires. For when they came to fall upon the meanes of raising and maintaining them, nothing but {117v} grievous complaints, moanings and bewailings were heard of the ruined and altogether wasted state of their countrey. Neither would they of the lower house hear of any impositions, taxations or contributions, all pretending inability and impossibility.

In this perplexity the spirituall estate, haveing befor consulted amongst themselves, arose and by the mouth of the Archbishop of Genesna made a long speach to the King and estates, the substance whereof was: that the Catholick church in Polland by the devout liberality and pious donations of their predecessours was brought into such a lustre as a more splendent was no where to be seene. Their office-bearers, monasteries and cathedralls so endowed with revenues, their churches so enriched with ornaments, that no kingdome of Europe could bragge of better. That seeing, by the iniquity of the tymes and prevalent power of so many enemyes, the state was redacted to so low a condition, they had considered what might or could be done on their part for giveing a vigorous supply and sussulcting the state in its present great necessityes. For, he said, as the church had hitherto been defended, and exspected still to be by their valours, so it were no more as reason that the church should affoord such helps {118} as was incumbent, that is to pray for them and give such maintenance as they were able. He said moreover that the publick revenues being morgaged, the people and countrey altogether wasted and impoverished, recourse must be had to extraordinary courses, not doubting but what they were about to do would be acceptable to God and imprint in the minds of them and their successours a pious remembrance of what they now did.

So ane act was condiscended to amongst themselves, that all the silver and plate which served rather for decorment then use, reserving only for each cathedrall two chalices and two patins, and for other churches but one, should be given to the state to coine money with, which came to some millions. The great prelates also gave large summes of ready coyne, which was done with such alacrity and so liberally, that it was not found needfull to impose any taxation on the people.

Thus let not statesemen or wor[l]dly persons envy or carpe at the riches of the church or the office-bearers therein. For it is always the surest anchor and pillar of a state and a certaine refuge for princes. Besides, the hospitality of the spirituality to all, and the lenity and ease they give to those who live in their lands, is very pleasant and profitable to a state, and it is well knowne that poverty bringeth {118v} contempt and misregard on persons of all qualities, especially on churchmen, which should by no meanes be, seing reverence and respect is due to men of their coat. And how can it be possible, that when churchmen ar in poverty and troubling their minds how to gett themselves provided of necessaries, but that they must be distracted from their devotions and be forced sometymes to use unseemly, yea, sometymes unlawfull shifts, which openeth a doore to confusion and atheisme?

Moreover the Polls concluded at this *seym* also to invite the King of Denmarke and Elector of Brandeburgh with other princes to a strict allyance against the Sweds, and resolve to prosecute the warr with all vigour. The Great Dukedome of Littaw, though makeing on body with Polland, yet in such cases of levies bringing up their quota proportionably, did by the same meanes levy a competent number of foot, horse and dragowns with great alacrity.

The garrison of Thorun haveing a designe upon Bramburgh, sent a strong party of horse and foot thither, and surpriseing the towne without any resistance, plundered it out, getting good booty.

Maior Generall Grodshitsky, lying in the Meve with the old regiments of Polls foot quartered there and thereabouts, {119} not to be idle, resolved to take Lissawes skonce and fortify it, thereby to put the Great *Werder* under contribution and hinder the intercourse of the Sweden from Marienburgh and other places to Dirshaw. So with great secrecy and silence drawing their forces together, they passed the Wistula and began to repair and fortify the skonce and to make a bridge over the Wistula working day and night thereat, w[hi]ch continuing for some dayes befor the Sweds were aware, had brought it to pretty good perfection.

But the Sweds getting notice hereof, drew together all the forces they could spare out of Marienburgh, Elbing and Dantziker Hooft, being in all about 3,000 foot and 800 horse, keeping the gates of these places in the meane tyme shutt, and causeing recognosce all along the Wistula. The generallissimus with most of the chieffe persons were present. Being come near to the fort and takeing a view thereof, they found it in better defence as they exspected and not easy to be taken by force. So they resolved to ruine the bridge and hinder all succours and provisions from those within, knowing they were not well provided of ammunition and provisions, which succeeded very well. For after some dayes were spent in makeing of batteries {119v} and cannoniring on the bridge, in which tyme Lt. Colonell Pflawme and diverse others were killed, at last the bridge was rendred uselesse, and all hopes of releefe taken away. So that these in the fort being unprovided of necessaries, beat the chamade, and not being able to obtaine other conditions of the Sweds, rendred themselves prisoners of warr.[318]

In the meane tyme Sapiha, who lay in Colum with the cavalierie of the Polls, getting notice, came downe as farr as Stum, where he surprised all the forragers of that garrison, by whom haveing gott intelligence that the fort was lost, without more ado he returned.

The King of Sweden haveing had the last harvest and this winter prodigious victorious progresses in Denmarke, forced that King to a very disadvantagious peace at Rotschild.[319] Amongst the articles one was for delivery of a good number of horse and foot to the Sweds, which being performed, 1,500 of these foot were sent by sea to Prussia under the command of Colonell Sinclair. Upon the same ships the Sweds returned the Polls (being about 700), who were taken in Lissawish skonse.

{120} Shortly after this the Elector of Brandeburgh, haveing made an offensive and defensive league with the Roman Emperour, Poll and Dane, entred in open hostility against the Sweds, both in Prussia and leading an army together with the Imperialists and Polls into Denmarke to the

---

[318] Cf. fols. 218–219.
[319] Roskilde. The Swedish army, led by the King, easily occupied Denmark, crossed the Store Baelt over ice and threatened Copenhagen. Peace was signed on 26 February 1658, but soon war broke out again with more success for the Danes.

assistance of that King, who being oppressed by the Sweds was forced to a breach with them againe. By this the Sweds garrisons in Prussia were more straitened and cut short of all contribution or livelyhood out of the high or maine land, and forced to subsist by the *werders* and the provisions in their store houses.

The Polls levyes being most compleeted towards the harvest, they drew their armyes together with the Imperialists and beleaguered Thorun. The *Woywod* of Sandomirs Koniecpolsky, being sent with 3 or 4,000 men to forme a leaguer near Marienburgh and keep a watchfull eye over the garrisons of Marienburgh and Elbing and straiten them so much as possible, which he did, encamping first betwixt Stume and Resenburgh[320] and afterwards at Christburgh[321].

A litle befor his comeing Feld Marshall Duglasse his lyfe company of Scots came from Strasburgh to Elbing, haveing done admirable good service the spring and summer, and at last were most of them taken prisoners and released for others, whom {120v} they had taken. But now the provisions growing scarse in that garrison, and the Polls lying very strong in the adjacent places, so that there was litle use for them there, which occasioned their being commanded from thence.

Betwixt the Sweds and Brandeburgers was litle or few actions of note at first, only partyes for provisions and forrage rideing hither and thither. The first of note was the takeing of Marienwerder, for the Sweds haveing notice of its being slenderly manned and guarded, sent a party from Marienburgh, who makeing some stay at Stume and getting some of that garrison along with them, came thither by day light, tooke it by skalado, fynding small resistance. The most of the burgers and few sojors retired to the church, which they maintained. The Sweds not dareing to stay long, packed up their booty, whereof they had good store, marched of and came safe to their garrisons.[322]

Shortly after this the Maior Generall Heuster, who was taken in the winter and kept in Marienburgh, escaped after this manner. He had had

---

[320] Riesenburg (German), Prabuty (Polish).
[321] Dzierzgoń.
[322] In August – see fols. 225 v.–226.

upon his writt or paroll liberty to ride out where pleased, and had hunted diverse tymes in company with the generallissimus. His lady had also come to him and stayed some weeks by him. But haveing plotted with his countreymen, {121} whilst they were yet in their quarters in the Warmish Bishopdome, and appointed a day when they should come with a party of horse and take both the generallissimus and him at hunting, this intelligence he sent with his lady when she returned.

This businesse, however, was not so closely caryed, but the Sweds smelled it, and afterwards by intercepted letters all being laid open, he was confined to close prison in the old castle of Marienburgh, yet so that every day with an officer and a guard he had the liberty of the castle and, being sent for, ated dayly at the generall[iss]imus his table. He had desired back his written paroll, and, as it was said, obtained it. Yet in the contest, w[hi]ch was afterwards betwixt him and the generall auditor[323], the Sweds would not have so constantly affirmed the contrary, if it had been given out. Yet being confined after that manner with a strong guard and not permitted further liberty as that of the castle, and that with a guard, he was *ipso facto* a close prisoner and not tyed longer to any paroll, seing he had required it, whither it was returned or not, so that he might very lawfully use meanes and make his escape, needing not to incurr blame of any thing he could do of that nature.

The old and new castles of Marienburgh are divided with a deep {121v} dry ditch, very broad and walled up on both sides, into which the houses of office of that syde of the castle, where the maior generalls lodgings were, were formed; and the provisions of wood for the castle were kept in the ditch, being brought into it by a great gate from that place of the towne called the *Freyheit*, behind which gate within was a swine-stall. This the m. generall had observed, and how that each Saturnday, being the market day, wood was brought into the ditch.

So haveing by his servants provided materialls for a compleete pawres habite, and made and fitted it in his owne chamber, on a Saturnday befor day light, haveing taken up a boord in the passage to the house of office,

---

[323] Highest rank in military court.

he convoyed himself with the helpe of his servants by a rope into the ditch, and then went into the swine-stall. Wood being brought and many pawres with waggons comeing into the ditch, he slipped out unseen and went out at the gate, as if haveing lost some thing he returned to seek it, and so unperceived of any, gott into the towne, where he stayed till after midday, when joyning himself with 15 or 20 pawres who with their waggons were rendevouzing to be gone. And so amongst the first of these waggons he slipped out at the gates unquestioned, and going to a village called Oldmarke, he hired there a pawre with a waggon who convoyed him to Rezenborgh, where makeing himself knowne, he was {122} furnished with cloaths and all things sutable, and so convoyed to the army then lying at the siege of Thorune.

The same day that he escaped from Marienburgh the generallissimus sending for him to dinner, his pages who lay by him in the roome excused his not comeing by saying he had been sick the whole night, had not slept and was now fallen asleep. At night also when the generallissimus sent to enquire of his health, his servants excused it upon the same pretext. The next day when it was near dinner tyme, the generallis[simus] sent againe to enquire of his health and desire him to dinner, which being then also excused, the generall auditor was sent with command to see and speak with himself. Then the servants seeing it could not be longer concealed, revealed all, and being strictly examined and threatened, told all the particulars of his going from thence. But how he gott out of the towne or whither he was gone they could not tell. Narrow search was made in Marienburgh, and horsemen sent out upon all the wayes, but nothing to be heard of him untill he was out of danger and their reach.

{122v} In the beginning of October the Brandeburgers sent a strong party of horse and foot towards the Nogat, and ferrying over a litle above Climent Fare entrenched themselves in the great *werder*, which boldnes the Sweds not endureing, presently sent out forces and with lesse danger or resistance as was exspected stormed and tooke their fort, killing some and getting therein Maior Denmarke, many officers and about 300 sojors.

Shortly after this a strong party of the Brandeburgers under the command of Maior Generall Gortsky advanced to Prusse Holland, w[hi]ch alaruming the Sweds, the generallissimus marched out with such forces as could be spared out of Elbing and Marienburgh and faced him near that place. The Sweds were much fewer in number as the other, yet nothing was done, so that haveing traversed hither and thither some dayes and faced other in unaccessable places, they marched of to their garrisons and quarters.

Upon this Koniecpolsky, the *Woywod* of Sandomirs, came downe from Thorun and encamped betwixt Stume and Rezenburgh, as is touched befor; where, by sending parties continually towards the Sweds garrisons, he straitened them very much. About the end {123} of November he removed to Christburgh, where falling sick he went up to Polland and dyed, leaving the command of the army to Jan Sobiesky, Crowne standard-bearer, who going also for Thorun, commanded the army to follow him under the command of N. Suchodolsky, *Starosta* Litinsky.

The Polls and Imperialists had from the beginning of July kept Thorun closely besieged. The Sweds had diverse tymes befor that attempted from Marienburgh to bring in some necessaries to them, but being blocked up, could not effectuate it. The Germans had their posts on the east and north syde, from the r[iver] to Jacobs gates, Jacobs mount and the Scots mount, and the Polls round the rest of the towne. All meanes usuall in these dayes were used both for offence and defence, trenches, approaches open and syled, batteries, mynes, granadoes, bombees, poysonable and venomous stuffe out of woodden morter pieces digged in the ground throwne into the towne. The besieged also with great and small shott, sallyes and false alarums did [what] could be exspected.

The Polls and Imperialists stormed it in diverse places many tymes and were repulsed. Yet in December in a generall storme they posted themselves

{123v} Dec[embe]r. by the Fishery and on another place of the earthen wall. The besieged, being now very few in number of whole and sound men and despairing of any succours, desired a parley, w[hi]ch ended in a treaty of surrendry upon the usuall conditions granted to persons, who had behaved themselves honourably. So on the 29th *Dec[emb]ris Graffe* Bent Oxensterne, Maior Generall Bilaw with the garrison marched out. They marched under 28 foot collours and 9 standards, being about 600 foot and not above 100 horse. Lt. Coll. Buck with about 1,500 sick and wounded men stayed in the towne. The garrison was convoyed to Marienburgh, and the wounded and sick men after some weeks stay thither also.

1659

On the first of January the King of Polland with the Queen (who had been here some months at the siege), the French ambassadour l'Ombres, the Field Marshall Lubomirsky, Lt. Gen-ll Susa (who commanded the Imperialists) with the Polls nobility made their entry into Thorun, and haveing stayed 8 dayes and given necessary orders and distributed the army in their winter quarters, they marched up into Polland. Most of the Polls foot and some of the cavaliery, who came to the campe latest, had their quarters {124} in Prussia, the Imperialists about Rava and Lovits, and the rest of the army had their assignations in diverse places of the countrey.[324]

{125} **1656**

[September]
Being come to Reden or Radzin, my servant, who from Thorun had been sickly, tooke his bed and two dayes thereafter dyed, and by the black and blew spots on his brest wee perceived that he dyed of the pestilence. For at this tyme the pestilence was in many places of Prussia, especially in Thorne and Elbing. Yet being no wayes afrayed, I caused bury him after the usuall way.

Haveing stayed some dayes in the towne, I gott my quarters in a village with two Scotsmen more. After a fortnights stay in these quarters, wee receiving orders to march, and haveing notice of two good horses the next doore, I caused my boy whom I had taken on in the same village to espy

---

[324] Fol. 124 v. is blank. At this point Gordon leaves his account of the course of the war and returns to his personal experiences. See fol. 79 v.

the conveniences of the house and stable, and after wee were conveened at Radzin I sent him back to bring the horses, who did his businesse neatly and brought the horses to me befor day.

This I confesse to be a most hainous crime, and punishable by all civill and even martiall law, yet at this tyme among the Sweden it was not only winked at, but allowed. And to speak the truth, it was impossible {125v} for the army to subsist without such shifts, and these who were either so conscientious, faint-hearted or lazy as not to use the lyke, were sure to be destroyed with vermine, or dy with hunger or cold. For pay, none was to be exspected, especially by the horsemen, and this countrey, albeit it was under our jurisdiction and contributed to the uttermost of its power for the maintenance of the army, yet the Sweds tooke their tyme of it and, according to their maxime, ruine and impoverish the countrey, and ar very indulgent to the citties and townes.

I will not insist here how farr such crimes may ly upon the actors as well as the superiour powers, much being to be said and many distinctions made upon this matter. Yet I say briefly that one can scarse be a souldier without being an oppressour and comitting many crimes and enormityes, albeit some more as others. So let no man presume to think himself guiltlesse or excusable by want of pay or other necessity. In this case it is better to cry *"Peccavi!"*[325], and {126} I would perswade all Christian souldiers, and those who intend to be so, first to seeke to serve under a lawfull prince or state in a good quarrell or cause, the defensive warr being always the most lawfull, or that made to recover or maintaine ones owne propriety and rights. But that warr made against ones owne religion, native countrey, or assisting rebells or those who upon the pretence of injuries do follow the way of conquest, such is impious and unlawfull. Next, to seeke such service where a constant pay is to be had, for there a man haveing a subsistance needs not to be driven by any necessity, if he guide well, to make any unlawfull shifts. For the cause or quarrell is many tymes imputed to the prince alone, but the guilt of impious and unlawfull actions doth always fall upon the particular actors.

---

[325] I have sinned (Lat.).

By day light I went to the *ruitm-r* and, shewing him what booty I had gott, I asked leave to go befor, the better to secure my {126v} purchase, which obtained, I made hast and rode befor to a small towne called Lashin[326] and lodged my self in a back street in a obscure house. In the evening the company came and quartered in the towne, and the next day buryed one Capt. Durham, who had dyed the day befor upon the way of the pestilence.

I haveing been ordered by the *ruitm-r* to meet the trowpe at Holland, kept on my course befor. Being come to Holland, I stayed a day and night, and then returning, found the trowpe quartering in a village a mile of. From hence some of our comorades went for Elbing and Brawnsberg. Two of those who went for Elbing, in their returne one of them by the way dying, the other, saying that he dyed of a fall from his horse, was not trusted, but put under a guard in a small cottage. Wee marching the next day, I stayed behind and had some discourse with him (whose name was Wallace). He said that his comorad, Rosse, at their comeing out of Elbing had bemoaned himself of a great paine in his head, which he said {127} proceeded of excesse of drink, and being then also drunk, he could not hold up his head, and at last falling from his horse, he dyed. This Wallace said also that he found no sicknes or paine in himself at all, yet he had a strong opinion and imagination that he must dy shortly. Which was verifyed the following night without the least sense of paine, and when visited the next day, no signe of any pestilentiall disease appeared upon him.

By easy marches wee passed through the Elbings *werder* and crossed the Nogat (being a branch or arme of the river Vistula) at a place called Climing-faire and quartered in Great Lesovits. Here I lodged with one John Burnet, and lying together were covered with a cloake which had belonged to Capt. Durhame, this Burnet haveing waited upon him in his sicknes, and after his death getting his cloake, caused boyle it to clear it of all pestilence. About midnight he began {127v} to be very sick, complaining especially of a paine in his head. I had at first no thought of any pestilentiall disease and so comforted him the best way I could, covering him and lying closse

---

[326] Lasin.

to him. But finding an exceeding heat from him, about day light I arose and went to another quarter, whither I had been invited the evening befor by my other comorades, to whom I was very welcome. I told not these nor any other any thing of John Burnets sicknes, or that I had lyen with him all night, fearing they would exclude me from company, the very conceit whereof would have killed me!

In this quarter were fowre of us, being a rich pawre, and had 4 *hoves*[327] of land. He had also two lively, lovely daughters, who after the fashion of this countrey were very coy. Which giveing occasion of discourse, brought on a wager that the pawre would give none of us any of his daughters, albeit he should know any of us to be an earle or lord. So to try conclusions, wee condiscended that Robert Steven, a pretty well bred gentleman who spoke good Dutch, should personate a lord, {128} which the Germans call *graffe*, and that wee should all attend and keep a great decorum and observance. So after a day or two both he himself and by us he broke the matter to the parents, who even as the daughters would by no meanes consent, excuseing themselves that their daughters were unfitt matches for such great persons, that they had a custome there to marry their daughters to their equalls, which was most reasonable and usually proved most happy. So with this comedy wee had good sport and merry discourse thereafter.

From this village wee removed to another, two miles further, where the fors[ai]d John Burnet dyed and was buryed. Here with my comorades Andrew Straitoune and Alex[ande]r Keith I made a pact not to desert on another in case any of us should be infected with ye pestilence. In this village dwelt the Scotsman, who in my journey from Braunsberg to Dantzick had so kindly offered to take me thither upon a waggon.

After some dayes stay in this village wee marched {128v} to a litle towne called Newteich, where wee dined but could not lodge all night because the Queens court were quartered here. So wee marched and lodged in a small village halfe a mile from thence, and the next day to another, larger, a mile further, where wee quartered 6 dayes.

---

[327] Hufe (German) – land measure; especially, a plot that could be ploughed in one day using one horse or a team.

Here wee had notice that Generall Duglasse was ordered to go by sea to Riga with 3 or 4,000 men to relieve it, it being besieged by the Tzar of Moskovia. And wee had orders to prepare to go along, the *ruitm-r* being allowed for transportance 3 horses, the cornet 2 and every trowper one. Whereupon many of our comorades sold their horses for halfe nought, I with some others only reserving ours untill wee should be ready to embarke.

Wee removed and quartered by the r[iver] Nogat, which crosseing, wee rendevouzed by Marienburgh and had our quarters assigned in Oldmarke, a large village, where wee were very well accommodated, I lodging in one house with James Birny and John Hurrey. After wee had been here {129} fyve dayes, whilst I was gone about some businesse to Christburg, a litle towne not farr of, my quarters was burnt of, wherein my linnens were lost. So at my returne I tooke up my quarters by the quartermasters, John Hurrey by the *ruitmaster* and James Birnie by his yonger brother John, the cornet.

Two dayes thereaft[er] I rode to Marienburg and bought linnens, and was very well entertained for my money in the signe of "The White Swane". Being returned, the next day I rode with some comorades to Stume, a litle towne and castle scituated in a lake, where wee were kindly entertained by a Scotsman called John Bull. At my returne it was my toure to go and remaine in the maiors quarters of Gen-ll Duglasse his regiment for orders, where haveing stayed 24 houres, I was releeved. In this Oldmarke 3 of our comorades dyed of the pestilence, and 4 who were {129v} sick recovered.

I rode to Elbing of purpose to enquire for letters out of Scotland by James Beverage and Thomas Smeton, Scots merchants there, but found none. The next day after my returne Andrew Straitowne being gott upon horseback to ride somwhere, as he was putting in his pistolls, being French workes, into the hulsters, I standing by and speaking something softly in his eare, the pistoll on the same side where I stood fired and shott through my breaches closse by my left thigh, without further harme as spoiling my breeches by the bottome of the hulster, which the shott forced out. For the safety from which danger God Almighty be praised! This same night

I had a quarrell with Walter Airth, a troublesome person,[328] which was however by the company composed.

Here wee stayed more as three weekes. On the evening befor wee had orders to march, being in the *ruitmasters* and at cardes, John Hurrey, who had been lying sick two dayes, arose and sitting downe by me, leaned upon my shoulder {130} to looke into my cardes, out of whose mouth proceeded such a strong stinking smell, that I was not able to endure it. So that haveing with great aversenes sitten halfe ane houre, and being ten aclock at night, I tooke leave and went home to my quarters, where fynding my comorades makeing merry, I tabled with them.

About midnight notice came that wee should march the next morning early, and ane houre thereafter that the afores[ai]d John Hurrey was dead. Being come to the *ruitmasters* quarters by day light, Patrick Dumbar and I were ordered to bury the s[ai]d John Hurrey, the trowpe marching to the rendevouz a mile of. Wee caused the *shults*[329] give people to make a grave and coffin, which being ready, wee with help of the deceasseds servant (for none of the pawres would come near him) prepared to put him in his coffin. He had on the sleeves of a buffe coat stitched with silver and sewed to linnen bodyes, {130v} which because of the buffe coat wee would faine have. But his armes were so stiffe and bowed towards his body that wee could by no meanes get them of. As wee were pulling at them, his shirt discovering his brest, I espyed some blewish spotts and imagined a strong sent to proceed from the corps. Wherefor without more ado wee put him in his coffin and nailed it fast, and with the help of a pawre, whom wee forced, caryed it to the church yard which was near by, the *ruitm-r* with the cornet and some horsmen comeing in the instant and giveing a salve or volley at his interring.

The cornet desireing us to come breakfast in his quarters, which was the *shults* house, I found my self so extraordinary sick that I was not able to stand upon my feet. And being afrayed that any should perceive, I went asyde and powred forth my prayers to God Almighty with many teares,

---

[328] Gordon was later on good terms with Airth, who followed him to Russia in 1661 and died there as major in 1678.
[329] Schulze (German) – village elder.

and afterwards used that which every morning and evening I had used since the infection or pestilence {131} came into our company, which was to drink a quantity of my owne urine, and now drunke of all what I made. Comeing in to breakfast, I was not able to tast any victuals. However lest any should take notice, I made a show of eating, letting all fall under the table.

Being ready to be gone, I was scarce able to gett upon horsebacke. However wee rode to Christburg, no body perceiving that any thing ailed me. Here wee did come in company with some Scotsmen and drunke largely at the French wine, w[hi]ch driveing exceedingly, made me go often aside, I drinking every tyme of a 3d part of what I made. Parting, wee marched about two miles to our quarters. By the way as often as I had occasion to go aside, I did as befor. In our quarters, being a gentlemans house and a large roome, wee did leaguer on the floore, with convenience of some fresh {131v} straw, where I sleeped very hard.

In the morning my comorade Alex[ande]r Keith expostulated very earnestly w[it]h me why I had groaned so terribly, and if I were not sick, I excuseing it by reason of our large quaffing the day befor, and denying any other sicknes as that w[hi]ch was ordinary to me after cups. And indeed I found my self, albeit not well, yet a great deale better, and so by the helpe of my gracious God every day thereafter on the mending hand.

Wee marched together with the generalls regiment of horse towards Libstat[330], where wee passed the river Passary, and being on our march 5 miles further, wee had notice of the Polls and Tartars being beat at Philippowa[331] and retired up into Polland. Herewithall wee received orders to returne, so that this same day wee marched two miles backward and downe towards Holland, not farr from which wee did meet with 43 Scots gentlemen, who were embarqued to have gon to Riga with the gen-ll. But the Moskovite haveing raised his siege, {132} they were contramanded, and haveing received horses, sadles, pistolls, hulsters and boots from the generall, were now enrolled in his lyfe company. Some others who were with us received the lyke, but I with most who brought along and had

---

[330] Liebstadt (German), Miłakowo (Polish).
[331] See fol. 86 v.

good mounting refused to take any thing, hopeing thereby to be the freer and not engaged to the company, wherein wee were deceived.

Wee marched through the Elbings *werder* and crossed the Nogat at Climings ferry, and so onwards by soft marches to Sienhagen, where wee rested some dayes and had good quarters, I being lodged in ye house of a Manist or Anabaptist, a Hollander called Bartholomeus Peters, who every morning presented me with a reichs thaler to be peacable, and at parting furnished me with good provisions. From hence wee marched towards the Hooft, where crossing another arme of the r. Vistula, wee encamped in the fields with other regiments, Gen-ll Duglasse being here with 3 or 4,000 men as well to further the compleeting of the workes of the fort, as to straiten the towne of Dantzick.

Being some dayes here, the Scots gentlmen who came last out of Scotland with the Lord Cranstownes {132v} regiment, being destitute of provisions and money, no pay falling, and they unaccustomed to make shifts, troubled the generall for a subsistance, so that the generall sent them againe into the great *werder* upon pretence of exequiring, as they call it, for nailes, under the command of one Maior Sinkler.

The first party wee did was downe into the Nering[332], where wee gott good provisions. The next party wee marched over the Vistula whereon a bridge was made, and downe into ye Dantzick *werder*. Being come a mile and a halfe, the trowpers and souldiers began to seek about for forrage, some whereof going to the left hand, were shott at by *snaphanes* or *bushcloppers*[333], as they call them, over a river, and some wounded. Whereupon Maior Generall Wirtsburg, who had the command of the party, drew downe to the river side and gave orders for makeing floates to transport and assaile them. In seeking through the houses I and another called John Kempe chanced upon a large tubb, wherein two men could have {133} place, and haveing gotten a long pole, wee rolled the tub to the river syde intending to go over therein. So haveing put it afloat, I embarqued with my pistolls and carabin. My comorade seing it go unsteady, and the water sipeing in, he being a heavy corpulent person refused to enter, and counselled

---

[332] Frische Nehrung (Vistula Spit).
[333] Snaphaan (Dutch), Buschklepper (German) – highwayman, brigand.

me not to venter. But I seeing the *snaphanes* and pawres on the other syde marching of, in hopes of getting the first booty, takeing the long pole in my hand, put of from land.

Being come in to the midle of the river, the streame did carry me downward, I rolling with the pole made no progresse forwards, the tub turning round and carryed downeward, the water also running into it apace. The maior generall and these at the rivers syde called and threatened to me that I should returne. I was sensible enough of my difficulty and danger, being alike destitute of the meanes of returning as going forward. In the meane tyme haveing my recourse to God, it came into my mynd to take the pole in the midle and erecting my self by short stroakes on both sydes, make way, which succeeding very well, {133v} I quickly reached the other syde, albeit over the knees in water.

Being on land, I was called to from the other syde to recover, if possible, a drove of cattell which the pawres were driving away. Whereupon I went through the yard, and opening a back gate see the pawres with their cattell a good way of, amongst whom I discharged my carabin, who being terrifyed with the shott and imageining, as I suppose, a great many Sweds to be come over, ran away and left the cattell, all which in full speed returned back into the *hoffe*[334]. I shutting the back gate againe, went into ye stable, where I found two mares, which I tooke and bringing them to the river syde, tyed them to a tree and called to my comorades over the river to come over with the first floate and take possession of the mares, whilst I went to see what more was to be had. Comeing into the provision house, I found a vessell with salt beefe, which with great difficulty I gott out and put it under a waggon whose wheeles were shoed with iron, laying my carabin thereon to keep possession of both. Then I went into the barne and found a great {134} deale of oates ready cleansed and 13 sackes ready filled. I carryed out the sackes on after another, all except two, and layd them by the waggon befor any came over.

The Sweds being come over, they made quick dispatch of what was to be had. Some comorades comeing by me, I desired them to looke to the

---

[334] Hof (German) – yard.

booty, untill I might go and fetch my mares. Whither being come, I found two *ruitm-rs*, Ziczenhoffe and Bober, of the field m[arshal] l[ieutenan]ts regiments untying them. I stept boldly forward to take them away. They made no resistance, only wording it they challenged them to belong to them, this place being assigned them for their quarters, which I not beleeving, pleaded my danger in hazarding, the prize made of all by those who could get the first possession, and priviledges allowed and approved in such cases. They followed me reasoning to the place where the other booty lay, where with high words they renewed their plea befor my comorades, by whose perswasion I yeelded to give them one of {134v} them, rather as to be further heard with them.

But when I would have given the slig[h]test, they would needs have the best, which I refuseing, they pulled the halters out of their heads and let them go, saying, "Then none of us shall have any of them". I makeing hast, recovered and brought them to the same place againe, whither also the fors-d *ruitm-rs* comeing, began to lay claime to them againe. But I being now throughly heated, would not consent to give any of them, so that some high words passeing, Ziczenhoffe called me for a *Barenheuter*[335], to which I answered, "Who calleth me so, he may be such a one himself!" Whereupon he offering to his sword, I drew myne and began to lay about me. They both drew, but could not keep stand with their small walking swords. Yet my comorades and other officers comeing in parted us.

I keeping my mares, prepared to gett over, putting my booty with help of my comorades in a large boat and swimming the mares at the boat syde, one whereof drowned. Being come {135} over, I went to our *ruitm-r* and informed him of what had passed, desireing to acquaint the generall therewith and represent to his Exc[ellency] that if every one should abuse us and take our booty from us, which with so great danger wee acquired, it would be impossible to us to subsist. Complaints comeing in on both sydes, the generall ordered the businesse to be heard the next day. Whither being come and examined, the witnesses being heard, and the maior

---

[335] Bärenhäuter (German) – idler, lazybones.

generall, who was present, relateing with what danger I had hazarded and recovered so many cattell, with other circumstances, the *ruitm-rs* were dismissed with a sharpe reproove, and I with a favourable warning to carry a greater respect to the officers in tymes comeing.

Some few dayes thereafter being one evening within the fort, and returning befor it was darke, as wee returned through Colonell Rutherfuirds regiment (commanded at that tyme by Maior Klinger), my *ruitm-r* {135v} and one Captaine Malcolme Hamilton going befor, and one Alex-r Keith and I at a distance after them, in passing, a serjeant with some others derided and spoke some disgracefull words of the *ruitm-r* and captaine. Which I overhearing, thought it might be objected to me thereafter that I had heard such words and did not resent them. And albeit my comorade, who was the *ruitm-rs* nephew, diswaded and counselled me not to take notice of it, yet being driven by I know not what destiny, I returned, and questioning the serjeant why he spoke such words; who answering disdainfully, and I falling to hott words, befor I was aware, one behind me caught me by the haire, and others comeing in, did so haile, pull and beat me with their fists and pieces of wood, that I was ready to fall downe. Yet straining my self, I gott free of him who had me by the haire, and drew my sword wherewith I made such roome that I cleared the coast of them, haveing wounded three of them grievously.

My comorades {136} comeing in, perswaded me to runne into the quarters of the regiments of horse w[hi]ch was hard by, but I being in great passion, could not recollect my self so as to be sensible of any danger, untill the main guard of that regiment comeing, tooke me and carryed me along. My *ruitm-r* and Capt. Hamilton hearing hereof, came and desired Maior Klinger to deliver me to them, promising to present me the next day, or then to keep me under his owne guard, promiseing withall all reasonable satisfaction, that it might not come to the generalls eares. But he being inexorable, went presently and complained to the generall, who ordered me (and those who were wounded also, at my *ruitm-rs* desire) to be sent to the generall *Gewaltiger*[336] or *profos*, where nothing vexed me more as to see these who had occasioned, begun the quarrell and so unmercifully beat me sitting free, and my self in irons.

The next day the generall comeing befor the lyfe company, who were ready {136v} drawne up, being to march upon a party with other regiments, said these words: "I would not have thought that Gordon would have done so. He may speake of luck if he come of with the losse of his right hand". Which, with the repulse which some ffriends who interceeded for me receaved, comeing to my knowledge, troubled me exceedingly. In the evening my *ruitm-r* gott diverse eminent persons to entreat the generall in my behalfe, who excused himself upon the point and account of justice, telling the *ruitm-r* that the next day he would cause call a counsell of warr.

The whole night I did not sleep, and by day light, seeing a page of the generalls come to the provost marshalls lodging, I really thought it was to cause bring me up to the counsell of warr. All my comorades hearing of my danger, intended with great earnestnes to desire my releasment, but the *ruitm-r* fearing lest by passionate words they might exasperate the generall worse, did {137} forbid them untill he should try his utmost. So going with the cornet very early in the morning to the generall, who as soone as he did see him, without exspecting what he would say, said to him, "I have commanded to let Gordon loose"; the *ruitm-r* rendring thankes, came immediately to the provost marshall to see me released.

Ane houre thereafter, haveing payed a ducate to the provost marshall and a doller to his assistant or servant, I was dismissed. My *ruitm-r* sent to Maior Klinger, desireing him to restore my sword, who showing himself very discontented, refused to give it. I went in the afternoone to render submissive thankes to the generall for the favourable punishment, and waiting an opportunity, at a turning on the wall I performed it, and withall complained that the maior would not restore my sword. He looked somewhat sever upon me, but s[ai]d nothing, only ordered a yong man to go along with me to the maior, commanding him to restore my sword. Being

---

[336] Head of military court (German).

so guarded, I went along, the maior with much reluctancy {137v} caused give me my sword, w[hi]ch haveing gott, I told him, I hoped to live the day to be revenged for his useing me so harshly, w[hi]ch words displeasing him, he threatened to complaine to the generall, but did not.

After some dayes stay in this leaguer wee had orders to march, most of our company being already in the great *werder*, takeing free quarters of the pawres, upon the account of defficiency for not bringing in nailes for makeing the bridge. So haveing taken some hearty and merry nights lodgings in this *werder*, wee marched altogether through Marienburgh and up to Marienwerder, where wee were billited upon the villages of that district, upon the acco[un]t of safeguards, because the army was to march that way towards Grawdents, where a bridge was to be made for passing over the army to the other syde of the Vistula, this district belonging to the Elector of Brandeburg, our faithfull confederate.

The place where I with W-m Midleton was sent to belonged {138} to a widdow gentlewoman, a kinsewoman to the *Graffe* von Dona, who had some foot sojors here lying on safeguard, which made us receive but a cold welcome and spare entertainment, and the next day so much as "Wee have no need of you". Whereupon wee marched of and quartered that night in a gentlemans house a mile from Marienwerder on the high way to Grawdents. Here also wee had more discourse and complements as reall and hearty entertainment.

The next day wee went to Marienwerder and there receaved orders, I to quarter in [...], where two other safeguards were, and my comorade in Campagnia, where were also two. Wee had allowed us every weeke a doller, and good free quarter, the generall finding these wayes to maintaine this company, most whereof were such who, not used and ashamed to make such shifts as the Sweds did, and not receiving any pay, were not able otherwise to subsist. In this place I used my old Varsavish trade, by getting my comorades to drive away cattell, and {138v} I for each relieffe received a doller, which without knowledge of my two comorades in the village (who were neer *simplices*[337]) was constantly practised twice a week.

---

[337] Simpletons (Lat.).

Whilst I was here the army marched by, and Coll. Ashemberg with his regiment quartered in this village, who tooke many horses along for his cariages, after whom I went to Grawdents and recovering them all, brought them back againe, which, with my vigilancy in recovering their cattell and horses from my comorades, gained me great good will and esteeme amongst the pawres.

Colonell Ashemberg, as he quartered here, was lodged in my quarters, and I forced to lodge in an outhouse with my horses. In the night tyme I heard the neighing of a horse hard by, and the next day causing my boy search, he found hedged in with sheaves of corne a very pretty black ston'd horse, which the landlord had hidd here for preventing being taken from him. When the colonell was gone, I perswaded the landlord to bring his horse into the stable, seing he was secure enough whilst I {139} was there. I would faine have bought this horse of the landlord, but he would not sell him by any meanes. Wherefor I bespoke my comorade W-m Midleton to send his servant in the night tyme, and myne should deliver him out to him, which had the desired effect as to the first part. But the servant bringing the horse first to Campagnia to his master and from thence to Marienwerder, and lastly to a *shafery*[338] halfe a mile from thence, the pawres gave notice thereof to my landlord, who was very sorry when he missed his horse. And albeit he durst not say it, yet perceived I by many circumstances that he suspected it to be a practice of myne. However perceiving by the path of the horse and getting notice from their neighbours, which way he was brought, he desired me to ryde along with his sonne to search after him, which I did. So wee went by their sure intelligence directly to the place where he was and brought him away.

{139v} Afterwards the pawres held a consultation intending, seing the danger of the armyes marching by was passed, to put of some of their safeguards. At this meeting most of the pawres were for keeping me alone and letting the other two go, but one said, "If you have a good horse and have a mind to be ridd of him, you may keep him", which made them conclude to part with me. So, paying me my dues, they dismissed me. I

---

[338] Schäferei (German) – sheepfold.

went immediately to the *ruitm-r* intending, if ever they should come in my way, to be avenged of their usage.

At this tyme our cornet John Birny dyed and was convoyed by such of the trowpe as were neer to Marienwerder and buryed in the cathedrall churchyard with the usuall military ceremonies.

Shortly after came an order for all the pawres of that *werder* to bring balkes or trees for building of a bridge over the Vistula by the Meve. About 70 waggons of these being conveened, I was sent to convoy them to the wood and leaguer by the {140} river, whither haveing brought them, I resolved to be even with them. So leaving them, I went to a market-tenter and finding some trowpers there drinking, I bespoke them to attack these pawres in their returne, it being now darke, and take some horses from them, whereof they were exceeding glad.

Whilst wee here stayed their departure, after much search they found me and desired me to returne and convoy them to their homes, which I refused, as haveing no orders, only to convoy them to the wood and leaguer. They smelling some designe, were very earnest that I should convoy them back againe, and when with words they could not prevaile, they promised to reward me. So takeing me aside, they from 4 pence for each waggon they advanced to pay me 12 pence, which I considered was better to take as run hazard of the other, and so putting handsomely of the former bargaine, I departed with [them] along the damme, I by their desire, for fear of some attact from the leaguer, rideing in the rear.

Being gone about a mile, I perceived the formost driving {140v} very hard, I began to doubt they intended to cheat me. So asking the hindermost how farr it was to the way where they were to part, and telling him that the last should be accountable for the rest, if any should run away, which the pawre takeing to consideration, told me I should do well to make hast, for he beleeved the formost were neer the parting way. Whereupon I made hast, and being gott to the parting way where they had covenanted to stay, I found them makeing what hast they could. Here leaving my boy to stop those who were comeing after, being the greatest part, I made hast to overtake the formost. But some being too farr gone, I returned with such as I found neer for fear of lossing all, and so made them one by one pay what they promised, and found by account that 17 had escaped. The next day returning to my quarters, I informed the *ruitm-r*, who was well satisfyed and heartily rejoyced at my being in some sort even with the pawres. {141}

Haveing stayed in these places about 5 weekes, wee had orders to march to Marienburgh, where haveing rendevouzed, wee marched back towards the Meve, and there upon the ice passed the river Vistula and quartered in the low countrey towards Dirshaw. Every regiment getting two houses, our company had one allowed. Here wee stayed two nights and then marching by Dirshaw, wee quartered in Gotteland in one house or *hoffe* with the generall; where, because the army was not as yet come up, wee were forced to keep a strong guard till past midnight. Whilst wee stayed here, I was out on diverse parties, as well for subsistance as intelligence, where nothing hapened either notable or considerable to my self.

Wee marched afterwards towards Dantzicker-Hooft and had our quarters in a village a large halfe mile from it. From hence I was sent with two other to be safeguard in Stiblaw.

[1657]

Whilst wee were here wee made diverse excursions towards Dantzick, in one whereof wee had very hott skirmishing with the Dantzickers, when the Kings lyfeguard and our company with assistance of some commanded men and voluntiers, in all not above 250 men, did all the service was done and resisted the Dantzickers, who were about 500 well mounted and armed men, and repulsed them many tymes, neither quitted ground {141v} untill some foot called *snaphanes* came up and galled them very sore with small shott, whereby they were forced to retire a litle.

At this tyme diverse were killed and many wounded, I receiving also a wound in the head with a sword. For being fewer in number and sometymes not well nor tymely seconded, wee were hard put to it, and once haveing charged the enemy home, wee in following too farr unadvisedly engaged our selves betwixt two reserves of the enemy. So that wheeling of, wee found our selves too farr of to be releeved by those whose turne it was to have done it, and were forced, befor wee could gett our armes charged, to wheele about againe, the enemy being closse in our rear, and so chargeing them desperately with our swords, wee forced one of these trowpes in upon the other and so put both to rout, but durst not follow them, it being sufficient to recover our sure standing. It drawing neer evening, both with mutuall consent as it were drew of, and wee came late into our quarters, haveing on the way received great thankes from His Majesty and commendation from all the generall persons. In this occasion I was wounded in the forhead, not knowing wherewith.[339]

{142} On Wednesday, January the 5th, according to my instructions, I convoyed some waggons with provisions belonging to two brothers, indwellers in Stiblaw called Swartswaldts. These haveing their wiwes and families in Dantzick, sent or brought once a week provisions for them, haveing obtained leave to do so, with an order to us to convoy them by Grebin, lest the garrison there might rob them. This being my toure or course, and passing Grebin about sunriseing, I was about returning, when these Swartswaldts were very earnest with me to go a litle further with them, pretending the fear they had lest some of the garrison might follow and rob them. I went about halfe a mile further, and in my returne not farr from the house of Grebin, being all alone, I did meet two horsemen, whom suspecting, I caused my horse leap a ditch to the right hand and with my pistoll in my hand demanded what they were. They smileing and not drawing their armes, answered, they were good Sweds, and I asking of what regiment, they said they belonged to Generall Duglasse, and therewithall stopping, they asked me wherefor I was so cautious so near our owne garrison, and entring into further discourse.

I being ashamed to be afrayed of those whom I tooke for our owne people, and out of a kind of youthfull bravery set {142v} spurres to my horse and made him leape the ditch againe. Being now closse with them, they began to perswade me to go along with them and seek after booty, whereto I not consenting, they as if resolving together said they would

---

[339] This engagement was fought on 4 January. Cf. above, fols. 91–91 v.

returne with me to the leaguer, and so rode back with me one on each syde.

I not suspecting any thing, and being come near some houses, which hindred the sight of the castle, they layd both hands on me, and in the same instant eight more starting out from behind one of these houses, I was not able to come to my armes or make any resistance, they presently mufling me in a long cloake which I had about me, and so hurryed me away in great hast. I considering the condition I was in, and remembring what I suffered in my former imprisonment, in the interim shifted my purse (wherein were 13 or 14 reichs thallers, one halfe whereof small Polls money) out of my pocket into a mor secret place in my breeches. When they thought themselves out of danger of the castle, they disarmed me and began to search me, finding only some small {143} money in my litle pocket. They searched narrowly in the neck of my doublet, the westband of my breeches and other places, still enquireing for more money. And albeit I told them that I had left such money as I had in my quarters, yet were they not satisfyed, thinking and saying it was impossible that I who had so good cloaths, horse and furniture, should be destitute of money.

Being come to the horse guards, my name was written downe, and being come a litle further, they bethought themselves of changing bootes with me, I haveing a paire of very good new English ones. So commanding me to light and render my bootes, I told them if they would deale so unhandsomely with me as to take my bootes, they might be at the paines to draw them of. Whereof they made no ceremony, and haveing taken them, threw to me a paire of theirs. I seing them and knowing by the fashion of them that the owners were pawres, it vexed me exceedingly to be so circumvented by such people, and could not containe my selfe from expressing {143v} my sence thereof, refuseing absolutely to put on their bootes, albeit because of the straitnes of my owne I had but linnen stockens on, and in such a cold day like to smart. They urged me and with their karabines pushed me in the back and breast to move me thereto. Notwithstanding which I stood to my resolution, and they seing my wilfulnes, made me sitt up againe, and so rode one untill near the utmost guards they made me alight againe and with great violence urged me to take their bootes. All which I endured, telling them I would not dishonour my self so much as to wear their old boots, and that if they brought me in so to their towne they would receive small thankes from their commendant, and exspect the lyke uncivill usage from us in the lyke cases. At last seing they could not prevaile, they restored my bootes.

Being brought to the commendant, Colonell Winter, the corporall brought me up, and after addresse was admitted. The commendant asked me of my quality, countrey and under what regiment, I telling him I belonged to {144} Generall Dowglasse his lyfe company of Scots, he rejoicing said, "O, have we catched one of these birds!" I told him that unlesse they had denyed their master, they had not catched me, whereat he turning to the corporall, asked him how he had taken me. He said that being near the castle of Grebin, and seing me well mounted and circumspect, it was impossible to take me otherwise. The colonell thereupon smileing said, "It is all one, by force or art to overcome". Then after some questions concerning the strength of the army, how long they intended to stay there and such lyke, he dismissed me with a souldier to the prison, my pawrish corporall convoying me also, of whom I desired nothing but a small booke which he had taken from me, being Thomas a Kempis[340] in Latine, but could not obtaine it. He however bought a loafe for me going up the street and told me that that and a stowpe, as they call it, of beer was to be my dayly allowance.

Being received, and my name enrolled in the prison howse, called sometyme Dowglasse *Thore*[341], but now the Hoogen *Thore*, {144v} I knew it was tyme for me to recover my purse and put it in its right place. The corporall brought me along the court to ane inne in the farthest part thereof, and in a pretty well furnished roome desired me to sitt downe behind the table, calling for a stowpe or pottle of beer. At the same table were some Dantzick trowpers, prisoners for some misdemeanours, and some Sweds officers walking in the roome. To these the corporall began to extoll and

---

[340] Thomas à Kempis, or Thomas Hemerken (ca.1380–1471), Netherlandish divine, author of the famous *De Imitatione Christi*.
[341] Tor (German) – gate. The name of this gate attests to Scottish influence in Gdańsk.

vaunt what good booty he had gott with me, as horse, cloake, armes etc. to the no small grudging of the trowpers.

Our beer being out and dying in my hand, I called for another pottle. The corporall then told me I was to have no allowance for that day, it being past noone, and that if I would drink now, I must resolve to fast the next day. But I telling him that I would pay for it, he asked me very earnestly if I had preserved any money. I being incensed with the hard usage I had from him, said, "You pawres ar not expert {145} enough in the sojor trade, you know not how to search a prisoner. See, I have preserved a 100 thallers (takeing out my purse and clapping it on the table) wherewith I will mount my self when I returne to the Sweds, and be even with you and your possessions!", which so amazed my corporall that he was ready to pull the haire out of his head, and moved such derision and laughter in the trowpers that, he being ashamed, without pledging me, went away in a chaffe; and as I heard two dayes thereafter, complained to the commendant that his prisoner had preserved 200 reichs thallers, and threatened to mount himself therewith, and to come and burne their houses, desireing that the money might be given to him. Whereat the commendant said, "That cannot be, for if he had preserved a 1,000 thallers, it cannot be taken from him now, farr lesse be given to thee".

{145v} On Saturnday wee were all called in to a great hall, where our names, nation and quality were called and read befor a reverend officer sitting in a chair at the upper end of a table and attended by some others. The businesse was to know who would take service and who not. I for my part answered I would not, yet more as three parts of fowre consented to take.

In this prison nothing was so irkesome as the stinking roome wherein wee lodged, for there being about 400 prisoners, and lodged in severall large roomes, whole, sick and wounded all through another, and about 50 in a roome. The stench was so great that a man comeing out of the fresh air into the roome could not only forbeare vomiteing but fainting. Every one had liberty in the day tyme to walke in the court and up and downe a turne pike from whence a faire prospect of the citty, countrey and Bishops hill was to be had. But in the evening at the ringing of a bell all must in to their respective roomes.

I haveing money, in the day tyme kept most in the inne, where because it was neither handsome nor permitted to stay without makeing the house the better, I was forced to buy beer, and being no lover of it my self, was glad to gett some body to helpe me out with it, and as glad they whose fortune it was {146} to do it. So passed I the tyme, sometymes walkeing in the court and up the turnepike, and then in to the roome, calling now and then for a small measure of beer, whereof I could not drink much, it being so strong. Here I found prisoner one John Gordon, who had been prisoner some weekes. He served for a trowper under the *Landt Graffe* van Hessens regiment, and had served for a single souldier and trowper upwards of 30 yeares, a simple dutchifyed person.

On Sunday and Moonday some handsome officers came to the prison house, calling for some of these who had refused to serve, and strove to perswade them. Being very earnest with me, showing the good usage, constant pay, and that many of my countreymen, especially a kinsman commonly called Steelhand, in good account served there, notwithstanding which I absolutely refused to engage.

On Tuesday morning by day light we were called out by name, 91 persons, and with a guard convoyed through the streets of Dantzick, where wee were reviled for kowstealers, horsestealers, robbers, sacrilegious, incendiaries and what not by the common people, some of ours answering them in their owne language. Being come without the towne, wee made a halt untill a coach {146v} and a ridewaggon with some officers came. Here againe being called by name, wee were delivered over to a guard of horse, and so went about a large halfe mile from the suburbes.

Wee made a litle halt at the maine horse guard, which was commanded by Patrick Gordon, commonly called Steellhand, who served for a *ruitmaster* here. Here the officers who had been prisoners, as Lt. Coll. Drummond, Maior Fulartowne, Lt. Scott and others, tooke their leave, and I comeing last would needs show my self, and was presently knowne by the *ruitmaster*, who asked me if I were not Achluichries his sonne. I answering "yea", he would perswade me to stay and take service there, but I excuseing my self tooke my leave, and so went along to the place assigned for the exchange of prisoners. On the Swedish syde was a lt. colonell and on the Dantzicker part was one Maior Thomsone, a Scottish man. Here wee stayed not long and in the evening came to the head quarters.

The next morning I showing my self to the generall, he was pleased to ask me how I was taken. I told all the truth and laid the blame on the pawres, who had perswaded to go further as was needfull, and insinuated so much as if it had been done out of designe. {147} The generall ordered me to go back to Stiblaw, and that the pawres would mount me againe. The next day accordingly I went thither accompanied with one Alex-r Keith, who had been a lieutennant in Scotland, and was now a voluntier and so glad of a temporary subsistance.

On Saturnday the 15th January the generall sent a corporall with some horsemen to me with orders, that if I had received satisfaction for my mounting, I should immediately march with him to the army. If not, I might stay till Moonday, but no longer, and then come to Marienburgh, where I should find orders by the *Graffe* van Dona what I should do. I showing the corporall that I had not received any satisfaction as yet, dismissed him, promiseing to conforme to his provisionall order.

After he was gone I caused conveen the pawres and began to treat concerning the price of my mounting, but not agreeing, they asked me if I would be content with my owne. I answered, "Yes, if restored in the same condition as they were taken from me". Whereupon they sent one to Dantzick to buy them out.

The same evening I gott such a great paine in my head and such a great heat {147v} all over my body, that the next day I was scarse able to stirr. In the afternoone two brothers of the Swartswalts came to me and told me that, the army being marched out of the Dantzick *werder*, they were afrayed that the Dantzickers should fall in and either kill or take me. So they perswaded me to go along to Great Lichtenaw and stay there by one of their brothers untill they procured my mounting or equipage.

I being exceeding sick and hardly able to sitt on horsebacke, rode with them and in the evening came to the village, and was received with my comorade in the house of Hans Swartswaldt. My sicknesse increasing, which was a violent hott feaver, and procured as I think by the great stench I had endured dureing my imprisonment in Dantzick. The people in the house were indifferent kind to me, and Alex-r Keith was a great comfort to me.

On Wednesday in the morning I was so ill that I desired a Catholick priest to be sent for, which I could not obtaine. On Thursday morning some of the pawres servants being at breakfast in the same roome, one knocked at the doore of the house very hastily, and one entring the roome and said something to the servants, whereupon they all in great hast {148} arose and departed, I being incapable of knowing or careing what it meant. A woman entring the roome came to me and told me that one was come from Stiblaw informing that the Dantzigers were near by, and that they should provide for secureing me. I not being able through the violence of the sicknesse to mind or weigh what she said, denied to rise, so that she departed. Immediately I heard the shutters or covers of the windowes makeing fast, and within a while a great tumult in the streets with shooting, and then some people striveing to breake open the doore of the forehouse and the windowes in ane after-roome of that where I did ly.

I haveing quite forgotten q[uha]t was told me of the Dantzickers, imagined y-t some unruly Swedish souldiers were makeing all this tumult. Yet moved by some tacite instinct, I resolved to arise, and with great difficulty haveing gott on my breeches, before I could gett to the doore I did fall twice or thrice. Being gott out and not knowing the conveniences of the house or where to hyde my self, and finding no body to direct me, yet by Gods gracious providence I went to the right hand, holding by the wall through the {148v} kitchen and in to a litle roome, where I laid me downe on the bench. And being now come to some sense of my condition, I remembred of some money which I had about me, and so takeing my purse wherein was a golden crosse, 2 ducats and about 3 reichs dollers in small money, I put it under the bench in a hole.

The woman of the house comeing in, would needs have me to ly downe in the landlords bed and say, if any came in there, that I was her husband and by trade a taylour, and I telling her that they would know me to be a sojor by my breeches, whereon were some silver lace and ribbands, shee in great hast pulled of my breeches and putting them under the bedstead layed me into the bed. And now haveing my ordinary recourse to God Almighty and the intercession of his Blessed Mother, I found evidently and miraculously Gods mercifull providence.

For I see the souldiers going to and fro by the windowes and heard them in the kitchen and other roomes, and as I heard often told thereafter, they left not a corner nor so much as a swinestall in that *hoffe* unsearched, carrying all with them and killing such Sweds as resisted, or for sicknes could not go along. {149} They tooke about 40 prisoners and killed 70, most sick men, and haveing stayed above two houres in the village, they marched of. My comorade Alex-r Kieth hidd himself in the barne among the sheaves of corne and so escaped, but lost all he had, as horse and armes. My horse and other mounting, w-ch my landlords had bought out of Dantzick, were taken away also.

Two dayes thereafter, my feaver being at the hight, I did fall into a sweat about midday, w-ch with great patience I endured till near midnight, being often ready to faint. So keeping my bed two dayes more, I recovered my health, but exceedingly extenuated and weake. I put my landlord in mynd of giveing me my horse and mounting according to the generalls order, w-ch he denyed to do, haveing as he said bought them out, and now at this tyme taken away againe. I alleadged the not haveing receaved them, and that if I had received them in Stiblaw, they had not been lost and I not runne such a hazard in the sacking of their village.

Hearing of the generalls returne to Marienburgh, I went thither very early and had entrance as his Excell. was going to rise. He wondred to see me so leane and weake, and haveing {149v} told him of my haveing been sick in Great Lichtenaw and the danger I had been in, he desired me to relate the particulars, which I did. Wherewith he seemed much moved, ordering me to go thither againe and get my mounting, but I told him that without a written order they would not obey. So he ordered me to come againe in the afternoone, which I did and received an order that they should restore to me my mounting under paine of military execution.

So haveing seen the *ruitm-r* and some of my comorades, as also my horses, I returned to my quarters and showed my order, w-ch the landlord desireing of me, sent it to Dantzick to his brothers who, it seemes, made but small hast to obey it, as not hearing any thing from them in 6 dayes.

It chanced that our company was to march through this village to Whitekirk, and two of my comorades knowing of my being here, came befor to give me a visitt. I hearing of the company being near the village, desired them to say that they were come to quarter in the village untill {150} they should restore to me my mounting, and sent one of them back to the *ruitm-r* to desire him to make a halt without or in the further end of the village, which he willingly did and sent the quarterm-r to the *shults* to that purpose. The *shults* comeing immediately to my landlord, they began to compound, and agreed with me to give me a good horse and 25 reichs dollers for my other losses. W-ch haveing received, and the *ruitm-r* a gratuity, I marched with the trowpe to Newkirch and from thence to Elbing to buy for my self necessaries.

At my returne I was with a convoy at Grebin about the exchange of prisoners where, being a truce, in conference, some of the Dantzickers knew me, and seing me well mounted, said it were tyme I were in Dantzick againe. I told them the turne was theirs now, that they should visitt Marienburgh.

After this wee returned and lay in the suburbs of Marienburgh. Being here, I with 5 more went one morning early and lay in wait on the way betwixt Marienburgh and Elbing for some booty, but could find no opportunity of adventuring, because the pawres came either too thick and many together, {150v} or accompanied with safeguards. So that it drawing neer night, wee marched into the Elbings *werder* and in a small village, where a Polls maior and *ruitm-r* had their locality, wee obtained a nights lodging, and were lodged in the *krue* or alehouse, each pawre sending a dish of meat and giveing us so much allowance of beer and brandy. But wee after supper falling in a merry veine, exceeded our allowances farr, so that in the morning the pawres with some reluctancy condiscended to pay it, and by no meanes would grant us our breakfast.

Wee mounted and went directly to the *shults* house and seing he would not order our breakfast, wee rode into the yard or *hoffe* and stabled our horses. W-ch when the *shults* had seen, he came to us and told us that wee should go two and two to a house and take our breakfast. So, as wee were drawing out our horses, the maior and *ruitm-r* (whose quarters that was) came with about 15 servants, their swords drawn, and with abusive words did fall on; W-m Midleton, Alex-r Langdels[342] and David Halyburton had only out their horses, I with ye two Keiths being not as yet come out. But the first three falling on in good earnest, Midleton haveing a long rapier and the other two good Scots {151} broad swords, which they so handled that the others had enough to do to defend themselves. And they now seeing us mounted with our pistolls ready cok't comeing up, tooke the flight and shutt the gate after them.

Our comorades recovering their horses, mounted, but wee could not get out any where. So as wee were considering w[ha]t to do, the maior and *ruitm-r* with their servants rushed in at the gate and fyred their pistolls at us. Wee being now on the defensive, and all the people of the village being gathered at the gate to hinder our getting out, and afrayed of a complaint to the generall, after some bickering and some skufling words wee were glad to capitulate and promise to be gone without more ado.

So wee marched away without our breakfast, which however wee gott in a house w-ch stood apart not farr of, for into a great village wee durst not go for fear of the lyke repulse. Haveing refreshed our selves, wee resolved to returne to Marien[burgh], fearing to be missed. As wee were on our way, wee perceived fyre in divers places of the great *werder* beyond Niewteich, and shortly after meeting a horseman, who told us that the {151v} Polls were fallen into the great *werder*, that the generalls with all their forces were marched towards them. This made us make what hast wee could.

Being come to our quarters and haveing enquired which way our trowpe was marched, 3 of us rode after them, the horses of the other three being weary. By the way accidentally meeting with the generall, he bidd us go feed our horses in the next village and then returne to the

---

[342] Alexander Landells, Patrick Gordon's gallant comrade-in-arms, was to follow him to Russia in 1661, served as his lieutenant colonel and fell in the heroic defence of Chigirin against the Turks in 1678. Gordon, always sparing in praise, called him "a very good and stout souldier".

towne. In our returne wee did meet the King in his coach, going towards Niewteich.

Haveing stayed some weekes here, wee marched with the generall towards Marienwerder, short of w-ch a mile wee quartered, and so onwards by Grawdents and Colum, beyond which a mile in a village orders came that our lieutennant with 30 horse should returne and force and bring up all those who were loitering behind in the villages. Wee marched back as farr as Marienwerder and brought up a Finns lieutennant and some others. The most, haveing heard of our coming, marched away in tyme.

Being returned, wee marched through Thorun, 98 men marching in rankes, being all yong, gallant, well cloathed, armed and horsed, w-ch made a gallant show. Neither was it lesse pleasant to see our servants and piedees[343] marching throw in a {152} trowpe, led by one Sinkler, who waited on the *ruitm-r*, and had drawne them up in good order with officers in their due places, they being all well armed and mounted, and above 200 in number.

The next night wee lodged in a gentlemans house a mile beyond Suleyova[344]. Here, it being my turne to make fyre and victualls ready and convenience for our horses, whilst the rest of my comorades were out seeking forrage and provisions, as I was beating in stakes for the horses, [came] one James Mongomery, a sonne of Skelmerlyes and nephew to the Marquisse of Ardgile, who from the battell of Varshaw had ridden in the trowpe. For he haveing been recommended by friends in Scotland to the Generall Dowglasse, and being a proper man in very good habite, the generall at first received him very kindly, gave him an excellent horse and a Dutch boy to wait upon him, admonishing him to behave himself well and learne the Dutch language soone, promiseing to advance him to an honourable charge.

This gentleman being high bended and not acquainted with the Germans fashions, nor complying with the generalls servants, whereby he began to be hated by them, and being delated, was reprehended by the generall, who alwayes loved to speake and tell the truth, to those especially

---

[343] Possibly a form of peage (Scots) – page or boy.
[344] Służewo.

whom he affected or tooke care for; {152v} which being ill taken by the said Montgomery, the generall began to neglect him, and his boy by hard usage being forced to runne away, and so in this condition after the battell of Varshaw was turned over to our trowpe. Where by his proud and high way of behaviour he gained nothing but neglect from the better sort, and from others ane aversnesse, whereby he keeped but seldome in company with the best, by whom he thought he gott not that respect which was due to him, but lodged and quartered with those of inferiour degree, where he was sure none would dispute the head of the table with him, and by whom or their servants his horse was taken ordinary care of.

This, so long as wee were in our locall and transeant quarters, where wee were well provided with all things necessary by the pawres, was not so grievous, irkesome or so much regarded. But when wee came to lodge closser or encampe in the field, where every one of us, who were not well provided of servants, must put our owne hands to worke if wee would have any thing to eat our selves, or our horses in a case to be ridden, and even the best without takeing care could be but slenderly provided {153} and soone go to ruine. Then it was that, every one haveing enough ado to furnish and maintaine himself, was wearyed of and shunned his company. Yet the winter over by shifting from one society to another, he had put of to this march, yet in a *krue* a myle short of Marienwerder his horse, which he had from the generall, and was indeed an excellent gelding, wanting all along the care and eye of his master, being hunger starved, dyed.

Here were the effects of pride and poverty to be seen! The first had procured the neglect and upon this occasion the derision of all person, and by the other he was incapacitated to come forward or help himself. He came to the *ruitm-r* and to diverse of us who had horses to spare, and in as submissive termes as his heart could permitt, craved the lend of a horse, but was put of every where with excuses.

When wee were on horseback ready to march, and I did see him standing befor the doore with his sadle and pistolls by him, for other baggage he had none, my heart pittyed him, and would have willingly affoorded him a horse, which I had to spare, had not the thoughts of being accounted too pittifull hearted (a passion, though, alwayes accompanying a generous mind, yet mistaken by meane capacities for faint-heartednes), {153v} as also feare to be burthened and so come in want afterwards my self; wee marched, and he, if he would not stay behind and runne the hazard of being knocked in the head by the pawres, must follow. So that, takeing up his sadle and pistolls on his back, he followed.

Being come to the generalls quarters wee halted, and Montgomery being come and seeing w-ch way the march did go, he walked on befor. The generall being ready, marched in his coach, and wee all after him. The generall being questionless informed of Montgomeryes condition, as he passed by, turned away his head and would not behold him. Wee passed by him also, with different passions. Halfe an houre thereafter, the *ruitm-r* takeing compassion of him, sent back a horse to him, whereon he mounted and jogged on.

This gentlman comeing to the place where, as I said befor, I was provideing convenience for my self and comorades in a gentlemans house a mile beyond Soleyewa, and alighting began to ty his horse to a stake, which I had newly beat in. I seeing that, began to rattle him up, telling him he might be ashamed, that he was become the refuse of the company, and that his behaviour had made him the object of derision and hatred to all; and asking him if he thought that any was {154} oblidged to worke for him; and told him he would procure himself the name of Skemler[345] Generall, which suited very well with his fathers stile or title (being Skelmerly); and that if he would put to his hand and do as he did see others must of necessity, and carry himself civilly sociable, every one would be glad of his company. For he might very well see that by his former high carriage, which no body cared for, he had gained ye contempt and neglect of every one. And much more of such matter I preached to him.

He hearing all with very great patience, and asking me now and then in a loveing way, why I was so ill to him? and what he should do? At last I told him, if he had a mind to eat, he must put to his hand and help to purchase and dresse it. And he againe asking me, what I would have him to do, and that he would most willingly do it, I asked him if he could flea

---

[345] Scots for sponger or parasite.

a sheep which lay there, being newly brought by one of my comorades. He answered yea, if he had a knife and any body to help to hold it, both which I affoorded him.

And so he did fall very handsomely to worke, which being so unexspected, I could not containe myself, but takeing a turne, I gott into the *ruitm-rs* quarters, who from his window had a fair prospect of the green whereon wee encamped. I told him I would show him a convert, {154v} and haveing showed him Montgomery fleaing a sheep, he much wondred and laughed heartily. I told him he should have but a litle patience, he should see him turning the spitt, which he did, haveing occasion to send the boy for water, and I being busy about other worke. After this there was none more dilligent and industrious in any society as he, so that thereafter some pleasantly called him my convert.

The next day wee marched and encamped two nights in the fields. The day thereafter wee lodged in a village to the left hand of Kuiavish Brest. Here wee stowed our selves and our horses in barnes. Here in the night tyme my best horse was stollne from amongst 40 which stood with him, which made me suspect dishonest dealing of some of the company. But not haveing any ground whom to challenge, I was forced to be quiet and make enquiry for him in the army, but in vaine.

Being past Cowalia, wee quartered about a mile further in a village by the edge of a wood. Here the *ruitmaster* takeing some along with him into these woods, gott good booty and brought a Catholick priest along to the quarters. I was sent with this priest to the generall, whom I found at his supper in Cowalia. After supper the generall asked him {155} some questions, and bidd me bring him back againe and take care that he should be brought to some sure place and there lett go free.

Haveing notice that the army was to march the next day by the way of Gostenin[346], where was a passe over a great marish, I thought it a fitt place to watch the armyes going over for my horse. So haveing obtained leave, the next morning befor I was well ready, I heard the trumpets of the avantguard sounding a march. At which tyme the sentryes and small

---

[346] Gostynin.

guards being drawne of, the free-booters and other loose people seek ordinaryly passages to be gone befor to purchase something. I made ready, and not waiting for a comorade and my boy, which were to go along w[i]t[h] me, hasted on befor and made such speed that I was gott quickly out of the noise and hearing of any.

So rideing all alone at leasure along by the syde of the wood, untill I was gott a great way of, and not hearing any body following me, whereas either my comorade or others, who usually made hast to gett befor, might have easily overtaken me. I began to suspect that the army was gone another way, which, being all alone and knowing all the countrey to be our enemyes, made me somewhat afrayed. So that being now come to the high land, I went into a small {155v} thicket a litle of the way, there to stay and see if any came that way. Here I heard cocks crowing and see the husband-men tilling and manuring the land in a very peacable manner.

Haveing stayed above an houre and a halfe here and not seeing any body come that way, I was more afrayed. Yet trusting to my horse, I resolved to returne the way I came, rather as with great danger take a short cutt to the way in which the army marched, which I knew must have inclined to the right hand. I had not ridden farr in the syde of the wood, when being afrayed of some suddaine assault out of the woods, I turned up to the hight, where I could see about me, and if I saw any danger, take the retreat or flight betymes.

I had not rode farr, when being on a milne damme by a small village, I saw one on horseback in Polls cloaths comeing towards me, and then another and a third. I would have gladly returned, but could not without bewraying an extraordinary and perhaps panick fear. So on I went, and being come neerer, I perceived them to be yong men belonging to the Sweds. I enquired of them w-ch way the army was marched, and they told me they had not seen the army in three dayes. One of them haveing a very fyne otter muffe on his hand, I asked him where he gott it. So he began to tell me a long story {156} how the day befor, being downe into the woodes, they happened upon some gentlmen with their familyes and goodes, who at the first sight of them had runne away. Yet that they not daring adventure to alight, had only from a tree snatched away that muffe.

I conceiving hopes that if the businesse were rightly handled, good booty might be gott, asked them if they would know the place and go along, and I would go with them. They willingly assented, only would have my promise that what wee gott should be equally shared amongst us, which I did. So back wee rode into the wood, and comeing to the place where they had been the day befor, found no body there. Only wee could perceive that there had been some good horses and trunkes with other baggage, which was carryed wee knew not whither. Wee alighted and began to seek about, and soone found out a good parcell of houshold linnen, a tunne of bier, the body of a very neat *kolesse*, and a while thereafter the wheeles. So that wee resolved to make up the *kolesse* and carry thereon the bier and such luggage as wee had gott to the army, makeing use of linnen for furniture for the horses to draw with.

In the meane tyme I going a litle further into the wood, did meet a couple of good lusty horses comeing in a foot roade, which I {156v} laid hold on and brought to the others to be yoaked in the *kolesse*, and takeing one of the biggest of the youths along with me to the foot road, wee rode further all along the syde of a great marish through very thick bushes. Being a good way of, I perceived a man standing on a tree, which being fallen, lay along in the marish. I alighted to have catched him, but he being aware escaped, though narrowly. Comeing further wee did see a smock, where I conjectured the gentlmen to be with their goods. Wee advanced very softly untill wee were gott unperceived within perfect wiew of them. I alighted and takeing my pistolls with me, desired the other when I should shout to shout also, as if wee called for our comorades, in the meane tyme not to forsake me in case I were put to it.

Being come to the place, which they had strongly barracadoed with great trees cutted downe round about them, I see ten or twelve gentlmen with their wiwes and children about a great fyre. I giveing a great showt and the other answering, I advanced in over the barricado. The Polls being surprised with fear and not knowing how many wee were, immediately ran away from the fyre. 4 or 5 gott to horseback, the rest with their wiwes and children befor them retired into the marish, haveing swords and karabins {157} by their sydes, and at great leasure, w-ch I seeing made no great hast, pretending as if I could not gett over untill I saw all clear. I came however in tyme enough to come betwixt them and two horses ready sadled and with pistolls. I gott up upon the best of them, being a yong horse and darke gray, and tooke the other in my hand. And hearing the great showting which these who had escaped did make, albeit there lay aboundance of all sorts of goods, trunkes, *skatolls*[347] and cloaths, yet durst wee not stay to looke for any thing. Only I tooke up in the going by a portmantle w-ch lay upon a trunke, and so made what hast wee could back againe, but in a larger way, w-ch he that was with me pretended to know.

Haveing ridden a great way and doubting how to find these wee had left makeing ready the *kolesse*, wee perceived a countrey fellow standing and hearkening. I rode up and befor he was aware had hold of him, and asking him what he was doing there, he without much ado told that, some gentlmen haveing notice of some Sweds entred into the wood, had sent him to see and informe them what number they were. He showed us also where the other two wee had left were. So takeing the pawre along, wee found our two youths ready with all, but in great fear by reason that the woods were rebounding with the clamours of the gentlmen, who haveing the alarum were, as it seemes, gathering from all quarters.

Wee {157v} set the pawre to drive the *kolesse*, who of purpose drove very often on upon trees to hinder us. Neither could wee by threats or fair words move him to keep the right way. So that if wee would not loose our *kolesse* and baggage, w-ch wee were loth to do, on[e] of the youths must sitt up and drive. Wee tooke, however, the pawr along with us lest he should give notice of our number.

By the way calling to mind that wee had passed the channell of a marish by a low bridge, and hearing the noise of the countrey people continuing and inclining that way, I conjectured that they were makeing hast perhaps to attackt us at that passage. Wherefor I thought fitt with another to make some hast befor to discover and secure that passage, and in good tyme, for 6 or 7 were even at it as wee came, whom wee skared away immediately, and rode about untill our *kolesse* came up and was safe over the passe.

---

[347] Szkatuła (Polish) – box or casket.

Being over, wee alighted and threw of the bridge, setting the trees afloat downe the streame.

Being near out of the wood and so of danger, whilst I stayed a litle behind, one of the youths shott at the pawre and killed him, pretending, when I was angry with him for it, that he had had ane intention to betray us. Whereas, I considered thereafter, it was meer simplicity, which in all his gestures he bewrayed, and might have easily escaped from us if he had been wise or pleased.

In the first village on the high ground wee alighted to bait our horses and eat something ourselves, one {158} being set on the toppe of the house sentry, who instantly called to us that 20 or 30 horsemen were comeing galloping out of the wood towards us. Wee mounted, and seeing them makeing great hast and in Polls habite, wee were in a quandary what to do. Yet trusting to our horses, wee resolved to know what they were, and so calling to them, after some enterchanges of dubious answeres wee knew them to be our owne people. They told us that they had been in the same woodes where wee had been, but further of, had killed many gentlemen and [got] good booty, but could not by reason of the great alarum in the woodes bring the halfe along with them.

They baited their horses a litle while with us, and then wee rode away together. Not farr of wee did meet with some straglers of the Sweds, who told us that the army was encamped a litle befor out to the right hand, and that they would the next day march over the passe at Gostenin; which wee beleeving and seeing a great many horsemen marching that way, turned of to the left hand and lodged in a small village halfe a mile short of that place. About midnight those whom wee did meet returned back into the woodes, and would have perswaded us to have gone with them, but it was Gods good providence that wee did not go, for as wee heard thereafter, they were all killed there by the countrey people.

Wee had notice that there were {158v} guards neer us, which made us more secure. So by day light setting forward, when wee came to the hight above the castle, wee perceived the guards were all marched away. So leaving the *kolesse* on that place, two of us rode downe to take a view of the castle, and wee had scarce entred the utmost gate, when wee perceived at a good distance 8 or 10 Polls standing by a fyre with their horses in their hands, drying themselves. They no sooner saw us, but they mounted, and whilst wee were bethinking our selves what to do, they ran away out at a back gate. Whereof wee were very glad, and made as if wee would have followed them, but returning speedily, wee made what hast wee could towards the way whither the army was marched.

In the first villages the pawres were all come and comeing out of the woodes, so that wee were in no small fear in going by these villages, for into them wee durst not go. On the fields I tooke a boy and made him to drive the *kolesse*. It was night befor wee gott to the army and the head quarters, comeing where the Kings *Trabants*, to whom these youths belonged, were lodged.

Wee according to bargaine divided all in 4 shares, the best horse with his furniture was reckoned for two, and being to cast lots, it was concluded, if myne {159} did fall to be one in him, I should receive 30 reichs dollers or any of the other two shares, which I pleased. The other horse with the furniture made the third share, and the *kolesse* with the two horses and other booty made the fourth, w-ch last was my luck to gett, wherewith I was very well satisfyed, it being worth double any other share, if I were but in any towne.

I lodged this night by a market-tenter, and the next morning early marched. I had not ridden above halfe a mile when I did meet with our trowpe, who were rejoyced to see me come with so good booty. That night wee quartered in a village not farr from Sobota. The next morning some of our comorades produced some Du[t]ch cloaths, which they had found in a hole, amongst which I knew my owne breeches, which had been taken from me not farr from this place near two years ago, when the pawres catched me sleeping, who must have been out of this village.

The same day I rode with a party along {159v} up the river. About a mile and a halfe wee came by a fort in the mooras, but could not come at it; there were some gentlemen and many pawres with their wiwes, children and goods in it. Here Generall Dowglas falling sick, was carryed to Lovits and so left us to all our great grieffe. He recommended us to the care of the Generall Adjutant Shoenleben, who indeed was very kind to us.

Wee marched to Peterkaw, and it being rendred, marched to Jendrzejowa, where in a Jesuits monastery I saw two very old Jesuits lying killed, one befor the great altar, the other above in a gallery, the altars all bared and deformed, which was a great pitty to see.

Here being on a party, I did first see the Hungarians, who being above 50 horsemen came in upon us in a gentlemans house, which had a mote and drawbridge. They put us in no small fear, wee thinking they were Polls. They told me in Latin that their army was not farr of, and would joyne with us {160} shortly.

Wee marched from Jendrzeyowa by the castle of Pienshowa and encamped in the fields. Maior Generall Wurts being come out of Crakow to the King, I did meet with many of my old acquaintances.

The next day, being sick and sitting in my *colesse*, the waggons of our trowpe takeing a near way, were necessitated to breake through the waggons of the left wing betwixt two regiments with great quarrelling and much ado. A coach being on the head of the other regiment, with a lady in it and 6 horses befor it, and my *kolesse* being at some distance from the other by reason of the bad way, the coachman driveing in befor me, and myne striveing to do the lyke, the postilion with his long whip strikeing at my servant, hitt me just on the face; which enraged me so that getting from my *kolesse*, I run after him and with my sword gave him such a stroke in the head that he did fall downe among the horses feet, and getting up, drove on my way. But hearing such a noise behind me, and being afrayed of being persued, {160v} I gott me to horse and in hast gott me to the army.

At the Kings meeting with the Prince of Transilvania, when they rode along the front of our army, the King takeing notice of our trowpe, shewed it to the prince, who looked upon us with great earnestnes.[348]

The army drawing near to Zavichost, it was my lott to be commanded by the waggons, and being on the right hand, wee must of necessity crosse through the left wings waggons to gett to our quarters, which was a mile below Zavichost in a gentlemans *hoffe*. Being come to the way, wee resolved to lett the regiment passe, which wee found on their march, and to breake

---

[348] This was on 31 March 1657, Gordon's 22nd birthday. See fol. 101.

then through betwixt it and the other. Which these waggonmasters of the regiments who were behind perceiving, advanced up with all the forces they could make to hinder our passage, and wee gathered ours, being about 15 comorades and 30 or 40 servants and boyes. The Germans were about 70 or 80 besides many fellowes come downe from the waggons {161} with clubbes and staves.

I seing their number increasing, and us without hope of more help, thought best to begin. So comeing up to them and telling them that wee must be thorow after that regiments waggons were past, they in a bragging way denying and threatening, and jeeringly calling us gentlemen, so wee came to sharper words. And I being in dispute with one of the chieffe of them, he in a rage called me trencher-licker, supposeing perhaps by my age and cloaths (which were neater as ordinary) that I was some noblemans or generalls page. Which heated me so that I drew and fell on, being not long unseconded by my comorades, who altogether falling on with our good Scots hearts and swords, in a trice put them to the runne, giveing many a bloody head and getting some. I was wounded in the forehead with one of their blunt swords.

In the meane tyme our waggons gott throw, and wee marched of to our quarters, where wee had abundance of forrage. In the night tyme, about one after midnight, a great fyre arose in the barne-yards where most of us were lodged, by what accident wee {161v} know not, and did great harme. I had lodged my self in one end of a barne of from the threshing-floore, and my horses by me. When the fyre had seized on the barne I was asleep, and dreaming that I was wrestling with another man who at every bout threw me to the ground, wherewith being vexed and with greater force intending reparation, I awaked – and found my self almost choaked with smocke. The cornes on the other syde of the threshing-floore being at the toppe all on fyre, I gott up and runne to the doores on each syde of the threshing-floore, which with great difficulty I set open. And then comeing back, with my sword I cut the halters of my horses and turned them all out into the threshing-floore.

By this tyme the fyre was so encreased that with heat and smocke I knew not almost where I was or what I was doing. Yet putting my naked sword under my arme and flinging my clocke over my shoulder, I thought to gett of my sadle, but catching hold only of one [of] the pistols, I drew it out and with great {162} danger and difficulty escaped out at the doore towards the fields; where I exspected to have found my horses, and that my servants, who were with my waggons within the yard, had brought out my *kolesse* and waggons, but found neither the one nor the other, all being burned.

Some lying on the threshing-floore, as one Lodovick Sinkler of Rosseline and others, being fast asleep and not hearing any thing, came out after me in their shirts, w-ch were burning on their backes. By this our trowpe was almost ruined as to horses and equipage, and which I could not recover all this march, haveing lost nine horses, much rich booty and all my mounting.

The next day a Dutch cornet challenged our lieutennant for affronting him, in vindication of some words he had spoken in disparagement of the Scots. The cornet at the second course was shott throw the back whereof he dyed halfe a yeare afterwards. The lieutennant was forced to lurke sometyme among the Hungarians.

The day thereafter I went a party on foot to find {162v} something to eat, and in the woods sped very well. I bought also a good yong nagge for 8 r. thalers, but could not gett a sadle for money nor good words no where, so that I was forced to make a shift some dayes without one.

Hearing of the bridge being ready, and the army to march over the next day, I thought it worth my paines to take ane exact acco[un]t of our new-come ffriends, of the number of them especially, haveing had some dispute about it with my comorades, who were of opinion that they were a farr greater number as I judged them to be. So accordingly (haveing mor attendants as convenience or businesse for them) I passed the bridge and tooke as particular ane acco[un]t of the number of them as I could, and reckoned of Hungarians well mounted, with servants and attendants marching under command, order and collours 12 or 15,000 horsmen; of foot, most whereof went under the name of Moldavians, 5,000; by the waggons and baggage of all sorts of people 5,000; by the artillery and {163} princes baggage 2,000; the guards and court 800; the Cosakes

6,000,[349] w-ch amounted not to one halfe of what they boasted to be. And even of these I beleeve there were many Polls, whom on their march they had taken and forced along with them.

Not farr from this place being on a party, I provided my self with a light waggon and a couple of good horses and other necessaryes. At Urzendowa, it being ordered that most of the baggage should be destroyed, the *ruitm-r* desired me to gett away with his befor to Lublin, and there to stay till either he should come or send to dispose of such things as he could not conveniently carry along. Being come to the suburbes of Lublin, I had not stayed above 3 houres when I receaved order to follow the march with all the waggons.

Two dayes thereafter, getting betymes befor the army with W-m and Alex-r Humes, wee rode here and there till midday and could not fynd any thing worth the takeing, when in our returne {163v} comeing to a large marish, on the other side whereof was a great thick wood of firres, as wee were passing through a long artificiall passage, wee did see on our right hand 15 or 20 persons comeing through the marish from the wood. I thinking that they had been in the wood seeking after booty, resolved to ride downe alongst the syde of the marish.

Wee had not ridden farr, when by a well wee found the footsteppes of Polls bootes very fresh, and rideing further, wee found their march into the wood, and then forward in a litle road or way w-ch wee followed. I rideing alone before and the other two at some distance, comeing near the place from whence wee did see these fors-d persons passeing through the marish, I see on the right hand of the way a man newly slaine, and a litle further another in the dead throwes, who lying on the way with his feet towards us, with his right hand, by moving it up and downe, seemed as I thought to diswade us from advancing any further. I looking upon him nearer, found him to be a Cosake by his foretoppe or tuft of haire, which the Cosakes use to wear on their forehead.

So turning {164} to my comorades, I asked them what they thought, if wee should go any further. At which Alex-r Hume answered, "I think wee

---

[349] Cf. fol. 99 v.

ar mad to go so farr, this being the third dead man of our owne people newly slaine!"; this indeed putting me in reall fear, being few and neither well mounted nor well armed either for a chase, charge or retreat.

Wee returned with greater hast and more circumspection as wee had advanced. On the way wee found a very pretty *kolesse* worth 20 or 30 r. thalers, which I would gladly have taken along, but my comorades would admitt no stay. Being come to the high way and meeting with some of these, who being upon their purchase had come over the same marish where wee had passed, they told us that at a village on the other syde they had seen some Cosakes, who told them that being in these woods they were surprised by about 50 Polls, from whom they had retired, and being hotly persued, were forced to quit their horses and gett through the marish on foot, haveing lost eight of their company.

{164v} The next day, wanting provisions and o[u]r waggons horses lykeing to faile, I with my comorade W-m Hume made a shift to gett befor the army againe. And being come to a gentlemans house on the skirt of a large hill, from whence a pleasant prospect into the countrey round about, wee perceived a great way of a man standing in a litle hight, to which place wee rode in great hast. Whither being come and finding no body there, I gave Hume my horse to hold and went in among some shrubes and bushes to looke after the man wee had seen. Haveing past through the bushes, among some faughed land I found 3 peasants lying not farr from another, whom I drove out befor me to the place where I left my comorade with my horse, who was gone from thence.

I went up on the hight and showted, but could not see him nor hear any answering, which put me in some fear and perplexity. Yet to be quite of the peasants, I came downe and pulled ane axe out of one of their hands and flung it as farr as {165} I could, and from the same fellow tooke a purse, which hung about his neck with some money in it. Then going to another to visitt him if he had any money, he caught hold of me and called his neighbours to assist him. So I began to strugle with him, and by Gods great mercy, who at this need gave me more as ordinary strength, I gott free of him and got out my sword, wherewith I drove him who had been in hands with me away, and set upon the other two, one whereof flung the axe (which he had fetched) at me, which I very happily avoided. Being enraged, I followed these two and at the entry of the bush overtooke one of them and gave him such a stroake on the head that he fell downe, and hearing a shouting within the bushes I made hast away.

Haveing run near a quarter of mile, I came to another litle hight from whence I at last espyed my comorad a great way of, to my great joy. I made hast and being come, chide him soundly as good reason. He excused himself {165v} by haveing seen and followed a woman who directed him to that place, where three horses were tyed in a thicket. Wee takeing these horses, marched of and in the evening came to the leaguer under Liatovits[350].

Nothing worthy of relateing did befall me on the march to Wengrova untill I came to Kamien, from whence I with 5 more went on a party towards Botczky[351]. By the way, being in a gentlmans house baiting our horses, 20 Hungarians chanced to come there also, with whom falling in discourse, they offered and desired that wee might go together. So being agreed on the ordinary lawes of partyes to share whatsoever wee should gett equally, being come to a house belonging to one of the Sapihaes, wee environed it and presently catched two gentlemen. A third escapeing into a garden, defended himself so well against 7 or 8 of these Hungarians with stones and the lyke, and at last with a long pole, that it was a wonder {166} and pleasure to see. But being wearyed and wounded, they mastered him and immediately cut of his head to my great grieffe, hateing such cruelty to a vanquished pretty man.

The other two wee examined to learne where any booty was to be had. One of them told us of a great company of gentlemen with their families, enclosed within a *waggonburg* in the wood not farr from thence, where was abundance of all sorts of goods and riches, and no great danger or difficulty in obtaining it, there being such a panick feare among them, that at the very first sight of us they would run away and leave all. After a particular and circumstantiall enquiry I found the businesse feasable and urged the prosecuting of it. The Hungarians at first seemed glad and well content,

---

[350] Latowicz.
[351] Boćki.

and tooke our march together that way. Wee were not past the gardens, when they halted and put in many difficulties, and by no perswasions could be moved to go forward. {166v} And so tying the two gentlemen, their hands behind their backes, to a hedge, they cut of their heades.

Wee marched to Botczky, the streets whereof wee found laid over with crosse trees, w-ch wee removed. And rideing a mile further, wee came to a gentlemans house where wee suddainly surprised some gentlemen, who had been carowsing. Upon our environeing the house they hide themselves in the barnes and outhouses, whither they being fetched and examined, they told that the gentlman to whom the house belonged was with many others in the woods within the marish, and all their substance with them; that they knew not of any thing hidd in the house or about it. 4 of those who said so they presently cut of their heads. The 5th being a youth of about 20 yeares of age, being terrifyed with such spectacles, and threatened with the same measure, told that he had heard of plate and other things hid in the house. And so bringing us from one place to another, {167} bidding us digg, where nothing was to be had, at last bringing us into the sellar, and finding nothing there, he declared that he knew not of any thing, and craved pardon for abuseing us, w-ch he said the desire of a litle longer tyme to live had moved him to do.

So he was brought out to the greene to be executed as ye rest, w-ch cruelty I hated much and was hugely grieved to see, and now seing this youth in this condition, used all meanes to save him, offering my share and at last all our shares of the booty (w-ch was considerable) for his lyfe. But the more urgent and earnest wee were to save him, the more obstinate they were, and threatened us as ffriends to the common enemyes and, as it were, in despight of us cruelly murthered him.

Being near evening, wee went out into the fields a large halfe mile from the house, and in a field among some bushes wee turned our horses to feed. Wee had {167v} with us a gentleman who was grieve of that place, out of whom by torture they hoped to gett more the next day. The Hungarians laid them all downe to sleep, leaving the care of their horses and prisoner to us. Wee then began to consult what was best to be done, for wee were all affrayed of our lives; they haveing threatened us diverse tymes, and now haveing good booty and in likelyhood of getting more, the greedinesse whereof might move them, who had neither fear of God or morall reason, to kill us indeed, they being 20 well mounted and armed fellowes, and wee 6, whereof 2 were but pittifull warriours.

To gett away from them wee could not, being affrayed of being intercepted by the Polls in our returne to the army. So that a motion being made of cutting their throats, it was approved by all, and discussed, was found easy to be done. For wee were masters of their horses and pistolls, and well armed with whingers, pistolls and good swords, and they all asleep {168} at some distance from another, perswading our selves that self-preservation, and the cruell murthers which they had committed in cold blood, would sufficiently justify us befor God and men. Yet when wee were even ready to put in execution what wee had determined, it was Gods pleasure not to permitt us to accomplish it, one of us even fainting, and wee all at the sight thereof relenting and changing our purpose.

Day being come, wee marched to the house againe and found that all the dead bodyes were carryed from thence. The Hungarians pined the *podstarost*, or grieve, exceedingly cruell by powring cold water in his mouth untill he vomited blood. He brought them to diverse places where he said things were hidden, but found nothing. At last in a low vault under the house they digged and found good booty, not permitting any of us to come neer. Yet one of our comorads peeping in unawares, did see them looking on some silver {168v} trenchers. So that by the case, which they brought out, wee perceived they had gott a good quantity of silver plate.

Afterwards they cut of the *podstarosts* head, and haveing provided waggons, loaded up 4 pipes of double brandy, 2 tunnes of meade and 5 of beer, w-ch bringing to the army on the march wee sold and dealt the money. As also wee shared 9 horses with sadles and pistolls, every one of us getting 28 reichs thalers, but two waggons with the best booty they had convoyed away. Wee had questioned them in the gentlmans house about the silver plate, w-ch they denyed and showed us some tinne trenchers, saying they had gott none other. At night wee told our *ruitm-r*, and he by meanes of Maior Generall Gawdy gott the prince to give strict order to enquire of the businesse, and do justice accordingly, w-ch was the trouble of 4 or fyve dayes, and at last gott nothing but some peuter vessell and other luggage of {169} small value, these faithlesse fellowes purging themselves by oath.

Being come to Littawish Brest, I went over the river Bug to Kodna[352], a small towne about 6 miles from Brest, where and in a house belonging to Sapiha wee had good booty, bringing 20 tunnes of beer and brandy to the leaguer. Wee brought also a pipe of cider, which wee sold for French wine to a sutler for 40 r. thal. Here I provided my self an excellent horse from James Burnet of Leyes, giveing him for him two horses and 12 r. thal.

Here our *ruitm-r*, being delated to the King by *Graffe* Jacob de la Gardie and Lt. Coll. Podkamer, was sent for by the King, and being questioned, he stood upon his justification, which so enraged His Ma-tie that with a litle walking sword he cut him twice in the head, giveing him many strokes over the shoulders, and then sent him under the guard by the generall *gevaltiger*, or provost marshall.

Here the King haveing notice {169v} that the King of Denmarke had declared warr and entred in action against him, resolved to returne.

The 2d dayes march I went on a party, where I had a quarrell with Lt. John Russell, which was taken up by our comorades.

Being come to the army and sold our booty, I went againe out with 7 others on the way towards Drogishin[353], and haveing ridden two dayes without finding any thing worthy transporting, towards evening, being in a thick wood by a marish and following a trodden way, wee came to a party of ours who had newly light upon a number of waggons full of all sort of houshold stuffe and provisions, the gentlmen with their families at the first sight of them running into the woodes and marish. They were about 30 or 4[0], all Finnes belonging to M. G-ll Fabian Barnes his regiment, and had such choice of booty, that wee seing them takeing only the most precious things, resolved to take what they left when they should be gone.

Whilst wee were on horseback looking {170} on, two of these Finnes brought a very beautifull virgin out of the marish, who by her habite and gesture assured us of her quality. They had no sooner brought her on dry

---
[352] Kodeń.
[353] Drohiczyn.

ground, when one of them began to strip her of her cloaths, leaving her in a white flannell petticoat and a bodies with silver py-holes. The Finne seing the silver presently tooke of the bodyes, and being taken with the fynnes of the flannell, would needs have the pettycoate of too. She all the tyme roaring and crying, that it would have moved a stone, and seing us better habited and complexioned as these rookes, called to us for help.

I had at the beginning diswaded him from useing her so roughly and uncivilly, which he minded not, and now my heart melting with pitty, I alighted from my horse and began to entreat him and these of his comorades by him, telling them that they had choice of rich booty besyde; that they should remember {170v} they were borne of women, and that it was neither Christian nor humane to discover a womans nakednesse. All which availed not, and now the yong gentlewoman seing me ready to stand for her, gott in behind me, and as the Finne would seize her againe, I in a friendly way put him by with my hands. Whereat he gave me such a blow on the neck, that I had much ado to keep my feet. Yet recollecting my self, and not used to put up such things, I drew my sword and gave him such a blow on the pate that he did fall to the ground.

His comorades seing this, 7 or 8 who were neerest did fall all upon me, so that I could not gett my self defended from getting some blowes. But their swords were so blunt that they did not cutt me, only in the right brow, which was by a thrust, I think. My comorades had all along diswaded me from medling with them, yet seing me now in this distresse, they gott all from their horses, and together with our good Scots swords {171} put them to a stand, and most of them being gott together, yet by the advantage of good hearts, hands, swords and straitnesse of ground wee made them give ground. And for the most part every right blow disenabling them of a man, they at last tooke them to their heeles. Wee did drive them a great way of into the woods, haveing possession of their horses and missile weapons.

Returning, wee consulted what to do, and albeit perhaps there were none killed, yet many of them being sore wounded, wee were afrayed of complaints. So wee resolved to take two or three of those who were wounded and all their horses along with us, so farr as wee could be sure they could not overtake us. At our returne wee seized on their horses and such of the booty as wee could in such a hast take. The yong gentlewoman, being all this while as it were in a extasy, and now seing us ready to be gone, came entreating us not to leave her to the cruelty of these pagans, which moved me so, {171v} that against my comorades will I sett her up behind me and tooke her along.

After wee were gott without the wood, wee marched about a Scots mile in the fields, and it being past sunsett, wee dismissed the wounded men with the horses back againe, haveing blind-folded the men all the way. The night being light, wee rode about 3 Dutch miles and then baited our horses in a gentlemans house about an houre.

About midday wee see some straglers and forragiers of our army, when wee concluded to divide our booty and separate. I put my yong lady in the habite of a Polls youth and dispatched her befor with my owne servant and another. Being come into the *hoffe* quarters, I did see my servant environed with some Polls on the street, and being come neerer, he told me that he was stop't by Koritsky[354] his people, who knew the lady and said she was their masters neere kinswoman.

I comeing near, Koritsky {172} himself came and very civilly desired to speak with me. I alighting, he told me that this gentlwoman was his very neer kinswoman; that I would be pleased to deliver her to him, that he would see her convoyed to a sure place in honour. I told him that he might have perhaps have understood from her or my servant, after what manner and what hazard I had been in to save her from dishonour; that my intentions were no other still as honourable; that she herself had desired to go along with me; that haveing obtained and cared for her so, I could not in honour part with her. He told me that the King was hard by, and that it would cost him but a word to the King for her. I being afrayed of haveing it come to much hearing, lest the other businesse should be discovered, yet told him, if I could be assured that she were really his kinsewoman and should be kept in honour, I would willingly part {172v} with her.

---

[354] See fol. 58 v.

In the meane tyme my comorade had told one of his servants that wee had gotten her for a share of rich booty, and so by parting with her should be at a losse. Which he telling to his master, he went in to the house and returning presented me with 10 ducats, saying, "I am informed that you have her as a share of your booty, wherefor be pleased to accept of this", which I refused, and seing some Polonian gentlewomen come out with him, without mor ado desired him to take her to him if she would go. Whereof she being glad, I desired only all might be kept quiet, promiseing to send some womens cloaths to him the next day, haveing gott good store at the shareing of our booty; which I sent accordingly, he giveing my servant a ducat for his paines.

{173} Being come to the river Bug not farr from Kamien, I went on a party againe with sixe comorads, rideing through Botcky to a village called Male Skripky, where in a garden wee found good booty digged by the root of a great oake tree, and hidd among some bushes a beautifull yong gentlewoman with her mother. I was not only willing but urgent to have them left there, but all, especially a marryed man, would needs have the yong woman taken along. After in our returne wee had ridden about two miles, I had perswaded them to consent to let her go, but wee being come then among the stragling partyes of the Sweds, she fearing to be seized on by others, who might use her mor uncivilly, refused to returne. So that wee were engaged to take her along, and being at a long and tedious dispute who should have the custody of her, at last it was allowed to me.

The next day comeing to Kamien, wee found the {173v} army marched towards Wengrowa. Wee lodged in a village about 4 miles from the Bug. In the night tyme a fellow whom I had taken in a village called Wielky Scripky runn away, takeing two good horses along.

By day light wee see some forrunners of the army and sutlers makeing back againe towards the r. Bug, who informed us that the army was to returne; as it did the same day, marching over the river and immediately sending out a strong party towards Czechanoftsa[355], who the next

---

[355] Ciechanowiec.

day returned with[out] getting notice of any enemy, who as it was said lay encamped at Sokoll. Only Felt Marshall *Graffe* Steinbock came to the army with a strong party of about 500 horse.

Hearing of the army being to stay here some tyme, and being by the yong gentlewoman, who was with me, earnestly entreated to bring her to some safe place, I resolved to bring her back to her fathers house; and getting some {174} comorades, a litle befor midday I rode from the leaguer, and passing through Botczky in the night tyme, wee came to Male Scripke by day light and delivered my charge of to her mother[']s sister.

Returning the same day through Botczky and comeing to the *Hoffstatt*, q-r the Hungarians had on our march to Brest cut of some gentlmens heads, I rideing downe by the house to the marish see a woman running away, whom I overtooke. She desired me to let her go and pointed to a litle bush in the marish. I alighted and in that bush found a peasant who, by threatening to cut of his head, told me he would bring us where the burgers of Botcky were keeping their horses. Haveing asked all the circumstances of the place, number of people and how armed, I found it feasable, and so going back to my comorades, found none there but one James Elphingstone, to whom I communicated the businesse. The rest of our comorades being so farr gone that {174v} there was no recalling of them, wee resolved our selves (haveing one servant only with us) to undertake it, promiseing freedome to the peasant at our returne to this place, and threatening to kill him if he brought us into any danger.

So marching through a very thick wood in a cutt out way above halfe a Dutch mile, wee came out among small bushes, where at length wee espyed the horses and some men walking among them with swords or simitars about them. Drawing neer wee gave a great shout and, advancing, they scarsely looking about them runne all into the marish, being about 25 or 30 men. I followed, making a show as if I would enter the marish, alongst which I rode too and fro to watch that they should not returne untill wee should seize the horses, whereof there were about a hundred. James Elphingstone standing sentry, I tooke 9 of the best, and the servant changed his, getting bridles ready hanging on a tree, and so haveing as many as wee could well guide, marched {175} of in great hast.

About sunsett wee came to the *Hoffstatt* and there tooke 4 litle boyes to guide our horses, letting the peasant according to promise go free, these boyes comeing with a heird of cattell very opportunely. Wee rode very hard changing horses, untill it was beginning to grow darke, and our horses beginning to faint, wee came by a village where wee were necessitated to bait our horses. Yet seing light in every house, wee durst not adventure to go in, only wee entered a barne w-ch stood a good distance from ye houses. Wee brought in our horses as quietly as wee could, and finding sheaves of rey wee fed our horses, but being exceedingly overtaken with sleep, wee resolved to sleep a few houres. So secureing the one door by lying downe within it, the other being shut with a great padlock, I watched first letting all the other sleep.

I could hardly {175v} containe my self wakeing ane houre and then called up my comorade, and haveing made him with all meanes fully awake, I rested, and awaking of my self found my comorade asleep, so getting up and calling on him and our servant and the boyes, suspecting them to be gone by a dreame, and finding the door a litle open. So searching and finding the boyes gone, in great hast wee drew out our horses and mounted, but not being able to guid[e] all our horses along, I resolved to hazard into the village on foot and entrap somebody. And so calling at the window of a litle house, counterfeiting the countrey accent, a litle youth made up the doore, whom I laid hold on, threatening him if he should make any noise. He seing he must go along and being asked for others, brought me to two other houses, takeing a boy out of either, such as I could medle with.

So comeing to our horses, wee mounted and about midday overtooke our comorades, who were in some perplexity, fearing the peasants {176} had killed us. Wee had concluded not to tell them the manner of our hazardous adventure, for then every one of them must have had an equall share with us. So wee made a tale, telling them that wee had chanced upon a party of the Brandeburghs, with whom going into the woods wee had gott these horses, and haveing gott two for our owne shares, wee had bought the rest of them; so makeing a *duane*[356], wee put two of our horses among the rest of our purchase.

Being come into the leaguer, the *ruitm-r* sent for me in the night and, makeing a heavy moane for want of money, I gave him 15 r. dollers, w-ch he tooke very kindly, being much more as he exspected. Two dayes thereafter he was released from his imprisonment, and being destitute of horses for his waggons, I gave him two of these I had purchased, and wee gave each of us a horse to mount the distressed brethren who were afoot.

{176v} Here wee were informed that our Generall Dowglas was ordered to go to Sweden and act against Denmarke, and that the King himself would shortly follow. This put us all to our wits end, knowing wee should have but bad dayes, when wee should be blocked up or besieged in garrisons; that the defensive party in a forreigne countrey, as wee were sure to be now, hath alwayes the worst of it; that there would be but small occasions of either getting riches or honour; that wee knew not of any patron and were not well beloved of the Sweds and Dutches. All these things considered, wee resolved to petition His Ma-tie that he would take us along, and by meanes of Lt. Coll. Arensdorff gott Field Marshall Steinbock to present our petition, w-ch was rejected.

Afterwards 4 of us were delegated to sollicite His Ma-tie. Wee tooke the opportunity of His Ma-ties haveing been abroad, and alighted from horse and spoke, saying wee came out of our owne countrey upon the acco[un]t of gaining honour and livelyhood; that wee {177} had engaged to serve under His Ma-tie and the command of Generall Dowglas; y-t wee doubted not but our service and behaviour were sufficiently knowne to His Ma-tie; that so long as wee had served His Ma-tie wee had not received a farthing of pay; that wee were not used, neither could make such shifts as those who were brought up with hard labour could; that being in ane army, which was master of the field, wee could hardly purchase so much as to keep lyfe and soule together, and if wee should be straitned to live within garrisons, wee foresaw all extremities; to prevent which wee humbly entreated His Ma-tie not to leave us behind him,

---

[356] This word has baffled the editor, who is not even sure what language it belongs to.

but take us along, where we would most willingly spend our lives in His Ma-ties service.

His Ma-tie haveing heard us out, turneing short, told us that good people must stay behind also, where there was honour to be wonne as well as where he was {177v} going. Wee replying that wee had rather seek honour in the fields as within walls, and *Graffe* Steinbock speaking something to His Ma-tie in our behalfe, His Ma-tie turning to him said, "I had rather cause sink them in the river with sackes about their neckes as give them their will!", which wee overhearing and so despairing of prevailing, desisted.

Two dayes thereafter the armies marched, the Hungarians on the west syde of the river Bug and the Sweds on the east. Being come to Poltowsko, I came about an houre or two befor evening in the leaguer, being detained at the passage of the river Narew. Being at my tent, the Cornet Robert Steward send for me, where I found 5 or 6 of our comorads. They all told me that they had intelligence of good booty to be had at a towne not farr of called Presnits[357], only quick expedition was necessary. I told them I was ready, so wee appointed our rendevous about {178} halfe a mile from the towne, N[orth]-west by a litle bush, whither wee came about halfe an howre after sunsett, being twelve and 7 boyes or servants.

Wee marched all night and by day light came to Presnits, where wee found many Sweds and Dutches befor us, who haveing sufficiently visited all places, told us there was nothing to be had but beer, whereof they would willingly have taken some tunnes along, but could find neither waggons nor horses or oxen to draw them. Wee put our horses however to feed, and in the meane tyme went up and downe seeking for what could be had. Some Germans galloping along the streets told us that some Polls were comeing out of the woods towards the towne. Wee mounted immediately, and being gott without the towne, see 8 horsmen rideing up and downe upon the fields, and advancing towards them, wee put them to a retreat and followed them over a small passe {178v} towards a wood.

---

[357] Przasnysz.

Wee had not followed them farr when, seing them makeing semblance as if their horses were wearied, yet when wee came neer them they could claw it away very swiftly; I suspected some stratagem by ambush and called often to Robert Steven, a very pretty man and well mounted, not to persue them farther, and comeing neer the wood wee kept up our horses, hopeing that he seeing himself alone, would returne. But he being eager in persuite, and wee unwilling to desert him, followed into the wood.

Wee had not gon farr, when 30 or 40 horse in a full carrier, and these few turning also, made towards us. Robert Steven would then have gladly retired, but being on a resty jade, she would not stirr back, and so was killed. Wee made what hast wee could over the fields to the passe, where some of our comorades, being afoot, shott at the Polls who persued us with their carabines, {179} and made them stand of, and wee being gott over, leap'd from our horses and threw of a small bridge.

Being gott to the towne and found the rest of our comorades, wee followed the Dutches who were gone befor. Being come over a passe and not overtakeing them, nor knowing w-ch way they went, wee held on the high way, and being come to a high ground, wee see a strong party of the Polls comeing out of the towne and takeing the high way after us. This put us in no small fear and made us hasten our pace.

Being come into a valley, wee happened upon about 30 horses feeding and with them 16 men and boyes, all whom wee seized upon and mounted them upon the best of the horses, giveing them our coats and hattes to make them appear strangers, and so drawing them in a troope with our worst-horsed comorades and the boyes by them, to keep them in good order; {179v} fowre of us keeping the arrear guard, to witt Cornet Stewart, Alex-r Landels, James Elphingston and my self, all exceeding well horsed and armed, Corporall Waugh and Thomas Hume had the van. By the trowpe were W-m Midleton, Alex-r Hume, Robert and Alex-r Areskins and David Halyburton, all except those two who had the van very ill horsed.

Haveing consumed some tyme in ordering our businesse, the Polls drew neer, and wee holding on our way w[i]t[h] as great hast as the horses and the keeping of good order could permitt. At their first comeing on they were about 30 or 40 horse, and seing such a strong, well ordered trowpe, they kept at a distance, pricking up and downe on both sides and in the rear. Wee knowing that our safety, next to Gods protection, consisted in stout resolution and not letting them know w[ha]t {180} mettall our trowpe was made of, wee did all wee could to keep them at as great a distance as possible.

Their numbers increasing to above 60 horse, they began to come up more closely to us, especially in the rear, but by our often wheeling and desperately charging up and fireing among them they were content not to engage so farr as to receive a charge of our trowpe, of whose weaknes if they had knowne as well as wee, all had been soon lost.

In the heat of this businesse our trowpe makeing a halt, I rode up to see what the matter was. So I found that one of the peasants who had undertaken to shew us the way to Mlave[358] and perswaded us that wee had no nearer no[r] safer retreat as to the Prussian borders, and wee seing great smoake on our left hand and towards that place, imagined that our army was marching thither. This peasant, {180v} I say, comeing to three sundry wayes, pretended not to know which was the right, neither could I or any other perswade him or any of the rest to tell us. At last I threatening to kill him, he seing the Polls hard by, leapt from the horse and run towards them. I knowing that it would cost us all our lives if he escaped to them, followed him, and by reason of the rough ground scarsely overtooke him befor he gott to them. I had no tyme to lay hold of him, neither was it safe for feare of his gripeing me. So with a back stroake with my sword I gave him enough, and so with difficulty escaped from those who came rideing in to his rescue. By chance, he being the guide and rideing with the foremost two, had none of our cloaths, which made us the lesse curious for recovering his body.

After wee had ridden halfe a mile further, there came about 15 horse more to them, so that divideing {181} themselves in three companies, they offered to charge us in the rear and both the flankes, which made us draw closser together and march faster, keeping ye midle of the three

---

[358] Mława.

wayes by good luck. Yet for all that they never offered to charge us in bodyes, only some of them comeing pricking out from their trowpes, w[i]t[h] whom wee could deale very well, keeping them always a pretty distance from our trowpe. Haveing ridden about a mile after this manner, being continually infested with their arrowes and carabine shott, wee of necessity spareing our shott, being not well stored with it, and seeing that they could not effect any thing, they marched away to the right and left hand, leaving about 12 or 15 in our rear.

Wee at first were very glad to be freed of them, but perceiving by a long tract of such trees as usually grow in marishes befor us that there was a passe, and that these who were {181v} gone from us were makeing great hast to two villages on the right and left hand, wee easily guessed that they intended to attact us at the passe, and to hinder our passage were gone to the other syde. This put us in some fear, but knowing that the contrary passion must help us, wee made all the hast wee could towards the passe, and then wee fowre who were in the reare passing by the trowpe desired them to stand to it now or never. I desired them to fight at least for a dry place to dy on, that it might not be said wee dyed in a gutter, w-ch was occasion of much good merriment thereafter.

Being joined to the two in the van, wee made hast through the marish, it being both deep and large. At the other syde, the ground being somewhat high, wee saw 15 or 20 of them already waiting for us, whom wee charged resolutely and without much ado put them to the flight, and made a free passage for our trowpe to march on.

After this they {182} did not molest us any more. Neither being come to a hight, from whence wee could see a great way, could wee discerne whither they were gone. So being exceeding glad to be rid of them, wee marched on towards Mlavy, from whence about halfe a mile wee alighted and in a gentlemans house baited our horses. Here wee were informed that about 2 miles from thence was the border of Prussia; that some of our army in their way to Prussia had been in Mlavy the day befor and, as they thought, lodged there last night. Haveing stayed about ane houre, wee dismissed our counterfeit trowpers and marched on securely towards the towne.

Being not come in sight thereof as yet, wee did meet ane old woman of whom wee enquired if any souldiers were in the towne. She told us that just now a number of Polls were come thither, whom wee conjectureing to be these who had persued us, halted {182v} and advised what to do. Wee asked the woman if there was any other way to the Prussian borders as through that towne. She told us that on the right hand their was a way which, if wee could hitt upon, would take us directly to the milne on the borders, and shew us the place afarr of whereabout wee should find this way. Wherewith wee wheeling about, marched with great hast through the village where wee had baited towards the wood, and by good luck light on the way the woman had told us of.

Wee had not marched farr into the wood, when wee did meet a peasant haveing on a waggon a litle tunne of bier, w-ch was a welcome guest to us, haveing suffered much thirst this day. This peasant informed us that he had bought the bier from the burgers of Mlavy who were here in the wood hard by; that they had a quarrell amongst themselves and were divided; that they had good armes and horses, being about 70 persons lying very secure. Wee takeing the peasant {183} along with us, resolved to fall in upon them, not doubting but that by our suddaine comeing they would quite their horses and run in to the wood. When all had assented, and that wee were even near and ready to attact them, these of our comorades who were ill horsed fearing that, getting a repulse, they should be left in the lortch, diswaded our advancing any farther.

So wee retired of, and fearing to be prevented of the passage at the milne, wee who were best horsed rode befor, and at the milne seized on a waggon with two horses, whereon a tunne of bier and some loaves of bread. When our trowpe was come, wee alighted and threw of the bridge and tooke our march towards Zoldaw[359].

In the evening wee came to a church and lodged ourselves in the church yard, and in good bier gratulated one anothers good fortunes for escapeing so many hazards that day, carowsing it so that, albeit wee had ordered good watch, yet all fell sound {183v} asleep and continued so

---

[359] Soldau (German), Działdowo (Polish).

till day light, when awakeing, wee found that all our horses were gone. So getting up, wee run out into the fields, and by the direction of a poor fellow wee found them about a quarter of a mile of. About midday wee divided our horses wee had gott, and some dissention and discontent falling out amongst us, wee divided and marched sundry wayes. Yet after some dayes march wee did meet at Capt. Straughan his house not farr from Stume.

Here wee consulted what to do and agreed to send to Elbing to Felt Marshall von der Linde to desire a passe to returne to the army, which obtained, wee marched from thence towards Thorne. The next day diverse consultations were held what course to take, most enclineing not to go back to the trowpe againe, whereof I would not hear. Yet seing them all so enclined, for fear of some force I dissembled, but the next morning made my escape from {184} them and with my boy onely tooke my jorney towards Thorne.

Being come to a litle towne called [...], I chanced to meet with Quarterm-r Forbes, who being come from Thorne assured me that the army was not come thither as yet, perswadeing me to go back with him to Elbingh and promiseing to returne with me to Thorne, whereto I consented, not knowing how to passe the tyme untill the armyes comeing. In our returne from Elbingh wee did meet some Scotsmen, who haveing gott their passes out of Thorne were going for Scotland.

Being come to Thorne, I found our trowpe there and went immediately to seek up the *ruitm-r*, but meeting first with the lieutennant (who never carryed any good will to me, and that in opposition to the *ruitm-r*), sent me over the river under the watch, alleadging that I with all the rest had runn away from the trowpe, neither would admit of any reason or excuse. I had not been {184v} long under the guard, when the *ruitm-r* caused release and sent for me. Being come into the towne, I did meet the lieutennant, who stomacked not a litle that I was freed, and with whom I had high words, w-ch he could never afterwards disgest.

Some dayes thereafter two Scots officers came and gave me a visitt at my tent, and whilst I sent my servant for bier to entertaine them, my best horse was stolne, being on a tedder hard by. I gott notice afterwards that a Scotsman of my Lord Cranstons regiment stole him, yet never could recover him.

The day befor the *ruitm-r* had me with fowre [others] to seeke up Robert Trotter and another Scotsman, who fainting for hunger in the woods was not able to come forward, and albeit wee had one Capt. Wallace with us, who had been in company with them and pretended to know the place where they stayed behind, yet notwithstanding all the paines and enquiry wee made, wee could not find them nor any token of them. And indeed the s-d Capt. {185} Wallace his horse brought him into the leaguer voyd of sense, which he did not rightly recover in a long tyme thereafter. Which was a pittifull case, that gallant men should be so used and brought to that passe, to dy for hunger, but not the least pay being given us, and many of these gentlemen not willing or knowing how to shift, were brought to the utmost extremityes. At this tyme a Polls nobleman called Koritsky marryed the widdow of the deceassed Palatine of Rava.

The King of Sweden at his departing from Thorne walked along the bridge on foot, being convoyed by many nobles and the magistrates of the towne.[360] At the farthest end of the bridge the magistrates tooke their leave of His Majesty, who immediately went into his coach. Being without the skonse, *Ruitm-r* Meldrum following by the right boot, His Ma-tie called him and giveing his hand to kisse, said to him so, "Meldrum, {185v} serve us as you have formerly, and you shall have our favour in as large a measure as ever".

After this wee marched alongst the bridge and with our trowpe lodged in the fields on the way towards Kowaleva, where I was in great necessity and straits, all my baggage and booty which I left behind me being lost, my best horse stolne, and forced to give out all the money I had for another, though farr short of that. So that getting no company to go upon party, and that was dangerous, all the countrey thereabouts being under contribution and provided with safeguards, I was forced many a tyme to dine with Duke Humfrey. At last wee were quartered in the towne where, through the pride of the burgers our landlords, wee had many quarrels

---

[360] On 4 July. See fol. 111.

and great vexation, so that wee wished for countrey cottages rather as these palaces.

Cornet Robert Stewart comeing to Thorn, was presently put under ye guard, and I the first put to watch him. {186} They required of him these gentlemen whom he had taken away from the trowpe. He excused himself saying that being come into Prussia they would not obey him, but went all sundry wayes. After some dayes detention by intercession of the Lords Cranston and Hamilton he was dismissed, yet stayed not long by the trowpe for shame, going away I know not whither.

Wee were sent to Kovalewa and staying two nights in that ruined castle, by order returned to Thorne and shortly thereafter marched to Strasburg, getting our quarters in the towne, and some villages on the other syde of the r[iver] Drevents allowed for our maintenance, out of which wee gott litle or nothing, all being ruined and scarce any body liveing therein.

I went with the *ruitm-r* to Marienburg, who sollicited for armes and some maintenance for the trowpe. After much sollicitation wee gott nothing but words and promises. Here I see {186v} Coll. Rose and Maior Klinger executed, and albeit the later had dealt with me very uncivilly at the Dantziker Haupt[361], yet seing his misfortune here my heart grieved and pittyed him.

Being returned to Strasburg wee went upon a party, haveing a designe upon a litle towne 7 miles from thence, where a faire was. Wee marched all night and came suddainly into the towne, scattering the people and getting good booty. In our returne, rideing of the way with some comorades, wee light upon a breed of wild horses and mares and drove them into a village and tooke diverse of them, I getting for my share a yong mare of an extraordinary beauty and grouth, whereof the commendant at my returne getting notice, used all meanes to gett her and spoke to me to sell her. I seing his earnestness, presented her to him and would not accept of any thing for her, which he tooke very kindly and promised {187} to do me a courtesy.

---

[361] See fols. 114, 135–137 v.

Wee went thereafter upon diverse partyes to gett something to live upon, and upon one, getting the *podstarost* or greeve of the lands w-ch were given us for maintenance, wee keeped him untill he promised and gave surety to contribute in a larger measure, and so let him go.

On the first of October, about eleven aclock befor noone, wee had ane alarum that the Polls were come within a mile of the towne, to the villages where some provisions of beere and bread were makeing for us. The trumpets sounding, I sadled my horse. In the comeing out my landlord, who had been ane old sojor, meeting me, told me the table was covered, I should dine first, and that meat and masse never hindred any yet, and that I might come in tyme enough to a badd bargaine. To which giveing no eare, I mounted, and comeing to the doore of the *ruitm-rs* lodging, I found him ready to sitt on horseback. He had an {187v} excellent gray or rather white horse of Dutch breed, very couragious, swift, tractable and well proportioned, who when the *ruitm-r* had mounted would by no meanes go out of doores, w-ch wee guessed to be a badd omen, yet no body spoke any thing.

Fifteene or 20 horse being come together, wee marched through the castle and round the towne. Over the r. Drevents some overtooke us, so that wee were 29 horse in all with officers and two boyes. Wee marched through the wood to a litle wast village, haveing sent befor us Corporall John Browne with six horsemen. Comeing through the next wood into ane open field, all being quiet and neither seing nor hearing of any body, the *ruitm-r*, takeing 3 or 4 along with him, ridd befor also, wee marching forward at leasure and very joyfully. One of our comorads staying behind a litle, in great hast came rideing up, telling us that the enemyes were {188} behind us, whereupon wee wheeled about and seeing them marching out of the wooddes and drawing up in a large front, wee sent notice to the *ruitm-r* who was already in the village, wee in the meane tyme marching back to meet them. Which they seeing, contracted their trowpes into a narrower front and marched directly forward in a chequer battell.

All this tyme such ignorance or fatality possessed the most p[ar]t of us, that they would not beleeve that they were enemyes (seeing them in Dutch habite), but that they were Coll. Niewmans regiment out of Newmark or at the worst a regiment of the Brandeburgers, which was said to be confederated or rebelled. I said diverse tymes, "They may be what they will, but without doubt they are enemyes, and wee will be forced to fight with them". However, seeing no body spoke any thing of retreating or makeing our escape, which was the only way to save us, I fearing to be taxed of cowardise, resolved, albeit I did see {188v} a certaine ruine and meanes to avoyd it also, not to say any thing, knowing I had but one lyfe to losse as well as others. So haveing my recourse to God Almighty and to the Blessed Virgin and to all the Saincts in heaven for their assistance and intercession to the Blessed Trinity, in as short and effectuall expressions as the tyme would permitt, I marched on with the rest.

Being come within a musquet shott of other, the quarterm-r desired two of us to ride up and enquire what people they were. Capt. James Kieth and I being upon the right hand of the first ranke, rode and being come neare called to them, "What ar you for people?" They answered, "Good Emperours". Wee replyed, "Wee are good Swedish"; whereupon they called to us to take quarters and render ourselves prisoners, and therewith let fly a volly of shott at us wherewith Capt. Kieth was killed, and I sore wounded in the breast under the left pape. And befor I could get my self recovered, one {189} of the officers befor the trowpe put his carabin into my brest, which did misserve him, otherwise he had surely killed me.

I returning to the trowpe said only, "You see now what people they are", and so joyned on the right hand of the trowpe, and together charged the formost trowpe of the enemyes; most of us breaking through it, but dispersed, and so each tooke a severall way. I tooke the way towards the wood, and being well horsed was in hopes to have escaped, but being followed by 10 or 12 horsemen, who continually shott at me and called however to me to take quarters. I had lost one of my pistolls and in my flight had gott the other charged, yet reserved it to the last. With one of their shotts they had wounded my horse in the sore legge, whereupon they gaining ground upon me, they shott me also in the left shoulder, they still calling to me to take quarters. So that seing no meanes to escape, I wheeled about and calling to {189v} them to give good quarters.

I fearing in the heat to be killed, closed in to one haveing a red cloake, judging him to be an officer, who protected me, neither could I perceive that they offered me any harme after I said I would take quarter. The person to whom I rendred my self tooke my sword and armes and my whinger, which I had under my coat. I was afrayed he should have taken exceptions at it, the Germans being very precise y-t no body carry any private weapon as pocket pistolls, durkes, whingers or rifled armes, saying these are treacherous and dishonourable weapons. One seing my coat new, albeit some holes therein with shott, opened my breast to have taken it of. I told him I had nothing under it but my shirt, and would perish without a coat in such cold weather, being also grievously wounded; which he nothing regarded, yet seing my shirt all bloody, he let it alone.

In my returne I did see a trowpe in a round shooting, {190} and on the way see sitting on the ground my good ffriend Alex-r Kieth, pittifully lamenting. I desired to be brought to him, saying he was my brother, w-ch they did. I asked him how he did, he said nothing, but tearing his haire cryed out, "Alace, alace, for this day I am a dead man!" I desired him to call upon God, and so w[i]t[h] many teares left him.

Being brought to the village, I found the *ruitm-r* on horseback, but very pale. He asked how I did. I told him I was twice wounded, yet was better in seing him alive. He replyed, "Yes, I am alive, but God knoweth how long". For upon the notice of the enemy he immediately came out of the village, and seing us broken and running, he neverthelesse charged one of their entire trowpes and brake thorow. And if he had made use of his horse to run, he might have escaped, being exceeding well mounted, but out of fatality or abundance of exasperated courage he wheeled about all alone and charged {190v} in among them, and was quickly environed by them. In a round, he wheeling his horse, discharged both his Scots and Dutch pistolls. A cornet offering to lay hold of him, he broke the Dutch pistol in many pieces on his face and freed himself of him, and haveing broken his halfe stockado[362] also, he was at last taken by force. He had many shotts in his cloathes, some whereof lightly touching his body, but the deadly shott

---

[362] A kind of thrusting sword (cf. estoc).

was in his crosse bone, which stopping the passage of his urine, was his death the 5th day thereafter. His horse was shott 10 or 12 tymes and his nearer hinder legge broken therewith, and was left on the place. Another horse being brought, the *ruitm-r* alighted and was takeing of his sadle to put on the other, which the officers hindred, causing a trowper sadle his horse.

The quarterm-r Alex-r Staker and the trumpeter escaped on horseback, Andrew Wilson on foot into the marish, ten were killed on the place, 14 {191} prisoners, most whereof wounded.

The Imperialists made no stay, fearing to be persued by the Sweds, and so in great hast marched away, giveing orders in case of a hard pursuite and being straitened to kill the prisoners rather as let them escape. This he who had the charge of me told, and counselled me in such a case to run away into the woods, and that I should not be afrayed although he did shoot at me, for he would do me no harme. This put me into a conceit of makeing my escape. However, it beginning to be darke, and in a large wood, yet not haveing eaten any thing that whole day, and fearing for hunger and losse of blood to faint and so be destroyed by the wild beasts or peasants, I left of such resolution and jogged on.

It being darke, wee came to a house where was some beer. I desired my convoy to get a piece of bread for me if possible. Whilst he went about it, one comeing by changed {191v} hats with me. It booted not to say it was ill done. Haveing gott a peece of bread wherein was straw of an inch long, and some beer, I was pretty well refreshed.

Being come to a gentlmans house, wee rested 3 or 4 houres and then marched two miles farther, where a su[r]geon comeing from the army dressed us. The next night wee were lodged within two miles of Plotsko, and the day thereafter brought in to Plotsko. Wee were lodged in the prison under the councell house. The next day a regiment of foot came marching in, amongst whom one Capt. Lesly, apparant heire to Count Lesly in Germany, was captaine,[363] who notwithstanding it was told him

---

[363] Captain James Leslie, nephew and heir of Walter Leslie (1606–1667). The latter distinguished himself in military and diplomatic service for the Habsburgs, becoming count and field marshal of the Holy Roman Empire.

wee were Scots prisoners, would take no notice of us, so verifying the old saying *"cum fueris felix"* etc.[364]

On Fridday the 5th, hearing that the *ruitm-r* was very weake, I made a shift to get up and go over the way {192} to him. When I come in he was very glad. Being come near him and takeing him by the hand, I perceived the cold sweat to be upon him, and told him he had best in tyme order his wor[l]dly effaires. He said to me, "Your Jesuits have been by me, they have given me good advice, I wish they were here againe". I said, "I would send for them". He said "Yes", but the Protestants who were present did not permitt.

He held me by the hand and told me softly what he would have written in his latter will, I and Corporall John Kempe telling John Browne, who did writt all downe, the summe whereof was: he left his arreares and his pretensions on the Crowne of Sweden for levying 84 horsemen, as also the goods in three trunkes, which were in Samoisky, to his sister in Scotland; his best horse, sadle, pistolls, sword and buffe coat to his lieutennant; his next best horse to John Browne; his third best horse and embroidered sword belt to me; a golden hatt string and his linnens {192v} to John Smith and another who had waited upon him since he was wounded; the rest of his horses and goods to be sold and distributed among his servants. He left also 10 ducats to the two Jesuits who had been by him, and 10 dallers to the landlady of the house. He constituted executors of his will my Lord Hamilton and *Ruitm-r* John Fryer. Haveing subscribed his will, and seeing many of us standing by him very sorrowfull, he said, "Do not grieve, my lads, all will be well, the Crowne of Sweden will releeve you".

By this tyme the roome was full of officers of the Imperialists, who all did show great signes of grieffe. He called then for some bier, and getting the kanne in his hand, he said first in Scots and then in Dutch, "Here is a health to all honest cavaliers!", and drunk a very hearty draught. After this he recommended himself very fervently to God Almighty, craveing forgivennes of his sinnes and professing great confidence in {193} Christ His

---

[364] "Cum fueris felix, quae sunt adversa, caveto; Non eodem cursu respondent ultima primis" (*Disticha Catonis*, I, 18). It translates: "When you are happy, beware of adverse things; The end does not always follow the same course as that begun".

mercy, and so gave up his ghost into the hands of his Saviour, all about very sorrowfully shedding teares. He was a very compleet gentleman, of a handsome stature, countenance and behaviour, and wanted only a litle experience to have been a good souldier.

The next day he was carryed by those of his owne trowpe to a litle chappell of the Jesuits and by their permission a 150 horse, who were on the party when wee were taken, convoying him and giveing 3 salvees when he was laid in the ground. The 50 Polls, being Massowrs gentlemen, who were with them had returned to their dwellings. Maior Generall Heuster was very civill to him, keeping him in his owne lodging and furnishing such conveniences as he needed, and was at such expences as useth to be at a souldier and cavaliers buriall. I was not able to convoy him, being very unwell of my wounds, swounding at every tyme I was drest.

After some dayes {193v} stay in this towne, the army marching towards Thorne, wee were taken out, and waggons given for us who were wounded, whereon I was not able to sitt for the great paine of my wounds. Wee marched 5 miles this day, and comeing through a wood of oakes, wee furnished ourselves with accornes, which at night stood us in good stead. For the baggage not being come up, wee could not gett any thing to eat, so y-t rosting these accornes in the fyre, chesnuts could not compare with them!

The next [day] wee marched and lodged at a gentlemans house called Gambart. Here wee stayed 10 or 12 dayes, being in the meane tyme well entertained by the bounty of the officers. For no allowance being given us, two went out twice a weeke to begg, and brought in more provisions as wee were able to destroy. One Sunday fowre of us were invited by a capt. called Ried, who sent his coach for us, and entertaining us very well, returned us againe. All this tyme by reasone of my grievous wounds I was exeemed from begging, {194} but now being pretty well recovered I was forced, much against my stomack, to begg also.

Wee removed afterwards to a village three miles from Thorne. Here wee had notice that a trumpeter from the Sweds had been in the head quarters, desireing our liberty upon ransome, and that the Imperialists said that wee had all taken service, which vexed us hugely, being to incurre blame for not holding out the usuall tyme. The Imperialists were alwayes solliciteing us to take service, which to be well used wee excused, saying that if the Sweds did not releeve us befor the usuall tyme of sitting was out, then wee would resolve what to do.

The Sweds expostulateing with the Imperialists for breach of the peace, they sustained that the Sweds were aggressours; and that when they came to Crakow to dislodge the Transilvanians, enemyes to the Empire, the Sweds in hostile manner did sally out with the Hungarians; {194v} and that they had dismissed such of the Sweds as were taken in these sallyes without harme or losse, whereas they might have been lawfully made prisoners of warr; and that in this last rencounter the Scots corporall who was killed gave first fyre at them. I being called to testify this, I declared that I could not positively and with good conscience averr, which or who had fyred first, but that upon our declareing our selves to be good Swedish, the Imperialist[s] had called to us to take quarters and render our selves prisoners, which being expressions used commonly in such occasions by professed enemyes, it was no wonder if the co[r]porall fyred, which howsoever I would nor could not positively say. Of this I heard no more.

Most of the army being gone over the river Vistula to the Generall Hatsvelt, who advanced to Thorne and made approaches and batteryes towards the skonces and outworkes made for defence of the bridge, and winter drawing on, they had quarters assigned them in Great Polland. So makeing a bridge over the river {195} Vistula at Dobrzin[365], the regiments on the Massours syde began to draw towards the bridge, the passages on the river Drevents haveing been all this tyme keeped with strong guards, who were now commanded to draw of.

The day befor wee marched, it being now more as 5 weekes since wee were taken, and so the prefixed tyme of remaining prisoners without releefe being expired, wee were desired by the officers to declare cathegorically if wee would take service or not. Wee excused our selves in as civill termes as wee could, telling them that wee were no ordinary trowpers, and so could not be confined to such a tyme of remaining

---
[365] Dobrzyń.

prisoners as others, they objecting that the Sweds neglected and cared not for us. Wee replyed that wee were otherwise informed, and that they had sent diverse tymes to the generall for our releasment, which they denyed. Wee desired then that one or two of us might be let go {195v} upon parole to the generallissimus wit[h] a prefixed tyme for his or their returne, and that if wee had no assurance of releeffe, then would wee most willingly serve the King of Hungaria and Bohemia, it being all one to us; that without this wee could not in honour (w-ch wee held dearer as our lyves) engage. This they refused and went away with threats of harsher usage.

In the morning befor wee marched wee found a paper wrapt about w[i]t[h] green silke, which being opened, wee found a great deale of nonsense in what wee could read, and other things wee could not read, with a name subscrived in blood, whereby wee concluded it to be a compact made by some body with the devill, and so buryed it in the channell. By and by the corporall who had the charge of us came and enquired very diligently for this paper, promiseing a good reward to him who should restore it. So after much search it not being found, the corporall was like to turne {196} distracted about it, calling out, "I am undone, I am undone!", which confirmed us in our opinion of its being a divelish compact.

As wee were on our march, 5 of my comorades came to me and after promise of secrecy they told me that they intended to make their escape, desireing me to bear them company. I told them that I had taken a resolution that if the Sweds did not releeve me, I would take service with the Imperialists. For haveing considered that the King of Sweden was glad to gett out of Polland with his credit; that he would fynd worke enough in Denmark; that the Roman Emperour had engaged in the Polls quarrell; that Brandeburgh, being first neutrall, was now engageing in a defensive and offensive league with Polland; that the Sweds haveing left scarce forces enough in Prussia to defend the p[rinci]p[a]ll garrisons; that their enemyes, being masters of the fields, would coup them up and straiten them in the townes, where haveing litle or no pay, they would {196v} be driven to great necessityes; and for my oune part, I doubted not to be well accomodated where I was.

Without telling them any thing of this, I only simply refused to go along. They entreated me not to betray them, which I sincerely promised and performed, but it seemes they had resolved otherwise. For haveing intended in the busy tyme of lodging themselves to go aside, as if to fetch wood, and then, it being darkish, to escape into the wood or marish, they offered no such thing.

In the 2d howre of the night, wee sitting all about a great fyre in a ruin'd village, two *ruitm-rs* came to us and began peremptorily to ask us why wee would not take service. Wee excuseing ourselves as befor, one of them told us that wee were more oblidged to serve the Roman Emperour as the Sweden, because the Sweden were in allyance with the archtraitour Cromuell; that ye Rom. Emp. had reseat our King[366] and maintained him in his dominions, when his neerest cousin of France and Holland had banished him; that all these who served the Sweden of the King of Great Brittaines subjects were to be looked {197} upon as traitours.

I finding this touching us so neerly, replyed that whatsomever oblidgements and courtesyes the Roman Emperour had conferred upon our King, he or his predecessours might have, perhaps, received the lyke or greater from our King and his; and that our King by Gods help comeing to his owne againe, may manyfoldly requite all; that such courtesyes being betwixt Princes either upon reason of state or otherwise usuall, could not put such a great engagement upon the subjects as to change or ruine their fortunes; that wee being free borne subjects of the King of Great Brittaine, and comeing abroad to seeke our fortune, had engaged in the service of the King of Sweden, which wee might very lawfully do without the least breach of loyalty to our owne prince; that being well accommodated there, wee could not staine our honour so farr as so soone to engage in anothers service, except wee had notice that wee were neglected by them, which wee were assured wee should not be. Wherewith they were so angred that they abused me, calling me milke-mouth and I know not what, threatening to {197v} delate me as the hinderer of the rest; and that they

---

[366] King Charles II of Great Britain (1630–1685) inherited the throne after the execution of his father in 1649 and was crowned in Scotland, but had to live in exile during Cromwell's regime.

would pinch our bellyes and libertyes; and that wee should be sent to digge in quarries and carry stones – and in great chaffing went away.

I fearing for my free speeches by their delation to be worse used, resolved to make my escape, and choosing out one John Smith as a nimble, able man, I went and sat me downe by him. And because every one was suspicious of another, I scarce could, without being taken notice of, get asked in his ear if he would this night go to his travells with me. He in a while telling me, "Yes, if you will", I then thereafter told him, "When you see me arise, then follow me". Every one watched another, that it was neer midnight befor I durst offer to rise, and then as if I went to ease my self. Being gone a litle way of among the thick high weedes, I stayed expecting my comorade, who stayed so long that I despairing of his comeing at all, was on the point of returning or going alone. At last he came, and so recommending our selves to God, wee made hast away.

The night was exceeding darke, {198} yet knowing the ground, and that the way towards Thorun would be best guarded, wee tooke our way forwards towards the army. Wee were not gott farr when a sentry called us on the right hand; wee declineing to the left, another at some distance called, so that with as much speed as wee could wee gott out betwixt them and downe to the marish. The sentryes rideing after us, one of them shott, which hastened us forward. Wee run in others hands through the wett ground, and ere wee were aware, were both over head in water. Yet recovering the other syde, our hearts were a great deale lighter, knowing horsemen could not follow us, and for foot wee did not care.

Being over the marish and on dry land, wee drew of our boots and wrung out our cloaths. And so at first, hearing a stirr in the leaguer and fearing to be followed, wee resolved to go directly to Strasburgh. Yet thereafter wee changed our purpose, doubting to find the way, and not being provided w[i]t[h] victualls to travell so farr. So intending for Thorun, wee went up the syde of the marish {198v} till finding it turne too farr to the right hand, wee crossed it againe, and being now near a mile from the quarters, wee drew to the high way and so hasted on, standing oftentymes still, listening if any did follow us, or if any were meeting us.

Wee went about the village wee had quartered, and then into the high way for fear of straying. But as wee were going on now someq-t securely, ere wee were aware it was daylight, and being in a plaine field, wee were someq-t troubled to find a sheltring place. At last wee saw towards the left hand on a high ground some bushes, whither wee ran and shrewded our selves. All the provisions wee had was one litle loave of grosse bread, one halfe whereof wee concluded to eat now and the other at night, resolving to stay here all the day, and in the night to set forward againe. This small portion of bread sharpened but our appetites, so that being exceeding cold and wet, wee could not containe from eating the other halfe, wherewith wee were scarce well satisfyed either.

It being a very darke, calme day, and the mist broken up, {199} wee looked out of the bush, and seing a village with a stone church, I presently knew where wee were, and that on the left hand was a wood, w-ch would bring us to the r-s Vistula and Drevents. Wee see also some horsemen rideing about the village, whom wee suspected to be horsemen sent in persuite of us. So that fearing to be found by them, as also to be benummed with cold and faint with hunger, wee resolved to hazard over the field into the wood.

Wee not haveing so much as a knife with us, broke of two long poles to serve for defence against the peasants or wild beasts, and so creeping over the fields on hands and feet wee gott into the wood, w-ch was so thinne that wee could not find any place to shelter our selves in. Wee runne from place to place, and comeing to a way, wee found the fresh print of many horses feet going towards Polland, and fearing to be discovered by some straglers, wee runne to a bush hard by and there in the water hid our selves. Staying here, wee saw diverse trowpers hastening up {199v} the same way after the rest.

So finding the coast clear, wee went on againe, but not dareing to keep any way, and by running to and fro to seeke out the thickest places of the wood, and the sunne not shineing nor wind blowing, wee had lost all mooths of the way. Yet I had a great guesse and against the opinion of my comorad chanced to go directly whither wee intended. Being come to the edge of the wood, wee did clime up into a tree and after diverse doubts at last discovered Thorun by the smocke above it. Intending to go along the edge of the wood to a village called the Fishery, and there passe the r. Drevents by boat or foord, perceiving the fresh prints of Polls boots and horses, fearing to be su[r]prised by the Polls, wee tooke our course directly downe to the river, knowing that by rivers are ordinarily marishes and places unpassable for horsemen.

As wee went by the rivers syde through bushes gathering slaes, wee espyed a peasant gathering wild aples. I giveing my boots to my comorade, with club in hand was on him {200} ere he was aware. I asking him from whence he was, he told, from the other syde of the Drevents, and that he came over the river at the Fishery in a boat belonging to our people (he takeing us to be Imperialists). I told him that wee were non of these, but belonging to Thorun, and desired him to assist us in getting over the river, and since wee could not go to the Fishery, that he would help us to bring boards or doores from the village, which was near, to make a floate to passe over upon. He telling us that the village was full of Imperiall trowpers, I remembred that the Polls had passed hereabouts and taken away the commendants horses. He said it was too deepe to wade, and the passage uneven and uncertaine, which however wee resolved to try, albeit he said the water would come to our chinne. Being come to the foord, and all our cloaths of, wee could neither with promise of rewards, good words nor threats perswade the peasant to lead us the way, and all he would do was to stand there and direct us, {200v} it being very crooked, and albeit my comorade was much taller as I, yet was I forced to go betwixt him and the streame, which run very swiftly.

So with our cloaths on our necks and our long clubs in our hands, recommending ourselves to God Almighty, wee, and with great difficulty and danger, gott thorow, my feet being thrice lift up from the ground by the strength and depth of the water, w-ch was lyke to choake me sometymes, in which case to have could swimme would have done well.

Being gott over and praising Almighty God, wee runne, naked as wee were, over all the low ground to the river Vistula under a hill, and so keeped under the hill till wee came neer the towne, and by a mill put on our cloaths and boots. Going in to the towne at Jacobs Gate, wee were not taken notice of. Wee went directly to the house of W-m Hume, an old comorade of mine, whose wyfe, being Glassa Gordons[367] daughter, in her husbands absence {201} gave me a paire of his shooes and stockens (my owne being all worne out).

Haveing refreshed our selves with victualls, wee went immediately to the commandant, Maior Generall Bilaw. He enquiring of us the usuall things, I told him that haveing been taken prisoners by Strasburgh the first of October last, wee had this last night about midnight made our escape from M. Gen-ll Hewsters regiment in a village about 4 miles from hence; that haveing drawne of their guards from the passages of the river Dreventsa, they were marched towards Dobrzin to crosse the Vistula there, and so march into Great Polland to their winter quarters. He asked me hastily, "What do these on the other syde of the river then?" I told him, "My lyfe for it, they will not stay above 3 dayes, for their chieffest strength consisting in commanded men, would not stay behind their collours going into quarters". He said, "I wish it may be so", and so giveing each of us a glasse of {201v} wyne, sent one to conduct us to Lieut. Coll. Brethawlt, who there commanded Felt Marshall *Graffe* Douglas his regiment of horse. He offered us a quarter, w-ch I declined, saying I had taken up my lodging by ane acquaintance.

The next day wee went to my Lord Hamilton and gave him the copy of the deceassed *Ruitm-r* Meldrum his testament. My Lord was very kind to us, takeing us along to the Governour *Graffe* Bengt Oxensterne, and procured for each of us 5 ells of gray cloth, w-ch selling for a reichs doller and a halfe the ell, stood us in good stead. I bought a horse for eight dollers and gave 4 in hand, and bought a stollen sadle and pistolls for one reichs doller.

Here I found one W-m Guild[368], who had been taken prisoner with us and convoyed away by the Polls, from whom he had escaped some weekes befor, and haveing the occasion of a party going by night to Strasburgh,

---

[367] One Henry Gordon de Glassauche is mentioned in an act of 1649 (Register of the Great Seal of Scotland, vol. IX, № 2093).

[368] William Guild was to serve under Gordon for both Poland and Russia. He died a lieutenant colonel in Moscow in 1685.

wee three rode along and came thither by {202} day light. Here I found any thing I had left disposed of and distributed, it being verily beleeved that I was killed. So that comeing in very early to Quarterm-r Streatowne as he was riseing out of his bed, he frighted and asked me if I were a ghost or not.

Albeit I was come here, yet I resolved not to engage or serve more under this trowpe, upon w-ch acco[un]t I neither would accept of a quarter in Thorne nor here. Makeing such shift as I could untill the lieutennant came, who haveing marryed in Elbing came at last, and upon my L-d Hamilton and *Ruitm-r* Fryers letters and the copy of the *ruitm-rs* will, delivered to me my horse, but not the embroidered belt, which the *ruitm-r* had left me.

I gott a passe from the commendant to go to the generallissimus in Elbing. On the way I tooke a couple of horses to bear my expences there, this being accounted neither sinne nor shame in that service. In the morning early I waited on the generallissimus as he came out of {202v} his chamber, and takeing an opportunity spoke to His R. Highnes after this manner: "May it please Your Royall Highnes. I haveing served in Generall Douglas his lyfe-company, and lately taken prisoner by Strasburg, have made my escape out of prison; and haveing never received of the Crowne of Sweden a farthing of money either of pay or for mounting, and haveing now lost all I had, I humbly entreat Your R.H. to take consideration of my condition and put me in a capacity of serving the Crowne of Sweden againe; and whereas out of the affection and desire I have to serve the Crowne, I have with great danger of my lyfe made my escape from the enemy, and am upon y-t acco[un]t become a free person, I desire also my passe from that company".

His R. H. answered, "I was informed you had all taken service". I replyed, "No, and that they exspected still to be releeved". Then His R.H. said, "I shall do my best, and as for you, I shall order something to you for to mount {203} you, but for your passe from that company you must go to your lt. coll. for it". I stayed some dayes there, exspecting to have gotten something, but being delayed, and wanting wherewith to maintaine my self, I resolved to returne.

But it being great folly and improvidence to returne empty, so with John Smith and our two servants wee went and lurked in a wood on the way betwixt Elbing and Marienburg, and by the marching by of a foot company from the Hooft to Elbing being hindred of many good bargaines. At last wee wentured upon two well horsed pawres and tooke with some difficulty their horses. But they giveing the alarum to the village near at hand, the pawres with great celerity way-laid us, so that wee could not go the way towards Marienburg whither wee intended, but were forced with some hazard returne back as farr as Lame-hand, and then up the drift to the right hand.

Makeing hast out of the *werder*, wee came {203v} about 9 aclock at night to a village on ye high land and lodged in the alehouse. The next morning, going not very early from thence, wee were alarumed by fyfteen pawres and some horsemen come from Marienwerder seeking after lost horses. Being come to Strasburg, wee sold our horses for 26 dollers.

18 *Dec-ris*. After 5 dayes stay I rode to Thorun and desired Lt. Coll. Brethault for my passe, who refused, showing me a postscript of the generalls to this purpose: "If any of my lyfe-company of Scotsmen who hath been an officer formerly desireth his passe, give it him, he putting as good a fellow as himself in his place". Whereupon the lt. coll. asked me if I had been an officer formerly and if I would put another in my place. I told him it was all a matter, whither I had been an officer or not, but that I had never received a farthing either of levy money or pay from the Crowne of Sweden, and that now haveing released my self out of prison, by all the lawes of the world I was a free man, and that Generall Douglas had not promised so {204} to us when wee engaged with His Excell., declareing further that, there might come q-t will, I would not serve under that company any longer, and so left him.

Being returned to Strasburg and shifting about some dayes, without engageing or takeing a quarter, the lieutennant one evening sent for me and asked me what I intended to do. I told him I would go back to the generallissimus, he haveing commanded me so if the lt. coll. did not give me my passe. He in passion then told me I should not go, but enter my self under the trowpe againe. I saying I would not, he commanded the quarterm-r to bring me to the castle and desire the colonell to put me under the watch. The quarterm-r going in first and telling his errand, I was called in. The colonell began to perswade me to enter my self under the company againe, which I refused, alleadging relevant reasons, wherewith the colonell being satisfyed, dismissed me, telling the quarterm-r he saw no reason to keep me under the guard, {204v} or why I should be forced to serve under y-t company any more against my will.

Befor I returned the lieut. had sent to my quarters and taken away the horse, which according to the deceassed *ruitm-rs* will he had given me. I stayed some dayes in the towne thereafter, and wanting a horse, I had my recours to the colonell, who in recompence of a brave yong mare, w-ch I gave him befor I was taken prisoner, gave me a horse. So in ane evening caused lead my horse out befor me, I went out quietly and tooke my way towards Elbing. On the way I went into Stume and visited Lt. Colonell Alex-r Anderson and my good ffriend Capt. Thomas Forbes.

Being come to Elbing, I had my recourse presently to the generallissimus, telling His R. Highnes that I had been by Lt. Coll. Brethault, who had denyed me my passe. His R. H. said, "Wee have no paper to writt passes on". I answered that I had not a mind to quite the Swedish service, only to be freed of that company and seek my preferment under another regiment. So calling Secretary Muller, he went {205} into a litle roome, and the Rentmaster Forbes with him.

I being called in, His R. H. said to me, "You will not then go out of the Swedish service?" I answering "no", and that I doubted not of my preferment under some other regiment, the gen-ll-m-s then asked the secretary if he knew not of a vacant ensignies place, who answering, "Yes, under Yo[u]r R. H. Lyfe Regiment of Dragownes". Then commanded he that the secretary should cause writt my passe from that company, and give me a letter to Lieut. Colonell Anderson to place me ensignie under that regiment.

I gave humble thanks, and waiting till the secretary came out, I went along with him and heard him give orders for my passe and letter. I entreated the writers not to delay me, who promised to have all ready the next day, which proved true.

[1658]

[January 1/11]

The secretary the next morning tooke my passe and letter along to be subscrived by His R. H., which done, they were brought back to the cancellary to be sealed, which was also presently done. So giveing the writers a reichs thaller for their pains, {205v} excuseing my self for giveing so litle, as being a ruined person, and protesting that I dealt all the money I had with them, they seemed well satisfyed.

I haveing now my passe, thought I was in another world, and calling to mind the great miseryes I had been in, the great necessityes and difficultyes I had been strugling with, the many unlawfull shifts I had been forced to use, and all to keep lyfe and soule together, and considering that there was litle good to be expected here in this service any more, resolved not to engage my self in hast with any. Yet I resolved to go to Stum and deliver my letter, yet no wayes not only not to urge, but not to desire, yea, rather to decline and shift of my enstallment. Knowing also that the positive order of the gen[eralissimu]s would displease the lt. coll., who by nature was a passionate man, and so minister occasion of breaking of, and thereby leave me blamlesse in case I should be questioned for not entring on my charge.

My passe was written in High Dutch, the substance whereof thus in English:

{206} **Translation of my passe** *verbatim*

Wee Adolph Johann, by the Grace of God *Palsegrave* by the Rhine, in Bavaria, of Gulick[369], Cleve and Bergen Duke, *Graffe* of Veldentz, Sponheim, of the Marck and Ravensburg, Lord of Ravenstein, His Royall Majesty of Swedens Generallissimus over the armyes and Upper Director of the Regall Prussian Palatinates, make knowne hereby that the shower

---

[369] Jülich.

hereof, Patrick Gordon, hath for the space of a year and a halfe under the lyfe garde of the Lord Field Marshall *Graffe* Douglas and the company of *Ruitm-r* Meldrum served for a free trowper (voluntier). In which tyme he hath so behaved himself as it beseemeth and belongeth to a souldier who loveth honour, but seing the *ruitm-r* being lately killed, and the company for the most part ruined, therefor the said Patrick Gordon intending to seek his advancement somewhere else.

So have wee hereby given him his passe and testimony of his good behaviour, requiring all and every one of His Royall Swedish Majesties high and inferiour officers, as also common souldiers to horse {206v} and foot, courteously and favourably to receive the said Patrick Gordon, and not only to suffer him with his servants, horses and baggage to passe freely, securely and unhindered, but also for his good behaviour and this our testimony and desire, to esteeme him recommended and worthy of all assistance and advancement.

In witnesse whereof wee have subscrived these with our owne hand and commanded to be sealed with Our Highnes secret seale. So done in Elbing the 1/11 of January *Anno* 1658.

(*L.S.*)[370]   Adolph Johan

Being come to Stum on a Sunday and first rideing in by Capt. Forbes whom I found at dinner, I sitting downe to dine with him, the lt. colonell sent for him, and asking who was come by him and to what purpose, he telling him that I had an order from the generalissimus to be installed ensignie, wherewith he was vexed. After dinner I went with the capt. to him and delivered my letter. He told me I had not done well, seing I intended to serve under his command, to go {207} to the generalissimus without acquainting him. I answered that I had not desired the gen-s for any place, farr lesse to be in any particular regiment. He asked me then what I would do for my ensignies place, and how many men I would levy. I told him I had done more as enough for it already, and would not levy the legg of a

---

[370] *Locus sigilli* – place of seal (Lat.).

man for it. Which vexing him, he in some passion s[ai]d, "Do you think so to start into an ensignies place? Where have you served befor?" I said I have served the Crowne of Sweden near three yeares under diverse regiments, and lately served under Generall Douglas his lyfe guard; and that for his ensignies place, which he valued so much, I cared not for it, not doubting to find that in every place where I had a mind.

And so desireing to be excused, I tooke my leave and went away to my lodging, and the next day returned from thence to Elbing. And hearing that one Lt. Hugh Montgomery had a locality in a village called Katsenaw, I rode thither to give him a visitt and {207v} consult what course to hold. I found here John Konning, John Cambell and David Sorrell. Wee resolved to take a transeant quarter up and downe the *werders* and make such shift as wee could.

The next morning, whilst wee were ready to go to breakfast, wee had a suddaine alarum that the Imperialists were hard by. Wee made hast to our horses and marched together out of the village, and seeing no body near, wee resolved to ride towards Elbing. And so taking to the damme by the Nogat, wee rode along it towards Climent-ferry, being with servants ten of us. The Imperialists had scattered themselves all along the *werder* towards Elbing, wee rideing by some houses where they were plundering, and seeing other[s] rideing very near us. At last they seeing us rideing the direct way and keeping closse together, suspected us to be no ffriends, and so made hast to Climent-ferry to meet us. Wee perceived their intentions and made great hast to prevent them, yet do what wee could, about 24 horsemen were gott befor us, so that no other remedy but fight. {208} With great resolution wee marched towards them, which they seeing, wheeled of befor wee came within carabin shott of them, whereof wee were exceeding glad.

So haveing the way clear befor us, wee marched a mile further and alighted at a pawres house, where wee found no body at home, but abundance of all things for man and horse. When I had stayed a while, I found a great tickling in my feet. So takeing of my boots and holding my feet to the oven, they began to swell and ake exceedingly, haveing frozen them by the way. For albeit I felt exceeding cold in them, yet being loth to alight for fear of being surprised at unawares, and so still rideing on, at last I did not feele any cold, so imagined they were returned to their naturall heat againe, when indeed the frost had benummed and made them sensles.

The next day wee removed to another quarter, and the day thereafter there brake out holes on the utmost side of my feet by my litle toes, whereout ran exceeding much matter, and the swelling {208v} aswaged.

I went to Elbing to a chirurgeon, with whom I agreed for ten reichs dollers to heale me. He said if I had, in steat [*sic*] of going in to a warme roome, rubbed my feet with snow, nothing would have ailed me. After he had me under cure two weekes I was nothing better, and had payed him the most part of his money, and because I could not stay in the towne, he gave me plasters along with me.

One night being lodged in a pawres house, as I was dressing my feet, an old woman in the house told me that was not the way to cure them, desiring me the next day to kill a rooke or crow and presently take out the braines and apply them to my feet, letting them stay 2 or 3 dayes if possible, and then apply another, and surely the 4th or 5th day they would be healed; and so gave me an oyntment for drawing on and hardening the skin, which I did, and by this meanes was perfectly healed.

The Imperialists lying encamped on the high ground hard by the *werder* in some villages, did roave abroad every day for provisions {209} and forrage. And wee were not idle, snapping them away where wee could find them, and gott good booty, I getting for my owne share in lesse as six weekes tyme one and twenty horsemens furniture, my share of prisoners being much more, wee giveing dragownes and others evill equipaged in with mounting and all. Two of which partyes, being most memorable, I shall relate.

Haveing agreed with 10 horsmen of Coll. Andrewes his regiment to ride a party, wee lodged together about a mile and a halfe from Elbing on the way to Marienburg, and rideing away two houres befor day, gott into a house about halfe a mile from the leaguer of the Imperialists undescryed. When it was day light, many went out of the leaguer diverse wayes in great and small trowpes to fetch provisions and forrage. So that wee rideing from thence scatteringly, gott into a drift or high way and rode forwards towards Elbing among them without ever being questioned, every one thinking us to be their owne and come from the campe. Wee rode {209v} on to get up to the formost.

    Being come to a village, wee found all the houses and barnes full, so that if none was gone further, wee resolved to get in to some house and stay untill most of them should returne, and then deale with the hindmost. But being come to the end of the village, wee perceived about 20 horsemen a good way of turning to the right hand of the way to a Hollanders house, which stood apart. So wee resolved to ride after those, and if no body followed us more as wee could well medle with, to fall upon these; which did fall out very luckily, for none stirred out of the village.

    Being come to the house, wee left one at the gate to give us notice if any approached to us, and wee being but 18 in all, wee found a great deale more as wee exspected, but all from their horses and scattered in the houses. 12 of us alighted, takeing our pistolls with us and giveing our horses to two to hold hard by the gate. Most of the horses being tyed to a long cribb in the midle of the yard, three rode about with their pistolls ready, not to suffer any come to horseback.

    Wee {210} who were on foot went first into the stove at the doore, whereof were standing about 20 muskets. Wee were no sooner entred ye roome, but wee bidd them take quarters and render their weapons. They tooke it to be jest at first, but were quickly put out of that conceit by wounding two or three of them with our swords, for to shoot wee were loth. So without much ado they rendred their swords, other weapons they had not. There being about 30 of them, wee asked them how many of [them] were here. They said, about 50 or 60. Wee commanded them to stay in the roome without makeing any noise, as they loved their lyves, and so leaving 3 with pistolls ready cok'd to guard the doore, wee went and seized on 8 or 10 more, who were seeking up and downe in the other houses, disarmed them and shut them into a low proviant house, wherein was but a small window, shutting the doore without. Wee tooke then the pistolls, which were in the hulsters, and secured them, but seeing more horses as wee had gott men, wee went to seeke after them, and found {210v} sixe in an out house, providing themselves of rootes and cabbage. These told us of some gone over to a small cottage not farr of, so thrusting them into the proviant house with the rest, wee went to looke for those who were gone to the cottage, who haveing their pistols with them were very opportunely returning. They being 8, wee seized upon them at the back gate and disarmed them without any resistance. Putting these also in with the other, wee tooke fyve more who had hidden themselves in a barne.

So calling for the trowpers first, wee caused them mount on the worst horses, and there being 23 of them, wee brought them out without the gate and put 6 to guard them. Wee caused the dragownes take their muskets and mounted them, takeing away their lunt from them, and so ranging them in the *hoffe* or yard, being 35 of them. And so guarding them befor and behind, and one every syde with pistolls cok't and swords ready drawne, threatening to shoot any who should but offer to stirr out of his ranke, and so our selves all behung with {211} swords and pistolls, wee hasted away towards Elbing, haveing also 3 spare horses of trowpers and 5 of dragowners, the riders whereof haveing hidden themselves, wee durst not stay to seeke.

When wee came near Elbing, wee gave to the dragownes their swords, and leaving in a taverne before the towne the trowpers horses, armes and cloakes, wee marched into the towne, the trowpers walkeing on foot befor, and the dragownes on horseback in order, getting a convoy of 12 musquetiers from the captaine at the gate, and so presented our selves befor Field-Marshall von der Lind his doore.

Montgomery, I and two of the Dutch men went up staires and found the generall in a roome looking out to the street. Wee addressing our selves to His Excel., told him that it had pleased God to blesse us on a party, and wee had taken and brought hither without the expence of any blood 23 horsemen and 35 dragowners; that as for the dragowners, because wee found them willing {211v} to serve the Crowne of Sweden, wee presented them to His Excel. with their horses and armes, as wee tooke them, and that he would be pleased to cause receive them, as also the horsemen from us. The field marshall thanked us very heartily, and asking how many were of us, wee saying "eighteene", he wondred and highly commended our wisdome, good conduct and courage.

Returning to the taverne, wee dealed our booty and tooke a hearty cup the most part of the night, whereat the Dutches had like to have quarrelled with us for delivering of to the field marshall ye horses and armes belonging to the dragounes, but they bethought themselves.

The next morning Lt. Montgomery and I went to ye field marshall, desireing an order to take a transeant quarter in the *werder*, untill wee should have convenience to returne to our respective garrisons, which he granted with an admonition to have a care of our selves. As wee did, lodging alwayes all in one house and giveing litle ease to our selves, where there was hopes of any {212} thing to be had, haveing very good fortune by getting many prisoners and good horses, cloakes and armes by them, which wee sold at very low rates, the money being scarce.

In the later end of February Capt. Forbes, who had been in detention and suffered a counsell of warr for killing a regiment quartermaster at a duell within the garrison of Stume, being pardoned, came to Elbing to give thankes to the generall persons there for their favour and intercession in his behalfe, and chanced on Saturnday with one W-m Fryer, a merchant, to lodge with us. In the morning I riseing early, went to my quarters w-ch was near by, intending to ride a mile of about some businesse. I was not well ready, when wee had an alarum that the Imperialists were hard by. I made hast to give my comorades notice, in the meane tyme the pawres running away with their horses told us that three were at hand robbing a sledge. I being ready, stayed not for any, but sending my servants to carry all I had to Elbing, rode towards them, who were from {212v} their horses busy plundring the sledge. As I came within two pair[371] of them with my pistoll ready cokt, my horse stumbling in a ditch, threw me out of the sadle and ran back to the houses, and I being glad to be no more taken notice of, as to be laught at by them, ran back also to recover my horse.

In the meane tyme Forbes and Montgomery being ready, came this way, and Forbes being formost, without great resistance tooke two of these, the 3d escapeing. I haveing recovered my horse, rode and overtooke Montgomery with a youth belonging to Capt. Forbes called Georg

---

[371] *Pair* of butts – Scots measure of distance.

Fermer. So hearing that Capt. Forbes, haveing taken two prisoners, was gone with them to Elbing, wee resolved to adventure forwards and try our fortune. And being come near the party, wee perceived one comeing after us, to whom wee turned and secured, and other two in the same way, whom disarmeing, wee put into a litle house, giveing Fermer their horses to hold at the doore with a ready cokt pistoll. Another wee tooke comeing directly from the party, {213} being sent to drive in the straglers; him wee secured also, and so mounting the rest, marched back towards the towne.

Wee had not ridden farr, when three came on our left hand within our reach. So takeing parole from these wee had taken, and setting them forwards with the boy, threatening if they offered to looke back, to leave the other and fall on them and without mercy kill them. So wee two going towards the three, and being within pistoll shott, wee called to them to take quarters. And presently I closeing with one of them, the other two tooke severall wayes, after whom Montgomery rideing, presently tooke one of them, and comeing near found me as yet strugling with him I had closed with. He discharged his carabin at us very unadvisedly, being as ready to kill me as the other. Whether this, or that I haveing gotten some advantage, discouraged my antagonist, I know not, but he presently rendred. And so takeing his pistolls, wee joyntly followed the third, who being a trumpeter, had fallen with his horse in a ditch and was taken without {213v} danger or hazard.

The Imperialists guessing by the shott they heard that enemyes were neare, sent out about 30 horsemen towards us. But wee haveing the advantages of being so farr befor them, and their takeing downe another way, easily escaped them, and they after halfe a miles pursuite returned. Wee overtooke Capt. Forbes at Himelreichs taverne befor Elbing, and takeing their horses, cloakes and armes from these our prisoners, brought them altogether and presented them to the field-marshall and Margrave von Baden, who was commendant, who heartily thanked and highly commended us.

This with diverse other exploits, which wee had done, gott the Scots such a vogue amongst the burgers and pawres, that whosoever brought in any prisoners or done any notable service against the enemyes, it was alwayes said to be the Scots. So that the Dantzickers, whom wee had infested very often, haveing intelligence of our lodging a mile from the towne, came with 60 horsemen and 100 dragownes {214} to surprise us. I being gone two dayes befor to Stume, they came first to my quarters, and environing the house, they shott diverse tymes in at a back window into ye bed where I used to ly. But understanding from the landlord that I was not there, they went directly to Montgomery his quarters, who with those that were w[i]t[h] him defended the house a while, and then were forced to retyre and hide themselves in the barne, lossing their horses and armes, John Campbell and two servants being taken. They were afrayed to stay long, and not haveing orders to raise fyre, otherwise they had taken them all.

Whilst wee lay in this *werder* a English ambassadour called Bradshaw, haveing been on his jorney to Moskovia, and not admitted,[372] returned this way and was lodged in Lame-hands taverne. Wee getting notice thereof, and thinking him to be that Bradshaw, who sat president in the highest court of injustice upon o[u]r soveraigne King Charles the First, of {214v} blessed memory, wee resolved, come what will, to make an end of him. And being about 15 with servants, six whereof might be accounted trusty wight men, the other also indifferent, wee concluded that doing the feat in the evening, wee could easily make our escape by the benefitt of the strait ground and darknes of the night; and so being resolved, wee tooke our way thither.

Being come near and asking a pawre come from thence some questions, he told us that just now some officers were come from Elbing to the ambassadour, and about 40 dragownes, who were to guard and convoy him to Marienburgh, which made us despair of doing any good, and so wee returned. Wee had resolved to make our addresses to him, as sent with a commission from Field-Marshall von der Linde to him, and being admitted, 7 or 8 of us to have gon in and stabbed him, the rest guarding

---

[372] After the execution of King Charles I Tsar Alexey Mikhailovich has greatly curbed English trading privileges in Muscovy and did not receive any embassies from the Commonwealth, while British royalists were readily accepted into his service, and the exiled court of Charles II enjoyed Russian support.

our horses and the doore, and so being come to horse, made our escape to Dantzick.[373]

{215} Capt. Forbes being to returne to Stume, perswaded me to go along and stay some dayes with him. The same night wee came there was an alarum, and so all must go to the wall to their respective posts and stations. I went along with Cap. Forbes to his parade place. About midnight the lt. coll. came visiteing the guards. Wee came out, and he drawing neer, I went and saluted him. He tooke the capitaine aside and desired him to perswade me to stay and accept of the ensignies place.

When the lt. colonell was gone, the capt. did begin to drink healths and perswade me to stay, telling me the lt. colonell had desired him to perswade me, which I would by no meanes heare of, haveing tasted of liberty and the contentments thereof, and haveing gained more in 6 weeks tyme as I had in a year befor, I was loath to be coped up in a garrison againe and be tyed to command and hard duty. Yet good company and the fruition of his company, who had been and was still my reall good and confident ffriend, and with whom I had contracted a brotherly familiarity, prevailed with me so farr that I gave my promise, w-ch {215v} however I repented the next day, yet would not passe from my word, and so was installed. A few dayes thereafter I gott leave to go to Elbing to fetch my baggage, where I understood of the misfortune Montgomery had had, which is mentioned befor, and to my great fortune had escaped.

In the tyme of my being in this garrison our pay was small and our duty hard, being every other night upon the guard and at the works every 3d day. Our pay was called a 3d part *lenung*, being for l[ieutenan]t and ensignie 6 reichs dollers and 2 3ds a month, the captaine 20 reichs dollers and somwhat more, and yet this was not duly payed. Our quarters could not affoord us any thing, the burgers being few and altogether impoverished. The single sojors had a reichs doller a month and commis[sion]s [of] bread and beer, viz. 2 pund of bread a day and a Scots pint of beer, wee being

---

[373] The conspirators were ready to sacrifice Swedish service to avenge their king, but they could have learnt of their mistake. The envoy was not John Bradshaw, judge of King Charles, but his brother Richard.

allowed also for our *hacke shutsen*[374], or attendants. Nether could wee make any other shifts, the countrey being all ruin'd round about us, and wee not dareing nor haveing any people to spare to hazard out with.

As to our politick way of liveing, wee {216} keeped a good formall ffriendship with the German officers, yet was there alwayes a jealousy, if not an undermineing of one another amongst us, which the [lt.] coll. fomented and occasioned, as a piece of policy – *divide et impera*[375]. He had a sort of antipathy from the beginning against Capt. Forbes, whither thinking his behaviour too lofty or that he was too wise and cunning, or both, upon which ground he sussulcted those who had any question or quarrell with him, and aggravated the least miscarriage of his. Yet knowing him to be ane active person, and knowne to all the generall persons, he bore fairer with him as he meaned. Which was seen by his carriage in that businesse of the regiment quarterm-r, who being an intollerable bragging fellow, at a feast had given Capt. Forbes great reason of offence, all which in respect to the lt. coll., who was present, the captaine did patiently beare. Yet he as if of purpose put on it, desisted not, neither did the lt. coll., as he in such case should have, command him silence. The capt. only after some retorsions told him that, carrying respect to the lt. coll. {216v} and company, he desired not to be heard there, but would see how he would answer these things to morrow.

The q-t-m-r haveing caroused the most part of the night, in the morning gott to horseback and fyred a pistoll into the doore of the capt-s lodging, and so rode out to a plaine befor the castle within the towne, the gates being shut. The capt. makeing ready rode out also, and going near the lt. coll-s lodging, was commanded by him to stay. The capt. said, "You suffered him yesternight to abuse me, and this day openly to provoke and bravade me. Now, come what will, he or I shall dy for it!", and so passed by, the lt. coll. darting a litle sword at him in the going by (wherein he had a singular art), yet did him no harme.

Being come to the open place befor the castle, they discharged their pistolls at other without any harme to either. So closeing with broad-swords,

---

[374] Presumably from German *Hacke(n)* (heel) and *Schutz* (guard).
[375] Divide and rule (Lat.).

the captaine wounded the other in the head and hand, so that he did fall from his horse, and his foot sticking in the stirrop, his horse dragged him to his quarters.

A guard {217} was presently put to the captaines lodging, and there being no chirurgeon in that place, the quarterm-r was carryed to Marienburg and dyed about midnight. Upon notice wherof the captaine was made closse prisoner in the castle and afterwards, brought to Marienburg, was by a counsell of warr condemned to be harquebussed. Yet being knowne to be a pretty man, and by the grandees well beloved, by the entreaty of a yong *Graffe* Oxensterne he was pardoned and restored to his place. The killing of the man was not so much regarded, because he had been provoked to it, as his disobedience of command and fighting w[i]t[h]in the garrison, which was by the lt. coll. aggravated to the hight. Upon his returne now the [lt.] coll. showed himself very ffriendly to him, and he dissembling as if he knew nothing of his instigateing so hard against him, carryed fair also.

This our lt. coll. was so passionate a person as ever I heard of. For at such a businesse as a man of setled judgment {217v} would not be moved, he would be so enraged, that flinging away his stick, gloves and cappe he would teare his owne haire, and that upon the streetes, so that I verily beleeved and used to say it was but a feigned passion to make people affrayed of him.

He tooke all the benefitt (which indeed was not great) to himself, and of 408 reichs dollars, which was brought to the garrison monthly, he tooke a 100 thereof to himself. For he tooke money for all the vacant places of the foure companyes and the staffe, excepting maior of a compleet regiment, which in the Sweds service is usually winked at, an officer takeing pay for all his servants and many more blinds besides, especially he who is chieffe in a garrison or commander of a regiment.

He kept a good ordinary table, and alwayes one or two or more officers at dinner, and then was very kind and familiar, but upon duty and in command very strict and severe, a very compleet souldier, vigilant and sober, liveing very frugally and provideing for his wyfe {218} and fyve daughters, which he had liveing in Pomeren. He was borne in Dantzick of Scots parents, and had been an ensignie in Moskovia.

The Polls lying in their quarters in ye townes by the river Vistula, and knowing y-t the Sweds had the best part of their subsistance and maintenance out of the Great *Werder*, designed to ruine it or put it under contribution, so that transporting themselves quietly over the Vistula, and had fortifyed the Lissawish skonce and made ready a bridge, befor ever the Sweds had notice thereof; who being alarumed herewith, the generallissimus drew such forces as could be spared out of Elbing, Marienburg and the Hooft, and with some cannon marched thither.

In the meane tyme orders were sent to our commendant to send a lieutennant or ensignie with 20 dragownes to recognosce alongst the Vistula towards Marienwerder, and make strict enquiry if the Polls were makeing preparations of vessells to transport themselves over the Vistula or Nagott {218v} into the *werder*, and returning once in 24 houres give notice to the commander in chieffe in Marienburg of what passed.

When it came to my turne, I marched out in the evening, as usuall upon the returne of the other party, directly to the Vistula and all along the river farther up as any had done before. In my returne, when it was day light, I found in diverse creekes 7 boats, 2 whereof could hold a dozen or 15 men, the other 5 but small, for 2 or three a piece. And albeit by the pawres, whom I had taken out of their houses in the night, I could not learne any thing of any forces to come that way, yet makeing hast to Marienburg, I informed the *Graffe* von Dhona of my dilligence and of these boats. His Exc. gave me many thankes in very ffriendly words and blamed those, who had been befor me and had not found or given notice of these boats; and so ordered me to returne, and he would send an officer with some musquetiers by water to fetch these boats away, which was done accordingly.

The Sweds in the meane tyme w[i]t[h] {219} much industry and vigour furthered their workes by the Lissawish skonce, and haveing in an opportune place raised a battery and planted thereon some cannon, they ruined the bridge, and so cutt of all hopes of succours from those in the skonce. Their Lieut. Coll. Pflawme being also killed, they came to an agreement and rendred upon discretion. There were about fyve hundred men in it, who were afterwards transported to Denmarke to the King of Sweden, where they did good service, and a regiment of Danes sent back to us. The skonce being taken, our recognoscing ceassed; the generall commissary or *pisars polny* of the Polls army Jan Sapiha being all this tyme in Colum with the greatest part of the cavalliery.

This passeing in the Passion Weeke, and wee presuming that the Polls, getting notice of the danger of their ffriends, would assuredly march to their releefe or to Marienburg, or into the Elbings *werder* for makeing a diversion, yet Easter Moonday {219v} being come, and wee hearing nothing of them, wee imagined they were keeping their Easter first. And so wee resolved the next day to send to a *hoffe* by Monto Spits and bring forrage, whereof some plenty was there. As also my captaine and I haveing clubbed for makeing a feast, wee sent our servants with 3 spare horses to bring some of our countreymen to the feast.

By day light wee sent away our forragers, about 70 persons, servants, towns people and some sojors. These being come to the *hoffe* and busy loading up hay and cornes, were suddainly environed by a great number of Polls commanded by one Michaelka, and all of them taken except two who hidd themselves among the straw, who upon the Polls leaving the *hoffe* came away and told us what had passed. They told also how that upon examination our servants had told that some officers were to come from Marienburg to a feast, and that Michae[l]sky had sent his lieutennant to intercept them at the milne halfe way betwixt Stum and Marienborgh. Whereupon wee all mounted, being 18 persons, ready to ride out as in such occasiones wee used to do. But the [lt.] coll. would not permitt us, saying he had a badd dreame, and that there was misfortune enough already.

Whereupon wee returned and unsadling our horses went to make preparation for reception of our guests, {220} and dinner being ready, wee went to the lt. coll-s lodging to desire him to come. Wee were not well there, when the watch from the steeple called out, "The Polls were takeing the dragowns horses away befor the gate!" So by the lt. coll-s permission wee gott to horse and rode out. Capt. Jacob Curas with most of the officers were out befor us.

My capt. and I meeting accidentally befor the gate, kept together and following closse alongst the topps of the hills for fear of being circumvented, wee at last perceived them in a valley on our right hand.

They were about 30 men and were driveing about 40 horses with them. Notwithstanding their strength wee rode up to them and fyred our pistolls at them diverse tymes, they letting at every tyme some of the horses go, without offering to follow us, when wee retired to charge our pistolls, only fyring at us as they marched, kept on their way makeing show of fear and doubt.

I diswaded my captaine from adventuring so closse to them or following them farther, telling him that if he or I or any of our horses chanced to be shott, wee should be both lost, and that by going too farr wee might be circumvented by an ambush, and that it was likely they were only enticeing us to follow them, they haveing no need to be so affrayed as they pretended. But the capt., being a violent eager person, would by no meanes be diswaded from persuing further.

{220v} Wee were by this tyme more as halfe a Dutch mile from the towne, and entering further among some birch bushes and shrubes, wee see them sending away their spare horses befor, and about a dozen of the best horsed staying together and retiring at more leasure. This I represented to the captaine as a certainty, that even these intended to fall back upon us, but he relying upon his being well horsed, could hardly be drawne to retire.

Yet at last wee stopped, which the enemy seing, returned to set upon us. Wee retired at leasure, keeping them at a distance, neither did they persue us eagerly. In the meane tyme one John Forbes, a serjeant, with a boy of mine came rideing up to us. The serjeant being drunk, notwithstanding commands and threats, rode by us and charged in among them, which necessitated us to returne and releeve him, which succeeding very well, the capt. giveing him a blow or two, sent him to drive homewards some horses w-ch the Polls had let go, and I sent my boy along with him.

All this tyme wee could see our officers standing in a trowpe on a hill without offering to advance towards us, albeit they might well perceive our manifest danger. The Polls beginning to persue us more boldly, wee mended our pace also, but on a suddaine out of a wood on the right hand some hundreds of Polls {221} came with full speed towards us, and then too late wee did see our errour! These whom wee had been persuing charged us now home, whom, however, wee keeping a distance from another, kept of a long tyme, letting our horses run at a strong gallop, spareing our shott, as being most spent, and wanting tyme to charge againe.

So, releeving other as need moved and looking and guarding alwayes behind us, wee minded not our way befor us, and so I was unexpectedly driven into a marish, where my horse stuck. I alighted from him, takeing out my pistolls, and gott him with great difficulty to follow me, yet being in the midle, he stuck againe. It being not broad, I was in hopes, after he had rested a litle, to gett him thorow, and the reeds being high and thick, I stayed there undiscovered.

In the meane tyme the captaine, seeing me fallen in the marish, turned to the left hand thinking to avoide it, but being overpowred by the multitude of persuers, was driven into the marish, wounded and taken. The Polls discovering me also, they began to shoot at me and called to me to take quarters; and seing them rideing about the marish, my horse haveing rested a litle, I rouzed him up so that he followed me, I holding the bridle, w-ch was long, in my hand.

Being come to dry land, three Polls were come so near, so that I could scarcely get to horse, whom however I kept of by presenting the wrong end of my pistoll, which in hast I could not get otherwise recovered; and {221v} being freed of these a litle, wee rode for it to the damme, wherein I gained ground of them, but on the damme was mett by about 20 others, who all made account to take me prisoner. I comeing near them, fyred a pistoll among them and so brake thorow with the losse of my sword and cappe; my sword hanging drawne by a ribband or band at my hand, one catched hold of the guards of it, the band broke. Another tooke hold of my cappe with haire and all, a good deale whereof he pulled out, which I did not feele then, but thereafter.

Being gott over the damme, my boy came to me, and I was gott a good way of towards the towne befor they were aware. But how soone they perceived I was gone, they followed me altogether. I was afrayed of nothing so much but that my horse, being a fyry nagge and haveing ridden over much deep ground and taken much paines, should faile me, I haveing as yet a large halfe German mile to the towne. Wherefor seing some of them gaining ground upon me, and being come to the hill where the officers stood (who how soone the ambush {222} breake loose marched of in great hast), I wheeled about and called out aloud for dragowners to advance, w-ch the formost of the Polls hearing, they wheeled of also, so that I had tyme to breath my horse and charge my pistoll. But a good company of the Pols being come up and seing non appear to my releefe, they breake loose againe.

So without keeping the high way I tooke the nearest cutt to the towne, which had almost been my ruine, for from the way to the right hand there was a cross unpassable ditch, w-ch if I had not in tyme perceived, and so in tyme crossed over to the high way, I had undoubtedly been killed or taken. Yet I was in great danger by the shotts I received in crossing their front and lossing the advantage of ground which I had. They persued me very hardly up to another hight, where I wheeled and called upon dragownes againe. But they were too wise to be gulled againe, w-ch I perceiving held on my way, they shooting continually with arrowes at me and often calling {222v} to me to take quarters.

At last I overtooke one Ensignie Quickfelt, and seing a Poll on a white horse a good distance befor the rest, I thought at the comeing downe of a hill to engage him, and called to the ensignie to second me. But he had no mind to it and said to me, "Oh, brother, he is hard, otherwise he would not persue you so". My horse being yet fresh, I could easily have passed by him and others too, but seing them heartles and not minding any resistance, I choose to keep the reare.

Being come near the towne, the Polls desisted from persuing us, fearing the cannon and musquetiers by the hedges. Divers shotts I had through my cloaths, and 3 arrowes sticking in them, and through Gods mercy had only a light wound with an arrow in my right thigh, albeit above a hundred were shott at me, and that very neere.

Being come where the officers stood, the lt. colonell rode at me with a cok't pistoll to shoot me for rideing so farr without orders. I did not stay to reason with him, only told him I could not leave my captaine. The takeing of my captaine, and to gett no more {223} thankes for comeing of so handsomly, did so vexe me that I was careles of my self and with haffe a desperate resolution rode into the fields betwixt our station and the Polls to seeke death in a manner. I, as the fashion, by swinging my pistoll about my head, provoked any of them out to change bullets. Diverse came out, but alwayes others takeing a compasse strove to entrappe me, w-ch I perceiving, retired to be at equall distance from my owne.

At last one came out to very equall ground. I advanced up to him, and being come pretty neare at the ordinary pace, he fyred his pistoll at me and wheeled of. At the shott my horse foundred almost to the ground, so that I thought he had been shott. Yet recovering, I followed him hard, untill I saw my self within danger of other three advancing to gett between me and my owne. So fyreing not so near as I intended or wished, my horse caryed me further in the danger, so that I was forced to turne downe towards the lake. The three Polls, being gott betweene me and my owne, persued me to the lake, {223v} where haveing a sight of the towne and, as I think, being affrayed of shott from the walls, they retired; non of our officers offering to help or releeve me, for which I upbraided them at my returne with some bitternes. About an howre thereafter the Polls marched of, and wee into the towne, where wee kept our feast with heavines.

The next day I desired the lt. coll. to writt to the generallissimus in the behalfe of Capt. Forbes and to intercede for his speedy releasement, lest by delay he might incurr danger. For when he was prisoner about a year befor in Conits, he made his escape by stabbing a sentry, and albeit a closs prisoner by the law of armes cannot be called in question or censured for any thing he doeth in the meanes of his escape, yet murther such as that was, taken in the strictest sense, is not allowable. However, at the desire of the generallissimus he was dismissed 6 weekes thereafter.

Some tyme befor the lt. coll., who could not endure a controller, had complained of the *podstarost* or *oeconomus*, that he did not manage the rents of the castle well, affoorded nothing thereof into the magasine, but converted all to his owne use, whereupon he was called from thence, and a writer only left to manage that businesse, w-ch was no wayes considerable. Upon the {224} returne of Capt. Forbes out of prison the generallissimus was said to intend the inspection of that businesse to him, the acceptance whereof I diswaded, telling him that it would be the ground of perpetuall dissention betwixt the commendant and him, and advised him to procure it for the lt. coll., who by many conjectures I perceived aimed at it, not so much for any benefitt which might accrue by it, as that he cared not to have any body in the towne who did not depend upon himself, or who could tell tales or looke in his cardes. And so accordingly, when the capt. came to the generallissimus, it was offered him, w-ch he declined and advised the giveing of it to the commendant, which was very well taken and an order to that purpose sent to him, as also a patent to be colonell, all which Capt. Forbes brought along with him, for which he was exceedingly welcomed and in great favour a good while.

This summer the Polls being quartered up and downe Prussia, and the Elector of Brandeburgh haveing declared himself our enemy, Thorun being blocquired also by the Imperialists and Polls, wee were continually molested, and hardly a week passed that the Polls did not come once or twice befor our garrison, trying to get away our horses and cattell. And albeit wee were very few who were in a capacity to ride out, yet wee {224v} never failed to shew our selves befor the gates within reach of our cannon, and very often on horsback skirmishing with them to the no small danger of our persons. Upon the Elector his declaration against the Sweds wee rode a party into the Dukedome as farr as Preus Marke and brought good booty of horses and cowes with us. But another party of free *ryters*, servants and such adventurers going out a weeke thereafter, were all taken except one, who betymes made his escape and brought tithings of the rest.

In May the coll. sent me to Elbing for our pay, which haveing obtained, I was employed thereafter every month to that purpose, being very well horsed, going and returning in the night for fear of the Polls, who continually almost lay at a mill halfe-way betwixt Stume and Marienburgh.

In July, comeing from Elbing to Marienburgh in the evening and feeding my horses befor the towne, by the negligence of my servant one of my horses breaking loose, I was hindred from rideing away in due tyme, so that when I came to the small brooke in the halfe-way it was day light. I used always to keep a byroad on the left hand of the mill. Yet suspecting nothing at this tyme, as I was {225} rideing at leasure and looking to the right hand, I thought I did see some red thing flying as it were along the valley towards me, w-ch minded me of makeing greater hast over that suspected place.

Being gott through the dale to the hight, I perceived a dozen of Polls comeing in full speed after me. I was well horsed and had a good advantage of ground befor them, yet haveing 408 reichs dollers, most in small money, behind me, and my servants horse none of the best, and fearing that some others were gone from the milne to the way w-ch led to the Marienburghs gate, I was in some perplexity. Yet keeping on the way and perceiving these behind me to gaine no ground of me, I was in better hopes. I was only affrayed of being waylaid by others, wherefor I resolved to take my way round the lake by Barlewits[376]; which succeeded exceeding well, for how soone I turned to the left hand, those who persued me, thinking as it seemes that I had mistaken the way, tooke the road towards the towne, so that I had gott a great advantage of them befor they perceived my {225v} intention of going round the lake, and then they followed me, but too late, for I kept the advantage I had of them and came safe to the towne.

A fortnight thereafter, the coll. haveing gott notice that a Scotsman in Elbing, by whom he had his goods and money in custody, was deceassed, he sent me thither to receive them and lay them in keeping by one Durham; which I did, and brought an acquittance of the reseat thereof. There were in two trunkes many good cloathes and much furniture, plate and money, to the value of above 4,000 dollers.

In August, haveing notice of the small garrison in Marienwerder, and that they lay secure, a party came from Marienburgh consisting of 200 foot and 50 horse, to whom from our garrison joyned Capt. Forbes with 40 men (for more wee could not spare). The[y] marched from Stume when it began to grow darke and befor daylight were gott to Marienwerder. They had ladders and all other things fitt for such an enterprise along with them, so that attacqueing it at 3 places, they tooke it by scalado without great resistance. The tyme consumed in breaking up the gates and secureing them gave the sojours of the garrison, as also the burgers with

---

[376] This village is marked as Warlitz on old maps of Eastern Prussia.

the readyest and best of their goods, leave to retire into the great church, which they defended so obstinately that it was thought fitt not to hazard men in takeing it. Only they besett the passages, {226} untill the souldiers had plundered out the towne, and then marched away in good order.

In the beginning of September, I being upon the watch at the south gate, I sent in the afternoone for a yong horse, which I had gotten in the Dukedome, and was not broken well as yet, and caused a souldier of Capt. Jacob Curas his company, who had some art in rideing, to ride him befor the gate a litle. This fellow had been trusted by his captaine to go out amongst the pawres, where he used to stay two or three weekes, and haveing engaged to serve, then run away with horses and bring them to his captaine; so that I had not the least suspicion that he should run away. But after he had ridden my horse up and downe neare the gate, and then rideing further and returning, at last he rode a good way of to a litle hight, from whence in a full gallop he rode towards the wood; whereof the sentry from the topp of the gate informing me, I went up myself, but he was already out of sight.

There were with me on the guard two Scotsmen sojours in our company, one called Wardlaw, the other Wadie. These offered, if I would let them take horses and give them swords, they would follow {226v} and bring him back againe. I knowing my horse to be yong and not able to run farr, permitted them to go. So they haveing gotten from other sojours two swords, and takeing two of my captaines horses who were befor the gate at the grasse, a drummer also tooke a horse of myne and followed, they hasted away, and haveing good horses, I was in good hopes that they should overtake him. By this tyme my lieutennant was come to releeve me from the guard, of whom I desired and obtained 4 men to convoy of the guard, that the men who were gone should not be missed.

Being come home, I sadled my best horse w-ch I kept always in the stable and rode out with intention to follow them, for now I began to suspect that these 3 were gone also, w-ch proved true. I was not farr from the towne, when I did meet my yong horse all in sweat comeing back againe. I made great hast, and was informed by such people as were earning in the fields which way they were gone, and also that they were not farr befor me.

So that befor they could gett to Rezenborgh I hoped to overtake {227} them. But do what I could, I could not, only I had a sight of the three one a hill not farr from the towne, and againe when they were near the gates. So that fearing to be taken my self, I returned, and now all my care was in case of meeting any Brandeburgers that I should not be taken. For my horse, I knew not how he would hold out if I were put to it to run, because I had ridden him so hard for three miles.

I resolved, however, it being near evening, to ride the direct way towards Marienwerder, another of the Dukes townes, so long untill it should be darke or untill I should be assured of the fields being clear. I had not ridden farr, when I did meet a party of ten or twelve horsemen with an officer, who only asked me from whence I came and whither I was going. I told them I was come from Resenborgh and was going to Marienwerder, and pretending hast lest I should be benighted, they let me passe without asking me more questions.

Haveing ridden halfe a mile farther, and ready to turne of to the right hand towards {227v} my owne garrison, I saw a trowpe of about 20 horsemen makeing great hast towards me. The officer asked me of what regiment, which company and whither I was going so alone. I told him I belonged to Coll. Shoneks regiment and *Ruitm-r* Langs[377] company, and was sent by the *ruitm-r* to Marienwerder about a businesse of his. It chanced that two of the same *Ruitm-r* Lang his company were there, who presently averred they did not know me nor had not seen me. I (haveing studied my lesson befor hand) answered that I was but lately come from Konigsberg to him, and so pretending hast, they let me passe.

When these were out of sight, resolving not to stand out more hazards of examination and finding a litle byroad, I made hast to Stume and came thither as it began to grow darke. The gates were shutt, and the coll. for no entreaty would cause open them, so that I was forced to stay under the bridge all night with my horse. When I came to my lodging in the morning and expected to be put in arrest or under a guard, {228} I heard not of any thing, so that I could not know what to think of it.

---

[377] Lang is a common surname both in German lands and Scotland.

The next day one of my comorades came and told me that the coll. had taken such offence at me that he would not hear of my remaining under the regiment any more. Neither that day nor the next, for all the entreatyes the officers and especially my countrey men made for me, could he be pacifyed; so that I began to think of takeing another course, and so caused desire only my passe, intending to engage for regiment quartermaster to Coll. Sinklairs regiment, which place was vacant and promised me befor, if I were free of this.

The coll. hearing of this, shewed himself mor easy, and because he had refused all entreatyes of others, it was conjectured that he expected I should speake for my self, which I was perswaded to do. So takeing the opportunity of his going out at the Marienburghs gate, and whilst he was leaning over the rails of the bridge, and few by him, I spoke to him, confessing my fault (which was in {228v} deed very great), and craved pardon, promiseing to take better head in tymes comeing. He made no scruple or ceremony of receiving me into favour againe.

The 20th of September a lieutenant w[i]t[h] 200 horse came to Stume by day light. This party was to go to Thorun with some money and provision. This towne had been now neer a year now and then blocquired, and now by the preparations made in Polland was expecting a formall siege. My colonell had 1,600 dollers lying by a Scotsman in Thorun called Robert Smart, for which he had his bond, and seeing the towne lyke to be taken from the Sweds, he thought this a good opportunity to fetch his money from thence. Wherefor he sent for me and desired me to go thither with this party, w-ch I willingly undertooke, so he gave me the bond and a letter to the merchant.

Being come with this party to Grawdents, wee gott certaine intelligence that a strong army of Polls and Imperialists were come to Thorun and laid a formall siege to it, which made {229} us returne in great hast, and because it was thought that another party would be sent thither againe, the colonell caused me keep all the writings by me, to be in readines to go along with the first good opportunity.

A weeke after this Capt. Forbes haveing had some difference with Capt. Michael Besum, I was sent to challenge this Michael out to fight.

Being come into the fields, Michael craved pardon of Capt. Forbes, which satisfaction I perswaded him to accept of, it being mor honourable as if he had wounded or killed him in the place. The quarrell was no sooner ended, when the colonell, haveing got notice, came out befor the gate, so I step't asyde a litle to shun the first brunt of his anger.

I rode to Elbing for our pay, and comeing in discourse with *Ruitm-r* Alex-r Smith about some debt owing me by Quarterm-r Andrew Straittowne, which he very unjustly and sullenly denyed me, wee did fall out and quarrelled upon the streets just befor the court of guard, but were not permitted to come in action by those who were present. Neither could I gett opportunity to meet him, he going that night to his quarters in the Great *werder*.

{229v} It were tedious to relate the many conflicts wee had with the Polls this summer, wee striveing to defend our horses and cattell feeding befor the gate, and they makeing suddaine onsets to gett them away, in two whereof I was in very great danger of being killed, and preserved only by Gods gracious providence and protection.

In October about 3,000 Polls came and encamped two miles from Stume. They were commanded by [...] Koniecpolsky, the *Woywod* of Sandomirs, and Jan Sobiesky, the Crowne standart-bearer. These sent parties continually towards Marienburgh, who in going and comeing forgott not to visitt us. So that wee were forced to raile in a piece of ground for safeguard of our bestiall befor the south gate, and be always in readines at the gate to sally out to releeve and defend them.

This month, going to Elbingh for our pay, I was almost taken by a party of the Brandeburgers commanded by *Ruitm-r* Lang, who had been at the gates of Marienburgh, but happily in their returning I discovered them befor they me, and so went aside and lurked among some bushes, untill the coast was clear.

{230} I must relate a businesse, which did fall out in the Aprill befor, because of a passage wherein I was concerned. There was a Dutchman who had served somwhere for an ensigny, and now had a subsistance by our regiment without being in actuall service or haveing any pay. This ensignie was sent to a village at the entry of the Elbings *werder* to ly upon safeguard there, where he was taken prisoner by a party of the Imperialists, who then quartered in the Bishopdome. After he had been in prison 4 or 5 weekes, and knowing that litle regard would be had in ransoming him, seeing he was not in actuall service, he did writt a letter to the generallissimus desiring to be releeved or ransomed, promiseing to deserve it with his service and blood thereafter. This letter, whither for want of opportunity or not, he did not send.

In the meane tyme the Imperialists proffered him an ensignies place if he would go with a party of theirs and show the meanes of takeing away the scout watch by Marienburgh. Whether he offered himself to this service or not is unknowne, for in the councell of warr thereafter he denyed it. However, he accepted of the service and came with a party (in which he had no command, only as a guide) to Marienburgh, yet by the vigilancy of the watch was disappointed.

This party, being 24 horsmen and commanded by a {230v} quartermaster, in returning lodged someq-t securely (as thinking themselves out of danger) in a village of the Dukedome, and in the night tyme were set upon and routed by a party of Sweds of 40 horse commanded by a lieutenant, who had been also upon adventures in the B[isho]pdome. The quarterm-r and 8 more were taken, amongst whom was the abovementioned ensignie, who in his returne from Marienburgh, comeing through the village out of which he had been taken, gave the letter he had written in prison to a pawre there, desireing him most earnestly to carry it to Marienburgh, which he did.

And now, the quarterm-r being brought to Marienburgh and examined, he told upon what acco[un]t he had been sent out, and with that the said ensignie had undertaken to show the meanes to gett away the utter guards or scoutwatch; and he himself being examined, denyed some circumstances, but could not the subsistence; which not agreeing with the professions he had made in his letter, after some dayes was sent to Stum with the deposition of the quarterm-r and other prisoners, as also the letter w-ch he had written to the generallissimus, with order to hold a counsell of warr upon him.

In this councell of warr, whereof I was a member, his chieffe plea was that, haveing been in prison 6 weekes and knowing that no regard would be had to {231} ransome him, because he had not been in charge, and the Imperialists offering him good conditions, if he would by such a piece of service give testimony of his fidelity and judgement, he thought he might lawfully engage in their service, haveing expected in prison releefe or ransoming such a space, as he conceived and had heard was allowable and practicable for men of his condition and quality. He understood also that by the law of armes a reformado ensignie was to be esteemed equivalent with an under officer in actuall charge and service, and the tyme prescrived by the articles or custome of warr for such a person to remaine in prison was 6 weekes; and if in such a tyme he were not releeved by the prince under whom he had served, he might freely take service, which tyme he had punctually observed.

As to that letter, he said he had written it in prison, and haveing it by him as he returned through that village where he had been safeguard, he desired one of his acquaintance to cary it and deliver it; that whilst he was in prison he could {231v} not find any opportunity to send it; and that now when he sent it he was of intention, when he returned, not to engage in their service untill he should hear if any course were taken for releeving or ransoming him.

Notwithstanding the sending of this letter was so aggravated by the president and most of the counsell that it was made the only occasion of sentencing him to death, I reasoned against it, and was therefor sharply taken up by the president. Yet when it came to voteing, I would not assent to his death nor subscrived the sentence, as is the custome, whereat the lt. coll. was displeased. It being Fridday, the subscrived sentence was sent the same evening to Marienburgh to the generallissimus, and ane answer returned the next day that he should be executed on Moonday betwixt 10 and 11 aclock.

On Sunday Capt. Jacob Curas went with his wyfe and sisters to Marienburgh to begg pardon for him, but could not get audience that day, nor the next befor 9 aclock, when without great entreaty or ceremony the generalliss[im]us was pleased to pardon him and {232} commanded an order to be sent immediately to that purpose. Yet it was so long delayed that it came too late, whether of purpose or not, God knoweth. And albeit great intercession was made on Moonday to the lt. coll., yet he durst not disobey. The execution, however, was protracted to 1 aclock, and about ane howre thereafter the pardon came. He dyed to all appearance very patiently and devoutly, desired that he might not be tyed to the post, nor his face covered, for he was shott or harquebussired, as the Dutch call it.

In November the Polls army removed to Christbur[g]h, from whence they continually infested us, especially one Michaelsky, a *ruitm-r* of voluntiers, who being a pawres son in Prussia, and knowing all the wayes and byroads and passages, did great mischieffe to the Sweds, for which he was nobilitated by the King of Polland.

{232v} On Sunday ye [17] of No[vembe]r our watch from the tower gave notice of some Polls being come to Barlewits, a small village not farr without the reach of our cannon. So Capt. Jacob Curas, Capt. Forbes and I rode to the south gate where wee found the colonell, of whom wee desired leave to ryde out. He told us he would not command us, but wee might go upon our owne hazard.

Wee rode keeping the low ground and came to the village undescryed, where wee found the Polls from their horses. Only two gott to horseback and, being well horsed, escaped to Peterswald. I persued them out into the fields, and returning found the captaines had taken 3 prisoners and more horses. They told me that some were gott into the houses to hyde themselves. I alighted and fetched out sixe, one by one, and so makeing them to mount, wee returned.

Wee were scarse out of the village, when about 50 or 60 horse came in full carrier from Peterswald, but wee had too great advantage of ground to be overtaken, and our musquetiers were {233} ready at the railling to assist us. A pawre fetcht out two prisoners, so that wee had eleven prisoners and 12 horses, one haveing hidd himself so that wee could not find him. The prisoners with all they had were given of to the guard in the castle till further orders.

Haveing notice that the colonell intended to take the best share of the booty to himself, to which purpose he delayed the giveing out the horses and other things, wee consulted on Wednesday what wee should do, and resolved the next day to desire him to give us the horses and other things; w-ch wee did, and he told us that after dinner wee should come and take them. Wee conveened at Capt. Jacobs house, and being assured that the colonell intended to take two of the best horses with the best furniture, w-ch was almost as much worth as all the rest, wee resolved to oppose and rather not take any thing as losse the best part of our booty, w-ch wee had gained at our owne and great hazard, and concluded that Capt. Jacob should speake, w-ch he was loth to do. Yet wee urged it, because he was eldest captaine, as also he was most earnest to contradict, as haveing a great familie, and in necessity.

{233v} I had also my owne designe in this, for my capt. haveing been under a cloud, I and others of my countreymen were looked upon asquint, and I knew his speaking would not be well taken and bring us in favour againe. Neither was he such a child as not to perceive this drift, and insinuated so much to us, yet could he not get it declined because of his precedency.

So over wee went to the colonell, and he caused the horses to be brought befor his doore, two of the best whereof with the best furniture were tyed to a post apart. When wee came out, he told us that those two were for him, and that wee should take the rest and deale them. To which Capt. Jacob answered, "You were not pleased to give us orders to go out, only permitted us to go at our owne hazards; so that wee have gained these with the great hazard of our lives and fortune. For if wee had failed and been taken prisoners, wee must have ransomed our selves. And now that you will take from us the best part of that w-ch wee have gained from our enemyes, being no free-*ryters* but officers, wee will not take any thing, and rather let you have {234} it all, as want that w-ch is only worth the haveing".

Wherewith the colonell was so incensed, that saying "You may thank God that I have not my sword by me, and I'll make you answer how you have behaved your self befor your enemyes" (for he had, by going further as he had orders, lost a party of 50 men about a year ago, and being taken prisoner, had ransomed himself, and the disobeying orders and the losse of the party hitherto connived at). So hastening into his chamber, he gave orders to drive all the horses away from befor his doore.

Wee being a litle surprized, especially Capt. Jacob, and not thinking that it should fly so high, wee consented to Capt. Jacobs desire and requested the coll-s *secretarius* to go in and tell him that befor he should be offended, wee would leave that which he had alotted for himself and take away the others. But he was so enraged that he would not accept of any thing, but commanded them all to be immediately taken away, or he would cause hogh the horses. So seeing this, I perswaded Capt. Jacob {234v} to let the horses be brought to his quarters, where by a cup of his beer wee would divide them, and since better could not be, take the byte and the buffet with it.

So wee went and shared the booty. I kept the best horse to myself and the furniture, and gave the other 3 to my capt. to mount dragowners upon. In the evening the coll. sent for Capt. Forbes from the guard and gave him the paroll or word, commanding thereby that none should obey Capt. Jacob Curas; wherewith wee were all sorry, not wishing or willing that it should have come so farr.

The next morning, being Fridday the 22d of November, returning from the maine guard, where I had visited my captaine, the sentry from the tower had given that about 15 or 20 horsemen were come to Barlewits. I made hast to horseback and rode to the south gate, where I found the colonell and 6 of our officers on horseback. How soone I came, the colonell told us wee should go the low way and strive to surprise them.

Wee rode along the {235} valley, and being come to the high ground not farr from the village, wee see them at a passe already out of the village. Wee left one upon the hill with orders, if any did appear from any other place, to shoot of his pistoll. So wee advanced downe to the skirt of the hill, where perceiving them to be about 20 men well horsed, wee thought it not safe to engage with them.

They had a waggon by them, which stuck fast in the marish, and two did alight to clear it, the rest being gott to the other syde. I seeing this, mad hast downe to engage these on foot in the marish, but befor I could come at them, they were cleared. Then 5 or 6 of these who were over turned and shott over the marish at me, it being not broad; my horse was yong, and the ground deep, so that by wheeling my horse for avoyding their sure aiming at me I wearyed him much.

In the meane tyme looking about, I see my comorades rideing in great hast to the village without giving any signe to me. I thought really they had seen some straglers in the village, whom they went to take, and knowing I could not do better service as to defend the passe and not permitt these to come over, {235v} I rode up and downe to that purpose, untill in an instant they alltogether returned with resolution to force the passage; which I seing, made hast to the village lest my comorades should be taken at disadvantage or unawares.

When I came to the high ground, I did to my great amazement see 2 or 300 men betwixt me and the towne, all in full carrier after my comorades, who being past the village had taken their course round the lake, haveing a great advantage of ground. I recollecting my self, and knowing my horse to be yong and almost wearyed, and so not able to hold out so farr as to ride round the lake, resolved to breake thorow the direct way to the towne. But putting my horse to it, he would by no meanes, and being headstrong, he caryed me forward to the village.

By this tyme some of the best horsed Polls were by a nearer cutt along the lake got befor me. I rode, however, as fast as I could, untill by some who persued me I was driven of the way, and comeing to a ditch on the right hand, {236} I forced my horse to leape it, but he failing, did fall therein. Yet I recovered my self, and crossing the way againe unperceived (for there were diverse Germans with the Polls), I rode towards the lake, intending by the benefitt or shelter of some bushes to escape unknowne; yet was discovered by those who were hindmost, and persued by about 30 or 40, most servants, whom however I kept of by presenting my pistoll to them. But being mett by 12 or 15 others, I was forced to take to the hill thorow some thornes, where, the hill being somq-t steep, my horse being quite wearyed stuck in a bush.

I dismounted and takeing out my other pistoll run towards the fields, to free my self of the scumme of them, and since I saw no other remedy but to be killed or taken, to fall among honest people. By this tyme a number were gott up the hill, some whereof shott at me with arrowes, others alighted from their horses and out of long gunnes shott at me ten or twelve tymes. I run hither and thither, not keeping any direct course, and by Gods mercy received no harme in my body, only two bullets through my coat.

{236v} It pleased God to bring two horsemen over the fields to me, who by appearance seeming to be gentlmen, I run towards them and called for quarters. But perceiving them to shun and hold of from me because of the pistolls I had, I threw them from me and ran to them, and very narrowly escaped the simitars of those, who now seing my pistolls gone, persued me hotly without fear.

One of those two being a *ruitmaster*, whose name was Dziallinsky and commanded the party, had enough to do to save me from the rable, of whom being ridd, he sent me with two horsemen back to the village. These takeing every one ane arme of me, galloped away so fast that my feet did scarcely touch the ground untill I was in the village, where they presently alighted and searched my pockets, and that only my least, not finding the biggest, wherein was by accident my passe, which I had from Duglasse lyfe guard, the letter from the colonell to the merchant in Thorun with his bond for 1,600 r. dollers, and a pasquill made in manner of a piquet upon the Sweds, and diverse small things.

The party being come together, I see *Ruitm-r* Michalsky, by whose contrivance this party was conducted. {237} Albeit they had followed the other officers to the gates of the towne, yet non was taken but a serjeant called Elias, being not well horsed. They put me on a litle naughty horse and upon my paroll let me ride without a guard, yet amongst them.

Wee lodged that night in a village, and was brought the next day to Christburg and delivered of to the Crowne Standard-bearer Sobiesky who, the Palatine of Sandomirs being gone from thence sick, had now the command. He haveing examined us of the strength of our garrisons, our store of ammunition and provision, with such like things, sent us to the maine guard to be kept there. Two dayes thereafter the Crowne standart-bearer departed towards Thorne, and the command remained in the person of [...] Suchodolsky, *Starosta* Litinsky.

The next day a trumpeter came from the generallissimus with a letter to the commander in chieffe of the Polls forces in Christburg, desiring an exchange or ransoming of prisoners, my name being first in the roll; which Suchodolsky excused by haveing the command but for a tyme and not haveing commission to deale in such matters.

[December.] After fowre dayes stay more wee marched from thence. The *starost* in the morning takeing my promise {237v} not to run away, gave me on[e] of his best horses to ride on, neither confined me to any place or guard, but let me ride by the army where I pleased. I lodged always in his lodging, satt at the table next to himself, and he gave me his clock to cover me in the night tyme and a *voylock*[378], or quilt, to ly upon, and being a very discreet gentleman, was very kind to me.

At Rezenburgh a drummer came from Coll. Anderson to that commendant, offering a Brandeburgish ensignie for me, and that they should use meanes to procure my liberty from the Polls. But the *starost* would not hearken to it, and so wee marched forward towards Thorne. On the way, considering the ruinous countrey, wee had pretty good accommodation.

The *starost* regrated very much the great expences he was at by keeping a free table, which was many tymes so well furnished with guests, that his owne servants suffered necessity. Neither could he gett preserved a drink of beer for himself, but all must go up, and then all want together. He told me that the charge he had was a great burthen to him, and that his pay, albeit duly payed, could not defray the halfe of the expences he was at; and that he served only upon that account, to gett his lands {238} saved from transeant quarter, and to gaine greater respect; seing it was a disparagement for any Polls gentleman not to serve or have served; neither was there amongst them a readyer and more honourable way to preferment, offices or riches, as by serving in the warres.

Being come to the army, I was put under a guard of dragownes belonging to Jan Sapiha, who quartered with the Crowne standard-bearer in one *Hoffe*. My entertainment here was very slender, getting no more allowance as a penny a day, and the bread was exceeding dear. Neither had wee any

---

[378] Wojłok (Polish) – felt.

vessell to bring water in, so that in a week I did not drink, and that by dry bread. This made me think of some other. So I told the corporall of the guard that I would desire liberty from Sobiesky to go with a sentry or sojor into the leaguer and visitt my acquaintances when I pleased. So takeing the occasion of his comeing out, I spoke to him in Latine, desireing that I might be permitted to go to the Roman Emperours army (w-ch lay hard by) and visitt my acquaintances with a sojor to attend me, to which he readily consented and gave orders to the corporall {238v} to send a sojour along with me.

This priviledge I made use of every day, and stayed abroad from morning to evening, finding many acquaintances by whom I was well entertained. Some gentlmen serving under Jan Sapiha were very kind to me also, especially one with whom I changed bullets by Stume the spring befor, that day when my captaine was taken, and I so narrowly escaped. He told me that I did wound him in the hip when he, haveing shott of his pistoll, retired.

I was acquaint here with one Capt. Lesly who served the Rom. Emperour, being a sone of Tullois and nevoy to Generall Count Lesly,[379] and with one Capt. Stewart and diverse others of our countreymen. I see also Maior Sacken, under whose guard I had been when I escaped out of prison from the Imperialists. He asked me, why I had run away from them?; I asked him, why they did not watch me better?, and that a prisoner under closse guard had nothing else to do but to devise how to escape; w-ch he acknowledging, nothing more was of it.

Haveing notice of some Swedish prisoners being under a guard by the Crowne and Field Marshall Lubomirsky, I {239} went and gave them a visitt. I found them by a maior called Pnewsky, who commanded the generalls lyfe guard of dragownes, where they had large allowance from the generalls kitchin. I was kept to dinner and desired, if I pleased, to come every day. The maior was very kind to me upon the acco[un]t of Coll. Gordon who had served under the Rom. Emp.,[380] under whose command

---

[379] Captain James Leslie of Tullos later inherited his unkle Walter's title and died in 1692.
[380] Possibly, Colonel John Gordon, commandant of Eger, who was involved in the

he had served cornett. He invited me to take service under Lubomirsky, assuring me of being accommodated and well used.

I had already considered that there was no possibility of my being releeved, as also that the Sweds were at a low ebbe, and all going to wrack with them; nothing to be expected but to be cop'd up in garrisons, to suffer hunger and all the calamities incident to besieged places, and was even glad to be ridd of their service with my creditt. So albeit that I made difficulty, yet I resolved to take service where I should see the best advantage.

Sobiesky offered me service and promised me a company of dragownes, which lay on his lands of Javorowa and thereabouts; which I excused, telling him that I being a yong man, was come out of my owne countrey to seeke honour, and that by lying upon lands and in quarters, nothing of that nature {239v} was to be expected; as also I perceived him to be a very niggardly person. He told me he had no other service for me. So I desired he would be pleased to deliver me of to the King or field marshall, saying I would willingly serve in the fields and be worth my meat; wherewith he was well pleased and said he would with convenience speake with Lubomirsky concerning me.

In the meane tyme Thorne being rendred on honourable conditions, the garrisone marched out, about 500 men. The wounded and sick by the articles of the treaty remained untill they could be gott conveniently convoyed to their owne garrisons.

[1659]

The King and Queen of Polland with the nobility made their entry into the towne on the first of Januar. I stayed still by the Crowne standard-bearer in his lodging, being now set at his owne table and well entertained.

All this tyme I had by me my colonells letter to Robert Smart and his note for the sixteen hundred reichs dollers, and now being here, I went to his house and delivered him the letter; which he accepted, and not

---

assassination of Prince Albrecht von Wallenstein in 1634.

knowing but that I was a freeman, desired to know when I would receive the money. I being acquainted {240} with him befor, told him that I was prisoner and had a sojor at the doore waiting upon me; that when I was taken, I had these writeings by me; that by good luck the Polls had not found them, and now I was to consult with him how to gett the money transported to ye colonel; wherewith the merchant was much surprised to see such fidelity and honesty in a poor sojor.

After diverse wayes considered, by bill of exchange was found the most sure. So I gott two of them, one whereof I delivered to Lt. Coll. Buck (who being wounded had stayed behind) and the other to Andrew Thomson, a merch-t, to be sent thereafter if that miscaryed. I did writt also to my colonell, showing what I had done and desireing to be ransomed. Upon the reseat of the bills of exchange I delivered the note to the merchant, who at last said he did not think there had been so much honesty in a necessitated sojor. I told him he was in a great mistake, for the ends of our two professions were different, ours being honour and theirs gaine, and that for his estate and ten tymes more I would not staine my honour.

{240v} The army being dismissed into their quarters, the King, Queen and nobility departed towards Varso. The Crowne standard-bearer, haveing spoken with Lubomirsky concerning me in the evening when he tooke his leave, the next morning by the breake of day he sent one Solkiewsky, a kinsman of his owne, with me to Lubomirsky. I staying in the utter roome, the gentleman went in, and after a litle stay I was called for. The field marshall asked me my countrey, name, and in what charge I had served, and then told me I should go along with him. There was a gentlman walking with him in the roome, who looked very earnestly upon me, who as I was told was one Morstein, and was betrothed to Lady Henrietta Gordon, a daughter of the House of Huntly[381].

All the generalls baggage being gone, I was showne into a large waggon covered with red cloth, which was called the cabinett waggon, wherein was the generalls bedding and furniture of the privy chamber. So all the

---

[381] The Marquis of Huntly was, of course, the Chief of the Gordons.

way I had this convenience with one of the pages, who by turnes had the oversight of this waggon.

Wee marched up on the Massowrs syde of the river Vistula and crossed the river by Sakroczin, and so to Varso, {241} and from thence to Janofsta[382]. Here, as on the way, I had my lodging in the dineing roome, not being confined or under any particular guard, because I gave my word not to run away. I dined at the table with the gentlmen, where the generall himself dyned also on festivall dayes, and wanted not for any thing of meat and drink.

After some weekes stay here the generall went to Lublin to the commission, whither the nobility who had any charge in the army, regiments or companies, as also the deputies from the army and commissioners for the treasury were conveened. Here were many meetings, great complaints of the oppression and insolencyes of the souldiery, and great feasting, yet nothing concluded. So that the powerfullest seized thereafter upon the collections and cesses in these countreyes and places, where they had greatest interest, to pay themselves the money which they pretended to have advanced for the souldiery and publick; and the weakest, especially the sojours of fortune and the common souldiers, gott nothing, only another commission was appointed to be in Russe Lemberg in May next, where satisfaction was promised. Here it first came out that the army intended to confederate and had nominated a directour, one Swidersky, in case they should {241v} not gett satisfaction, and this I heard him and the deputies of the army publickely owne at a feast by the field marshall.

Here were Lt. Coll. Henry Gordon[383] and Maior Patrick Gordon, alias Steele Hand, and some other of our countrey men, to whom I did not, however, show or reveale my self, being loth they should know my condition or necessityes. In the meane tyme the generall offered me the ensignies place to the lyfe-company of his regiment of foot; which I refused, saying I had served for ensignie to dragouns under the Crowne of Sweden and would not serve for ensignie to no prince in Christendome any more.

After some dayes he caused tell me that he was to have a regiment of

---
[382] Janowiec.
[383] Youngest son of George, 2nd Marquis of Huntly. He served the Poles until 1663.

dragownes, and that he would give me the regiment quarterm-rs place. I seeing him to be a very noble person and the nobleman of greatest power and esteeme among all the Polls, ablest to protect and help those who served under him and nearest his person, readily embraced the offer, being even glad to be so ridd of the Swedish service with my credit. For albeit there were no right cartell or articles erected or agreed on betwixt the Polls and Sweds, yet men of quality observed usually the ordinary tyme prescrived in the former German {242} warr for remaining prisoner without takeing service, w-ch, if not precisely kept sometymes, was not, neither should be, so precisely looked into except in generall and other persons of great quality. Because many reasons might move and excuse the not staying the prefixed tyme, as the case was now with me.

For haveing been prisoner at first in Sandets by the Polls 18 weekes, and albeit the Sweds used meanes, yet the Polls would neither give me for ransome nor exchange, so that I was forced in a manner to beg service. Then, being taken againe at the battell of Varso, and behoved to take service the 4th day thereafter, for haveing had no charge under the Polls, I knew I should not be taken notice of, and rott in prison befor I should be asked for.

And now I had been eleven weekes in prison. The Sweds, whilst I was in Prussia, had sent twice to releeve me, but were refused, so that I had no hopes of liberty that way. And now if I omitted this tyme and opportunity, I was sure to be sent to some remote place, and be no more taken notice {242v} of till the peace. And what I, being a stranger, should receive of recompence for my sufferings, was very uncertaine, yet certaine enough not to be so much as to countervaile the loss of so much tyme.

Besydes I had my other considerations, as being a sojor of fortune and a stranger to both nations, my interest was nothing in the one or other, whereby I should be oblidged to serve or suffer more for the one or the other. Only religion made me encline more to the Polls as the other. So that by all meanes, so farr as my honour could permitt, I behoved to seek my advanc[e]ment and strive to make some fortune, w-ch as the case stood now with the Sweds was very unlikely, yea, impossible to do amongst them.

For they had now the Roman Emperour, the Kings of Denmark and Polland, the Moskovite[384] and Elector of Brandeburg in their topp, any whereof was almost able to cope with them; and now nothing was to be exspected in Prussia but to suffer hunger and all the calamities and necessityes incident to besieged and blocquired places. The pay being so small, {243} as it was impossible to subsist with it, the service so heavy, and the rewards, when the peace should be made, not like to be great, seing by all probability, haveing so many enemyes in their topp, they were at the best to be no gainers by the warr.

It is true that the good discipline amongst them, the respect given to all according to their charge, with their justice in preferring men of meritt are great incitements for aspireing minds to embrace and stay in that service and comport with the difficulties thereof.

On the contrar, I had observed so much both befor and now, that strangers in Polland lived very well, and a man of good government could be soone in a possibility of makeing a fortune. And albeit the pride of the generality of the Polls would not suffer them to give such due respect to strangers as was requisite, yet the nobility and the more civilized were not deficient in any thing of that nature. And truly, it is in vaine for a stranger {243v} to think that he can be in equall esteeme with the natives of alike quality and condition, unlesse the republick stand very much in need of military persons, or that his services have been very eminent. And even then for the most part the respect is more formall as materiall, and continueth but so long as your employment is active, or you enter into competition with any. And it is well knowne that every one is good to their owne, and no reason but that a native *ceteris paribus*[385] should be advanced befor an alien.

Indeed, in such places where their chieffe profession is military, and the natives not much enclined thereto, as in Holland, strangers are much looked upon, and have been often preferred befor the natives, of purpose

---

[384] Gordon did not yet know that the Russo-Swedish war was already effectively over after the Truce of Valiesar (20 December 1658), although peace was not signed until 1661.
[385] Other things being equal (Lat.).

to oblidge and encourage them. Yet even there of late wee have seen high military charges put by strangers of better and greater, and bestowed on natives of lesser meritt.

It were tedious to cite presidents, only this {244} I must relate. When Gustav Adolph, King of Sweden, invaded Germany, most of his chieffest and best officers, as is well knowne, were Scottishmen, to whose great and active valour he owed the best part of the good fortune he had there.[386] Yet afterwards, when his Sweds by experience had attained to a reasonable knowledge in the warrs, many of these cavaliers, being disoblidged, quitted the service, and very few of so great a number at the peace receaved rewards suitable to their services.

But to returne, I did see the Polls strongly confederated, levying a considerable force of stranger regiments, viz. 22, and shortly lyke to be, with Gods grace, in a capacity to regaine their owne. And being now offered a stepp of preferment with ane advantagious place, and being knowne to so great a person, who had the ruling of all military and a great influence on the politick affaires also, I promised to my self a bettering of my fortune, intending to use all endeavours, and by industry, diligence and good behaviour draw from {244v} every one a good opinion; assureing my self that my religion, knowledge in the languages, especially the Latine, and being knowne to be a gentleman, would be no small helps in such a countrey and among such people, where learning, nobility and vertue make way to the most eminent honours and fortunes.

Haveing given my word to serve, the field marshall caused bring me into his chamber befor day and asked me himself if I would accept of the regiment quarterm-rs place. I answering "yes", he told me he was to have a regiment of dragownes shortly, to the which I should be reg. quarterm-r. In the meane tyme I should stay by his lyfe-company, and he would see me

---

[386] This is largely true. One contemporary wrote that King Gustav Adolf "immediately after the battel at Leipisch [Breitenfeld, 1631] in one place and at one time had six and thirty Scotish colonels about him" (Sir Thomas Urquhart of Cromarty, *The Jewel*, Edinburgh, 1983, p. 94). Alexia Grosjean, modern expert on the subject, estimates the Scottish contingent serving Sweden at the peak of the Thirty Years' War to have reached about 20,000.

accommodated. So ordering to give me a hundred reichs dollers to mount me, he tooke me by the hand and dismissed me.

The treasurer giveing me a note to one Mr. Cuthbert, a Scotsman and borne in Aberdeen, I went and immediately receaved the money, wherewith I bought such things as I stood in most need of, as linnens, clocke, pistoll, sword, boots, shooes and other necessaryes. The Maior {245} Pnewsky gifted me a good nagge, which he had promised me befor if I would take service, and now keeped his word. The *Ruitm-r* Dziellinsky getting notice that I had engaged to serve, restored to me my sadle, which at my being taken prisoner he had gott, and protested, if the rest of my mounting were in his power, he would have given me all.

Index of persons and places

A

Aberdeen, 4, 7, 282
Achmade, 5
Achridy, 5
Adolf Johann, Prince, Swedish Generalissimus, 89, 90, 94, 96, 97, 99, 100, 101, 102, 140, 154, 155, 157, 164, 166, 167, 168, 234, 240, 241, 242, 243, 244, 255, 260, 261, 267, 268, 274
Airth, Walter, Trooper, 174
Alehous, wagonmaster, 71
Alexey Mikhailovich, Tsar of Russia, 28, 100, 127, 128, 129, 173
Allagrett ab Allagretis, Envoy, 100, 127
Allan, Margaret, widow, 4
Altenburg, 89
Altenburg, Duchess of, 89
Altmark, 161, 167, 173
Anderson, Alexander, (Lt.) Colonel, 123, 124, 125, 146, 147, 155, 242, 243, 244, 245, 252, 253, 254, 255, 256, 259, 260, 261, 262, 264, 265, 266, 268, 269, 270, 271, 273, 274, 276, 277
Andrew, servant, 23
Andrews, Colonel, 246
Anhalt, Johann Georg, Prince, 37, 39
Anholt (Anout), 8
Antwerp, 22
Archisefsky, Podstarosta, 107, 108, 109, 122
Arensdorf, Lt. Colonel, 218
Areskin, (Erskine) Alexander, Trooper, 220
Areskin, (Erskine) Robert, Trooper, 220
Argyll, Marquis of, 195
Aschemberg, Colonel, 133, 182
Auchluichries, 4

Auchluichries, Easter, 4
Augustow, 129
Austria, 143, 148

B

Baden, Margrave of, 97, 98, 99, 154, 155, 250
Baltic Sea, 27
Banier, Colonel, 29
Barlewitz, 262, 269, 271
Barnes, Lieutenant, 72, 73, 74
Bartenstein (Bartoszyce), 92
Barthman, Jacob, skipper, 7
Bavaria, 243
Beerenklau, President, 39, 134
Będzin, 62
Berends (Barnes), Fabian, Major General, 29, 212
Beresteczko, 93
Berg, 243
Bernsdorf, 30
Besum, Michael, Captain, 265
Beverage, James, merchant, 173
Biecz, 88
Birnie, James, Trooper, 173
Birnie, John, Cornet, 173, 174, 180, 183
Blackhall, Robert, priest, 9, 11
Blunia, 118
Bober, Rittmeister, 178, 179
Boćki (Botczky) 209, 210, 215, 216
Bockum (Bockhune), Johann, Colonel, 112, 114
Bohemia, 143, 145, 147, 148, 149, 153, 159, 234
Bomesdorf, Lt. Colonel, 160
Boote, Herman, Colonel, 25
Bornholm, 8

Bosa, Samuel, Colonel, 98
Bötticher (Betker), Major General, 29, 34
Bourman, Colonel, 29
Bowle Hans, Lieutenant, 86
Bow, Major, 55, 56, 57, 58, 68
Bradshaw, John, 251
Bradshaw, Richard, Ambassador, 251
Brandenburg, 17, 31, 89, 100, 101, 102, 109, 123, 129, 135,
    138, 139, 140, 147, 148, 154, 157, 158, 163, 164, 181,
    234, 261, 280
Braunsberg (Braniewo), 9, 10, 13, 18, 90, 136, 171, 172
Bremen, 28, 29, 81, 130
Brethault, Lt. Colonel, 239, 241, 242
Bretlach, Christian von, Colonel, 29, 49
Broberg, Major, 29
Bromberg (Bramburg, Bydgoszcz), 101, 154, 159, 163
Brown, Andrew, schoolmaster, 6
Brown, John, Corporal, 227, 231
Brześć (Brest) Kujawski, 141, 198
Brześć (Brest) Litewski, 19, 144, 145, 212, 216
Buck, Lt. Colonel, 169, 277
Buck-shants, 123
Bug, 102, 144, 212, 215, 219
Bull, John, 173
Bülow (Bilaw), Major General, 154, 155, 168, 239
Burnet, John, Trooper, 171, 172
Burnet of Leys, James, Trooper, 212

C

Campagnia, 181, 182
Campbell, John, 245, 251
Canasilius, 27
Canterstein, Lorenz, Secretary, 105, 107

Carolen, 33
Carpathians, 65, 137, 149
Cato, 3
Charles I, King of Great Britain, 251
Charles II, King of Great Britain, 235
Cherkassky, J. K., Prince, 128
Chigirin (Czegrin), 92
Chmielnitsky, Bogdan, Hetman, 64, 92
Christburg (Dzierzgoń), 165, 168, 173, 175, 269, 273, 274
Christian IV, King of Denmark, 100
Christina Augusta, Queen of Sweden, 26, 28
Ciechanowiec, 215
Climent Fare, 167, 171, 176, 245
Cockenhausen, 127, 129
Collof, Anton, Commander, 149
Columby, 94, 95
Comineanus, General, 150, 152
Copenhagen, 8
Copernicus, Nicolaus, astronomer, 9
Courland, 27
Coyet, Envoy, 100
Crakau, Colonel, 25
Cranston, Lord, 101, 120, 133, 156, 176, 225, 226
Crimea, 146, 152
Cromwell, Oliver, 28, 235
Cruden (Crochdan), 4, 6
Cujavia, 64
Curas, Jacob, Captain, 256, 263, 268, 269, 270, 271
Cuthbert, 282
Czarnetsky, Stefan, Commander, 55, 59, 62, 94, 96, 100, 101, 106, 113, 137, 138, 145, 146, 147, 149, 154
Czersk, 99
Częstochowa, 63, 138, 147

D

Dankwort, Major General, 135, 154, 155
Danzig (Dantzick, Gdańsk), 13, 14, 16, 89, 91, 101, 130, 131, 132, 133, 134, 135, 136, 137, 138, 185, 187, 190, 193, 254
Danziger Haupt (Hooft), 16, 101, 131, 134, 154, 155, 164, 176, 184, 226, 241, 255
De la Gardie, Countess, 89
De la Gardie, Jacob, Count, 212
De la Gardie, Magnus, Count, 89, 90
De la Gardie, Pontus, Count, 50, 51, 65
Dembe, 59
Denmark, 8, 100, 138, 139, 140, 145, 148, 154, 155, 163, 164, 212, 218, 234, 255, 280
Denmark, Major, 167
Despauters, Jean, grammarian, 4
Dick, John, 18
Dirschau (Tczew), 16, 132, 136, 155, 156, 157, 163, 184
Dobczyce (Dupshits), 73
Dobrzyń, 233, 239
Dona, Count von, 181, 190, 255
Donaldson, John, 9
Donklaw, Rittmeister, 68, 69
Dorflinger, Major General, 130
Douglas, Madam, 107
Douglas, Robert, Field Marshal, 38, 53, 54, 55, 56, 58, 60, 61, 89, 94, 95, 101, 102, 107, 115, 116, 119, 120, 121, 123, 129, 131, 134, 135, 136, 140, 142, 154, 159, 165, 173, 175, 176, 178, 179, 180, 181, 184, 185, 187, 190, 192, 194, 195, 196, 197, 198, 203, 218, 239, 240, 241, 244, 245, 273
Dracheim, 31
Drake, Colonel, 156
Drohiczyn (Drogishin), 212
Drwęca (Dreventz), 156, 159, 226, 227, 233, 237, 238, 239

Drummond, Lt. Colonel, 189
Dubald, Colonel, 91
Duderstatt, Colonel, 35, 155
Dumbar, Patrick, Trooper, 174
Dunajec, 65
Duncan, James, Rittmeister, 34, 51, 52, 64, 69, 70, 72
Durham, 262
Durham, Captain, 171
Dvina, 129
Dzialinsky, Rittmeister, 273, 282
Dzialinsky, Starosta, 101

E

Elbing (Elbląg), 12, 89, 91, 100, 139, 155, 161, 165, 168, 169, 171, 193, 224, 240, 241, 242, 245, 247, 248, 250, 252, 255, 261, 266
Elias, Sergeant, 273
Ellon, 5
Elphinston, James, Trooper, 216, 217, 220
Engel, Colonel, 29, 36
England, 100, 155
Europe, 162

F

Falkenburg, 30
Falsterbo (Valsterboom), 8
Ferdinand III, Emperor, 64, 88, 89, 100, 127, 136, 138, 139, 143, 147, 275
Ferguson, James, 21
Fermer, George, 250
Ferquhar, Robert, 21
Filipów, 130, 175
Fishery, 238

Fittinghof, Colonel, 89
Forbes, John, Sergeant, 257
Forbes, Quartermaster, 224
Forbes, Rentmaster, 242
Forbes, Thomas, Captain, 242, 244, 249, 250, 252, 253,
    254, 256, 257, 258, 259, 260, 261, 262, 265, 266,
    269, 270, 271, 275
Forgell, Georg, Colonel, 51, 52, 104, 105, 107, 125
France, 100, 141, 155, 235
Franz, Duke of Sachsen-Lauenburg, 24, 29, 49, 52, 64
Frauenburg (Frawensberg, Frombork), 9, 11, 129, 131
Frazer, Alexander, schoolmaster, 6
Frederik III, King of Denmark, 8, 140, 145, 163, 164, 165, 212, 280
Freyerwald, 30
Friedrich Wilhelm, Elector of Brandenburg, Duke of Prussia, 17, 31,
    89, 90, 91, 100, 101, 102, 103, 109, 115, 123, 129, 131, 135, 136,
    138, 139, 140, 147, 148, 154, 157, 158, 159, 163, 164, 181, 261,
    264, 280
Friedrich, Landgrave of Hessen, 64, 189
Frish Haf, 9, 10, 16, 131
Fryer, John, Rittmeister, 231, 240
Fryer, William, merchant, 249
Fularton, Major, 189
Fyn (Funen), 140

G

Gąbin (Gambin), 19
Gambart, 232
Gardin, Major, 23
Gardin, Rittmeister, 22, 23, 24, 34, 39, 40, 41, 49, 52, 53, 64
Garioch, Alexander, 6
Gawdy, Major General, 145, 154, 211
Gembetsky, Paul, 33

Gerfelt, Colonel, 89
Gerlechofsky, Colonel, 86
Germany, 28, 77, 143, 230, 281
Gliniany (Glinam), 92
Gniezno, 35, 101, 162
Gniezno, Archbishop of, 162
Gnoyova Gora, 105
Gołąb (Columby, Goluby), 155
Gonsiewsky, Wincenty, Hetman, 102, 129, 130, 158
Gordon of Auchleuchries, John, Patrick's father, 4, 5, 6, 7, 21, 189
Gordon of Glassa, 239
Gordon, Colonel, 275
Gordon, George, Patrick's brother, 4
Gordon, Henry, Lt. Colonel, 278
Gordon, John, Trooper, 189
Gordon, Lady Henrietta, 277
Gordon, Patrick, 'Steelhand', 189, 278
Gortsky, Major General, 145, 167
Gostynin, 198, 202
Gottland, 132, 184
Grabia, 72, 73, 74
Graudenz (Grudziądz), 17, 89, 123, 132, 137, 154, 155, 161, 181, 195, 265
Great Britain, 27, 235
Great Lesovits, 171
Great Lichtenau, 135, 190, 192
Great Lumny, 108
Great Poland, 19, 64, 100, 101, 103, 108, 110, 123, 138, 139, 158, 159, 233, 239
Grebin (Grybów), 101, 132, 133, 135, 136, 185, 187, 193
Gribowa, 87
Grodshitsky, Major General, 163
Grudzinsky, Andrzej, Wojewoda, 33, 154
Guild, William, Trooper, 239

Gustav II Adolf, King of Sweden, 27, 281
Gutland, 101
Gyorgy II Rakoczi (Ragotsky), Prince of Transylvania, 64, 95, 102, 125, 136, 137, 138, 139, 140, 141, 142, 143, 144, 145, 147, 149, 150, 151, 153, 154, 204, 206, 211
Gzin, 18

H

Halberstadt, Rittmeister, 72, 73
Halyburton, David, Trooper, 194, 220
Hamburg, 21, 25, 29
Hamilton, Lord, 226, 231, 239, 240
Hamilton, Malcolm, Captain, 179
Hanau, Count, 29
Hatzfeld, Melchior, Field Marshal, 152, 233
Hedwig Eleonora, Queen of Sweden, 100, 131, 140, 172
Heidelberg, 89
Heidelberg, Elector of, 89
Heinrichsdorf, 30
Hel (Heel), 8
Helsingor (Elsenure), 8
Henderson, Sir John, Major General, 111, 117
Hessen, Colonel, 34
Heuster, Madam, 166
Heuster, Major General, 153, 160, 161, 165, 166, 167, 232, 239
Hoffstet, 31
Holland, 27, 91, 102, 135, 136, 148, 235, 280
Holstein, Duchess of, 89
Holstein, Johann, Trooper, 59, 80, 81, 85, 86, 87
Holy Roman Empire, 127, 143, 148, 233
Hony-Crook, 5
Hoode, Friedrich, Corporal, 81, 87
Horn, Henrik, General, 29, 154

Hume, Alexander, Trooper, 207, 220
Hume, Thomas, Trooper, 220
Hume, William, Trooper, 207, 208, 209, 239
Hungary, 137, 143, 145, 147, 148, 149, 153, 159, 234
Huntly, 277
Hurrey, John, Trooper, 173, 174

I

Innes, Franciscan Provincial, 86, 87
Inowłódz, 50, 53
Inowrocław (Winowratsaw), 34
Isbrandt, Ambassador, 135
Islam Geray, Khan of Crimea, 92
Isola, Franz, Minister, 136, 158, 159
Israel, Madam, 99
Israel, Major General, 99, 129

J

Jan II Kazimierz, King of Poland, 26, 27, 31, 32, 33, 36, 37, 38, 39, 46,
 54, 55, 59, 63, 64, 73, 78, 87, 88, 90, 92, 93, 94, 95, 102, 104, 105,
 106, 107, 110, 111, 112, 113, 114, 115, 116, 117, 119, 127, 131,
 132, 134, 137, 138, 139, 146, 147, 148, 149, 153, 154, 158, 160,
 162, 169, 269, 276, 277, 280
Janowiec (Janofsta), 278
Jaroslaw, 88, 93, 95, 96
Jawicky, Castellan, 145
Jaworów, 276
Jędrzejów, 55, 204
Jeżów, 49
Jordan, Governor, 73
Jülich (Gulick), 243
Jutland, 8

K

Kalisz (Calish), 32, 33, 123, 125, 158
Kamień, 209, 215
Kamieniets Podolsky, 92
Kannenberg, Christoph, Major General, 90, 91, 116
Karl of Sweden, Prince, 89
Karl X Gustav, King of Sweden, 25, 27, 28, 29, 30, 32, 33, 36, 37, 38,
    39, 45, 49, 52, 53, 54, 55, 58, 59, 62, 63, 64, 65, 86, 88, 89, 90, 91,
    92, 94, 95, 96, 97, 100, 101, 102, 103, 109, 113, 114, 115, 116, 121,
    123, 124, 127, 129, 131, 132, 133, 134, 135, 136, 138, 139, 140,
    141, 142, 143, 144, 145, 146, 147, 149, 154, 155, 156, 158, 164,
    184, 185, 195, 203, 204, 212, 214, 218, 219, 225, 234, 235, 243,
    244, 255
Kashubia, 139
Katzenau, 245
Kazimierz (Casimirs), 58, 59, 61, 64, 72, 73, 94, 149
Keisermark, 101
Keith, Alexander, Trooper, 172, 175, 179, 190, 191, 192, 194, 229
Keith, James, Captain, 228
Keith, Trooper, 194
Kempis, Thomas a, 187
Kemp, John, Corporal, 176, 231
Kiev (Kyow), 62
Kleparz (Clepars), 56
Kleve, 243
Klinger, Major, 157, 179, 180, 181, 226
Kodeń, 212
Kole, 8
Kollet, Captain, 79, 80, 96
Koło (Colla), 39, 42
Koniecpolsky, Aleksandr, Wojewoda, 61, 94, 165, 168, 266, 273
Königsberg, 9, 10, 90, 91, 103, 264
Konigsmark, Count, Colonel, 37, 42, 43, 44, 61

Konigsmark, Count, General, 130, 131
Konigsmark, Kurt Christoph, Count, 29
Konigsmark, Major, 52
Konin, 36, 37
Konitz (Chojnice), 101, 131, 133, 139, 155, 159, 260
Konning, John, 245
Koritsky, nobleman, 95, 214, 215, 225
Kościan (Kostzian), 32, 64
Kosichewa, 62
Kowal, 19, 141, 198
Kowalewa, 155, 225
Krakow, 49, 50, 55, 56, 58, 59, 61, 62, 63, 64, 65, 66, 71, 72, 73, 74, 79, 88, 93, 102, 119, 123, 125, 136, 142, 143, 145, 153, 154, 204, 233
Krakow, Bishop of, 66, 70, 104
Krone, 31
Krosno (Crosna), 73
Krzemień, 144, 145
Książ (Xiaz), 55
Kulm (Culm, Chełmno), 15, 17, 161, 195
Kulmsee (Chełmża), 123

L

Laeso (Lezow), 8
Lame-hand, 241, 251
Łańcut (Landshut), 88, 142
Landels, Alexander, Trooper, 194, 220
Landskoronsky, Stanislaw, Hetman, 89, 106
Landskron, 61
Langenau, 131
Lang, Rittmeister, 264, 266
Larkin, Colonel, 29
Lashin, 171
Lawder, William, Lieutenant, 42, 59

Leczko, 132
Łęczyca (Lenshits), 37
Leopold I, Emperor, 143, 145, 147, 148, 149, 153, 159, 164, 228, 234, 235, 275, 280
Lesczinsky, family, 19, 106
Leslie, Avraam (Alexander), General, 128
Leslie, James, Captain, 230, 275
Leslie, Walter, Count, 230, 275
Leslie of Tullos, 275
Leszno (Lissna), 100
Liatovits, 209
Liebstadt, 175
Lighton, Rittmeister, 65
Linde, Lorenz von der, Field Marshal, 90, 154, 155, 224, 248, 249, 250, 251
Lindsay, James, 21
Lipinki, 155, 160
Lissau, 163, 164, 255
Lithuania (Littaw), 19, 28, 93, 127, 129, 140, 163
Little Poland, 103, 123
Livland (Liefland), 25, 26, 127, 129, 138, 140
Loewenhaupt, Major General, 89, 100
Logan William, schoolmaster, 4
L'Ombres, Ambassador, 133, 148, 169
Lonsky, Major, 142
Louis XIV, King of France, 88, 100, 235
Lowicz (Lovits), 20, 36, 49, 99, 118, 123, 142, 169, 203
Lubawa (Libava), 18
Lübeck, 24, 26, 29
Lublin, 88, 93, 94, 95, 100, 144, 207, 278
Lubomirsky, Constantin, 65, 78, 88, 107
Lubomirsky, family, 88, 142
Lubomirsky, Jerzy, Prince, Field Marshall 88, 96, 98, 101, 136, 137, 142, 146, 149, 150, 169, 275, 276, 277,

278, 281, 282
Luboml, 99
Ludwig, Lt. Colonel, 29
Lwów (Lemberg), 64, 88, 93, 94, 95, 278

M

Maesdam, Ambassador, 135
Male Skripky, 215, 216
Małogoszcz (Malogost), 54
Maly Lumny, 107, 108
Marck, 243
Mardefeld, Colonel, 33
Mardefeld, Major General, 89
Maria Ludovica, Queen of Poland, 102, 112, 169, 276, 277
Marienburg (Malbork), 16, 89, 90, 91, 101, 102, 134, 135, 136, 139, 140,
    155, 157, 160, 161, 163, 164, 165, 166, 167, 168, 169, 173, 181,
    184, 190, 192, 193, 194, 226, 241, 246, 251, 254, 255, 256, 261,
    262, 266, 267, 268
Marienwerder (Kwidzyń), 17, 137, 165, 181, 195, 196, 241, 262, 264
Mazovia, 64, 157, 159
Mecklenburg-Güstrow, 89
Mecklenburg-Güstrow, Duchess of, 89
Mehmed IV, Sultan of Turkey, 146
Mehmed Geray, Khan of Crimea, 149, 150
Meldrum, John, Rittmeister, 98, 123, 159, 171, 173, 174, 178, 179, 180,
    183, 184, 192, 193, 195, 196, 197, 198, 207, 211, 212, 218, 224,
    225, 226, 227, 229, 230, 231, 232, 239, 240, 242, 244
Menzies (Menezes), Alexander, priest, 10
Menzies (Menezes), Thomas, 9, 10
Mewe (Gniew), 16, 132, 155, 163, 183, 184
Mezeboze, 151
Miaskowsky, Maximilian, 33
Michalko (Michalsky), Rittmeister,159, 160, 256, 269, 273

Middleton, General, 136
Middleton, William, Trooper, 181, 182, 194, 220
Miechow, 55
Miedzibeze, 144
Międzyrzecz (Mezeritz), 32
Mill, John, 5
Mitlach, Zacharias, Captain, 87
Mława, 221, 222
Montau Spitz (Monto Spitts), 16, 155, 160, 256
Montecuccoli, Raimondo, Count, 152
Montgomery, Hugh, Lieutenant, 245, 248, 249, 250, 251, 252
Montgomery, James, Trooper, 195, 196, 197, 198
Montgomery of Skelmorlie, 195, 197
Moravia, 83
Morstein, John, Envoy, 27
Morstein, gentleman, 277
Moscow, 89, 129, 148
Muller, Burhard, Major General, 29, 37, 63
Muller, Secretary, 242, 243
Münde, 8
Munkacs (Monchats), 137
Murovanie Goslin, 33
Murray George, schoolmaster, 5
Muscovy, 173, 251, 254

N

Nairn, Colonel, 89
Narew, 102, 219
Nassau, Wilhelm Adolf, Count, 144
Nemerowitz, nobleman, 95
Nering, 176
Neuenburg (Nowe), 17
Neukirch, 134, 193

Neuman, Colonel, 227
Neumark, 31, 154, 155, 227
Neus, 8
Neuteich, 135, 136, 172, 194, 195
Neuwedel, 31
Nida, 55
Nieporent, 109, 112, 114
Nogat, 16, 167, 171, 173, 176, 245, 255
Norway, 8, 154
Noteć, 30, 33
Nowy Dwór (Novodwor), 102, 107, 109, 119, 146

O

Odense, 140
Oesel, 26
Ogilvie, Mary, Patrick Gordon's mother, 4, 6, 7, 21
Oliwa, 101
Opalinsky, 21
Opalinsky, Krzysztof, Wojewoda, 33
Oparów, 45
Opoczno, 52, 65
Opole (Opolia), 64, 148
Ossolinsky, family, 107
Oświęcim, 62
Oxenstierna, Bengt, Count, 107, 116, 134, 154, 155, 168, 239
Oxenstierna, Count, 29, 254
Oxenstierna, Erik, Count, Chancellor, 90, 91, 131
Oxenstierna, Gustav, Major General, 154

P

Parczew, 145
Passarge (Passary), 10, 175

Pelplin, 159
Perceval, General, 136
Peters, Bartholomeus, 176
Peterswald, 269
Pflaume, Lt. Colonel, 164, 255
Piaseczno (Piositsna), 116
Piątek, 20
Piliavtsy (Pilavets), 92
Pilica (Pilcza), 50
Pillau, 91, 100, 101, 131, 135
Pińczów (Pienshow), 204
Piotrków (Peterkaw), 142, 149, 204
Pleitner, Colonel, 155
Plock (Plotsko), 123, 230
Pnewsky, Major, 275, 282
Podkamer, Lt. Colonel, 212
Podolia, 149
Poland, 15, 18, 20, 25, 26, 27, 28, 29, 30, 31, 32, 33, 36, 37, 38, 39, 40, 46, 55, 59, 64, 73, 81, 84, 86, 87, 88, 90, 91, 92, 93, 94, 95, 101, 102, 104, 106, 107, 111, 112, 113, 114, 115, 127, 129, 131, 132, 134, 136, 137, 138, 139, 140, 141, 142, 143, 145, 146, 147, 148, 149, 150, 152, 153, 154, 155, 157, 158, 160, 162, 163, 168, 169, 175, 234, 237, 265, 269, 276, 280
Pomerania (Pomerell), 8, 24, 25, 31, 38, 90, 101, 125, 130, 131, 133, 136, 138, 139, 143, 154, 155, 156, 157, 254
Porte (Turkey), 138, 146
Potocky, Stanislaw Rewera, Hetman, 88
Pottingen, Franz Eusebius, Count, 64, 100
Poznań (Posna), 19, 20, 32, 33, 34, 35, 41, 158
Prague (Poland), 97, 100, 110, 114, 115, 117
Preussisch Holland (Pasłęk), 91, 103, 136, 167, 171, 175
Preussisch Mark, 261
Priaskowsky, Wojciech, 33
Proszowice (Prossowits), 73

Prussia, 13, 17, 27, 61, 81, 88, 89, 90, 94, 101, 103, 122, 129, 130, 135, 136, 138, 139, 140, 142, 143, 145, 154, 155, 156, 158, 159, 164, 165, 169, 222, 226, 234, 261, 269, 279, 280
Prust, 101, 132
Przasnysz (Presnits), 219
Przedbórz, 46, 54, 142
Przeimsky, Christophorus, Envoy, 38, 39
Przemyśl (Premisl), 95
Przeworsk, 88
Puchar, Colonel, 155
Puchar, Johann Baldwin, Commissary, 107, 116
Puck (Putsk), 25, 101
Pułtusk (Pultovsko), 102, 124
Pyzdry (Pisdra), 36

Q

Quickfelt, Ensign, 259

R

Racibórz (Ratibor), 148
Radom, 97, 98, 99
Radoszyce (Radoshits), 54, 142, 143
Radzievsky, Hieronim, Under-Chancellor, 28, 32, 33, 34, 37, 89, 104, 105, 139
Radziwill, Boguslaw, Prince, 129, 130
Radziwill, Jan, Prince, 18, 19, 93
Rajgród, 129
Ratzeburg, 24
Ravensburg, 243
Ravenstein, 243
Rawa, 49, 142, 169, 225
Redden (Radzyń), 89, 90, 123, 169, 170

Rhine, 243
Ried, Captain, 232
Riesenburg (Prabuty), 165, 167, 168, 264, 274
Riga, 26, 100, 127, 129, 173, 175
Rimanowa, 65, 72, 74
Riter, Lt. Colonel, 98
Roan, 8
Rosa, Colonel, 29, 139, 157, 226
Roskilde (Rotschild), 164
Ross, John, 109
Ross, Trooper, 171
Rusische Moule, 30
Russell, John, Lieutenant, 212, 224, 231, 240, 241, 242
Russia, 100, 127, 129, 149
Rutherford, Colonel, 179
Rzeszów (Reshowa), 88

S

Sacken, Major, 275
Sącz (Sandets), 59, 65, 74, 77, 96, 279
Samogitia, 100, 127
Samptra, 33
San, 88, 95, 96
Sandomierz (Sandomirs), 88, 89, 94, 95, 96, 142, 143, 165, 168, 266, 273
Sapieha, Commander, 113, 115
Sapieha, family, 209, 212
Sapieha, Jan, Commander, 61, 161, 164, 256, 274, 275
Sapieha, Pawel, Hetman, 142
Saxen, Major, 31
Saxony, 89
Saxony, Elector of, 89
Saxony, Electress of, 89
Scepusia (Zips), 59, 73

Schlachte, Major, 29
Schleswig-Holstein, 89
Schleswig-Holstein, Duke of, 89
Schlippenbach, Count, General, 97, 134, 138
Schlochau (Sluchow, Człuchów), 101, 133, 159
Schoenleben, General Adjutant, 203
Schönbergen, gentleman, 25
Schonek, Colonel, 264
Schwarzwald, brothers, 185, 190
Schwarzwald, Hans, 190
Schwarzwasser, 17
Schwerin, Otto, Baron, 159
Scotland, 6, 15, 19, 23, 156, 173, 176, 190, 195, 224, 231
Scott, Lieutenant, 189
Scrogges, Alexander, 5
Sienhagen, 176
Silesia, 50, 59, 62, 64, 73, 92, 93, 94, 95
Sinclair, Colonel, 164
Sinkler, Colonel, 265
Sinkler, David, Colonel, 29, 94, 110, 116
Sinkler, Major, 176
Sinkler, servant, 195
Sinkler of Rosslin, Lodovick, Trooper, 206
Skagen, 8
Slangfeld, 107
Sleich, Robert, merchant, 18
Slichting, gentleman, 66
Slomniki, 55
Słupca, 36
Służewo (Soleyewa), 141, 195, 197
Smart, Robert, merchant, 265, 276, 277
Smeton, Thomas, merchant, 173
Smith, Alexander, Rittmeister, 266
Smith, John, merchant, 17

Smith, John, Trooper, 231, 236, 238, 241
Snide mills, 30, 34
Sobiesky, Jan, Commander, 61, 94, 168, 266, 273, 274, 275, 276, 277
Sobigorsky, gentleman, 136, 142
Sobota, 46, 141, 142, 203
Sokoly (Sokal), 145, 216
Soldau (Działdowo), 223
Somnitz, Lorenz, Commissioner, 159
Sorrell, David, 245
Spanko, Colonel, 161
Sparr, Colonel, 90
Sparr, Otto Christoph, Lt. General, 110
Sparr, Field Marshal, 152
Sponheim, 243
Środa, 20, 34, 35, 41
St[ ]felt, Captain, 50
Stade, 24, 101
Staker, Alexander, Quartermaster, 230
Stanislawsky, gentleman, 136, 142
Stargard, 160
St. Brzeziny (Bresini), 50
Stein, Rittmeister, 52
Stenbock, Gustav Otto, Field Marshal, 38, 49, 64, 89, 90, 101, 130, 135, 140, 145, 216, 218, 219
Stettin (Szczecin), 24, 25, 36, 39, 40, 131, 154
Steven, Robert, Trooper, 172, 220
Stewart, Captain, 275
Stewart, Lt. Colonel, 65
Stewart, Robert, Cornet, 219, 220, 226
Stiblau, 101, 132, 184, 185, 190, 191, 192
Stotsky, Jan, gentleman, 77, 78, 82, 83
Stradomia, 59, 62
Straiton, Andrew, Quartermaster, 121, 172, 173, 240, 266
Strasburg (Brodnica), 89, 154, 155, 159, 165, 226, 236, 239, 240, 241

Straughan, Captain, 224
Studt Hof, 133
Stuhm (Sztum), 155, 161, 164, 165, 168, 173, 224, 242, 243, 244, 249, 251, 252, 256, 261, 262, 264, 265, 266, 267, 275
Stuhmsdorf, 26, 27
Suchodolsky, Starosta, 168, 273, 274
Suider mills, 30
Sulzbach, Philipp, Count, 54, 140, 147, 154
Susa, Lt. General, 153, 169
Sweden, 25, 26, 27, 31, 32, 33, 38, 39, 59, 62, 64, 86, 88, 90, 91, 92, 94, 95, 96, 100, 101, 102, 103, 107, 109, 113, 116, 123, 127, 129, 131, 132, 133, 134, 135, 136, 137, 138, 139, 140, 141, 142, 143, 144, 145, 146, 147, 148, 149, 154, 155, 156, 158, 160, 163, 164, 170, 218, 225, 231, 234, 235, 240, 241, 243, 245, 248, 255, 278, 281
Swidersky, gentleman, 278
Świecie (Swets, Schwetz), 15, 17, 155
Święty Krzyż, 144

T

Taube, Colonel, 29
Tempelsburg, 31
Thomson, Andrew, merchant, 277
Thomson, Major, 190
Thorn (Toruń), 17, 18, 19, 89, 100, 106, 137, 140, 155, 160, 161, 163, 165, 168, 169, 195, 224, 225, 226, 232, 236, 238, 240, 241, 261, 265, 273, 274
Tolkemit (Tolkamet, Tolkmicko), 136
Tom, Hary, schoolmaster, 5
Torren, Count de, 127
Trago, 30
Tramburg, 30
Transylvania, 64, 89, 95, 102, 125, 138, 139, 141, 142, 143, 144, 146, 149, 150, 153, 154, 204

Trindell, 8
Trotter, Robert, Trooper, 225
Tuchel (Tuchola), 155, 159
Tykocin (Tikotzin), 102
Tyniec (Tenits), 125

U

Uchtenhagen, 30
Ujazdow, 107, 117
Ujście (Ustzie), 30, 33, 34
Ukraine, 149
Uniejów (Uniewa), 37, 43
Urzędów, 144, 207

V

Valdemar, Prince, 100
Ven (Ween), 8
Venceslaus de Lesno, Bishop, 158
Verden, 28, 29
Versen, Fabian, Colonel, 29
Veze, 31
Vienna, 148
Vilnius (Vilna), 93
Visniovetsky, Dimitry, Prince, 133
Vistula (Wistle), 14, 16, 55, 58, 59, 94, 95, 96, 97,
    101, 102, 108, 109, 123, 131, 132, 135, 137,
    139, 144, 146, 147, 149, 156, 160, 163, 164,
    171, 176, 181, 183, 184, 233, 237, 238, 239,
    255, 278
Volyn (Volhynia), 93
Vonsovits, brothers, 66

W

Wadie, Soldier, 263
Waldeck, Count, 157
Waldeck, Count, General, 129, 130, 140, 157
Wallace, Captain, 225
Wallace, Trooper, 171
Wangerin, 30
Wardlaw, Soldier, 263
Warka (Varky), 97, 99, 115, 116
Warmia (Wermeland), 10, 90, 103, 139, 161, 166
Warsaw, 19, 37, 49, 52, 65, 88, 89, 93, 94, 96, 97, 99, 100, 101, 102, 103, 104, 107, 109, 114, 116, 119, 120, 124, 125, 129, 134, 143, 144, 145, 146, 147, 149, 161, 195, 196, 277, 278, 279
Warta, 20, 36, 37
Watson, James, 21
Watson, John, Major, 98
Waugh, Corporal, 220
Węgrów, 144, 209, 215
Welau, 158
Weldenz, 243
Westertown of Auchleuchries, 5
Weyer, Jacob, Wojewoda, 136
Weyer, Ludowick, Wojewoda, 31, 125, 126
Weyershof, 14, 31
White, James, 21
Whitekirch, 135, 136, 193
Wielky Skripky, 215
Wilczitsky, teacher, 22
Wilson, Andrew, Trooper, 230
Winter, Colonel, 187, 188
Wiśnicz (Wisnits), 59, 74, 75, 76, 84, 88
Wistul-munde, 89

Wittenberg, Arvid, Field Marshal, 29, 30, 31, 32, 33, 34, 35, 36, 49, 52, 100, 105, 107, 134
Wladislaw IV, King of Poland, 25, 26
Wojnicz (Voynits), 59
Wolgast, 29
Woyna, Officer, 145
Wrangel, Karl Gustav, Field Marshal, 38, 100, 101, 102, 134
Wresovitz, Major General, 63, 126
Wulffe, Colonel, 62
Württemberg, 89
Württemberg, Duke of, 89
Wurtz, Paul, Major General, 29, 65, 102, 143, 153, 204
Würzburg, Major General, 154, 155, 176, 177, 179

Y

Yurgen, Hans, Trooper, 69

Z

Zadzik (Zadzecky), Great Chancellor of Poland, 26
Zakroczym (Sacroczin), 123, 124, 145, 146, 147, 278
Zamość (Zamostze), 88, 95, 104, 125, 231
Żarnów, 53
Zator, 62
Zawichost, 144, 204
Zbaraż, 92, 93
Zborów, 92
Ziczenhof, Rittmeister, 178, 179
Żnin (Snin), 101
Zolkiewsky, gentleman, 277
Żwaniec, 92